Advanced Applications of NLP and Deep Learning in Social Media Data

Ahmed A. Abd El-Latif
Menoufia University, Egypt & Prince Sultan University, Saudi Arabia

Mudasir Ahmad Wani
Prince Sultan University, Saudi Arabia

Mohammed A. El-Affendi
Prince Sultan University, Saudi Arabia

A volume in the Advances in
Social Networking and Online
Communities (ASNOC) Book Series

Published in the United States of America by
    IGI Global
    Engineering Science Reference (an imprint of IGI Global)
    701 E. Chocolate Avenue
    Hershey PA, USA 17033
    Tel: 717-533-8845
    Fax: 717-533-8661
    E-mail: cust@igi-global.com
    Web site: http://www.igi-global.com

Library of Congress Cataloging-in-Publication Data

Names: Abd El-Latif, Ahmed A., 1984- editor. | Wani, Mudasir Ahman, 1987-
   editor. | El-Affendi, Mohammed, 1971- editor.
Title: Advanced applications of NLP and deep learning in social media data
   / Ahmed A. Abd El-Latif, Mudasir Ahman Wani, and Mohammed El-Affendi.
Description: Hershey, PA : Engineering Science Reference, [2023] | Includes
   bibliographical references and index. | Summary: "The primary objective
   of this book is to build a better and safer social media space by making
   human language available on different social media platforms
   intelligible for machines with the blessings of AI. This book bridges
   the gap between Natural Language Processing (NLP), Advanced Machine(AML)
   and Deep Learning (DL), and Online Social Media. This book connects
   various interdisciplinary domains related to Natural Language
   Understanding, Deep machine Leaning Technology and will be highly
   beneficial for the students, researchers, and academicians working in
   this area as this book will cover state-of-the-art technologies around
   NLP and DML techniques and their role in Social Media Data Analysis.
   Furthermore, the OSN service providers will take the advantage of this
   book to update, modify and make better social platforms for its users.
   Psychiatrists and clinicians will also be beneficial as this book's main
   focus are to analyze the user behavior in Online Social networks which
   play a key ingredient in several psychological tests"-- Provided by
   publisher.
Identifiers: LCCN 2022040870 (print) | LCCN 2022040871 (ebook) | ISBN
   9781668469095 (h/c) | ISBN 9781668469101 (s/c) | ISBN 9781668469118
   (eISBN)
Subjects: LCSH: Natural language processing (Computer science) | Deep
   learning (Machine learning) | Semantic computing. | Sentiment analysis.
   | Web usage mining. | Social media.
Classification: LCC QA76.9.N38 A336 2023 (print) | LCC QA76.9.N38 (ebook)
   | DDC 006.3/5--dc23/eng/20221110
LC record available at https://lccn.loc.gov/2022040870
LC ebook record available at https://lccn.loc.gov/2022040871

This book is published in the IGI Global book series Advances in Social Networking and Online Communities (ASNOC) (ISSN: 2328-1405; eISSN: 2328-1413)
British Cataloguing in Publication Data
A Cataloguing in Publication record for this book is available from the British Library.

All work contributed to this book is new, previously-unpublished material.
The views expressed in this book are those of the authors, but not necessarily of the publisher.

For electronic access to this publication, please contact: eresources@igi-global.com.

Advances in Social Networking and Online Communities (ASNOC) Book Series

ISSN:2328-1405
EISSN:2328-1413

Editor-in-Chief: Hakikur Rahman, Ansted University Sustainability Research Institute, Malaysia

MISSION

The advancements of internet technologies and the creation of various social networks provide a new channel of knowledge development processes that's dependent on social networking and online communities. This emerging concept of social innovation is comprised of ideas and strategies designed to improve society.

The **Advances in Social Networking and Online Communities** book series serves as a forum for scholars and practitioners to present comprehensive research on the social, cultural, organizational, and human issues related to the use of virtual communities and social networking. This series will provide an analytical approach to the holistic and newly emerging concepts of online knowledge communities and social networks.

COVERAGE

- Introduction to Mobile Computing
- Learning Utilities
- Knowledge as a Symbol/Model of Development
- Knowledge Chains
- Epistemology of Knowledge Society
- Flourishing Knowledge Creation Environments
- Current State and Future Development of the Institutional Knowledge Management
- Supporting Virtual Communities of Practice and Interest Networks
- Advanced Researches in Knowledge Communities
- Importance and Role of Knowledge Communities in R&D and Innovative Knowledge Creation

IGI Global is currently accepting manuscripts for publication within this series. To submit a proposal for a volume in this series, please contact our Acquisition Editors at Acquisitions@igi-global.com or visit: http://www.igi-global.com/publish/.

Titles in this Series

For a list of additional titles in this series, please visit:
http://www.igi-global.com/book-series/advances-social-networking-online-communities/37168

Community Engagement in the Online Space
Michelle Dennis (Adler University, USA) and James Halbert (Adler University, USA)
Information Science Reference • ©2023 • 364pp • H/C (ISBN: 9781668451908) • US $215.00

Handbook of Research on Bullying in Media and Beyond
Gülşah Sarı (Aksaray University, Turkey)
Information Science Reference • ©2023 • 603pp • H/C (ISBN: 9781668454268) • US $295.00

Handbook of Research on Technologies and Systems for E-Collaboration During Global Crises
Jingyuan Zhao (University of Toronto, Canada) and V. Vinoth Kumar (Jain University, India)
Information Science Reference • ©2022 • 461pp • H/C (ISBN: 9781799896401) • US $295.00

Information Manipulation and Its Impact Across All Industries
Maryam Ebrahimi (Independent Researcher, Germany)
Information Science Reference • ©2022 • 234pp • H/C (ISBN: 9781799882350) • US $215.00

E-Collaboration Technologies and Strategies for Competitive Advantage Amid Challenging Times
Jingyuan Zhao (University of Toronto, Canada) and Joseph Richards (California State University, Sacramento, USA)
Information Science Reference • ©2021 • 346pp • H/C (ISBN: 9781799877646) • US $215.00

Analyzing Global Social Media Consumption
Patrick Kanyi Wamuyu (United States International University – Africa, Kenya)
Information Science Reference • ©2021 • 358pp • H/C (ISBN: 9781799847182) • US $215.00

Global Perspectives on Social Media Communications, Trade Unionism, and Transnational Advocacy
Floribert Patrick C. Endong (University of Calabar, Nigeria)
Information Science Reference • ©2020 • 300pp • H/C (ISBN: 9781799831389) • US $195.00

701 East Chocolate Avenue, Hershey, PA 17033, USA
Tel: 717-533-8845 x100 • Fax: 717-533-8661
E-Mail: cust@igi-global.com • www.igi-global.com

Table of Contents

Detailed Table of Contents

Chapter 1
    Deepali Dhaka, Jamia Millia Islamia, India
    Monica Mehrotra, Jamia Millia Islamia, India

Social media is a widespread source of diverse forms of data. Information is diffusing so fast that any fascinating news is so rapidly spread through social media that it can be accessed by millions of users in seconds. Spammers are also part of these networks. Conventional spam detection approaches focus either on an individual message or individual account to classify them as spam or legitimate. However, these spam or spammers might be part of a group or controlled by some other accounts for a specific purpose called a campaign. Spam campaigns have become a great threat to social network services. They are more adversarial than individual spam accounts as they target many users on the network. Spam campaigns follow a stealthier approach than spammers to prevent themselves from detection. So, this study highlights various spam campaigns so far detected in the literature, their detection techniques, and the features used to build campaigns. It also highlights various issues and challenges that need to be picked up while detecting spammers.

Chapter 2
    Neha Kumari, Jawaharlal Nehru University, India

India was hit by the devastating second wave of COVID-19 with a sudden surge in cases in April 2021. It was far more severe and catastrophic than the first wave. Several models tried to gauge the severity and peak of the second wave but were successful only to some extent. The current scenario highlights the urgent need to forecast the trend and magnitude of the third COVID-19 wave with reasonable accuracy. It will significantly aid the COVID-19 preparation and planning by government and non-government organizations. The present research work forecasts the temporal trends of the second wave of COVID-19 in India's 10 most affected states using the autoregressive integrated moving average model (ARIMA). The model is trained using COVID-19 confirmed cases from March 14, 2020 to March 30, 2021 for India's 10 most affected states (i.e., Bihar, Delhi, Gujarat, Haryana, Karnataka, Madhya Pradesh, Maharashtra, Rajasthan, Tamil Nadu, and Uttar Pradesh). Performance evaluation of the model suggested that time series models can predict forthcoming COVID-19 waves by temporal analysis of previous waves.

Marcellus Amadeus, Alana AI Research, Brazil
William Alberto Cruz Castañeda, Alana AI Research, Brazil

Social media data has changed the way big data is used. The amount of data available offers more natural insights that make it possible to find relations and social interactions. Natural language processing (NLP) is an essential tool for such a task. NLP promises to scale traditional methods that allow the automation of tasks for social media datasets. A social media text dataset with a large number of attributes is referred to as a high-dimensional text dataset. One of the challenges of high-dimensional text datasets for NLP text clustering is that not all the measured variables are important for understanding the underlying phenomena of interest, and dimension reduction needs to be performed. Nonetheless, for text clustering, the existing literature is remarkably segmented, and the well-known methods do not address the problems of the high dimensionality of text data. Thus, different methods were found and classified in four areas. Also, it described metrics and technical tools as well as future directions.

Akib Mohi Ud Din Khanday, United Arab Emirates University, Al Ain,
  UAE
Syed Tanzeel Rabani, Baba Ghulam Shah Badshah University, India
Qamar Rayees Khan, Baba Ghulam Shah Badshah University, India
Fayaz Ahmad Khan, Cluster University of Srinagar, India

Modern networks, like social networks, can typically be characterised as a graph structure, and graph theory approaches can be used to address issues like link prediction, community recognition in social network analysis, and social network mining. The community structure or cluster, which is the organisation of vertices with numerous links joining vertices of the same cluster and comparatively few edges joining vertices of different clusters, is one of the most important characteristics of graphs describing real systems. People post content on social media platforms and others comment, share, and like their messages. There are various approaches in finding the communities on online social networks. In this chapter an overview of community structure is provided. A critical analysis is being done on various community detection algorithms.

Recognition of emotional information is essential in any form of communication. Growing HCI (human-computer interaction) in recent times indicates the importance of understanding of emotions expressed and becomes crucial for improving the system or the interaction itself. In this research work, textual data for emotion recognition is used. The proposal is made for a neural architecture to resolve not less than eight emotions from textual data sources derived from multiple datasets using google pre-trained word2vec word embeddings and a multi-head attention-based bidirectional LSTM model with a one-vs-all multi-level classification. The emotions targeted in this research are anger, disgust, fear, guilt, joy, sadness, shame, and surprise. Textual data from multiple datasets are ingested such as ISEAR, Go Emotions, and Affect dataset. The results show a significant improvement with the modeling architecture with good improvement in recognizing some emotions.

Chapter 6

Humans learn new concepts from a few observations with strong generalisation ability. Discovering patterns from small samples is complicated and challenging in machine learning (ML) and deep learning (DL). The ability to successfully learn and generalise from relatively short data is a glaring difference between human and artificial intelligence. Because of this difference, artificial intelligence models are impractical for applications where data is scarce and limited. Although small sample learning is challenging, it is crucial and advantageous, particularly for attaining rapid implementation and cheap deployment costs. In this context, this chapter examines recent advancements in small-sample learning. The study discusses data augmentation, transfer learning, generative and discriminative models, and meta-learning techniques for limited data problems. Specifically, a case study of convolutional neural network training on a small dataset for classification is provided. The chapter also highlights recent advances in many extensional small sample learning problems.

Chapter 7

Anil Kumar, RD Engineering College, India
Abhay Bhatia, Roorkee Institute of Technology, India
Arun Kashyap, GL Bajaj Institute of Technology and Management, India
Manish Kumar, Ajay Kumar Garg Engineering College, India

The world wide web (WWW) is an advanced system with an unmatched amount of digital data. Today's internet usage is accessible through common search engines like Google and Yahoo. Cybercriminals have become more assertive on social media. As a result, numerous commercial and trade websites are hacked, leading to forced trafficking of women and children as well as a number of other cybercrimes. Due to this, it is important to identify social media crimes as soon as possible in order to avoid them. To do this, a machine learning technique to detect crimes early must be proposed. Long short-term memory networks are a type of recurrent neural network that can pick up order dependency in problems involving prediction of sequence.

Chapter 8

Vibhor Sharma, Swami Rama Himalayan University, India
Lokesh Kumar, Roorkee Institute of Technology, India
Deepak Srivastava, Swami Rama Himalayan University, India

Useful information can be extracted through the analysis of Facebook posts. Text analysis and image analysis can play a vital role towards this. To predict the users' involvement, text data and image data can be incorporated using some machine learning models. These models can be used to perform testing on advertisements that are posted on Facebook for users' involvement prediction. Count of share and comments with sentiment analysis are included as users' involvement. This chapter contributes to understand the users' involvement on social media along with finding out the best machine learning model for prediction of users' involvement. The procedure of prediction with both text data and image data by suitable models is also discussed. This chapter produces a predictive model for posts of Facebook to predict users' involvement that will be based on the number of shares and comments on the post. The best models are obtained by using the combination of image data and text data. Further, it demonstrated that random models are surpassed by the models that are integrated for prediction.

Tawseef Ahmad Mir, Baba Ghulam Shah Badshah University, India
Aadil Ahmad Lawaye, Baba Ghulam Shah Badshah University, India
Akib Mohi Ud Din Khanday, United Arab Emirates University, Al Ain,
UAE

Social media, a buzz term in the modern world, refers to various online platforms like social networks, forums, blogs and blog comments, microblogs, wikis, media sharing platforms, social bookmarks through which communication between individuals, communities, or groups takes place. People over social media do not only share their ideas and opinions, but it has become an important source through which businesses promote their products. Analyzing huge data generated over social media is useful in various tasks like analyzing customer trends, forecast sales, understanding opinions of people on different hot topics, views of customers about services/products, and many more. Different natural language processing (NLP) techniques are used for crawling and processing social media data to get useful insights out of this. In this chapter, the focus is on various NLP techniques used to process the social media data. Challenges faced by NLP techniques to process social media data are also put forward in this chapter.

Ovais Bashir Gashroo, Jamia Millia Islamia, India
Saima Saleem, Jamia Millia Islamia, India
Monica Mehrotra, Jamia Millia Islamia, India

Before the development of information and communication technology, social connections were confined by narrow cultural borders. User-generated multimodal information, online social networks, and rich data related to human behavior have all undergone a revolution as a result of these social technologies. However, the abuse of social technology, such as social media platforms, has given rise to a brand-new type of cyber-crimes such as cyberbullying, cyberstalking, cyber trolling, identity theft, etc. Such crimes result in a breach of privacy, a security lapse, financial fraud, and harm to public mental health and property. This chapter discusses various automated methods and systems driven by machine learning, deep learning, and fuzzy-logic-based algorithms for tackling various types of cybercrimes on various social media platforms. It then highlights various issues and challenges pertaining to the existing methods, which offer new study avenues for researchers to investigate.

Artificial intelligence (AI) systems perform critical tasks in various safety-critical (e.g., medical devices, mission-control systems, and nuclear power plants). Uncertainty in the system may be caused by various reasons. Uncertainty quantification (UQ) approaches are essential for minimising the influence of uncertainties on optimisation and decision-making processes. Estimating the uncertainty is a challenging issue. Various machine-learning approaches are used for uncertainty quantification. This chapter comprehensively views uncertainty quantification approaches in machine learning (ML) techniques. Various factors cause uncertainty, and their possible solutions are presented. The uncertainty analysing approaches of the different machine learning methods, such as regression, classification, and segmentation, are discussed. The uncertainty optimisation process is broadly categorised into backward and forward approaches. The subsequent sections further classify and explain these backward and forward uncertainty approaches.

Preface

Welcome to the captivating world of *Advanced Applications of NLP and Deep Learning in Social Media Data*. This comprehensive book delves into the intriguing intersection of NLP, DL, and the analysis of social media. In this preface, we embark on a detailed exploration of the subject matter, shedding light on its various dimensions and intricacies.

Within the pages of this book, we embark on a fascinating journey into the realm of NLP and DL, focusing specifically on their advanced applications in analyzing social media data. As technology continues to evolve at an unprecedented pace, the ability to understand and interpret the vast amounts of textual information generated on social media platforms has become increasingly crucial. NLP and DL techniques provide powerful tools for extracting meaningful insights from this massive volume of unstructured data, enabling us to uncover valuable knowledge and make informed decisions.

OVERVIEW OF THE SUBJECT MATTER

Natural Language Processing (NLP) lies at the core of numerous everyday tools and applications. From virtual assistants like Siri to language translation software, chatbots, spam filters, search engines, and language correction tools, NLP has become an indispensable technology. By combining the knowledge of linguistics and the powerful AI algorithms of computer science, NLP enables machines to comprehend the rules, structure, and meaning of human language. It encompasses various aspects, including syntax, semantics, pragmatics, and morphology, to analyze and extract meaning from text and speech.

NLP, when combined with advanced Machine Learning (ML) algorithms, transforms artificial systems into artificially intelligent systems. This fusion of ML and NLP is instrumental in creating systems that can understand, process, and interpret information in a user-friendly manner. Social media platforms serve as rich sources of textual data, with users sharing their personal, social, and professional experiences.

Analyzing this vast and heterogeneous social media data requires advanced ML, DL, and intelligent tools and techniques. This book focuses on applying advanced NLP and DL approaches to collect, analyze, visualize, and process social media data to address a wide range of real-life challenges.

DESCRIPTION OF WHERE THE TOPIC FITS IN THE WORLD TODAY

In today's interconnected world, social media platforms play a crucial role in shaping public opinion, influencing behavior, and fostering connections among individuals. The sheer volume and diversity of data generated on these platforms present both immense opportunities and significant challenges. Researchers, academicians, and professionals need advanced techniques to receive, process, and interpret this information effectively, ensuring that social media interactions are safe, reliable, and beneficial for users.

The advanced applications of NLP and DL in social media data analysis offer a solution to these challenges. By leveraging the power of NLP and DL, we can gain valuable insights into sentiment analysis, semantic aspects, toxicity, emotion detection, fake news detection, influential nodes, propaganda identification, hate speech detection, opinion mining, user behavioral analysis, and much more. By exploring these topics, this book provides a roadmap for researchers and practitioners to navigate the complex landscape of social media data analysis, fostering a better understanding of its impact on society and facilitating the development of robust tools and systems.

DESCRIPTION OF THE TARGET AUDIENCE

This book is designed for a diverse audience with an interest in NLP, DL, social media analysis, and artificial intelligence. The target readers include:

Researchers and Academics: Professionals actively engaged in the field of NLP, DL, and social media analysis will find this book invaluable in expanding their knowledge and staying up-to-date with the latest advancements. It provides a comprehensive overview of advanced techniques, methodologies, and case studies, enabling researchers to contribute to the advancement of the field.

Professionals and Practitioners: Industry professionals, data scientists, analysts, and AI practitioners who work with social media data will discover practical insights, best practices, and real-world applications in this book. It equips them with the necessary knowledge and tools to tackle the challenges posed by social media data and harness its potential.

Students and Educators: This book serves as a valuable educational resource for students pursuing courses in NLP, DL, social media analysis, and related disciplines. It offers a solid foundation of theoretical concepts, practical techniques, and case studies, helping students understand the intricacies of social media data analysis.

As the editor of this book, I am honored to bring together a distinguished group of researchers and experts who have contributed their knowledge and expertise to this comprehensive compilation. Their collective insights and innovative approaches will undoubtedly enrich the readers' understanding of NLP and DL applications in social media data analysis.

The book is a collection of 11 chapters that cover different topics related to data analysis, Natural Language processing, and machine learning. A very brief description of each chapter is given as follows:

Chapter 1 provides an overview of social spam campaigns and their detection techniques, which is an essential area for social network services. The chapter presents various spam campaigns detected in the literature, their detection techniques, and the features used to build campaigns, highlighting various issues and challenges that need to be considered while detecting spammers.

Chapter 2 focuses on the forecasting of the COVID-19 second wave in the ten most affected states of India. The chapter explains the significance of predicting the trend and magnitude of the third wave with reasonable accuracy. The chapter uses the Autoregressive Integrated Moving Average Model (ARIMA) to forecast the temporal trends of the second wave of COVID-19 in India's ten most affected states. The performance evaluation of the model suggests that time series models can predict forthcoming COVID-19 waves by temporal analysis of previous waves.

Chapter 3 discusses clustering methods and tools to handle high-dimensional social media text data. The chapter presents various challenges of high-dimensional text datasets for NLP text clustering and how dimension reduction needs to be performed. The chapter also describes different methods found and classified in four areas, along with metrics and technical tools, and future directions.

Chapter 4 provides a critical review of community detection algorithms. The chapter provides an overview of the community structure, critical analysis of various community detection algorithms, and how graph theory approaches can be used to address issues like link prediction, community recognition in social network analysis, and social network mining.

Chapter 5 presents the proposal of a neural architecture for emotion recognition from textual data sources derived from multiple datasets. The chapter explains the importance of understanding emotional information in any form of communication and how the proposed architecture can resolve not less than 8 emotions from textual data sources using Google pre-trained word2vec word embeddings and a Multi-head attention-based bidirectional LSTM model with a one-vs-all Multi-Level Classification.

Chapter 6 focuses on learning from small samples in the age of big data. The chapter explains the ability of humans to learn new concepts from a few observations with strong generalization ability and how discovering patterns from small samples is complicated and challenging in machine learning (ML) and deep learning (DL). The chapter provides an overview of various learning techniques from small samples and their applications in the field of computer science.

Chapter 7 presents the architecture of a deep learning model for skin cancer detection, which explains the importance of early detection of skin cancer and how the proposed model can be used for the same. The chapter also provides a dataset consisting of two different skin lesions, i.e., benign and malignant.

Chapter 8 focuses on the evolution of IoT and its role in enabling edge computing. The chapter explains the significance of IoT in enabling edge computing and how it can revolutionize the field of computer science. The chapter also provides an overview of various architectures and approaches for implementing edge computing in IoT networks.

Chapter 9 presents an overview of blockchain technology and its applications in various fields. The chapter explains the significance of blockchain technology in ensuring transparency, security, and reliability in various applications and how it can revolutionize the field of computer science.

Chapter 10 provides an overview of the challenges and opportunities in implementing AI in the healthcare industry. The chapter explains the significance of AI in healthcare and how it can revolutionize the field of medicine. The chapter also provides an overview of various challenges and opportunities associated with the implementation of AI in healthcare.

Chapter 11 discusses the applications of machine learning in natural language processing (NLP) and presents various techniques for NLP. The chapter explains the significance of NLP in various fields, including healthcare, social media, and financial services, and how machine learning can be used to extract insights from large datasets.

This book makes a significant impact on the field of data analysis and machine learning by addressing a wide range of topics and providing valuable insights into various subject matters. Each chapter focuses on a specific aspect of data analysis, highlighting its importance and offering novel approaches and techniques to tackle the challenges associated with it.

The chapters in this book contribute to the subject matter by delving into diverse areas such as social spam campaign detection, COVID-19 forecasting, text clustering, community detection algorithms, emotion recognition, small-sample learning,

LSTM networks, user involvement prediction on social media, NLP techniques for processing social media data, and addressing cybercrimes in online social networks. By covering these topics, the book provides a comprehensive overview of the latest advancements in the field and offers practical solutions to real-world problems.

One of the key contributions of this book is the exploration of cutting-edge techniques and methodologies that can be applied to analyze and interpret large volumes of data generated from social media platforms. With the proliferation of social media, understanding user behavior, sentiment analysis, and extracting meaningful insights from text and image data have become crucial tasks for businesses and organizations. The chapters dedicated to NLP techniques, emotion recognition, and user involvement prediction shed light on the potential of machine learning models in extracting valuable information from social media data.

Additionally, this book addresses the challenges associated with learning from small samples, a topic of great significance in machine learning and deep learning. It highlights various techniques such as data augmentation, transfer learning, generative and discriminative models, and meta-learning, which enable effective learning and generalization from limited data. This aspect of the book is particularly valuable as it provides insights into techniques that can be applied in scenarios where data availability is scarce.

Moreover, the book contributes to the field by discussing the detection and mitigation of cybercrimes in online social networks. The chapters that explore trolling, cyber-stalking, cyber-bullying, and identity theft shed light on the methodologies and techniques that can be employed to combat these threats. By discussing automated methods driven by machine learning and deep learning algorithms, the book provides valuable insights into the development of systems that can effectively address these issues and safeguard privacy and security.

In conclusion, this book significantly impacts the field of data analysis and machine learning by offering a comprehensive overview of various topics and providing practical solutions to complex problems. Its contributions to the subject matter are far-reaching, as it addresses critical issues such as spam campaign detection, COVID-19 forecasting, text clustering, community detection, emotion recognition, small-sample learning, social media data processing, and cybercrime detection. Researchers, practitioners, and professionals in the field will benefit greatly from the insights and techniques presented in this book, paving the way for advancements and innovations in data analysis and machine learning.

We hope that this book serves as a valuable resource for readers seeking to deepen their understanding of NLP, DL, and their applications in the analysis of social media data. We extend our gratitude to all the authors and contributors who have shared their expertise and insights, making this comprehensive exploration possible.

This book was not possible without the efforts of many people. First and foremost, I would like to extend my heartfelt thanks to IGI Global for publishing this book. Your dedication to promoting cutting-edge research and knowledge dissemination has provided a platform for researchers and practitioners to share their expertise and contribute to the advancement of the subject matter. Your commitment to quality publications and scholarly works is commendable, and I am grateful for the opportunity to be a part of this endeavor.

To the authors of the book, Deepali Dhaka, Monica Mehrotra, Neha Kumari, William Alberto Cruz Castañeda, Marcellus Amadeus, Ny Akib Khanday, Syed Rabani, Qamar Khan, Fayaz Khan, Vishwanath Kamath, Jayantha Sarapanahalli, Ishfaq Rather, Shakeel Ahamad, Upasana Dohare, Sushil Kumar, Anil Kumar, Abhay Bhatia, Arun Kashyap, Manish Kumar, Vibhor Sharma, Lokesh Kumar, Deepak Srivastava, Tawseef Mir, Aadil Lawaye, Akib Khanday, Ovais Gashroo, Saima Saleem, and Ratneshwer Gupta, I extend my deepest appreciation for your remarkable contributions. Your expertise, dedication, and hard work are evident in each chapter of the book. Through your research and insights, you have made significant contributions to the field, addressing critical challenges, and providing valuable knowledge that will shape the future of data analysis and machine learning.

I would also like to express my gratitude to the reviewers who dedicated their time and expertise to ensure the quality and rigor of the book. Your valuable feedback, suggestions, and critical insights have been instrumental in refining the content and ensuring its scholarly excellence. Your commitment to maintaining the highest standards of academic work is greatly appreciated.

Last but not least, I want to extend my heartfelt thanks to the other editors who have worked tirelessly to bring this book to fruition. Your guidance, expertise, and meticulous attention to detail have been invaluable in shaping the structure, coherence, and overall quality of the book. Your dedication to maintaining the integrity of the research and ensuring its relevance and significance is truly commendable.

Once again, I would like to express my deepest appreciation to everyone associated with this book, directly or indirectly. Your collective efforts have contributed to the advancement of knowledge in the field of data analysis and machine learning, and your work will undoubtedly have a lasting impact on researchers, practitioners, and policymakers in this domain.

Thank you all for your exceptional contributions, and I look forward to witnessing the continued success and impact of your work.

Enjoy this journey into the advanced applications of NLP and deep learning in social media data!

Best Regards,

Ahmed A. Abd El-Latif
Menoufia University, Egypt & Prince Sultan University, Saudi Arabia

Mudasir Ahmad Wani
Prince Sultan University, Saudi Arabia

Mohammed A. El-Affendi
Prince Sultan University, Saudi Arabia

Acknowledgment

We gratefully acknowledge the collaborative efforts and contributions of numerous individuals in bringing this edited book to fruition. Without their support, expertise, and unwavering dedication, this project would not have been possible.

First and foremost, we express our deepest gratitude to the authors whose insightful chapters enrich the pages of this book. Your knowledge, research, and expertise have made a significant impact on the field, and we are honored to have your work included in this volume.

We extend our heartfelt appreciation to the reviewers who dedicated their time and expertise to provide invaluable feedback and suggestions. Your meticulous attention to detail and constructive criticism have greatly enhanced the quality and rigor of the book. We are immensely grateful for your commitment to scholarly excellence.

Our sincere thanks go to the editorial team for their hard work and dedication throughout the editing and production process. Your meticulousness, professionalism, and attention to detail have played a crucial role in shaping this book into its final form. Your commitment to maintaining high standards of quality is commendable.

We would like to express our gratitude to the publishing staff who have been instrumental in bringing this book to the public. Your support, guidance, and expertise have been invaluable in navigating the various stages of publication. We appreciate your commitment to disseminating knowledge and promoting academic discourse.

Additionally, we would like to thank our families, friends, and colleagues for their unwavering support and understanding during the countless hours we dedicated to this project. Your encouragement and belief in our abilities have been a constant source of motivation.

Finally, we extend our deepest gratitude to the readers of this book. It is our hope that the chapters presented within these pages inspire thought, provoke discussions, and contribute to further advancements in the field. Your interest and engagement make our efforts worthwhile.

Once again, we express our sincere appreciation to everyone who has played a part in making this edited book a reality. Your contributions and support have been invaluable, and we are truly grateful for the opportunity to collaborate with such talented individuals.

Thank you.

Ahmed Abd El-Latif, Mudasir Wani, Mohammed El-Affendi

Dr. Mudasir Wani would like to extend a special acknowledgment to my 9-month-old son (*Zohan*) for his incredible patience throughout the process of creating this book. Although you may not fully comprehend the complexities of this endeavor, your unwavering support and understanding have been truly remarkable.

To my dearest son, I want to express my deepest gratitude for your patience, love, and unwavering support. You have taught me the importance of balance, resilience, and finding joy in the journey. As you grow older, I hope this book serves as a testament to the profound impact you have had on my life and work.

In addition to acknowledging my 9-month-old son for his patience, I would like to express my heartfelt gratitude to the individuals who have been taking care of him during the process of creating this book. Dear *Kashish*, your dedication, love, and support have been invaluable, allowing me to focus on my work with peace of mind. Thank you for shouldering the responsibility of caring for our son while I immersed myself in the demands of this project.

Thank you for being an integral part of our lives and for your selflessness in caring for our precious little one.

With all my love and gratitude,

Mudasir Wani

Chapter 1

A Comprehensive Study to Detect Social Spam Campaigns

Deepali Dhaka
Jamia Millia Islamia, India

Monica Mehrotra
Jamia Millia Islamia, India

ABSTRACT

Social media is a widespread source of diverse forms of data. Information is diffusing so fast that any fascinating news is so rapidly spread through social media that it can be accessed by millions of users in seconds. Spammers are also part of these networks. Conventional spam detection approaches focus either on an individual message or individual account to classify them as spam or legitimate. However, these spam or spammers might be part of a group or controlled by some other accounts for a specific purpose called a campaign. Spam campaigns have become a great threat to social network services. They are more adversarial than individual spam accounts as they target many users on the network. Spam campaigns follow a stealthier approach than spammers to prevent themselves from detection. So, this study highlights various spam campaigns so far detected in the literature, their detection techniques, and the features used to build campaigns. It also highlights various issues and challenges that need to be picked up while detecting spammers.

INTRODUCTION

Social media is undoubtedly a part of almost everyone's life in one way or another. It is omnipresent in our digital lives and has made communication with anyone,

DOI: 10.4018/978-1-6684-6909-5.ch001

anywhere so easy, provided we have an internet connection and a device. People share their views and emotions on various issues through social media, and these views are so powerful they can reveal the personality and values of those users (Kakar et al., 2021a). Social media has become a platform for getting famous, running businesses, and more. It is an enormous source of information. However, this ease of use comes with a price sometimes, as these platforms are invaded by spammers (Dhaka & Mehrotra, 2019) who aim to gain monetarily from phishing, advertisement, pornography (Dhaka et al., 2022), malware distribution, identity theft, etc.

Mostly, spam approaches focus on either an individual message or individual account to classify them as spam or legitimate. However, these spammers or spam might be part of a group or controlled by some other accounts for a specific purpose called a campaign. Campaigns have become a great threat to social network services. A spam campaign is a group of spammers working in an organized and active way intended to achieve a goal. Spam Campaign is more adversarial than individual spam accounts as they target many users on the network. So, the main motive of social spam campaigns is to spread malicious content effectively to as many users as possible. Spam campaigns follow a stealthier approach than spammers to prevent themselves from detection. Generally, a spam campaign possesses two properties that help detect them. The first property is the distributive property, which refers to the spam campaign's ability to distribute its content to a large number of users in a short period. The second property is bursty behavior, which refers to the sudden increase in activity or frequency of messages from the spam campaign. By monitoring these two properties, social media platforms can detect and prevent the spread of spam campaigns, thereby protecting their users from malicious content.

Campaigns are groups of accounts formed to send information in bulk to other existing users on the network. However, these accounts that form campaigns are sometimes hijacked and manipulated to send unwanted and illicit information. Generally, campaigns can be classified into three categories –

1. **Legitimate Campaigns:** These are the groups of legitimate users who aim to work coordinately for a genuine reason such as campaigns running during a natural crisis to create awareness among people for their benefit, social campaign videos can be used to spread awareness among users regarding cyber sexual harassment (Rumahorbo & Mutiaz, 2023).
2. **Promotional Campaigns:** These campaigns aim to promote an event or product, generally for advertisement, or to gain more visibility on their target websites.
3. **Spam Campaigns:** These can be groups of spammers, botnets, or compromised accounts that are intended to send deceptive and malicious information to as

many users as possible for monetary profit or to direct users through URLs to phishing sites or malware.

We can further categorize spam campaigns as social spam campaigns and email spam campaigns as shown in Figure 1.

Figure 1. Taxonomy of campaigns

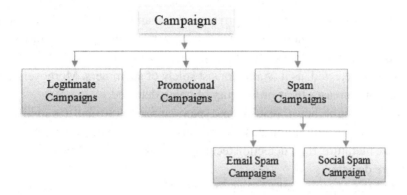

The Motivation Behind the Study

Spam campaigns are often carried out by organized groups with more resources and technical expertise than individual spammers. These groups may be more difficult to detect and track, making them a more significant threat to social media users. Spam campaigns on social media can have a significant impact on the platform's reputation and user trust. Users may be less likely to use a platform if they feel that it is not secure and that their personal information is at risk. This can lead to a decrease in user engagement, which in turn can negatively impact the platform's revenue and growth.

Additionally, spam campaigns may use various tactics to evade detection, such as creating multiple fake accounts, using URL shorteners to obscure malicious links, or using content that is difficult to distinguish from legitimate content. As a result, detecting and mitigating the impact of spam campaigns on social media can be a challenging task that requires a more comprehensive approach than just identifying individual spammers.

Studying spam campaigns can also help us understand information diffusion (Kakar et al., 2021b), which, in turn, can aid in developing more advanced detection algorithms.

Contribution

Despite considerable research having been done on the detection of spam and spam accounts, not much work has been done in studying the relationship among spammers i.e., how they exist in groups. To appear more genuine, spammers form a close-knit group whose members collaborate, resulting in a high clustering coefficient (Yang et al., 2012).

To gain greater insight into the activities of spammers, we need to identify their behavioral characteristics, which can be better understood by analyzing their existence in groups. As the reciprocity rate of the spammers is low, they tend to form a sparsely connected network with genuine users. To evade this feature, they may make dense connections among themselves, but a group like this would be more likely to be detected, as it would consist solely of spammers. Moreover, their similar behavior increases their probability of being detected.

This paper highlights how threatful these spam campaigns are and it is significant to detect them. This study highlights the various spam campaigns that have been detected in the literature, their detection techniques, and the features based on which campaigns are detected.

The rest of the paper is sectioned as follows- The first section discusses email spam campaign and their associated issues. The next section covers social spam campaigns, their classification based on the clustering features, and a summary of past work. Finally, the paper concludes with a discussion of the findings and their implications.

EMAIL SPAM CAMPAIGN

Email spamming is a conventional spamming method that has seen significant growth on the internet. Simply blocking spam emails is not an effective solution since spammers may find ways to evade such blocking techniques. Therefore, it is crucial to understand the behavior of spammers, which can be achieved by identifying and studying spam campaigns. Clustering spam emails into small groups based on a similarity metric can help in discovering these campaigns. By characterizing spam campaigns, we can gain insight into the behavior of spammers and develop effective prevention strategies (Sheikhalishahi et al., 2015).

The clustering of spam emails can be categorized into the following groups, as illustrated in Figure 2.

Figure 2. Clustering email spam campaign

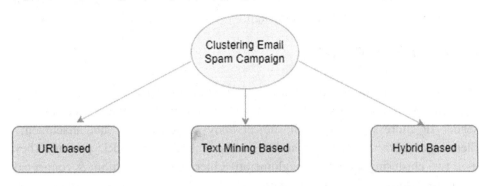

URL-Based Spam Email Clustering

To cluster spam emails into campaigns, a technique called spamscatter (Anderson et al., 2006) is used to extract URLs from the emails. These links are then followed to their destination server sites and websites that are graphically similar using the Image Shingling technique are grouped into one cluster. This method is often used to focus on scam infrastructure that is sustained by spam.

Another type of spam campaign is the botnet-based campaign, which involves a network of compromised computers controlled as a group with malicious intentions. These spamming botnets can be identified by analyzing the URLs they spread and their bursty and distributed properties. To identify botnet-based spam campaigns, a framework such as AutoRE (Xie et al., 2008) can be used. AutoRE generates automatic URL signatures of groups of similar URLs and focuses on email patterns that are bursty and distributed, without requiring labeled training data.

Text Mining-Based

Spam email texts can be analyzed using various techniques to cluster similar emails into campaigns. (Zhuang et al., 2008) used the shingling method to cluster spam emails with similar content into spam campaigns. Two campaigns could be merged if the spam message sending host participates in both spam campaigns. Mostly supervised learning is used to label campaigns.

(Qian et al., 2010) introduced an unsupervised text mining-based campaign identification framework called SCA SpamCampaignAssassin. This approach extracts campaign signatures and performs spam filtering based on them. They utilized LSA (latent semantic analysis) to group spam emails into clusters. (Calais et al., 2008) extracted attributes such as layout, language, and URL fragments from spam email messages to build a frequent pattern tree. Messages that share a common frequent path are clustered into a single campaign.

Hybrid Feature-Based

(Wei et al., 2008) discovered that many spam emails have no content but only attachments. To cluster such emails, they identified eleven attributes: message_id, sender_IP_address, sender_email, subject, body_length, word_count, attachment_ filename, attachment_MD5, attachment_size, body_URL, body_URL_domain). They used two clustering methods - agglomerative hierarchical algorithm & connected component with weighted edges algorithm. If the first algorithm was found to be weak, the second algorithm was applied.

The clustering algorithm used by (Sheikhalishahi et al., 2015) is named as Categorical Clustering Tree (CCTree). This algorithm forms a tree with a root consisting of all the attributes and then data is divided based on the attribute with the highest entropy among all.

ISSUES WITH EMAIL SPAM CAMPAIGN

Text mining-based and URL-based spam clustering strategies are common but not suitable for various reasons. Firstly, as spam emails keep changing their content, these strategies can become less effective. Secondly, the active period of a URL is usually short, and it can be challenging to cluster URLs due to the URL shortening service.

Szpyrka et al. (2023) uses campaign metrics such as click count, opens count, and hard bounces count instead of analyzing email content to detect campaigns.

To address these issues, Calais et al. (2008) proposed a new approach to cluster spam emails based on IP addresses resolved from URLs. This method is effective as IP addresses are not easy to change, but it can be a costly affair.

However, the main problems with these approaches are scalability and privacy. In the aforementioned work, there is no emphasis given on the privacy of email content, also approaches are not scalable enough to handle big data. To overcome these challenges, AlMahmoud et al. (2017) develop Spamdoop, a platform built on top of a standard Map Reduce facility. Spamdoop can handle a large amount of email data while maintaining the privacy of email content.

SOCIAL SPAM CAMPAIGNS

Social spamming is more successful than email spamming because spammers exploit the trust-based relationship between users on social networking sites (SNSs) (Chu et al., 2012; Stringhini, 2010).

Click-through rates of spam on SNSs are also observed to be much greater than that of email spam (Grier et al., 2010). This makes SNSs more lucrative for spammers than email. However, email-based spam filtering techniques are insufficient to protect other web services from spam. Email spam occurs in short-lived campaigns, while spam on other SNSs occurs in long-lasting campaigns (Thomas et al., 2011).

Instead of detecting spam messages or spam accounts individually, spam can be clustered into groups based on various similar features to detect campaigns, as listed below and shown in Figure 3.

1. URL-based
2. Content-based
3. Crowd retweeting
4. Hybrid feature-based
5. Phone number based

Figure 3. Social spam campaign clustering

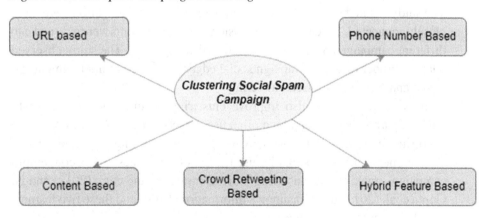

URL-Based

According to the work done so far, there are two ways to study spam campaigns. The first way is to cluster incoming messages, such as wall posts on Facebook or tweets on Twitter, based on some shared URLs, and then extract candidate campaigns from those clusters based on ground truth or spamming properties. This clustering cum classification approach has been adopted by several studies, including Gao et al. (2010), Grier et al. (2010), Chu et al. (2012), Zhang et al. (2012), and N. Gupta et al. (2012). The second approach is to first classify spammers/spams as either spam or ham based on some extracted features. Then, spam campaigns are extracted by clustering spam messages or spammers into groups based on URLs. This approach has been used by studies such as Stringhini (2010) and Gao et al. (2012).

1. URL-based clustering
    The use of URLs as a feature for grouping spam messages and spam accounts is independent of the context in which they are used. According to the existing literature, URL is considered an important feature to group similar spam messages and spam accounts. In a study (Stringhini, 2010) bots were grouped into a campaign if they advertised URLs pointing to the same site. The study found that the behavior of bots varied across different campaigns. Spammers use URL shortening services to evade OSNs filtering techniques, particularly if the URL directs to a hostile site. To overcome this, URLs can be crawled to reach their redirect chains, and the final URL can be used for blacklisting. However, this process can take time, which allows spammers to continue spamming for extended periods (Grier et al., 2010).
    Yang et al. (2012) analyzed the inner and outer social graphs of criminal accounts and criminal supporters to identify the characteristics of spammers. The study found that spammers belonging to the same organization were more closely connected. To reach this conclusion criminal accounts were grouped into different campaigns based on URLs advertised by them. The study observed a large number of intra-campaign social edges compared to inter-campaigns.

2. URL- and timestamp-based clustering
    Temporal features can also improve clustering accuracy when used with URLs. Spammers in a campaign often use botnets to auto-post messages in a short time interval to reach as many users as possible. This temporal activity of spammers with URLs can be used to group messages and accounts into campaigns, making the clustering more accurate. Zhang et al. (2012) and N. Gupta et al. (2012) used Shannon's information theory and these two features to link accounts with similar purposes.

3. URL- and content-based clustering
    Clustering techniques are used to group those messages that share a similar textual description and URL destination (Gao et al., 2010; Egele et al., 2017). Chu et al. (2012) do not only rely on URLs but also consider other features like content and behavior. To detect compromised accounts, Egele et al. (2017) built a behavioral profile from user's messages. They modeled seven features

to build the behavioral profile mentioned in Table 1. The study focused on compromised accounts, which are more harmful than profiles made specially to disseminate spam, as these compromised accounts can easily gain the trust of other legitimate users because of their profile history. To detect large-scale compromised accounts, messages are grouped based on two similarity measures: message content similarity using n-gram analysis and URL similarity. For each group, the proposed system checks all accounts to determine if messages deviate from the account's behavioral profile. If messages in a group deviate from the account's behavioral profile and exceed a threshold, then the group is considered suspicious.

Using semantic similarity may result in computational overhead for a real-time system. Therefore, an alternative is required for an online spam filtering system like text shingling. An online spam filtering system is required for the early detection of spam or spammers, with a minimal time lag. Gao et al. (2012) developed an online spam filtering system deployed on the OSN service provider side which checks every incoming message before sending it to its intended receiver. To overcome the online clustering overhead, the study used incremental clustering and parallelization. Incoming messages are clustered into one group based on text shingling and URL comparison. Then, based on OSN-specific features and a few general features of the spam clusters formed so far, messages are classified as spam or legitimate.

Content-Based

To detect a spam campaign, most of the work revolves around URLs, but a tweet or text-based models also have great potential in optimizing spam campaign detection methods followed by a deep learning approach (Mostafa et al., 2020). Lee et al. (2013) found a graph-based content-driven method to extract and identify campaigns on large social media platforms. The main idea is to find the correlation between messages at the user level. According to their hypothesis, a campaign is defined as a set of users, and the messages they posted belong to a common talking point. It has also been observed that spam campaigns use hot topics which are trending i.e., hashtags, and exploit them to hide malevolent URLs (Antonakaki et al., 2016). Studying how information diffuses in and out of a campaign help in understanding the behavior of spammers. A post that is posted many times by the same account can be considered spam. Ghosh et al. (2011) studied such posts having embedded URLs to get to know about their retweet dynamics using an entropy-based classification approach. Compared to human retweeting, automatic retweeting has a lower time interval entropy.

Crowd Retweeting-Based

The social connections of crowd retweeting-based campaigns differ from those of other existing spam campaigns. These campaigns have adopted a crowdsourcing system to spread spam, posing a significant threat to OSNs as they take advantage of the inherited property of microblogging sites and evade traditional detection approaches. They try to appear as normal as possible by creating attractive profiles, following legitimate accounts, and updating their tweets frequently. There are two types of crowd-retweeting spammers: spam initiators and spam workers.

Spam initiators pay spam workers to retweet target spam messages. Profile features, social relationships, and retweeting behavior of both spam initiators and spam workers are some significant features.

Spam initiators are connected non-reciprocally and behave more like normal users and spam workers are more closely connected and their retweeting behavior differs from normal users.

They spread spam by retweeting and a campaign can reach a large number of users through an online social network and its mention network (Liu et al., 2018).

Hybrid Features-Based

A spam campaign can also be identified based on a set of different categories of features. According to Ahmed and Abulaish (2013), features like friends, followers, pages, hashtags, and URLs are important for classification. An undirected social graph can be formed, consisting of nodes as spam profiles, and edges between two profiles are weighted based on the information contained in the identified features. The Markov clustering algorithm is then applied to group similar spam profiles, which are further analyzed to find campaigns. This work was done to find campaigns on both Twitter and Facebook networks. Fazil and Abulaish (2020) modeled the multi-attributed profile features of a user using a graph-based approach to detect coordinated campaigns.

Phone Number-Based

Most spam campaigns are detected based on URLs present in the messages. However, there are malicious messages which do not contain URLs, making URL-based detection insufficient. To detect a broader range of spam messages, we should focus on aggressively advertising phone numbers over social media and the associated messages (Jere et al., 2021).

Spammers are exploiting the phone numbers advertised on social networks to run spam campaigns. Spam attacks can be done by calling or sending SMS to legitimate users. Phone number-based spam campaigns use one channel to disseminate information like OSN, and other channels like the phone to attract users via call or SMS.

Although URL-based spam attack has been extensively explored, using phone number over URLs appears to be a better option to run campaigns because –

- Telephony medium is easily used by users, and their inherent trust property makes them a better choice.
- Fewer phone numbers are required compared to URLs to bypass the filtering mechanism.
- It is difficult to detect a phone-based attack because it requires cross-channel analysis, i.e., phone and web, while URLs involve only one channel (web).

This area has not yet been explored much, but recently, few works have been done in this context.

One way to lure users to call a number controlled by spammers is by aggressively advertising them on social media. This category of spam that gains monetary profit through telephony channels is called outgoing phone communication attacks (P. Gupta et al., 2018). Tech support scams and credit counseling scams are examples of two phone advertising spam campaigns.

Some campaigns exploit the phone number information across multiple platforms to reach more users with the same effect. With the convergence of two media, telephony, and the internet, the phone channel has become an attractive medium for spammers to spread spam. These days attackers instead of calling victims directly, spread a toll-free phone number across different platforms associated with some alluring text. When a user calls this number, the spammer convinces them to take the service and in return asks for money in advance or gains remote access to the user's machine with deceptive intentions. Such kinds of spammers work in groups to form a campaign. Depending on the value of the Jaccard coefficient between the corresponding set of posts, two phone numbers are kept together in a cluster, which will eventually form a campaign. If information about such spam accounts/spammers is shared across different platforms, it may aid in spammer detection (S. Gupta et al., 2018).

Microblogging networks like Twitter can be modeled as heterogeneous information networks (HIN) to detect spam campaigns using meta paths between two users. To know the similarity between two users, a metric called Hierarchical Meta-Path Scores (HMPS) is used (S. Gupta et al., 2018). The study focused on tweets containing phone numbers. As their spammer and non-spammer classes are highly imbalanced, they did feedback-based active learning using an SVM-based one-class classifier.

A prototype tool called COMPA was developed to detect compromised accounts and their campaign. COMPA detected spam campaigns that do not contain URLs but lure victims to call a phone number. Additionally, it is also capable of detecting "Get more followers" scams and worms (Egele et al., 2013).

Table 1 shows a summary of a few works mentioned in the manuscript based on techniques and features used to detect spam campaigns.

Table 1. Summary of a few important works

Reference	Social Network	Time	Data Source &Statistics	Technique	Features Used	Observation
(Xie et al., 2008)	Hotmail	3 months	Emails from Hotmail, identified 7,721 botnet-based spam campaigns & 340,050 unique botnet host IP addresses.	A framework called AutoRE generates URL signatures to identify botnet-based spam campaign.	Content-based – Using URLs in an email (URL having distributed yet bursty property.	Botnets are evolving, so we need to evolve with those features which cannot be easily evaded by spammers.
(N. Gupta et al., 2012)	Twitter	Not available	2000 URLs are randomly picked from the Tweets2011 corpus.	A graph-based approach to get candidate campaign, MCL algorithm is used to distinguish between spam and promotion campaign.	URL and timestamp CHECK REF-Zhang2016	Based on the SVM classifier, the clusters were first categorized by URLs and time interval of tweets and then classified with 87.6% F1-measure and 90.3% Precision
(Egele et al., 2017)	Twitter, Facebook	3 months (Twitter), 2 years (Facebook)	By accessing Twitter streaming and RESTful API services, 1.4 billion messages from Twitter have been collected, 106 million messages from Facebook (used already existing dataset of the year 2009)	COMPA is the first system designed to detect individual compromised accounts as well as large-scale compromises called a campaign. COMPA leverages anomaly detection approaches.	For behavioral profile-Time (hour of the day), Msg source, Msg text, Msg topic, link in the message, direct user interaction, proximity. Campaign – message content and URL.	Detected 383,613 compromised accounts on Twitter and 11,087 compromised accounts on Facebook also detected large-scale compromises.
(Ahmed & Abulaish, 2013)	Twitter, Facebook	Not available	320 Facebook and 305 Twitter profiles (Java API parser) Manual labeling Facebook: 165 (spam), 155 (normal) Twitter: 160 (spam), 145 (normal)	Machine learning was used for classification, MCL algorithm is used on a weighted graph to find spam campaigns	Hybrid feature set -Interactions-Driven, Posts/tweets-Driven, URL-Driven Facebook &Twitter Features, Tags-Driven Facebook Features	The best classification result is obtained by using the J48 algorithm using a combined dataset. Spam campaign detection accuracy can be improved further by identifying more features.
(Gao et al., 2012)	Twitter, Facebook	January 2008 to June 2009 (Facebook), June 2011 to 21 July 2011 (Twitter)	187 million Facebook wall messages and 17 million tweets.	The decision Tree algorithm was used to classify spam messages from spam campaigns, and text shingling and URL comparison was done to construct a campaign from spam messages.	Hybrid feature set-OSN-specific features -Sender Social Degree, Interaction History. General features -Cluster Size, Average Time Interval, Average URL Number per Message, Unique URL Number. Campaign feature – URL, text shingling.	After the deployment of the online spam filtering system, it has been seen that it requires low maintenance cost also system achieves high accuracy, low latency & high throughput.

continued on following page

Table 1. Continued

Reference	Social Network	Time	Data Source &Statistics	Technique	Features Used	Observation
(Chu et al., 2012)	Twitter	3 months, February to April 2011	50 million tweets (developed a crawler in PHP which taps to Twitter streaming API and search API).	Random forest is used for classifying campaigns and tweets are clustered into campaigns based on the same final URLs in tweets.	Classification features. Tweet level – spam content proportion, URL redirection, URL blacklisting. Account level features – account profile, social relationship, account reputation, account taste, Lifetime Tweet Number, Account Registration Date, Account Verification, and Account Protection. Campaign-level features - Hashtag Ratio, Mention Ratio, Content Self-similarity Score, Posting Device Makeup.	This work effectively classifies campaigns into spam and legitimate ones by the Random Forest algorithm using both content and behavioral features with 94.5 accuracy.
(Jere et al., 2021)	Tumblr, Twitter, and Flickr	4 months	18,000,000 posts	LDA with cosine similarity	Phone related keywords like call me, call us etc.	Total of 519 phone numbers were found, responsible for spam campagns across these thre platforms.
(Sharma et al., 2021)	Twitter	To access covid19 tweetsMarch 1 to July 22, 2020.	312 of the Russian coordinated trolls' accounts with their 1.2M tweets, and also includes 1713 normal accounts. Post with covid19 keyword - 119,298 active accounts with 13.9 million tweets.	An unsupervised generative model for coordination detection.	Temporal activity of accounts like -posting original content, replying,re-sharing, or reacting to other posts.	Detected coordinated accouts based on their behaviors. Their model is independent of the language, hence can be used across platforms.
(Gao et al., 2010)	Facebook	April and June 2009	187M wall posts crawled from roughly 3.5 million users.	Clustering of messages sharing similar text and URL destination.	Those URLs and text cluster into the Spam campaign having bursty and distributed properties.	Threshold-based techniques for spam detection identified 200,000 posts from 57,000 malicious accounts. Most of the attacks are phishing attacks.
(Mostafa et al., 2020)	Twitter	Not available	150,000 Tweets	Several machine learning classifiers, such as SVM or naïve Bayes or random forest are used.	Tweets transform into a vector representation, then the Manhattan lstm model is used to find their similarity.	They found 58 candidate campaigns with an average F1 measure of 94.6. In the future they will consider Tweet timestamp to improve text similarity.
(Antonakaki et al., 2016)	Twitter	3 months Tan-March 2014	150 million tweets	lightweight classifier	Total no. of tweets, hashtags, user mention, URLs, followers, followee.	Detected 73.5% of spammers with a low FPR of 0.25%

OBSERVATIONS

1. The content-based clustering approach may not be effective as spammers can easily manipulate content. Therefore, it is recommended to use more comprehensive similarity measures like text shingling to detect spam campaigns.

2. Instead of only considering URLs, the landing pages of the URLs should also be analyzed as spammers can use URL shortening services to evade URL -based detection.

3. Detecting campaigns on social media platforms like Twitter and Facebook can be challenging due to their large user base and the contextual meaning of the short post is difficult to determine.

4. A user-centric approach to detect spam campaigns is more robust than analyzing individual messages.

5. Spammers tend to be closely connected within their social community compared to normal users.

6. Within the spammer social community, spam workers tend to follow each other to form a small world, while spam initiators tend to be connected nonreciprocally and exhibit behavior similar to legitimate users.

7. Spam workers are more likely to retweet the tweets of their followees, especially for one-hop retweeting, compared to normal users.

8. Studies have shown that spammers tend to have more followees and followers compared to normal users.

9. Malicious accounts tend to perform loosely synchronized actions in various social network contexts.

10. Campaigns help in persuasive communication. Their impact on users is such that they deflect their opinions about an issue.

11. Botnets are threatening as they spread spam campaigns. They can be controlled by a single individual or group and can control more than one campaign. Therefore campaigns running by the same entity are more crucial (Patel, 2022).

CONCLUSION

The problem of detecting and combating spammers on social media platforms is indeed challenging, as spammers are constantly evolving and adapting their tactics to evade detection. While many detection techniques focus on individual spammer account detection, it is important to consider how spammers work in groups or campaigns to reach as many users as possible with malicious intentions. This manuscript provides an overview of various techniques for detecting spam campaigns and classifies the literature based on the feature used to detect them. However, the study focuses on campaigns on a single platform, and it is important to note that some campaigns may target users on multiple platforms. Cross-platform studies could be an interesting avenue for future research in this area.

Overall, effective spam detection and prevention requires a combination of techniques, including content-based clustering, analysis of final landing pages, user-centric detection, and analysis of the behavior of spammer groups. By staying vigilant and constantly adapting to new tactics, social media platforms can work to protect their users from the harmful effects of spam campaigns.

REFERENCES

Ahmed, F., & Abulaish, M. (2013). A generic statistical approach for spam detection in Online Social Networks. *Computer Communications*, *36*(10–11), 1120–1129. doi:10.1016/j.comcom.2013.04.004

AlMahmoud, A., Damiani, E., Otrok, H., & Al-Hammadi, Y. (2017). Spamdoop: A privacy-preserving Big Data platform for collaborative spam detection. *IEEE Transactions on Big Data, 7790*, 1–1. doi:10.1109/TBDATA.2017.2716409

Anderson, D. S., Fleizach, C., Savage, S., & Voelker, G. M. (2006). *Spamscatter : Characterizing Internet Scam Hosting Infrastructure*. Academic Press.

Antonakaki, D., Polakis, I., Athanasopoulos, E., Ioannidis, S., & Fragopoulou, P. (2016). Exploiting abused trending topics to identify spam campaigns in Twitter. *Social Network Analysis and Mining*, *6*(1), 1–11. doi:10.100713278-016-0354-9

Calais, P. H., Pires, D. E. V., Guedes, D. O., Wagner, M., Hoepers, C., & Steding-Jessen, K. (2008). *A Campaign-based Characterization of Spamming Strategies*. Ceas.

Chu, Z., Widjaja, I., & Wang, H. (2012). Detecting social spam campaigns on Twitter. Lecture Notes in Computer Science, 7341, 455–472. doi:10.1007/978-3-642-31284-7_27

Dhaka, D., Kakar, S., & Mehrotra, M. (2022). Detection of spammers disseminating obscene content on Twitter. *International Journal of Business Intelligence and Data Mining*, *21*(3), 265–289. doi:10.1504/IJBIDM.2022.125210

Dhaka, D., & Mehrotra, M. (2019, February).: Cross-Domain Spam Detection in Social Media: A Survey. In *International Conference on Emerging Technologies in Computer Engineering* (pp. 98-112). Springer. 10.1007/978-981-13-8300-7_9

Egele, M., Stringhini, G., Kruegel, C., & Vigna, G. (2013, February). Compa: Detecting compromised accounts on social networks. NDSS.

Egele, M., Stringhini, G., Kruegel, C., & Vigna, G. (2017). Towards Detecting Compromised Accounts on Social Networks. *IEEE Transactions on Dependable and Secure Computing*, *14*(4), 447–460. doi:10.1109/TDSC.2015.2479616

Fazil, M., & Abulaish, M. (2020). A socialbots analysis-driven graph-based approach for identifying coordinated campaigns in twitter. *Journal of Intelligent & Fuzzy Systems*, *38*(3), 3301–3305. doi:10.3233/JIFS-182895

Gao, H., Chen, Y., Lee, K., Palsetia, D., & Choudhary, A. (2012). *Towards Online Spam Filtering in Social Networks*. NDSS. doi:10.1016/j.carbon.2015.04.031

Gao, H., Hu, J., Wilson, C., Li, Z., Chen, Y., & Zhao, B. Y. (2010). Detecting and characterizing social spam campaigns. *Proceedings of the 10th Annual Conference on Internet Measurement - IMC '10*, 35. 10.1145/1879141.1879147

Ghosh, R., Surachawala, T., & Lerman, K. (2011). *Entropy-based Classification of "Retweeting" Activity on Twitter*. https://arxiv.org/abs/1106.0346

Grier, C., Thomas, K., Paxson, V., & Zhang, M. (2010, October). @ spam: the underground on 140 characters or less. In *Proceedings of the 17th ACM conference on Computer and communications security* (pp. 27-37). ACM.

Gupta, N., Bhaskar, M., & Gupta, D. K. (2012). Macroenvironmental influence on Hepatozoon lacertilis infectivity to lizard Hemidactylus flaviviridis. *Journal of Environmental Biology*, *33*(1), 127–132. doi:10.1145/0000000.0000000 PMID:23033655

Gupta, P., Perdisci, R., & Ahamad, M. (2018). Towards Measuring the Role of Phone Numbers in Twitter-Advertised Spam. *ASIA CCS '18 (ACM Asia Conference on Computer and Communications Security)*. 10.1145/3196494.3196516

Gupta, S., Khattar, A., Gogia, A., Kumaraguru, P., & Chakraborty, T. (2018). *Collective Classification of Spam Campaigners on Twitter: A Hierarchical Meta-Path Based Approach*. doi:10.1145/3178876.3186119

Gupta, S., Kuchhal, D., Gupta, P., Ahamad, M., Gupta, M., & Kumaraguru, P. (2018). Under the Shadow of Sunshine: Characterizing Spam Campaigns Abusing Phone Numbers Across Online. *Social Networks*, 67–76. Advance online publication. doi:10.1145/3201064.3201065

Jere, R., Pandey, A., Singh, M., & Ganjapurkar, M. (2021, January). Leveraging Phone Numbers for Spam detection in Online Social Networks. In *2021 IEEE 19th World Symposium on Applied Machine Intelligence and Informatics (SAMI)* (pp. 119-124). IEEE.

Kakar, S., Dhaka, D., & Mehrotra, M. (2021a). Value-Based Behavioral Analysis of Users Using Twitter. In *Inventive Communication and Computational Technologies* (Vol. 145, pp. 283–294). Springer. doi:10.1007/978-981-15-7345-3_23

Kakar, S., Dhaka, D., & Mehrotra, M. (2021b). Value-based retweet prediction on twitter. *Informatica (Slovenia)*, *45*(2), 267–276. doi:10.31449/inf.v45i2.3465

Lee, K., Caverlee, J., Cheng, Z., & Sui, D. Z. (2013). Campaign extraction from social media. *ACM Transactions on Intelligent Systems and Technology*, *5*(1), 1–28. doi:10.1145/2542182.2542191

Liu, B., Ni, Z., Luo, J., Cao, J., Ni, X., Liu, B., & Fu, X. (2018). Analysis of and defense against crowd-retweeting based spam in social networks. *World Wide Web (Bussum)*, 1–23. doi:10.100711280-018-0613-y

Mostafa, M., Abdelwahab, A., & Sayed, H. M. (2020). Detecting spam campaign in twitter with semantic similarity. *Journal of Physics: Conference Series*, *1447*(1), 012044. Advance online publication. doi:10.1088/1742-6596/1447/1/012044

Patel, C. (2022). *Visual Analysis of Spam Campaigns based on Network Modelling*. Academic Press.

Qian, F., Pathak, A., Hu, Y. C., Mao, Z. M., & Xie, Y. (2010). A case for unsupervised-learning-based spam filtering. *Performance Evaluation Review*, *38*(1), 367–368. doi:10.1145/1811099.1811090

Rumahorbo, K. A., & Mutiaz, I. (2023). In-Press: Adolescent Responses to the Social Campaign Video on Kemdikbud. RI Account about Cyber-sexual Harassment. *Indonesian Journal of Visual Culture, Design, and Cinema*, *2*(1), 107-116.

Sharma, K., Zhang, Y., Ferrara, E., & Liu, Y. (2021, August). Identifying coordinated accounts on social media through hidden influence and group behaviours. In *Proceedings of the 27th ACM SIGKDD Conference on Knowledge Discovery & Data Mining* (pp. 1441-1451). ACM.

Sheikhalishahi, M., Mejri, M., & Tawbi, N. (2015). Clustering Spam Emails into Campaigns. *Proceedings of the 1st International Conference on Information Systems Security and Privacy*, 90–97. 10.5220/0005244500900097

Stringhini, G. (2010). *Detecting spammers on social networks*. https://dl.acm.org/citation.cfm?id=1920261.1920263

Szpyrka, M., Suszalski, P., Obara, S., & Nalepa, G. J. (2023). Email Campaign Evaluation Based on User and Mail Server Response. *Applied Sciences (Basel, Switzerland)*, *13*(3), 1630. doi:10.3390/app13031630

Thomas, K., Grier, C., Ma, J., Paxson, V., & Song, D. (2011). Design and evaluation of a real-time URL spam filtering service. *Proceedings - IEEE Symposium on Security and Privacy*, 447–462. 10.1109/SP.2011.25

Wei, C., Sprague, A., Warner, G., & Skjellum, A. (2008). Mining spam email to identify common origins for forensic application. *SAC '08: Proceedings of the 2008 ACM Symposium on Applied Computing,* 1433–1437. 10.1145/1363686.1364019

Xie, Y., Yu, F., Achan, K., Panigrahy, R., Hulten, G., & Osipkov, I. (2008). Spamming botnets: Signatures and characteristics. *Computer Communication Review*, *38*(4), 171–182. doi:10.1145/1402946.1402979

Yang, C., Harkreader, R., Zhang, J., Shin, S., & Gu, G. (2012). Analyzing spammers' social networks for fun and profit: a case study of cyber criminal ecosystem on twitter. *WWW '12: Proceedings of the 21st International Conference on World Wide Web*, 71–80. 10.1145/2187836.2187847

Zhang, X., Zhu, S., & Liang, W. (2012). Detecting spam and promoting campaigns in the Twitter social network. *Proceedings - IEEE International Conference on Data Mining,* 1194–1199. 10.1109/ICDM.2012.28

Zhuang, L., Dunagan, J., Simon, D. R., Wang, H. J., Osipkov, I., Hulten, G., & Tygar, J. (2008). Characterizing botnets from email spam records. *Proceedings of the 1st Usenix Workshop on Large-Scale Exploits and Emergent Threats, 2*, 1–9. https://static.usenix.org/events/leet08/tech/full_papers/zhu ang/zhuang.pdf%5Cnpapers2://publication/uuid/A045FDFA-4186-4 754-BD44-EB30103D1F2F

Chapter 2
ARIMA Modeling and Forecasting of COVID–19 Second Wave in the 10 Most Affected States of India

Neha Kumari
Jawaharlal Nehru University, India

ABSTRACT

India was hit by the devastating second wave of COVID-19 with a sudden surge in cases in April 2021. It was far more severe and catastrophic than the first wave. Several models tried to gauge the severity and peak of the second wave but were successful only to some extent. The current scenario highlights the urgent need to forecast the trend and magnitude of the third COVID-19 wave with reasonable accuracy. It will significantly aid the COVID-19 preparation and planning by government and non-government organizations. The present research work forecasts the temporal trends of the second wave of COVID-19 in India's 10 most affected states using the autoregressive integrated moving average model (ARIMA). The model is trained using COVID-19 confirmed cases from March 14, 2020 to March 30, 2021 for India's 10 most affected states (i.e., Bihar, Delhi, Gujarat, Haryana, Karnataka, Madhya Pradesh, Maharashtra, Rajasthan, Tamil Nadu, and Uttar Pradesh). Performance evaluation of the model suggested that time series models can predict forthcoming COVID-19 waves by temporal analysis of previous waves.

DOI: 10.4018/978-1-6684-6909-5.ch002

INTRODUCTION

The COVID-19 pandemic emerged as a global challenge for humanity, demanding adequate attention from researchers, policymakers, and the government. When the nation struggles with a health crisis and a crumbling economy, it is imperative to understand its complex dynamics to offer early warning systems and help government officials take essential measures to alleviate it (Adiga et al., 2020).

India experienced a catastrophic second wave of COVID-19 with a record of thousands of new confirmed cases every day, demanding adequate attention from all stakeholders. Different mathematical and data-driven approaches, including government SUTRA (Susceptible, Undetected, Tested Positive, and Removed Approach), tried to gauge the second wave's severity but were somewhat successful (Koshy, 2021). Modeling virus spread is an interplay of numerous factors, including mobility, geographic variations at the local level, health conditions of susceptible populations, intervention strategies, following lockdown protocols like masks, adhering to Social distancing procedures, etc. (Adiga et al., 2020; Koshy, 2021).

There was an apparent disparity in temporal trends of the second wave in different states (Katoch & Sidhu, 2021). Understanding the temporal variations of previous waves and forecasting forthcoming waves and their severity is the need of the hour (Roy et al., 2021; Wu et al., 2018). The present study explores the ARIMA model for temporal analysis of past Covid waves to validate and predict future waves. The study elucidates the importance of time series analysis for analyzing temporal trends of the second wave, and the present research can pave the way for forecasting future Covid waves.

Epidemics are spatiotemporal in nature. So, before modeling epidemics, it is imperative to understand the nature of virus propagation in both space and time and then design the appropriate model (Wang et al., 2022). Spatiotemporal Data Analysis is complicated owing to challenges posed by the complex data. Spatiotemporal dependencies between the incidence cases, heterogeneity, and missing values are some of the challenges that must be addressed before modeling.

In this context, this chapter highlights simple mathematical models with spatiotemporal data instances and then elaborates ARIMA model to gauge the temporal prediction of Covid 19. The author also accentuated models' role and importance in different stages of epidemic modeling. Literature demonstrated that simple forecasting models like ARIMA can gauge temporal correlations between incidence cases. State-of-the-art also highlighted the use of Recurrent Neural Networks for the Temporal study of epidemics. RNN has a vanishing gradients problem. Even simple regressive methods can model real world epidemic data (Ceylan et al., 2020; Chaurasia & Pal, 2020; Cong et al., 2019; He & Tao, 2018; Hyndman & Athanasopoulos, 2018; MK et al., 2022).

Simple regressive methods can ascertain temporal observations in real-time data like epidemics. The chapter also elaborates that simple mathematical models like SIR(Susceptible- Infected – Recovered) can also identify peak, the population at risk, epidemic size, and other epidemic parameters (Hyndman & Athanasopoulos, 2018).

These mathematical models represent the risk change rate from differential equations theory. The present research work forecasts the temporal trends of the second wave of Covid-19 in India's ten most affected states using the Autoregressive Integrated Moving Average Model (ARIMA).

Role of Models

The spread of infectious diseases is complex, and it is crucial to understand the nature of epidemic observations before modeling them (Wang et al., 2022). In recent years, with the emergence of geographical information systems, a deluge of data regarding location and environment has unfolded many opportunities to explore geographic variations of disease concerning space and time. Mathematical, agent-based, network, and machine learning models have been addressed in the recent work to understand the nature of the virus and critical dynamics of an epidemic like the peak of the epidemic curve, incubation period, R0, serial generation time, etc. (Ceylan et al., 2020; Chaurasia & Pal, 2020; Cong et al., 2019; He & Tao, 2018; MK et al., 2022). Classical compartmental models were used extensively in the literature. The simplest mathematical model is the SIR model (Susceptible Infected-Recovered). The idea of the model is the assumption of three groups among the homogeneous population, i.e., Susceptible, Infected, and Recovered. Differential equations model the transitions between compartments. However, these models are insufficient for addressing spatiotemporal challenges posed by epidemic data.

Epidemic Stages and Modeling

Different epidemic stages require different modeling strategies and data-driven methods to understand the spread of disease. The question of interest for epidemiologists varies across phases of a pandemic. For instance, machine learning models can help short-term forecast projections (Adiga et al., 2020). If the epidemic has roots in the country, we have transitioned to the acceleration stage (Adiga et al., 2020). And at this stage, it is crucial to identify the temporal trends in confirmed cases, trends of mortality rates, and epidemic size predicting the future time course of an epidemic. Models at this stage require time-series datasets of disease cases, mortality rates, and hospitalizations. Autoregressive models (AR) and their different variants have been extensively used in previous epidemics to study temporal patterns (Cong et al., 2019; He & Tao, 2018). They use historical data for forecasting, and model parameters can be tuned using updated past values over time.

Deep Learning and Temporal Trends of the Epidemic

Epidemic data can be categorized as spatiotemporal disease outbreak event data. An event can be described as a point, location, and time, i.e., when and where the disease cases happened.

This event can be represented as tuple $<c_i, t_i>$, where c_i is the case happening at a particular time stamp t_i (MK et al., 2022; Wu et al., 2018). Recurrent neural networks can capture temporal correlations in spatiotemporal data. A recurrent Neural Network (RNN) forms connections between nodes to form a sequential directed graph. Recurrent Neural Network has memory to store sequences. Recurrent Neural Networks convert independent activations into dependent by assigning same weights and biases to the layers.

The major drawback of RNN is the problem of vanishing gradients. Hence, the simple model of ARIMA model is used in this research work to identify temporal correlations in epidemic case observations.

BACKGROUND

The government needs to respond to the pandemic stages and thus relies on different data-driven and statistical techniques to plan and respond. A substantial literature has tried various methods ranging from time series-based predictive models to advanced machine learning models like support vector machines, wavelet neural networks, and mathematical models like SIR models for contact tracing (Ceylan et al., 2020; Chaurasia & Pal, 2020; Cong et al., 2019; He & Tao, 2018; Hyndman & Athanasopoulos, 2018; MK et al., 2022).

Previous epidemics suggested many forecasting methods to analyze the temporal patterns in contagious diseases like Tuberculosis, influenza, SARS, Ebola, and Dengue (Roy et al., 2021). ARIMA model was the most widely used forecasting technique in the state-of-the-art methods with a Time series forecasting perspective (Ceylan et al., 2020; Chaurasia & Pal, 2020; Cong et al., 2019; He & Tao, 2018; Hyndman & Athanasopoulos, 2018; Kaunain Sheriff, 2021; MK et al., 2022).

In a paper, Wu et al. (2018) developed a deep learning-based framework to find epidemic parameters in time series data. Early detection of epidemic parameters is an essential problem in public health. The paper addressed two challenges of epidemic prediction - the temporal dependency between disease cases and the need for real-time prediction. Limited training data is an open challenge in real-time epidemic prediction with Time Series forecasting perspective. The author combined the strength of convolutional and recurrent neural networks.

for robust prediction. He and Tao (2018) elucidated the idea of Richards's curves and performed trend analysis in China Covid 19 cases. Ceylan et al. (2020) forecasted the epidemic trend of Covid -19 occurrence in critically affected countries of Europe. Cong et al. (2019) predicted the trend of the epidemic-confirmed cases in Italy and forecasted that Covid -19 epidemic curve would take the shape of a plateau in 40-55 days. Tyagi et al. (2020) predicted the number of Covid cases till June and projected the number of ICU beds, ventilators, and other health requirements.

Tandon et al. (2020) implemented the ARIMA model to forecast exponential increases and declines in cases, considering social distancing and sanitization efforts. Ceylan et al. (2020) predicted the temporal trend of COVID-19-confirmed cases for four Indian states, Maharashtra, Tamil Nadu, Andhra Pradesh, and Karnataka. The major limitation of this paper was that predictions of confirmed cases were based on past values ignoring local spatial geographic variations. In Kraemer et al. (2022), the author modeled the real-time data of Monkey Pox. The author in Sheel (2021) highlighted second-wave Covid 19 trends.

OBJECTIVES

COVID-19 waves have obfuscated temporal patterns. The major objective of this study is to validate the applicability of a simple ARIMA model trained on the patterns of the first wave for upcoming waves prediction.

METHODOLOGY

Dataset

Data was curated from Covid-19India.org. The dataset comprises confirmed cases, active cases, recovered cases, and the mortality rates of Covid 19 from all Indian states and Union Territories. This state-level data is provided by the Ministry of Health and Family Welfare department of the Government of India. Daily confirmed cases of COVID-19 were considered for ten states. These states were the ten most affected states in India. Different states witnessed the second wave differently. As it started in states like Maharashtra and Delhi, it later reached southern India in states like Tamil Nadu, and the situation in Andhra Pradesh was unclear. The second wave is not uniform in all the states, and many states have yet to witness a peak in daily cases. Based on this unusual behavior of the second wave, the states selected for study are Bihar, Delhi, Gujarat, Haryana, Karnataka, Madhya Pradesh, Maharashtra, Rajasthan, Tamil Nadu, and Uttar Pradesh (Cong et al., 2019).

Model Selection

Time series analysis of previous waves can help forecast future waves' temporal trajectories. The temporal nature of epidemic waves and the need for real-time alerts categorize this as a time series forecasting problem (Tandon et al., 2020).

Auto-Regressive Methods

Autoregressive methods are popular for time series forecasting. State-of-the-art techniques suggest Autoregressive methods can perform better in predicting as they require a small number of parameters when limited training instances are available (Wang et al., 2022).

ARMA model combines two models, the autoregressive model with order p and the moving average model with order q are applicable for stationary time series. Usually, with real-time data, time series do not exhibit stationarity as they have no fixed mean (Wang et al., 2022). For the case of non-stationarity, the ARIMA model was used, including differencing (Wang et al., 2022).

In Autoregressive model:

$$Yt = \alpha + \beta 1 Yt - 1 + \beta 2 Yt - 2 \ldots + \beta p Yt p + \varepsilon 1 \tag{1}$$

The predicted value Y_t depends on previous lags; the error is the difference between the actual and expected outcomes.

Moving Average

Moving average model uses past forecasting errors in a regression model:

$$Yt = c + \varepsilon t + \theta 1 \varepsilon t - 1 + \theta 2 \varepsilon t - 2 + \cdots + \theta q \varepsilon t - q \tag{2}$$

Here ε_t is white noise, and Y_t represents the weighted moving average of some of the past forecast errors.

ARIMA model comprises three parameters (p, d, q), where p represents the order of autoregression, d is the degree of trend difference, and q is the moving average order. ARIMA model is an applied stochastic time series model. It uses the linear combination of past values and errors for future predictions (Wang et al., 2022).

The complete model ARIMA (p, d,q) is represented as:

$$Yt = \alpha + \beta 1 Yt - 1 + \beta 2 Yt - 2 + \ldots \beta p Yt - p + \theta 1 \varepsilon t - 1 + \theta 2 \varepsilon t - 2 + \ldots + \theta q \varepsilon t - q \tag{3}$$

MODEL DEVELOPMENT

The model is trained using COVID-19 confirmed cases from March 14, 2020, to March 30, 2021, for all the ten states considered. During this duration, India witnessed a peak of daily confirmed cases of 100,000. Cases started retreating till April, which saw a sudden spike in the confirmed cases in Delhi and Maharashtra. During this period, the country grappled with the first wave of the pandemic.

After a decline in the number of cases in March 2021, the epidemic curve saw an abrupt increase from the first week of April 2021. Hence, we tested our model using daily confirmed cases of Covid 19 from March 31, 2021, to June 16, 2021, for all the states considered. April and May saw a devastating increase in the number of cases, but the curve flattened out in June. However, India flattened out a very high plateau in the case of a second wave (Katoch & Sidhu, 2021).

EXPERIMENTAL DESIGN

Experiments were performed in python. Parameters of the model are tuned using the gridSearchCV function under the model selection package of sci-kit learn. Optimal ARIMA parameters were selected according to the model performance after hyperparameter tuning.

The predicted values and the data of confirmed second-wave cases were plotted with time to verify the model performance. RMSE(root-mean-squared error) was taken as the performance criteria to analyze model accuracy (Table 1).

Results and Observations

Table 1 summarizes the parameters(p,q,d) of the ARIMA model and RMSE values indicating the model performance on the Covid-19 data of the second wave in different states.

The graph is plotted between actual and predicted values of Covid 19 confirmed second-wave cases. From the above results following inferences could be made:

1. The table indicates that Karnataka and Maharashtra have higher RMSE values. Graphs of these states (Figures 5 and 6) saw numerous temporal variations. They witnessed a sudden surge in cases before any intervention measures. The model's accuracy is higher for Gujrat (Figure 3), Tamil Nadu (Figure 9), and Madhya Pradesh (Figure 7), with lower RMSE values. The accuracy of models in these states is attributed to vaccinations and lockdown protocols implementation before reporting cases started.

Table 1. Parameters of the ARIMA model

State	Order (p,q,d)	RMSE
Bihar	(6,2,0)	905.654
Delhi	(0,1,0)	1749.126
Gujarat	(0,2,1)	310.095
Haryana	(2,1,2)	704.799
99Karnataka	(0,2,2)	3376.062
Madhya Pradesh	(1,2,0)	447.23
Maharastra	(8,1,0)	4009.84
Rajasthan	(0,2,2)	818.498
TamilNadu	(4,2,2)	578.085
Uttar Pradesh	(10,2,0)	1736.406

Figure 1. The second wave predicted vs. actual for the state of Bihar

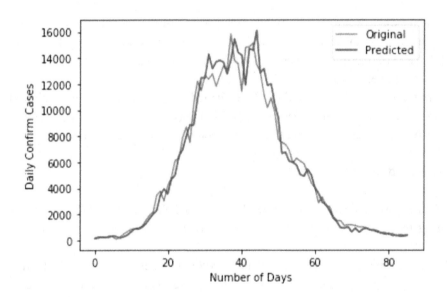

2. As evident from the Graph, several temporal variations in the second wave spread and peaked in Delhi (Figure 2), Bihar (Figure 1), and Uttar Pradesh (Figure 10). Despite several efforts of second-wave prediction by all the stakeholders, some questions remain unanswered, like the cause of the difference in temporal trends across other states of India and variations in severity from the first wave (MK et al., 2022).

Figure 2. The second wave predicted vs. actual for the state of Delhi

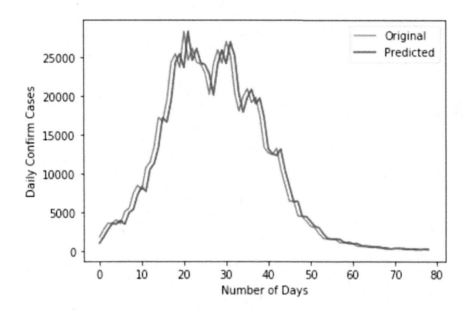

Figure 3. The second wave predicted vs. actual for the state of Gujarat

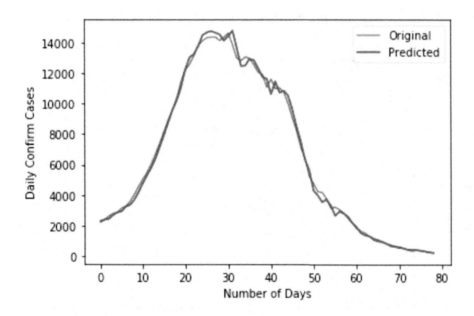

Figure 4. The second wave predicted vs. actual for the state of Haryana

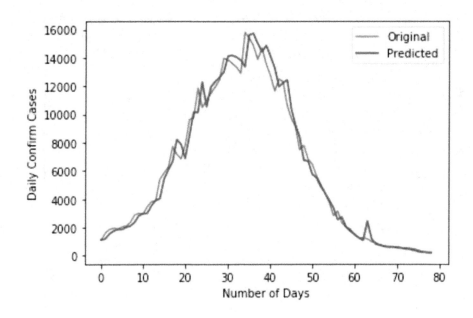

Figure 5. The second wave predicted vs. actual for the state of Karnataka

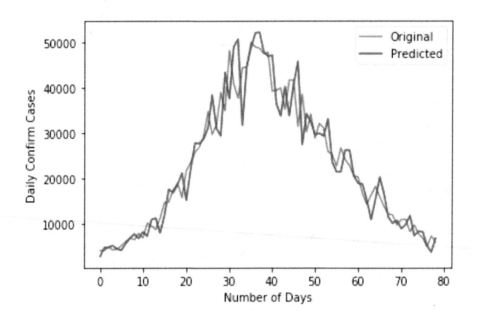

Figure 6. The second wave predicted vs. actual for the state of Maharashtra

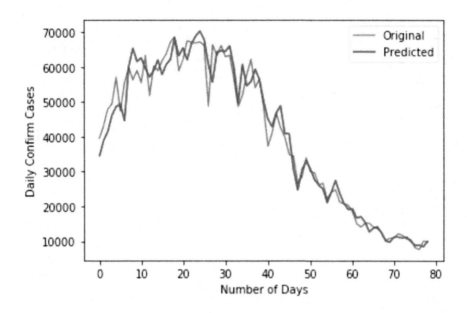

Figure 7. The second wave predicted vs actual for the state of Madhya Pradesh

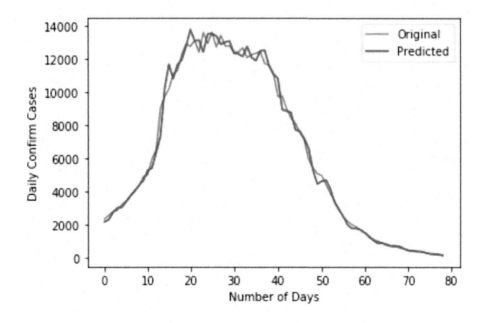

Figure 8. The second wave predicted vs. actual for the state of Rajasthan

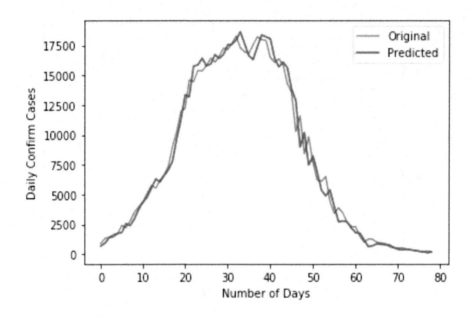

Figure 9. The second wave predicted vs. actual for the state of Tamil Nadu

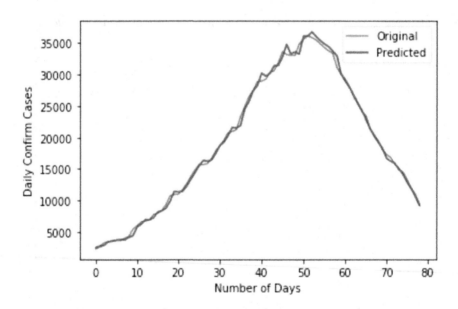

Figure 10. The second wave predicted vs. actual for the state of Uttar Pradesh

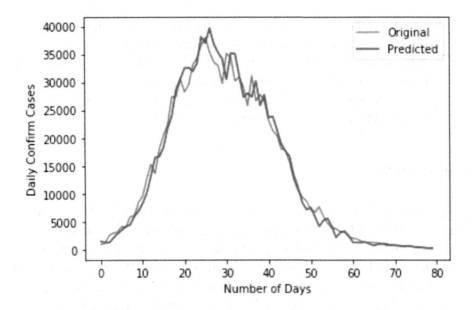

3.   Predictions are affected due to variations at the local level, like non-reported cases, number of testing, and number of vaccinations, especially at the grassroots. Complex epidemic parameters and spatial heterogeneity contribute to this disparity. Also, the virus's behavior, other variants, and asymptomatic patients contribute to the parameter beta and increase the number of infections that vary from place to place.

Substantial literature validated ARIMA models for the temporal modeling of epidemics of similar patterns (Adiga et al., 2020; Ceylan et al., 2020; Chaurasia & Pal, 2020; Cong et al., 2019; He & Tao, 2018; Katoch & Sidhu, 2021; Koshy, 2021; MK et al., 2022; Roy et al., 2021; Wu et al., 2018). Literature demonstrated significant evidence of using simple forecasting models for analyzing temporal dynamics of epidemics like Influenza, SARS, and Ebola. Although it is difficult to compare one epidemic to another model-wise, virus propagation differs in every epidemic. Further external factors like airborne or waterborne, environmental factors and risk factors are different.

But, regarding temporal variations, our results validated the literature. Results corroborated that even simple forecasting time series models can predict future waves. Here the author has tried to map the temporal risk of upcoming waves through the stochastic process of the regression model.

LIMITATIONS

1. We have taken the same time frame for all the states, but reporting cases started late in some states, and few witnessed their peak in May.
2. ARIMA model is sensitive to outliers and doesn't consider noise. So, it can be suitable for short-term but not long-term forecasting.
3. We have made temporal predictions only based on past values and not considered geographical local variations and behavior of the virus.

CONCLUSION

The study investigates the applicability of the ARIMA model to predict the second wave of Covid 19 in India. The paper elucidates the idea of time series analysis of previous waves to predict the temporal trajectory of future waves. The concept can further pave the way for third-wave peak prediction. Results revealed that the ARIMA model could accurately predict the forthcoming waves by using past temporal correlations. Graphs also indicated a disparity in temporal trends of the second wave in different states attributed to the behavior of the virus, number of testing, number of reported cases, and mobility. The spread of infectious diseases depends on many parameters. The model only considered temporal correlations ignoring local geographic variations and heterogeneity.

FUTURE RESEARCH DIRECTIONS

1. Virus propagation is a complex phenomenon and interplays many factors. Apart from temporal correlations, it is essential to integrate local geographic variations or spatial heterogeneity to understand disease spread.
2. Prediction accuracy can be further improved using deep learning models for capturing longer temporal correlations in epidemic data.
3. Here, data instances as a tuple or sequence is considered. Considering data instances as spatial maps and using convolutional neural networks can also be explored in the future.

DATA AVAILABILITY

The data analyzed has been taken from https://data.covid19india.org

ACKNOWLEDGMENT

This research has been partially supported by the School of Computer and Systems Sciences, Jawaharlal Nehru University, New Delhi, India. I want to thank my institution for providing me with the resources to perform research activities. I would also like to thank my lab mates for their valuable feedback on this work.

REFERENCES

Adiga, A., Chen, J., Marathe, M., Mortveit, H., Venkatramanan, S., & Vullikanti, A. (2020). Data-driven modeling for different stages of pandemic response. *Journal of the Indian Institute of Science*, *100*(4), 901–915. doi:10.100741745-020-00206-0 PMID:33223629

Ceylan, Z., Bulkan, S., & Elevli, S. (2020). Prediction of medical waste generation using SVR, GM (1, 1) and Arima models: A case study for megacity Istanbul. *Journal of Environmental Health Science & Engineering*, *18*(2), 687–697. doi:10.100740201-020-00495-8 PMID:33312594

Chaurasia, V., & Pal, S. (2020). Application of Machine Learning Time Series analysis for prediction COVID-19 pandemic. *Research on Biomedical Engineering*, 1–13.

Cong, J., Ren, M., Xie, S., & Wang, P. (2019). Predicting Seasonal influenza based on SARIMA model in mainland China from 2005 to 2018. *International Journal of Environmental Research and Public Health*, *16*(23), 4760. doi:10.3390/ijerph16234760 PMID:31783697

He, Z., & Tao, H. (2018). Epidemiology and Arima model of a positive rate of influenza viruses among children in Wuhan, China: A nine-year retrospective study. *International Journal of Infectious Diseases*, *74*, 61–70. doi:10.1016/j.ijid.2018.07.003 PMID:29990540

Hyndman, R. J., & Athanasopoulos, G. (2018). *Forecasting: Principles and practice*. OTexts.

Katoch, R., & Sidhu, A. (2021). An application of Arima model to forecast the dynamics of COVID-19 Epidemic in India. *Global Business Review*. Advance online publication. doi:10.1177/0972150920988653

Kaunain Sheriff, M. (2021). *Explained: What has changed in the second wave of Covid-19*. https://indianexpress.com/article/explained/explainedwhats-changed-in-second-wave-7289002/

Koshy, J. (2021). *Scientists see flaws in govt-backed model's approach to forecast the pandemic.* https://www.thehindu.com/news/national/governmentbacked-mode l-to-predict-pandemic-rise-and-ebb-lacks-foresightscientists /article34479503.ece

Kraemer, M. U. G., Tegally, H., Pigott, D. M., Dasgupta, A., Sheldon, J., Wilkinson, E., Schultheiss, M., Han, A., Oglia, M., Marks, S., Kanner, J., O'Brien, K., Dandamudi, S., Rader, B., Sewalk, K., Bento, A. I., Scarpino, S. V., de Oliveira, T., Bogoch, I. I., ... Brownstein, J. S. (2022). Tracking the 2022 monkeypox outbreak with epidemiological data in real-time. *The Lancet. Infectious Diseases*, *22*(7), 941–942. doi:10.1016/S1473-3099(22)00359-0 PMID:35690074

MK, M. VAtalla, SAlmuraqab, NMoonesar, I.A. (2022). Detection of COVID-19 Using Deep Learning Techniques and Cost Effectiveness Evaluation: A Survey. *Frontiers in Artificial Intelligence*, *5*, 912022. doi:10.3389/frai.2022.912022 PMID:35692941

Roy, S., Bhunia, G. S., & Shit, P. K. (2021). Spatial Prediction of COVID-19 epidemic using Arima techniques in India. *Modeling Earth Systems and Environment, 7*(2), 1385–1391. doi:10.1007/s40808-020-00890-y

Sheel, A. (2021). *Global covid trends: The second wave and where we are headed.* https://www.livemint.com/opinion/online-views/global-covid-t rendsthe-second-wave-and-where-we-are-headed-11623168003670. html

Tandon, H., Ranjan, P., Chakraborty, T., & Suhag, V. (2020). *Coronavirus (COVID-19): Arima based time-series analysis to forecast near future.* arXiv preprint arXiv:2004.07859.

Tyagi, R., Dwivedi, L. K., & Sanzgiri, A. (2020). *Estimation of effective reproduction numbers for COVID-19 using real-time bayesian method for India and its states.* Academic Press.

Wang, S., Cao, J., & Yu, P. S. (2022). Deep learning for Spatio-Temporal data mining: A survey. *IEEE Transactions on Knowledge and Data Engineering*, *34*(8), 3681–3700. doi:10.1109/TKDE.2020.3025580

Wu, Y., Yang, Y., Nishiura, H., & Saitoh, M. (2018). Deep learning for epidemiological predictions. The 41st International ACM SIGIR. doi:10.1145/3209978.3210077

APPENDIX: ABBREVIATIONS

ARIMA: Autoregressive Integrated Moving Average Model.
RMSE: Root Mean Squared Error.
RNN: Recurrent Neural Networks.
SIR: Susceptible- Infected-Recovered.
SUTRA: Susceptible, Undetected, Tested Positive and Removed Approach.

Chapter 3
Clustering Methods and Tools to Handle High-Dimensional Social Media Text Data

Marcellus Amadeus
Alana AI Research, Brazil

William Alberto Cruz Castañeda
 https://orcid.org/0000-0002-9803-1387
Alana AI Research, Brazil

ABSTRACT

Social media data has changed the way big data is used. The amount of data available offers more natural insights that make it possible to find relations and social interactions. Natural language processing (NLP) is an essential tool for such a task. NLP promises to scale traditional methods that allow the automation of tasks for social media datasets. A social media text dataset with a large number of attributes is referred to as a high-dimensional text dataset. One of the challenges of high-dimensional text datasets for NLP text clustering is that not all the measured variables are important for understanding the underlying phenomena of interest, and dimension reduction needs to be performed. Nonetheless, for text clustering, the existing literature is remarkably segmented, and the well-known methods do not address the problems of the high dimensionality of text data. Thus, different methods were found and classified in four areas. Also, it described metrics and technical tools as well as future directions.

DOI: 10.4018/978-1-6684-6909-5.ch003

INTRODUCTION

The Big Data era has forced different industries to rethink computational solutions to obtain useful insights in real-life scenarios. The attention has been focused on the design of algorithms for analyzing available information. Although the analysis of this massive volume of data brings challenges for extraction of meaningful information due to those data being in different forms.

Currently, Social Media Data (SMD) has changed the way how is used in big data. The amount and types of data available (text, audio, image, video) offers richer and more natural insights expressing feelings or emotions that make it possible to find relations, language expressions, track trending topics, as well as other social interactions (Kauffmann, et al., 2020). Therefore, to efficiently utilize SMD from various sources for decision-making and innovation, industries must use big data analytics to handle information. For example, (Chatterjeea, et al., 2019) use a dataset of 17.62 million tweet conversational pairs to model the task of understanding emotions as a multi-class classification.

Typical applications of big data analytics for social media include monitoring activities to measure loyalty, keeping track of sentiment towards brands or products, observing the impact of campaigns, the success of marketing messages, identifying and engaging top influencers, and social media analytics. However, most existing approaches to social media analysis rely on Machine Learning (ML) techniques that include text analytics and available unstructured and qualitative text data. Thus, text analytics requires inspecting the target textual document (corpus) to turn it into structured information.

To process a text corpus, a general framework for text analytics proposed by (Hu & Liu, 2012), consists of three consecutive phases: text preprocessing, text representation, and knowledge discovery. Text preprocessing makes the input documents consistent to facilitate text representation for text analytics tasks. Traditional text preprocessing methods include stop words, removal, and stemming. Text representation transforms documents into sparse numeric vectors. Basic text representation models are Bag of Words (BOW) or Vector Space Model (VSM). Knowledge discovery, after text corpus transformation into numeric vectors, it is applied the existing ML methods like classification or clustering.

Hence, Natural language processing (NLP) is an essential and fundamental tool for such a task. NLP promises to scale traditional methodologies of supervised and unsupervised methods that allow the automation of tasks such as document classification, content analysis, sentiment analysis, part-of-speech tagging, machine translation, and information retrieval in new social media data. Standard tasks carried out by NLP are text mining, which encompasses association, categorization, and clustering. However, before implementing, and considering the general framework for text analytics, it is required to perform preprocessing and representation of texts as indexing and encoding.

The process of text indexing consists of segmenting a text into a list of words, and three basic steps allow it. The first one is tokenization, which is the operation of segmenting a text by white spaces or punctuation marks into tokens. The second is stemming or lemmatization, in which each token is converted into its root form using grammar rules. The third is stop-word removal, in which removing grammatical words such as articles, conjunctions, and prepositions performed. Nevertheless, tokenization is the prerequisite for the next two steps, but stemming and stop-word removal clouds are switched with each other, depending on the situation.

The list of words, results from indexing, is given as the input to the text encoding. The process of text encoding refers to mapping a text into the structured form of a numerical n-dimensional vector. This vector is constructed by assigning values to features with the reference to the text. A vector with high dimensionality means that many features, relatively hundreds, are required for maintaining the system's robustness. Therefore, a corpus is a source from which feature candidates are generated. For example, research works such as (Jaggi, Mandai, Narang, Naseem, & Khushi, 2021) and (Schubert & Feher, 2021) has been exposed the use of Reuter21578 and 20NewsGropus datasets as typical text corpus. Each dataset consists of 20,000 texts, and more than 20,000 vocabularies are extracted as feature candidates. Implementing one of the state-of-art schemes to select features or reduce dimensionality as wrapper approach, principal component analysis, or singular value decomposition will be built a 20,000 by 20,000 matrix, in which is difficult to trace the results from classifying and clustering texts methods.

The dataset dimension corresponds to the number of attributes/features that are measured on each observation. A dataset with a large number of attributes is referred to as a high-dimensional dataset. One of the challenges of high-dimensional datasets for text clustering problems is that, in certain cases, not all the measured variables are important for understanding the underlying phenomena of interest, and dimension reduction need to be performed. Consequently, it's essential to understand that text differs from other kinds of data due to text is inherently high dimensional. Exemplifying, assume a sample of documents, each of which are w words long, and suppose that each word is drawn from a vocabulary of p possible words. Then the unique representation of these documents has dimension p^w. For ML models, training in high-dimensional spaces can become difficult due to high computational complexity as well as raise issues like inaccurate classification, visualization, or clustering. The challenges related to training ML models due to high dimensional data are referred to as the curse of dimensionality, which has two important aspects: data sparsity, which means that training samples do not capture all combinations, and distance concentration, where distances in the space converging to the same value.

Training a model with sparse data could lead to high-variance or over-fitting condition as well as in clustering or nearest neighbors' methods, the concept of proximity or similarity of the samples may not be qualitatively relevant in higher dimensions. To mitigate the problems associated with the curse of dimensionality the suite of techniques used are subspace clustering and dimensionality reduction. Subspace clustering it's following the idea of correlation in high dimensionality where for some data items features are correlated, but for others, the same features are not. By contrast, dimensionality reduction is divided into feature extraction and feature selection techniques. Feature extraction transforms the original dataset into a new reduced dataset by removing redundant and irrelevant features. Thus, the new feature set preserves the maximum information of the original dataset. For feature selection, the techniques select the subset of features from input data that are most relevant to the given problem. In Information Retrieval (IR) and text mining, feature selection techniques are usually called term selection. Usual IR and indexing techniques for reducing dimensionality are stop word removal, stemming, or lemmatization. Less common techniques are term strength and term contribution.

Dimensionality Reduction Techniques (DRT) are organized into linear and non-linear. Linear Dimension Reduction Techniques (LDRT) use simple linear functions to transform high-dimensional data into lower dimensions. Non-Linear Dimension Reduction Techniques (NLDRT) work with applications that have complex non-linear structures. In models' relations that appear in the data in a non-linear manner, kernel methods are used. These kernel models avoid explicit mapping to learn a non-linear function.

Alternatively, as an unsupervised TM technique applied to terms instead of documents, term clustering is a technique for dimensionality reduction. More precisely, when it's used as a VSM, e.g., BOW obtains a term-document matrix D where rows of D are documents and columns of D are terms. Therefore, clustering columns instead of rows could be applied to the usual row clustering techniques on D^T. In essence, these techniques need to be able to manipulate the high dimensional space efficiently to decrease the dimensionality. Reducing dimensionality improves speed, and precision as well as converts the data into an expressive representation with lower dimensions that can be easily processed, analyzed, and visualized.

Explicitly, dimensionality reduction is the process of transforming the high-dimensional representation of data into low-dimension representations. Mathematically expressed, given a dataset x_i of $x_i \in R^D$ with a very large D, the goal is to find a mapping $f : R^D \mapsto R^d$ $s.t. d \ll D$. The implementation procedure of the dimensionality reduction concept transforms the original dataset having high dimensionality and converts it into a new dataset representing low dimensionality while preserving the original meanings as much as possible. Formally, DRT transforms the high dimensional data $Y = \left[y_1, y_2, \ldots, y_m \right] \in R^{m \times p}$ to $Z = \left[z_1, z_2, \ldots, z_m \right] \in R^{m \times k}$ having p dimensions and m observations into low dimensional data, where $k \ll p$. Moreover, DRT tends to reduce over-fitting (or high variance), in which if the dimensionality of data is D and there are N examples in the training set, then it is good to have $D \approx N$ to avoid over-fitting. Note that DRT sometimes might remove important information, in other words, the aggressiveness of reduction is D / d.

As already stated, a simple and flexible approach to text representation modeling for extracting features from documents is BOW or VSM. Afterward, into the knowledge discovery phase, one of the activities that can be applied is Text Clustering (TC). The goal of TC is to assign text content to a group whose other elements are similar to each other to those belonging to other groups. This means, obtaining groups as homogeneous as possible internally and as heterogeneous as possible externally, for some measure. In TC, a cluster is represented by a collection of similarities and dissimilarities between texts that are calculated using metric or semi-metric functions. There are three main types of text similarities in which a cluster is represented: similarity between two text contents, the similarity between two text content collections, and similarity between text content and a text content collection.

As an example, let $X = \left\{ T_1, T_2, \ldots, T_n \right\}$ be the set of texts to be clustered. Using the VSM, each text is measured for a set of m initial attributes $A_1, A_2, \quad, A_m$ (a set of relevant characteristics of the analyzed text) and is therefore described by an m-dimensional vector $O_i = \left(O_{i1}, \ldots, O_{im} \right), \in R, 1 \leq i \leq n, 1 \leq k \leq m$. Thus, VSM is based on the notion of similarity. The similarity between two text contents encompasses measures like distance-based similarity, cosine similarity, and distributed-based similarity that are used for discriminating texts for any metric function d.

For distance-based similarity, the text content is represented as a vector in the VSM. To measure text content similarity is used the distance between two vectors in vector space. The smaller distance between these vectors, the greater the similarity of the text contents. The commonly used distance metrics include *Euclidian, Manhattan, Chebyshev, Minkowski, Mahalanobis*, and *Jaccard*. For example, using the *Euclidian distance*, let O_i and O_j be the vector representations of two text contents, and the distance d is defined as follows:

$$d\left(O_i, O_j \right) = d_E\left(O_i, O_j \right) = \sqrt{\sum_{l=1}^{m} \left(O_{il} - O_{jl} \right)^2} \tag{1}$$

where equation 1 is a special case of Minkowski's distance, with $p = 2$.

$$d_p\left(i,j\right) = \sqrt[p]{\sum_{l=1}^{m}\left|O_i - O_j\right|^p} \tag{2}$$

thus, the similarity between two text contents O_a and O_b is defined as

$$sim\left(\overrightarrow{O_a},\overrightarrow{O_b}\right) = \frac{1}{d\left(\overrightarrow{O_a},\overrightarrow{O_b}\right)} \tag{3}$$

For cluster analysis, similarity measures, as equation 3, are used to identify non-trivial groups in a large dataset, organizing text data and retrieving information. Although, the curse of multidimensionality has some peculiar effects on clustering methods, i.e., how distances (or dissimilarities) between points are computed. Otherwise stated, the behavior of distances in high-dimensional data is critical. For illustrative purposes, the usefulness of the nearest neighbor algorithm for certain distributions is discussed by (Angiulli, 2018). In equation 4 is showed that the relative difference of the distances of the closest MinDist and farthest MaxDist data points of an independent selected point tends to 0 as dimensionality increases:

$$\lim_{d\to\infty} \frac{MaxDist - MinDist}{MinDist} = 0 \tag{4}$$

In such circumstances, the notion of distance becomes meaningless. The result has been extended to examine the absolute difference MaxDist − MinDist, by considering different metrics. In the case of Minkowski's distance, in equation 2, it has been shown that, for d = 1, MaxDist − MinDist increases with dimensionality, for d = 2, MaxDist − MinDist remains relatively constant, and for d ^{3} 3, MaxDist − MinDist tends to 0 as dimensionality increases. Discovered for the nearest neighbor algorithm, the result reveals a general problem in clustering high-dimensional data, at least when the data distribution causes the usual distances between points to become relatively uniform.

Additionally, in TC, text vectors are characterized by high dimension, sparsity, and correlation among dimensions, which involves improvements to the clustering algorithm to process high-dimension text. Taking as an example, according to equation 1, the K-means algorithm aggregates points and this implicitly means that the data lie in a Euclidean space. To overcome this limitation, the kernel-based clustering methods presented in (Balbi, 2010) apply to compute distances using a non-linear kernel function, defined in equation 5 as:

$$d_2^k \left(O_i, O_j \right) = \sqrt{\sum_{l=1}^{m} k^2 O_{il}^2 + k^2 O_{il}^2 - 2k \left(O_{il} - O_{jl} \right)^2} \tag{5}$$

In the previous notations $K : R^d \times R^d \rightarrow R$ is the kernel function, which is a similarity function having the property that, for any O_i, $K\left(O_i, O_i \right) = 1$, as the distance between O_i and O_j increases, $K\left(O_i, O_j \right)$ decreases. The kernel distance enables the clustering algorithm to capture the non-linear structure in the data.

Nonetheless, for TC, the existing literature is remarkably segmented, and the well-known methods do not address the problems of the high dimensionality of text data. Methods are unable to find robust and effective results across datasets. This happens because in high-dimensional space the distances among randomly selected points tend to concentrate near their mean value. Thus, different methods for high-dimensional text clustering are discussed in the subsequent sections. Figure 1 depicts the organization of the detected methods, from classical, deep learning-based to the most recent meta-heuristic and short text clustering methods.

Figure 1. Organization from classical to most recent cluster methods for high-dimensionally

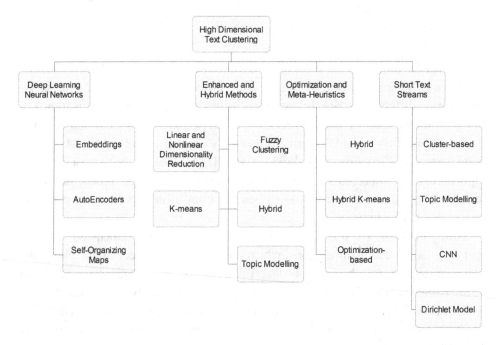

Thus, this chapter intends to guide researchers in the current methods and techniques applied to high-dimensional text clustering tasks. It also highlights metrics and recent technical tools to handle high-dimensional text clustering. Its look first, Section II describes current research methods classified into four categories according to the implemented algorithms and methods found: Deep Learning Neural Networks, Enhanced and Hybrid Methods, Optimization and Meta-heuristics, and Sort Text Streams. Section III describes metrics and technical tools that enable development applications derived from the founded categories. Section IV presents conclusions, as well as challenges.

TEXT CLUSTERING METHODS FOR HIGH-DIMENSIONALITY

One can observe that DRTs focused in convert the data from a higher dimensional space into a lower dimensional space for better text analysis retaining most of its essential attributes in its original form. Since DRTs are classified into feature extraction and selection, the objective is to find methods that describe features usefull in high-dimensional text clustering with effective accuracy. In this manner, this section focused on outlining methods and algorithms that scientific works have proposed. It was detected four relevant areas for high dimensional text clustering techniques: Deep Learning Neural Networks, Enhanced and Hybrid Methods, Optimization and Meta-heuristics, and Short Text Streams.

Deep Learning Neural Networks

With the use of data-driven models and the exploration of several data streams, deep learning has become increasingly important due to the discovery of a helpful representation of data by neural networks. Jointly optimizing Deep Neural Networks (DNN) with an unsupervised clustering algorithm has been becoming an active research field.

Embedding-Based Methods

Accomplished dimensionality reduction via deep learning and K-Means Clustering (KMC) was proposed by (Yang, Fu, Sidiropoulos, & Hong, 2017). This approach can work well for a broad class of generative models. An optimization criterion joins DNN-based dimensionality reduction and KMC. This criterion is a fusion of three parts: dimensionality reduction, data reconstruction (implemented using a decoding network), and cluster structure-promoting regularization. (Wang, Liao, Zhu, Zhou, & Jia, 2020), proposes a low-dimensional text representation learning method inspired by the skip-gram model (Word2vec). The proposed model considers texts as learning units and makes use of similarity relations rather than the contexts of words to preserve the pairwise similarity relations. The main contribution of (Zhang, et al., 2018) is the development of a polynomial function-based kernel KMC method with the incorporation of Word2Vec model. The research of (Wang, Zhou, & Li, 2019) explores KMC, Hadoop, and Spark to propose an algorithm based on the parallelized KMC. Word2vec was adopted to calculate the weights of word vectors, and thus reduce the dimensionality of massive text data. Canopy algorithm was introduced to cluster the weight data, and identify the initial cluster centers for the KMC.

A detected problem in existing text clustering algorithms based on the BOW models is that ignore text structural and sequence information. For this reason, Guan, et al. (2020) propose a Deep Feature-based Text Clustering framework that includes pre-trained text encoders into text clustering tasks applying classic KMC algorithm to extracted features. The Bag of Word Clusters approach is proposed by Rui, Xing, and Jia (2016), which consists of a text representation where groups semantically close words and considers them as one dimension in the representation space. For each dimension, it was used dynamic k-max pooling method. Words are grouped by performing s clustering algorithm on word embeddings. Unlike Latent Semantic Indexing (LSI), Latent Dirichlet Allocation (LDA), and Probabilistic Latent Semantic Indexing (PLSI), the method finds new feature space from larger and independent texts.

Recent studies have combined NLDRT and DNN with hard-partition clustering to achieve reliable results. These methods cannot update the parameters of dimensionality reduction and clustering at the same time. Li, Ni, Xue, and Jiang (2021) found that soft-partition clustering combined with deep embeddings, and the membership of Fuzzy c-Means can solve the problem. In this sense, it was built a continuous objective function that combines the soft-partition clustering with deep embedding. A unified deep learning framework for text data mining using deep adaptive fuzzy clustering and word embedding is proposed by Praveen and Priya (2020) that consist of four layers: feature vector construction, fully connected layer, max pooling layer, and softmax. Hyperparameter obtained with softmax function are optimized using quantum annealing. In the study of Kotte, Vuppu, and Thadishetti (2021) it's proposed a deep random prediction dimensionality reduction framework with Stacked-Random Projection (SRP) in combination with a greedy layer-wise architecture. Dimensionality compression technique was used to minimize the high-dimensional text feature dimensions. After that, it was used Naive Bayes classification algorithm to calculate the number of dimensions before using KMC.

AutoEncoders-Based Methods

In the context of AutoEncoders (AE) the research of Zhang, Sun, Eriksson, and Balzano (2017) uses a MIXture of AE (MIXAE) to identify a non-linear mapping suitable for a particular cluster. AE is trained simultaneously with a mixture assignment network to take concatenated latent vectors as input and infers the distribution over clusters. In this respect, the study of (Kushwaha & Pant, Textual data dimensionality reduction - a deep learning approach, 2020) proposes a dimensionality reduction method based on Deep AE Neural Network (DRDAE) to provide optimized and robust features for text clustering. DRDAE selects less correlated and salient feature space from the high dimensional feature space.

Shah and Koltun (2018) presents a deep continuous clustering algorithm to perform nonlinear dimensionality reduction and clustering jointly. In the algorithm, data are embedded into a lower-dimensional space by a deep AE to optimize the clustering process. Diallo et al. (2021) proposes a deep embedding clustering framework based on contractive AE (DECCA) to learn document representations. Furthermore, to grasp relevant documents or word features, the Frobenius norm helps the AE to perform better. In this way, the contractive AE apprehends the local manifold structure of the input data and competes with the representations learned by existing methods. A denoising AE for dimensionality reduction is presented by Leyli-Abadi, Labiod, and Nadif (2017). The proposed AE can discover the low-dimensional embedding, and as a result, reveal the underlying effective manifold structure. The visual representation of this embedding suggest perform the clustering on the set of documents relying on the expectation-maximization algorithm for Gaussian mixture models. Inspired by Stacked AE (SAE), Sun and Platos (2020) propose a deep random projection framework, which incorporates random projection as its core stacking element. The framework enables to reduce the dimensionality as well as spectral clustering and fast search to find density peak clustering.

Self-Organizing Maps-Based Methods

Alternatively, Self-Organizing Maps (SOM) have been used as a tool for mapping high-dimensional input data into a low-dimensional feature map, which has significant advantages for text clustering applications. In this manner, to overcome the issue of high dimensionality using SOM, Fraj, Hajkacem, and Essoussi (2020) proposes a new multi-view text clustering method to capture and integrate information from each view onto low-dimensional space and maintain both syntactic and semantic aspects of the text. Investigating an effective way to cluster large-scale text collection, Liu, Wu, and Chen (2015) puts forward a vector reconstruction-based clustering algorithm, which repeats two sub-processes until it converges. The first one is partial tuning, in which feature weight are fine-tuned by an iterative process similar to SOM. The second one is overall tuning, where features is reallocated among different clusters. In this sub-process, the unnecessary features are removed from clusters' representative vector.

In a practical manner, Sarkar, Ejaz, and Maiti (2018), using topic modeling and SOM to train input binary data, reduce the dimensions and preserve the topology of the original data on a two-dimensional grid, where each unit is associated with a prototype vector. Subsequently training SOM on the input binary data, the final set of prototype vectors of the SOM grid is extracted with KMC algorithm. Another SOM approach is proposed by Rafi, Waqar, Ajaz, Ayub, and Danish (2017) using multi-layer and multi-feature to cluster documents. SOM performs autonomous self-organization of high dimension feature space into low-dimensional projections using four layers containing lexical terms, phrases, and sequences. It was concluded that SOM with multi-features and multi-layers is effective in producing high-quality clusters on large document collections.

Enhanced and Hybrid Methods

Research related to high-dimensional text document classification and clustering is usually limited to the application of traditional distance functions. In this regard, are described contributions considering the word distribution in documents, novel functions, state-of-the-art dimensionality reduction techniques variants, embedding methods, and enhanced/hybrid models. State-of-the art on DRTs and their suitability for different types of data and applications are presented by Ayesha, Hanif, and Talib (2020). The work brings the properties of DRT and explores which are used for text clustering as well as the positive and negative aspects of each technique.

The survey of Tjøstheim, Jullum, and Løland (2021) exposes four parts in the embedding of high-dimensional and nonlinear data structures. The first part covers nonlinear methods such as principal curves, multidimensional scaling, local linear methods, ISOMAP, graph-based and kernel-based methods. The second part is concerned with topological embedding methods, in particular mapping topological properties into persistence diagrams. The third part exposes how to embed such data in a vector space of moderate dimension to make the data amenable to traditional clustering and classification techniques. The final part deals with embedding in $\mathbb{R}^2$. Lastly, three visualization methods are presented: t-SNE, Uniform Manifold Approximation and Projection (UMAP), and LargeVis based on methods in parts one, two, and three, respectively.

Linear and Nonlinear Dimensionality Reduction-Based Methods

Comparing the advantage and disadvantages of three-dimension reduction algorithms for text clustering, Principal Component Analysis (PCA), Nonnegative Matrix Factorization (NMF), and Singular Value Decomposition (SVD), Mohamed (2020) present an effective dimension reduction algorithm for Arabic text clustering using PCA. For that purpose, a series of experiments have been conducted using two linguistic corpora, English and Arabic. In the context of emergency department, and involving high dimensional, noisy, and sparse text data, Li, Zhu, Qu, Ye, and Sun (2019) propose a Semi-Orthogonal NMF (SONMF) method for continuous and binary design matrices to bi-cluster patients and words into a lower dimension of topics. The method benefits are: (a) generates uncorrelated basis topics, and (b) the topics provide a clear and rich interpretation.

Abuzeina (2019) evaluates and measures the accuracy of the Arabic text clustering using two feature types: the complete word form and the microword form. PCA was used to reduce the feature vector dimensions while the K-means algorithm is used for clustering purposes. As part of an aviation safety reporting system, Irwin, Robinson, and Belt (2017) makes use of latent semantic analysis, reduces narratives, truncates vectors for a two-dimensional projection through the application of isometric mapping, and visually renders the result with geographic information systems software.

A novel similarity function for feature pattern clustering and high-dimensional text classification introduced by Kotte, Rajavelu, and Rajsingh (2020) to carry out supervised learning-based dimensionality reduction. An important characteristic of this study is that the word distribution before and after dimensionality reduction is the same. An approach for feature representation and dimensionality reduction of text documents is described by Kumar, Srinivasan, and Singh (2018). This approach retains the original distribution of features, and the output is a hard representation matrix. The hard matrix is used to obtain the low-dimensionality document matrix, which is the input for clustering.

Taking into account ISOMAP, Locally Linear Embedding (LLE) and SVD, Salem (2017) suggest a framework based on manifold learning that merges Random Forest (RF) with dimensionality reduction techniques to increase the accuracy of predictive analysis for big text data. The framework exploits the problem of text classification performed by support vector machines and RF. (Gupta & Begum, A Comparative Study on Feature Selection Techniques for Multi-cluster Text Data, 2018) describe that feature selection techniques show better clustering results than techniques that rank features independently. Moreover, it compared two feature selection techniques: TF-IDF and Multi-Cluster Feature Selection (MCFS). The experimental results show the superior clustering results of MCFS over traditional TF-IDF.

The efficient MCFS (EMCFS) method proposed by (Gupta & Begum, Efficient multi-cluster feature selection on text data, 2020) preserves the multiple cluster structure of the data. Implements the anchor graph to build the adjacency matrix to reduce the dimension of the feature space. A comparison with MCFS reveals that EMCFS improves accuracy and makes it a promising method for high-dimensional datasets. In the study of Bharti and Singh (2015), two different feature selection methods were used to select relevant feature sublists: term variance and document frequency. In addition, it introduced a merging approach to choose top-ranked and usual features from the considered sublists. Besides, the feature extraction method and PCA are applied to refine the selected feature space. Finally, the clusters of documents are created with reduced feature space to assess effectiveness.

A sentence ranking approach proposed by Sreelekshmi and Remya (2018) find the relevant terms in documents to improve feature identification and selection. Document vectors are mapped into a lower dimensional space using SVD. Is used k-rank approximation method to minimize the error between the original term-document matrix and its map. The similarity matrix converted into a fuzzy equivalence relation by calculating the max-min transitive closure. Finally, it was applied fuzzy rules to cluster documents. Adopting a membership function, Reddy (2016) achieves a feature extraction process projected onto their similar low dimensional representation in feature space algebraic rules and transformations. The objective is to find an optimal transformation matrix equivalent to the input high-dimensional document feature matrix. The approach is compared to feature selection technique, Information Gain (IG), and results prove that the dimensionality reduction accomplishes better when compared the original distribution of words per document.

Proposing a high-level framework, Trad and Spiliopoulou (2021) implements a compact data representation in a latent feature space derived with non-parametric topic modeling. The approach encompasses the following components: (1) a method of latent semantic representation of texts in a low-dimensional dense feature space after vectorizing with word unigrams, (2) a method for deriving authorial clusters in this feature space in two variants for the learning model.

K-Means-Based Methods

Huang, Chen, and Ye (2020) proposes a clustering method that combines feature selection form information theory criteria to establish clustering rules. Improved K-Means it used to generate basis clustering. The cluster method it tested on standard datasets, and its performance is compared with the K-means ensemble. Aoyama and Saito (2021) presents a K-means clustering algorithm architecture for a large-scale and high-dimensional sparse dataset. The architecture employs an invariant centroid-pair (ICP) based filter to decrease the similarity calculations between a data object and centroids of all the clusters. To maximize the ICP performance, the architecture exploits for a centroid set an inverted file that is structured to reduce pipeline hazards.

The research of Sangaiah, Fakhry, Abdel-Basset, and El-Henawy (2018) proposes a model for text clustering using Arabic datasets. Three approaches were implemented: unsupervised, semi-supervised, and semi-supervised with dimensionality reduction to construct a clustering-based classifier. After document preprocessing, the unsupervised technique impalements K-means and incremental K-means. On the other hand, the semi-supervised technique uses threshold +K-means and K-means with dimensionality reduction. After the K-means algorithm was applied, dimensionality reduction is obtained by calculating the score for each term in each class and selecting the ratio manually to reduce the score. F-measure, entropy, and SVM calculate the accuracy.

Proposed by Kadhim and Jassim (2021), a technique that combines chi-square with K-means for clustering website documents. It was compared with IG on BBC sport and BBC news datasets. The experimental findings show that the chi-square combined with K-means improves the performance of document clustering. Wu, Lin, Fu, and Wang (2015) proposes a K-Means algorithm based on SimHash to calculate the feature vectors extracted as well as the fingerprint of each text obtained. SimHash not only reduces the dimension of the text but also directly calculates the Hamming distance between the fingerprints as the vector distance.

Topic Modelling-based Methods

In the work of Tseng, Lu, Chakraborty, and Chen (2019) is reduced the dimension and used Latent Semantic Analysis (LSA) activated by SVD. In a separate experiment, it used topic modeling using LDA. Clustering is done using K-Means. After dimension reduction by LSA and LDA, the ground truth for documents in two clusters was verified manually, and the results were compared. By manual inspection, it was verified that the comments are grouped into positive and negative. LDA can extract meaningful topics. The number of topics could also be made smaller, like 50 to 100 compared to what we had using LSA.

Applying an ensemble clustering approach (Zhao, Salloum, Cai, & Huang, 2017) produces robust clusters with LDA and FG-K-Means soft sub-space clustering algorithm for the same corpus. The integrated method implements topic modeling to get a two-level features representation of text data as a basis for subspace clustering. In addition, topic modeling generate diverse ensemble components of the same data. By using both topics and words to cluster text data, is obtained more interpretable clusters. A user behavior model based on topic model from document classification problems is presented by Leng, Liu, Pan, Zhou, and Niu (2015). The study exploit

TF-IDF to form a high-dimensional sparse feature matrix. Then LSA is applied to reduce the latent topic distribution and generate a low-dimensional dense feature matrix. K-means++ is applied to obtain the dense feature matrix, and interpretable user clusters.

Hybrid-Based Methods

The synchronization-inspired clustering algorithm (Sync) can accurately cluster datasets with any shape, density, and distribution. However, a high-dimensional dataset with high noise and redundancy bring new challenges resulting in increased clustering time and a decreased clustering accuracy. To address these challenges, an enhanced synchronization-inspired clustering algorithm (SyncHigh) was developed by Chen, Guo, Liu, and Zha (2021) to cluster high-dimensional datasets quickly and accurately. A PCA-based dimension purification strategy is designed to find the principal components in all attributes. A density-based data merge strategy is constructed to reduce the number of objects participating in SyncHigh thereby speeding up clustering time.

When the size of textual data increases, there is a need for an approach that combines advantages of statistical and semantic features to give accurate results within an acceptable range of time. In this context, Mehta, Bawa, and Singh (2021) propose a Stamantic Clustering as a text clustering technique to combine the effectiveness of the statistical features (using TF-IDF) and semantic features (using lexical chains). The technique uses a fewer number of features while maintaining a comparable and even better accuracy for the task of document clustering.

Focused on detecting text messages that borrow similar meaning or relate to the same event, Fomin and Belousov (2017) design an algorithm based on the VSM. Text-to-vector transformation is performed with TF-IDF. To reduce the dimension PCA is used. In the reduced vector space, is used the agglomerative hierarchical clustering and cluster merge using the closest linkage algorithm. Merging clustering are stopped when the distance between two nearest clusters exceeds a threshold value given to the algorithm as a parameter. Presenting an ensemble clustering technique, Khan, Ivanov, and Jiang (2016) describes a low-dimensional component data generation method by FastMap. The advantage is that preserves the clustering structure of the original data.

Fuzzy Clustering-Based Methods

The research conducted by Karami (2017) investigates the application of fuzzy clustering as a dimensionality reduction method based on the Unsupervised Feature Transformation (UFT) strategy to collapse the BOW matrix and provide a lower-dimensional representation of documents instead of the words in a corpus. The evaluation shows that fuzzy clustering produces better performance and features for PCA and SVD.

Optimization and Meta-Heuristics

Clustering analysis, as an optimization task, involves the minimization or maximization of dissimilarity within a cluster or between clusters. Meta-heuristic methods are preferred to traditional-based approaches for solving high-dimensional data clustering problems due to their superior convergence speeds and ability to obtain quality solutions (Boushaki, Kamel, & Bendjeghaba, 2018). The systematic review of Ezugwu, et al. (2021) presents nature-inspired meta-heuristic algorithms used for automatic clustering analysis. Also is discussed the trends from traditional to meta-heuristic algorithms. The focus is on meta-heuristic algorithms to solve clustering problems over the last three decades. Table 1 shows the nature- inspired meta-heuristic algorithms applied to solve non-automatic and automatic clustering.

Table 1. Nature- inspired meta-heuristic algorithms applied to solve non-automatic and automatic clustering

Type	Algorithms
Clustering with swarm intelligence-based algorithms	- Particle swarm optimization (PSO), - Firefly algorithm (FA) - Artificial Bee Colony (ABC) - Ant Colony Optimization (ACO) - Symbiotic Organism Search (SOS) - Bacterial Evolutionary Algorithm (BEA) - Grey Wolf Optimizer (GWO) - Sine–Cosine Algorithm (SCA) - Cuckoo Search (CS) - Bat Algorithm (BA) - Bee-inspired Algorithm (BeeA)
Clustering using the plant-based algorithm	- Flower Pollination Algorithm (FPA)
Clustering using breeding-based algorithms	- Differential Evolution (DE) - Genetic Algorithm (GA) - Invasive Weed Optimization (IWO)
Clustering with the social human behavior-based algorithms	- Teaching Learning-Based Optimization (TLBO) - Imperialist Competitive Algorithm (ICA)
Clustering with physics based algorithms	- Gravitational Search Algorithm (GSA) - Harmony Search (HS) - Black Hole Algorithm (BH)
Clustering with miscellaneous sources of inspiration algorithms	- Membrane computing - Dynamic local search - Action-set learning automata - Artificial Immune System (AIS)

The survey of Abualigah et al. (2021) presents meta-heuristic optimization algorithms in text clustering applications, including fundamental, modified, hybridized, and multi-objective methods such as PSO, GWO, CS, FA, Krill Herd Algorithm (KHA), Social Spider Optimization (SSO), GSA, Whale Optimization Algorithm (WOA), ACO, GA, HS. In addition, bring a review of local search techniques used to solve text document clustering problems as Heuristic Local Search (HLS), K-Means, C-Means, and Hybrid Clustering.

Ezugwu (2020) present a survey on nature-inspired meta-heuristic algorithms used to solve automatic clustering problems as well as a comparative study of several modified well-known global meta-heuristic algorithms for the same problem. Three hybrid swarm intelligence and evolutionary algorithms (Particle Swarm Differential Evolution, Firefly Differential Evolution, IWO Differential Evolution) are proposed to deal with the task of automatic data clustering.

Hybrid-Based Methods

A novel feature selection method is introduced by Abualigah et al. (2021) to tackle the problem of high-dimensional features in text clustering. A parallel membrane-inspired framework is proposed to enhance the performance of the KHA combined with the swap mutation strategy (MHKHA). The hybrid KHA strategy is incorporated with K-means to cluster documents. Proposed to solve the feature selection problem in text clustering an hybrid intelligent algorithm developed by Bharti and Singh (2016), combines Binary PSO (B-PSO) with opposition-based learning, chaotic map, fitness-based dynamic inertia weight, and mutation. Fitness-based dynamic inertia weight is integrated with the B-PSO to control the movement of the particles. Mutation and the chaotic strategy enhance the global search capability of the algorithm. An opposition-based initialization generates opposite position of the best particle to get rid of the stagnation in the swarm.

To compute redundant/irrelevant features in high dimensional sample data exploration based on feature selection calculation with data granular, Kolli and Sreedevi (2021) propose a Novel Granular Feature Multi-variant Clustering based GA (NGFMC-GA) model. This model consists of two phases, first, based on the theoretic graph grouping procedure that divide features into different clusters, and second, select strongly representative features from each cluster to match a subset of features. To solve the text clustering problem, Mustafa, Ayob, Albashish, and Abu-Taleb (2020) proposes a Memetic Differential Evolution algorithm (MDETC) to address the effect of the hybridization between the differential evolution mutation strategies with the memetic algorithm. This hybridization intends to enhance the quality of text clustering and improve the exploitation and exploration capabilities of the algorithm.

Mustafi, Mustafi, and Sahoo (2022) proposes a novel clustering algorithm using a weighted combination of several criteria as its fitness function. The algorithm leverages the Nearest Neighbors Separation (NNS) method to enhance the separation of the clusters. A new parameterized fitness function provide more weightage to the traditional metrics based on intra-cluster distances. An evolutionary genetic algorithm perform the actual clustering, and the results obtained were compared with the traditional K-Means algorithm.

Hybrid K-Means-Based Methods

In Rashidi, Khamforoosh, and Sheikhahmadi (2022), the MkMeans++ algorithm is combined with FA, CS, and KHA algorithms to produce new algorithms called FireflyMkMeans++, CuckooMkMeans++, and KrillM-kMeans++ to specify the optimal centroid of the cluster, better separate users, and avoid local optimal. In the proposed hybrid clustering approach, the initial population of FA, CS, and KHA algorithms is initialized through the solutions generated by the MkMeans++ algorithm, and it makes use of the benefits of FA, CS, and KHA.

An intelligent weighting K-means clustering (IWKM) algorithm based on swarm intelligence is presented by Tao, Gu, Wang, and Jiang (2020). The degree of coupling between clusters is presented to enlarge the dissimilarity. Weights and features are used in the weighting distance function to determine clusters. To eliminate the sensitivity of initial cluster centers, swarm intelligence find initial cluster centers, weights of views, and weights of features. Precise perturbation is proposed to improve the optimization performance of swarm intelligence. As a consequence of the K-means inability to process high-dimensional data, Sun and Platoš (2020) propose an SRP-DR framework and an enhanced K-means algorithm based on the improved density peaks algorithm to determines the number of clusters and the initial clustering centers.

A novel K-means variant is proposed by Rezaee, Eshkevari, Saberi, and Hussain (2021) called a game-based K-means (GBK-means) algorithm. This algorithm leverages the power of bargaining game modeling into K-means. In this novel setting, cluster centres compete with each other to attract the largest number of similar objectives or entities to their cluster. Thus, the centres keep changing their positions so that they have smaller distances with the maximum possible data than other cluster centres. The approach of Jagatheeshkumar and Selva Brunda (2018) aims to find an optimum solution for text clustering based on K-means and Lion Optimization Algorithm (LOA) with feature selection (K-LOA). The proposal discovers the initial point using the fitness function. Consequently is implemented feature selection method to find the optimal subset of attributes. The fitness function is used not only for data fit but as well as improve cluster performance. Using the Lion optimization algorithm is possible to find cluster centroids.

Abualigah, Khader, Al-Betar, and Alomari (2017) proposes three feature selection algorithms: GA, HS and PSO with feature weight scheme and Dynamic Dimensionality Reduction (DyDR) for the text document clustering problem. DyDR reduce the number of features used in clustering and thus improve the performance of the algorithms. K-Means is used to cluster the set of text documents based on the terms (or features) obtained by dynamic reduction. Experiment analysis with K-means shows that PSO with length feature weight and dynamic reduction produces the optimal outcomes for almost all datasets tested. Link-based Binary PSO (LB-PSO) with the integration of a new neighbor selection strategy to solve feature selection problem in text clustering is proposed by (Kushwaha & Pant, Link based BPSO for feature selection in big data text clustering, 2018). LB-PSO algorithm introduces a new updating strategy to learn from the neighbor's best position instead of the global best. Takes the original text dataset as input and produces the new subset of prominent features. The K-means clustering algorithm takes these features as input to evaluate the feature selection method. The proposed feature selection algorithm enhances the text clustering algorithm results by making more similar groups.

Optimization-Based Methods

A dynamic and incremental approach for document clustering based on the recent CS optimization and LSI was proposed by Boushaki, Kamel, and Bendjeghaba (2018). Experiments on four high-dimensional text datasets show the efficiency of the LSI model to reduce the dimensionality space with more precision and less computational time. In addition, the proposed CS-LSI determines the number of clusters automatically by employing a proposed index, focused on a significant distance measure. The widely used K-means algorithm becomes slow with large and high-dimensional datasets, such as document collections. Recently Fast Partitional Clustering (FPAC) proposes an improvement in the speed reducing the quality of the clustering results. Bejos, Feliciano-Avelino, Martinez-Trinidad, and Carrasco-Ochoa (2020) introduce an improved FPAC algorithm that achieves better clustering results than FPAC, without highly increasing the runtime.

An enhanced Detailed Dimensionality Reduction (DDR) technique is proposed by Abualigah (2019) to obtain a subset of features that improves the performance of the text clustering with KHA. The proposed technique reduces non-useful features from the initial ones that comes from the selection method. Based on the β-hill climbing technique, an algorithm is proposed by Abualigah et al. (2017) for text feature selection to improve text clustering. β-hill climbing obtains the optimal low-dimension subset of informative features with low-dimension space. The results of the proposed method and original Hill climbing are examined using the K-means text clustering and compared with each other.

To reduce the dimensionality of large volume of text documents, Janani and Vijayarani (2020) proposes a new FA for feature selection. The algorithm optimize the set of high-dimensional features, and a classification task is used to selected features. Thirumoorthy and Muneeswaran (2021) implement the Hybrid Jaya Optimization algorithm for text Document Clustering (HJO-DC). The proposed work is compared with partitioning techniques such as KMeans and K-Medoids and meta-heuristic techniques such as GA, CS, PSO, FA, and GWO. Purushothaman, Rajagopalan, and Dhandapani (2020) purpose the use of a hybrid GWO and Grasshopper Optimization Algorithm (GOA) to select the text features. GWO selects local characteristics of text documents, and GOA selects the best global qualities from local functions. The hybrid approach minimizes un-informational functions for enhancing text classification algorithm quality. It also used the Fuzzy C-Means (FCM) algorithm to cluster the document after the selection of global text features.

Short Text Streams

Short-text streams are generated at large volumes from different sources. Clustering these streams consists in assigning a text to a new cluster or one of the existing ones as it arrives. Organizing these text streams is an important step toward discovering trends or finding groups over time. Therefore, short text stream clustering is a challenging task due to the lack of context contained. To achieve results in short-text clustering, three main factors must be considered: document representation, document similarity, and document clustering. The objective of Kongwudhikunakorn and Waiyamai (2020) was to identify the combination of document representation, document distance, and document clustering that produces the best clustering quality. The proposed method creates a vector representation for vocabularies in short text document datasets from the learned model on an external text corpus. Clustering is performed by K-means, and the similarity of the documents is calculated by a document distance function.

Topic Modelling-Based Methods

A comprehensive review conducted by Qiang, Qian, Li, Yuan, and Wu (2022) in short text topic modeling techniques reveals three categories of methods based on: Dirichlet Multinomial Mixture (DMM), Global Word Co-occurrences (GWC), and Self-Aggregation (SA). Zheng, Meng, and Xu (2015) proposes a short-text-oriented analysis approach to cluster and extract hot topics. This approach consists of three stages: First, generate a feature vector for each sample to obtain the high-dimensional

VSM. Secondly, use SVD to achieve the DR. Lastly, apply cosine similarity and the K-means method to cluster samples on a low-dimensional matrix and extract the hot topics for each cluster.

Lossio-Ventura et al. (2021) trains state-of-the-art topic modeling and clustering algorithms on short texts from two health-related datasets. LSI, LDA, LDA with Gibbs Sampling (GibbsLDA), Online LDA, Biterm Model (BTM), Online Twitter LDA, and Gibbs Sampling for Dirichlet Multinomial Mixture (GSDMM), as well as the k-means clustering algorithm with two different feature representations: TF-IDF and Doc2Vec. Internal indices evaluation suggests that online twitter LDA and GSDMM as the best, while external indices suggest that LSI and K-Means with TF-IDF are the best. Curiskis, Drake, Osborn, and Kennedy (2020) evaluate techniques for document clustering and topic modeling on three datasets from Twitter and Reddit. Concerning clustering methods were selected: (a) KMC using Euclidean metric, (b) k-medoids algorithm with starting centroids sampled with a uniform distribution, (c) hierarchical agglomerative clustering algorithm with Euclidean metric and Ward linkage, and (d) NMF algorithm. It tested the DBSCAN clustering algorithm with a range of hyper-parameters but found that it delivered a poor performance for all feature representations. It was demonstrated that K-means clustering provided the best performance with Doc2vec embedding.

In short text clustering, the BOW-based methods have limitations to the sparsity of text representation. Many sentences embedding-based methods fail to capture the document structure dependencies within a text corpus. Jin, Zhao, and Ji (2020) proposes a Topic Attention Encoder (TAE). This encoder assumes the document-topic vector to be the learning target. The concatenating vector of the word embedding and the corresponding topic-word vector are the inputs. A self-attention mechanism is used in the encoder to extract weights of hidden states and encode the semantics of each short text document. With captured global dependencies and local semantics, TAE integrates the superiority of BOW methods and sentence embedding methods.

Dirichlet-Based Methods

Chen, Gong, and Liu (2020) proposes a Dirichlet process biterm-based mixture model (DP-BMM), which can deal with the topic drift and the sparsity problem in short text stream clustering. The major advantages of DP-BMM include (a) exploiting the word pairs constructed from each document to enhance the word co-occurrence pattern in short texts, and (b) dealing with the topic drift problem of short text streams naturally. Besides, it was also proposed an improved algorithm of DP-BMM with forgetting property (DP-BMM-FP), which can delete biterms of outdated documents. The study of Kumar, Shao, Uddin, and Ali (2020) proposes an Online Semantic-enhanced Dirichlet Model for short text stream clustering (OS-

DM). When compared with the existing approaches, has the following advantages: (a) allows the processing of each arriving short text in an online way, (b) integrates semantic information for model-based online clustering to handle term ambiguity, and (c) equipped with Poly Urn Scheme, the number of clusters are determined automatically in the cluster model.

Kumar, Kumar, Haq, and Shafiq (2020) proposes a bridge framework between the clustering model and the language translation component. Includes the non-parametric Dirichlet clustering model (NDML) to cluster the temporal short text data and identify the events based on the change in the probability distribution. The temporal data is split into a fixed window, and at that point, the DM updates the existing model by merging each instance into an existing cluster or creating a new one. Working with streaming unlabeled text data, Suprem (2019) presents two-fold approaches. The first one avoids dimensionality problems creating an evolving map of the live data space. The second one leverages high-confidence labels to generate weighted training sets, update existing deep learners to change decision boundaries, and create new deep learners for unseen regions of the data space. Each data point is encoded as a vector and dimensionality is reduced with t- SNE. Studying the problem of user clustering in the context of short text streams to infer users' topic distributions over time, Zhao et al. (2016) proposes a dynamic multinomial Dirichlet mixture user-clustering topic model (UCT). The method extracts word pairs in tweets and forms a word-pair set for each user to capture word co-occurrence patterns.

Cluster-Based Methods

In short text clustering, the high-dimensional sparseness of text matrix representation becomes a challenging problem. For this reason, Dai, Li, Li, and Li (2020) proposes a deep embedded method for feature extraction and clustering allocation using AE of sentence-distributed embedding. This method maps from data space to low-dimensional feature space and iteratively optimizes clustering targets. The method of Rakib, Zeh, and Milios (2020) clusters the streams of texts based on the frequently occurring word pairs in texts. It detects outliers in the clusters and reassigns the outliers using the semantic similarity based on the dynamically computed similarity thresholds.

Grey system theory (GST) provides better results in numerical analyses with insufficient data but has not yet applied to short-text clustering. The purpose of Fidan and Yuksel (2020) was to develop a short-text clustering model based on GST applicable to small datasets. The grey relational clustering, hierarchical and partitional algorithms were applied to small datasets separately. A Sentiment Word Co-occurrence and Knowledge Pair Feature Extraction based LDA short text clustering algorithm (SKP-LDA) is proposed by Wu, Yang, and Shen (2021).

The co-occurrence can handle different short texts of a microblog endowed with emotional polarity. Furthermore, the knowledge pairs feature of topic special words as well as topic-related words are extracted and inserted into LDA for clustering by K-Means. Thus, semantic information can be found more accurately and the clustering center is optimized iteratively.

Considering the problem of clustering short texts, Peng, Pavlidis, Eckley, and Tsalamanis (2018) proposes a subspace clustering algorithm that relies on linear algebra to cluster such datasets. The algorithm obtains vector representation for the n product names through TF-IDF. In order to form meaningful clusters in such datasets is used the concept of principal angles, which is an appropriate measure of dissimilarity that allows the merging of the previously identified subspaces. Applying PCA is obtained an orthonormal basis for each subspace. To retrieve the final set of K clusters was applied the spectral clustering algorithm that uses the Gaussian kernel on pairwise distances/dissimilarities.

CNN-Based Methods

Wan, Ning, Tao, and Long (2020) proposes a short text clustering ensemble algorithm based on CNN. Word2vec preserves the semantic relationship between words and obtains the multi-dimensional vector representation. The feature is extracted from the original vector combined with the CNN and clustering methods are used to cluster vectors. The Gini coefficient measures the reliability of clustering. In this respect, a flexible Self-Taught CNN (ST-CNN) framework for short text clustering and traditional unsupervised dimensionality reduction methods are proposed by Xu et al. (2017). In the ST-CNN raw text features are firstly embedded into compact binary codes using an existing unsupervised dimensionality reduction method. Hence, word embedding was explored and fed into CNN to learn deep feature representations, meanwhile, the output units fit the pre-trained binary codes in the training process. Finally, it has obtained the optimal clusters by implementing KMC to cluster the learned representations.

METRICS AND TRENDS IN TECHNICAL TOOLS

The survey of Ezugwu et al. (2022) provides an up-to-date comprehensive review of the different clustering techniques, cluster analysis properties, and quality measures to evaluate how the resulting set of partitions fits the input data. Tables 2, 3, and 4 summarize the properties, similarity measures, and cluster validation measures required for evaluating the performance of clustering algorithms.

Table 2. Evaluation properties for the performance of clustering algorithms.

Evaluation Property	Description
Scalability measures	Involve running time and memory requirements for executing the clustering algorithm. A priority due to the ever-increasing data. Linear or near-linear complexity is highly desirable for all clustering algorithms.
High dimensionality	Measures the algorithm's ability to handle data with many features in the dataset. Identifies relevant features or capture the intrinsic dimension importance for described data structure.
Robustness	Ability to detect and remove possible outliers and noise in the data set.
User-dependent K	Ability to specify the correct number of clusters. The algorithm should determine the number of clusters based on the data properties. Therefore, clustering algorithms are considered an optimization problem that can be solved using meta-heuristic algorithms.
Parameter reliance	Practical guidance in the self-determination of parameters by the algorithm itself or incorporating schemes that decrease reliance of algorithms on user-dependent parameters.
Irregular cluster shape	Ability to discover or detect irregular cluster shapes.
Order dependence	Maintain the order of input patterns in a dataset to achieve correct clusters. Such characteristic is commonly in incremental or online (stream) data.
Visualization	Enhance the proper interpretation of the clustering output and also aids the extraction of useful information.
Mixed data types	Clustering algorithms are expected to be capable of handling input with different attributes as well as flexible enough to handle any data type in the dataset.

Cluster similarity measure provides the degree of separation or closeness of the relationship between data points. All cluster methods define relationships among data that plays a significant role in the clustering method's success. Table 3 presents the frequently used similarity measures in proposed clustering techniques.

Nonetheless, how to evaluate the resulting clusters? Cluster validation criteria are usually internal or external validation. The internal validation criteria measure the intra-cluster compactness and the inter-cluster separation after the dataset partitioning by the clustering algorithm. External quality criteria require that knowledge about the dataset, the structure, and the number of clusters embedded in the dataset need to be matched. Table 4 summarizes internal and external quality criteria measures for clustering techniques.

Technically, relevant practical tools to implement current methods in high dimensional text clustering are exposed to enable applications or algorithms deployments. Furthermore, findings of these technical approaches are organized into the fields of Deep Learning Neural Networks, Enhanced and Hybrid Methods, Optimization and Meta-heuristics, and Short Text Streams involving tools and

Table 3. Similarity measures used for clustering techniques.

Similarity Measure	Description
Euclidean distance	Considered the standard or used metric for numerical data. Accepted by many clustering problems, it is the default distance measure used with the K-means algorithm.
Cosine distance	Provides the angle between two data vectors, and A, B are n-dimensional vectors. Have an excellent application in document similarity.
Jaccard distance	Measures the similarity between two data objects by evaluating the intersection divided by the data objects' unions. Applied in ecological clustering species.
Manhattan distance	Measures the absolute differences between coordinates of pairs of data objects. Results in hyper-rectangular-shaped clusters.
Chebyshev distance	Determine the absolute magnitude of the differences between the coordinates of a pair of data objects and is Chebyshev's objective.
Minkowski distance	A significant advantage is when the embedded clusters in the dataset are compacted or isolated. Otherwise, it performs poorly.
Average distance	A modified version of the Euclidean distance, which improve the drawback.
Weighted Euclidean distance	Modified Euclidean distance that can be used when each attribute's relative importance or weights is available.
Chord distance	A variant of the Euclidean distance that gives two normalized or non-normalized data points within a hypersphere of radius one, the chord length joining the points.
Mahalanobis distance	Extract hyper ellipsoidal clusters and solve the issues caused by linear correlation among features measured.
Pearson correlation	Great application in clustering gene expression data. Evaluates the similarities in the shape of gene pattern.
Multi Viewpoint-Based Similarity Measure	Excellent advantages in document clustering. Multiple viewpoints can be used to make a more informative assessment of similarity.
Bilateral Slope-Based Distance	Time-series clustering measure that combines a simple representation of time series, the slope of each segment of the time series, Euclidean distance, and the dynamic time warping.

Table 4. Internal and external quality criteria measures for clustering techniques.

Validation Measure	List of Standard Measures
Internal validation criteria	Sum of squared error (SSE), Scatter criteria, Condorcet's criterion, C-criterion, Category utility metric, Bayesian information criterion (BIC) index, Calinski–Harabasz index, Davies-Bouldin index (DB), Silhouette index, Dunn index, NIVA index, Gamma Index, Score function, C-Index, Sym-index, COP Index, Negentropy Increment, SV-Index, OS-Index, The modified Hubert statistic, SD validity index, Dbw validity index, Root-mean-square standard deviation (RMSSTD), R-squared (RS), Compact-Separated (CS) index, Bal-Hall index, Banfeld-Raftery index, Det Ratio index, Baker-Hubert Gamma index, GDI index, G-plus index, Ksq_DetW index, Log_Det_Ratio index, Log_SS_Ratio index, McClain–Rao index, PMB index, Point-Biserial index, Ratkowsky-Lance index, Ray-Turi index, Scott-Symons index, Tau index, Trace_W index, Trace_WiB index, Wemmert-Gançarski index, Xie-Beni index
External validation criteria	Mutual Information-Based Measure, Rand Index, F-measure, Jaccard Index, Fowlkes-Mallows Index, NMI measure, Purity, Entropy, Relative validation

Table 5. Tools used to implement proposed methods

Method Approach	Tools	Description
Deep Learning Neural Networks	Keras, Scikit-Learn, TensorFlow, Gensim, Scrapy, FastText, Beautiful Soup, Natural Language Toolkit (NLTK), Pytorch, Theano.	Most researches are focused on constructing a network structure and training with the support of Scikit-learn, Keras, TensorFlow, and PyTorch tools. Others researches are concentrated in take advantage of techniques to collect data from the internet through web scraping tools like Scapry and Beautiful Soap. Tools like Gensim, fastText, NLTK, and Theano reduce the size of text, implement preprocessing tasks, and vector optimization and representation respectively.
Enhanced and Hybrid	R packages (Rtsne, Trend, BNPmix, IMIFA), libraries written on C++ (SHTEClib), SciPy and mpmath libraries, PyTorch, Matlab.	R environment as well as their packages are the most suitable among the researches to perform functions associated with high dimensionality. C++ library was designed to confront the sparseness and high dimensionality of short texts. Other researches adopt SciPy and mpmath for numerical complex processing. PyTorch and SpaCy to process large text data.
Optimization and Meta-heuristics	Keras, OpenAI toolkits-resources, Keras-RL, Scikit-learn, NLTK, R packages (igraph, blockcluster, textcat), Porter stemmer.	R packages perform multidimensional analysis of texts. Keras, Keras-RL, and OpenAI Gym are used to develop deep reinforcement learning for clustering. NLTK pre-processing tasks as well as Scikit-learn to implement clustering algorithms.
Short Text Streams	Gensim, Tweepy, R package (tm), Scikit-learn, NLTK, MOA framework, Snowball	Scikit-learn, and Gemsim most used tools for online text stream operations. Other tools support text data acquisition, processing, and stemming such as Tweepy and Snowball. Two data mining frameworks MOA and WEKA are used to implement clustering algorithms.

computational execution environment. Table 5 synthesize tool used to implement or deploy the proposed methods.

CONCLUSION AND FUTURE RESEARCH DIRECTIONS

This chapter concludes, in Table 6, with a comparative analysis of the advantages and disadvantages of the six top most used tools. The scientific literature was explored to discover novelty and gaps in high-dimensional text clustering methods. The chapter summarizes the literature from 2015 to 2022. Diverse methods, including standard, basic, modified, and hybrid are reviewed. Most of the retrieved research papers describe high-dimensionality methods regarding high dimension, dimension reduction, sparsity, and subspace clustering used in text clustering applications. Identified Deep learning methods are related more with high dimension, dimension reduction, and sparsity. On other hand, the advent of methods in optimization and

Table 6. Comparative analysis of advantages and disadvantages of six top most used tools

Tool	Advantages	Disadvantages	Alternative
Scikit-learn	- Implements several non-neural net-based algorithms. - Offer several tools for data manipulations and utilities such as metrics functions, and artificial dataset generations. - Versatile, handy, and serves real-world purposes like a prediction. - Well-documented	- Creates a convenient abstraction that could encourage more junior data scientists to go without an understanding of the fundamentals. It is not the best choice for in-depth learning	- PyTorch - Keras
Gensim	- Classified as NLP / Sentiment Analysis and Machine Learning tool. - Provides convenient facilities for text processing. - Handle large text files even without loading the whole file in memory. - Doesn't require costly annotations or hand tagging of documents because it uses unsupervised models. - Robust, easily plug-in input corpus or data stream. - Easy to extend with other vector space algorithms.	- Facilities provided by Gensim for building topic models and word embedding are unparalleled with scikit-learn and R.	- NLTK - Keras - fastText - SpaCy - TensorFlow
NLTK	- Leading platform for building python programs to work with human language data. - Supports various languages and named entities for multi-language.	- Does not have any support for word vectors. - Difficult to learn and use. - Slow. - Splits text by sentences, without analyzing the semantic structure - No neural network models	- SpaCy - Gensim - TensorFlow - PyTorch - Scikit-learn
Keras	- User-Friendly and fast deployment. - Quality documentation and large Community Support. - Multiple backend and modularity. - Neural networks API and pre-trained models. - Multiple GPU support - Convolutional networks support. - Allows for easy and fast prototyping - Recurrent networks support	- Problems in low-level API - Need improvement in some features (data pre-processing tools) - Slower than its backend	- PyTorch - TensorFlow - Scikit-learn
TensorFlow	- Graph visualizations - Rich ML algorithms - Debugging, Parallelism - Scalability, Pipelining - Keras friendly, architectural support - High performance	- No GPU support for Nvidia and only language support - Missing symbolic loops - No support for Windows - Architectural limitation, Inconsistent	- PyTorch - Keras
R	- Support for data wrangling - Array of packages - Quality plotting and graphing - Highly compatible, platform-independent - ML operations, eye-catching reports	- Data Handling - Lesser Speed - Spread across various packages - Basic security	

meta-heuristics concentrate on automatic clustering, feature selection, co-clustering, document clustering, and clustering improvement due to the algorithms had proven its performance in solving different text clustering problems.

The detected deep networks based methods present better external clusters validation measures in terms of Adjusted Rand Index (ARI), Normalized Mutual Information (NMI), and Fowlkes-Mallows Index (FMI) for dimensionality reduction methods, and enable spectral clustering and fast search as well as find density peak clustering to process high-dimensional data. For optimization and meta-heuristics-based methods, the algorithms set proper weight schemes for solving text feature selection problems and dimension reduction to create a new low-dimension subset of text features to improve performance. Also, a dynamic incremental approach for document clustering resolves shortcomings of conventional high-dimensional text datasets clustering to make the model incremental and enhance the document representation with precision and less dimension.

On the other hand, enhanced and hybrid methods, increase the performance of the clustering algorithm in terms of precision, recall, F measures, and accuracy. It is clear that the proposed methods obtain the optimal low-dimension subset of features with low-dimension space. Thus, hybrid methods select a subset of features compared to single-dimension reduction methods. Hence, they improve the performance of the clustering method significantly. Also, top-ranked and common features are necessary for document representation. Finally, the accuracy of the clustering method is improved by refining the feature subspace. Short-text stream methods were evaluated with a traditional clustering method and three dynamic user clustering models. The reported precision, NMI, and ARI values average the performance of state-of-the-art textual features models. These methods are characterized by having fixed vocabularies regardless of the corpus size, which is extremely important in text mining systems. In addition to handling the space-challenging problem, the proposed approaches improve the problem of uncommon words as the corpus words are decomposed.

Thus, this chapter aims at the research work in the domain of high-dimensional text clustering describing how the algorithms and methods have been used and providing their effectiveness, advantages, and disadvantages. Directions suggested by this chapter for future research on high-dimensional text clustering are meta-heuristics optimization algorithm with short text streams, hybrid methods by combining two or more deep learning approaches, and scalability, concept drift adaptation of text streams in order to achieve scalable performance. The technical vision provided in this chapter examined, analyzed, and identified the practical tools to perform a tangible implementation of algorithms for clustering tasks on high-dimension text datasets. It was found that classification in each area highlights specific tools to implement practical solutions.

It was observed that the most implemented tool is Sciki-learn, followed by Gensim, NLTK, R packages, Keras, and TensorFlow. These tools include features and algorithms to handle neural networks that embed words in a lower-dimensional vector space. Clustering algorithms are also incremented with the flexible TensorFlow ecosystem to easily build and deploy ML-powered applications. Future directions might be to examine implemented algorithms in a deep manner into the different areas to develop and deploy new hybrid algorithms to provide improved clustering performance.

REFERENCES

Abualigah, L., Alsalibi, B., Shehab, M., Alshinwan, M., Khasawneh, A., & Alabool, H. (2021). A parallel hybrid krill herd algorithm for feature selection. *International Journal of Machine Learning and Cybernetics*, *12*(3), 783–806. doi:10.100713042-020-01202-7

Abualigah, L., Gandomi, A., Elaziz, M., Hamad, H., Omari, M., Alshinwan, M., & Khasawneh, A. (2021). Advances in Meta-Heuristic Optimization Algorithms in Big Data Text Clustering. *Electronics (Basel)*, *29*(2), 101. Advance online publication. doi:10.3390/electronics10020101

Abualigah, L. M. (2019). *Feature Selection and Enhanced Krill Herd Algorithm for Text Document Clustering*. Springer. doi:10.1007/978-3-030-10674-4

Abualigah, L. M., Khader, A., Al-Betar, M., & Alomari, O. (2017). Text feature selection with a robust weight scheme and dynamic dimension reduction to text document clustering. *Expert Systems with Applications*, *84*, 24–36. doi:10.1016/j.eswa.2017.05.002

Abualigah, L. M., Khader, A. T., Al-Betar, M. A., Alyasseri, Z. A., Alomari, O. A., & Hanandeh, E. (2017). Feature Selection with β-Hill Climbing Search for Text Clustering Application. In *International Conference on Information and Communication Technology* (pp. 22-27). IEEE. doi:10.1109/PICICT.2017.30

Abuzeina, D. (2019). Exploring bigram character features for Arabic text clustering. *Turkish Journal of Electrical Engineering and Computer Sciences*, *27*(4), 3165–3179. doi:10.3906/elk-1808-103

Anderlucci, L., & Viroli, C. (2020). Mixtures of Dirichlet-Multinomial distributions for supervised and unsupervised classification of short text data. *Advances in Data Analysis and Classification*, *14*(4), 759–770. doi:10.100711634-020-00399-3

Angiulli, F. (2018). On the Behavior of Intrinsically High-Dimensional Spaces: Distances, Direct and Reverse Nearest Neighbors, and Hubness. *Journal of Machine Learning Research, 60*. https://jmlr.csail.mit.edu/papers/volume18/17-151/17-151. pdf

Aoyama, K., & Saito, K. (2021). *Structured Inverted-File k-Means Clustering for High-Dimensional Sparse Data.* doi:10.48550/arXiv.2103.16141

Ayesha, S., Hanif, M., & Talib, R. (2020). Overview and comparative study of dimensionality reduction techniques for high dimensional data. *Information Fusion, 59*, 44–58. doi:10.1016/j.inffus.2020.01.005

Balbi, S. (2010). Beyond the curse of multidimensionality: High Dimensional Clustering in Text Mining. Statistica Applicata - Italian. *Journal of Applied Statistics*, 53–63. https://www.researchgate.net/publication/272350422_BEYOND_THE_CURSE_OF_MULTIDIMENSIONALITY_HIGH_DIMENSIONAL_CLUSTERING_IN_TEXT_MINING

Bejos, S., Feliciano-Avelino, I., Martinez-Trinidad, J., & Carrasco-Ochoa, J. (2020). Improved fast partitional clustering algorithm for text clustering. *Journal of Intelligent & Fuzzy Systems, 39*(2), 2137–2145. doi:10.3233/JIFS-179879

Bharti, K., & Singh, P. (2015). Hybrid dimension reduction by integrating feature selection with feature extraction method for text clustering. *Expert Systems with Applications, 42*(6), 3105–3114. doi:10.1016/j.eswa.2014.11.038

Bharti, K., & Singh, P. (2016). Opposition chaotic fitness mutation based adaptive inertia weight BPSO for feature selection in text clustering. *Applied Soft Computing, 43*, 20–34. doi:10.1016/j.asoc.2016.01.019

Boushaki, S., Kamel, N., & Bendjeghaba, O. (2018). High-Dimensional Text Datasets Clustering Algorithm Based on Cuckoo Search and Latent Semantic Indexing. *Journal of Information & Knowledge Management, 24*(03), 1850033. Advance online publication. doi:10.1142/S0219649218500338

Chatterjeea, A., Gupta, U., Chinnakotla, M., Srikanth, R., Galley, M., & Agrawal, P. (2019). Understanding Emotions in Text Using Deep Learning and Big Data. *Computers in Human Behavior, 93*, 309–317. doi:10.1016/j.chb.2018.12.029

Chen, J., Gong, Z., & Liu, W. (2020). Dirichlet process biterm-based mixture model for short text stream clustering. *Applied Intelligence*, 1609–1619. doi:10.1007/s10489-019-01606-1

Chen, L., Guo, Q., Liu, Z., & Zha, S. (2021). Enhanced synchronization-inspired clustering for high-dimensional data. *Complex & Intelligent Systems,* 203-223. doi:10.1007/s40747-020-00191-y

Curiskis, S., Drake, B., Osborn, T., & Kennedy, P. (2020). An evaluation of document clustering and topic modelling in two online social networks: Twitter and Reddit. *Information Processing & Management, 21*(2), 102034. Advance online publication. doi:10.1016/j.ipm.2019.04.002

Dai, Z., Li, K., Li, H., & Li, X. (2020). An Unsupervised Learning Short Text Clustering Method. *Journal of Physics: Conference Series, 1650*(3), 1–7. doi:10.1088/1742-6596/1650/3/032090

Diallo, B., Hu, J., Li, T., Khan, G., Liang, X., & Zhao, Y. (2021). Deep embedding clustering based on contractive autoencoder. *Neurocomputing, 433*, 96–107. doi:10.1016/j.neucom.2020.12.094

Din, S., & Shao, J. (2020). Exploiting evolving micro-clusters for data stream classification with emerging class detection. *Information Sciences, 507*, 404–420. doi:10.1016/j.ins.2019.08.050

Ezugwu, A., Shukla, A. K., Agbaje, M. B., Oyelade, O. N., José-García, A., & Agushaka, J. O. (2021). Automatic clustering algorithms: A systematic review and bibliometric analysis of relevant literature. *Neural Computing & Applications, 33*(11), 6247–6306. doi:10.100700521-020-05395-4

Ezugwu, A. E. (2020). Nature-inspired metaheuristic techniques for automatic clustering: A survey and performance study. *SN Applied Sciences, 57*(2), 273. Advance online publication. doi:10.100742452-020-2073-0

Fidan, H., & Yuksel, M. (2020). A Novel Short Text Clustering Model Based on Grey System Theory. *Arabian Journal for Science and Engineering, 45*(4), 2865–2882. doi:10.100713369-019-04191-0

Fomin, S., & Belousov, R. (2017). Detecting semantic duplicates in short news items. *Business Informatics*, 47-56. doi:10.17323/1998-0663.2017.2.47.56

Fraj, M., Hajkacem, M., & Essoussi, N. (2020). Self-Organizing Map for Multi-view Text Clustering. In *International Conference on Big Data Analytics and Knowledge Discovery* (pp. 396-408). Springer. 10.1007/978-3-030-59065-9_30

Guan, R., Zhang, H., Liang, Y., Giunchiglia, F., Huang, L., & Feng, X. (2020). Deep Feature-Based Text Clustering and Its Explanation. *IEEE Transactions on Knowledge and Data Engineering, 13*. Advance online publication. doi:10.1109/TKDE.2020.3028943

Gupta, A., & Begum, S. (2018). A Comparative Study on Feature Selection Techniques for Multi-cluster Text Data. In N. Yadav, A. Yadav, J. Bansal, K. Deep, & J. Kim (Eds.), *Harmony Search and Nature Inspired Optimization Algorithms. Advances in Intelligent Systems and Computing* (pp. 203–215). Springer. doi:10.1007/978-981-13-0761-4_21

Gupta, A., & Begum, S. (2020). Efficient multi-cluster feature selection on text data. *Journal of Information and Optimization Sciences*, 1583-1598. doi:10.1080/02522667.2019.1703259

Huang, X., Chen, L., & Ye, Y. (2020). Information-Theoretic Based Clustering Method for High-Dimensional Data. *Journal of Physics: Conference Series, 10*(2), 022115. Advance online publication. doi:10.1088/1742-6596/1533/2/022115

Irwin, W., Robinson, S., & Belt, S. (2017). Visualization of Large-Scale Narrative Data Describing Human Error. *Human Factors and Ergonomics Society*, 520-534.

Jagatheeshkumar, G., & Selva Brunda, S. (2018). An Improved K-Lion Optimization Algorithm With Feature Selection Methods for Text Document Cluster. *International Journal on Computer Science and Engineering*, 245–251. doi:10.26438/ijcse/v6i7.245251

Jaggi, M., Mandai, P., Narang, S., Naseem, U., & Khushi, M. (2021). Text Mining of Stocktwits Data for Predicting Stock Prices. *Aoolied System Innovation, 22*(1), 13. Advance online publication. doi:10.3390/asi4010013

Janani, R., & Vijayarani, S. (2020). Text Classification Using K-Nearest Neighbor Algorithm and Firefly Algorithm for Text Feature Selection. In T. Sengodan, M. Murugappan, & S. Misra (Eds.), *Advances in Electrical and Computer Technologies. Lecture Notes in Electrical Engineering* (p. 13). Springer. doi:10.1007/978-981-15-5558-9_47

Jin, J., Zhao, H., & Ji, P. (2020). Topic attention encoder: A self-supervised approach for short text clustering. *Journal of Information Science, 17.*

Kadhim, A., & Jassim, A. (2021). Combined Chi-Square with k-Means for Document Clustering. In *International Scientific Conference of Engineering Sciences* (p. 14). IOPScience. doi:10.1088/1757-899X/1076/1/012044

Karami, A. (2017). Taming Wild High Dimensional Text Data with a Fuzzy Lash. In *International Conference on Data Mining Workshops* (pp. 518-522). IEEE. doi:10.1109/ICDMW.2017.73

Kauffmann, E., Peral, J., Gil, D., Ferrandez, A., Sellers, R., & Mora, H. (2020). A framework for big data analytics in commercial social networks: A case study on sentiment analysis and fake review detection for marketing decision-making. *Industrial Marketing Management*, *90*, 523–537. doi:10.1016/j.indmarman.2019.08.003

Khan, I., Ivanov, K., & Jiang, Q. (2016). FastMap Projection for High-Dimensional Data: A Cluster Ensemble Approach. *International Journal of Database Theory and Application*, 311-330. doi:10.14257/ijdta.2016.9.12.28

Kolli, S., & Sreedevi, M. (2021). A Novel Granularity Optimal Feature Selection based on Multi-Variant Clustering for High Dimensional Data. *Turkish Journal of Computer and Mathematics Education*, 5051-5062. doi:10.17762/turcomat. v12i3.2031

Kongwudhikunakorn, S., & Waiyamai, K. (2020). Combining Distributed Word Representation and Document Distance for Short Text Document Clustering. *Journal of Information Processing Systems*, *24*. Advance online publication. doi:10.3745/ JIPS.04.0164

Kotte, V., Rajavelu, S., & Rajsingh, E. (2020). A Similarity Function for Feature Pattern Clustering and High Dimensional Text Document Classification. *Foundations of Science*, *25*(4), 1077–1094. doi:10.100710699-019-09592-w

Kotte, V., Vuppu, S., & Thadishetti, R. (2021). High Dimensional Text Document Clustering and Classification using Machine Learning Methods. In *International Conference on Intelligent Computing and Control Systems* (pp. 1612-1617). IEEE. 10.1109/ICICCS51141.2021.9432128

Kumar, J., Kumar, R., Haq, A., & Shafiq, S. (2020). A Non-Parametric Multi-Lingual Clustering Model for Temporal Short Text. In *International Computer Conference on Wavelet Active Media Technology and Information Processing* (pp. 58-61). IEEE. doi:10.1109/ICCWAMTIP51612.2020.9317342

Kumar, J., Shao, J., Uddin, S., & Ali, W. (2020). An Online Semantic-enhanced Dirichlet Model for Short Text Stream Clustering. In *Annual Meeting of the Association for Computational Linguistics* (pp. 766–776). ACL. 10.18653/v1/2020.acl-main.70

Kumar, K., Srinivasan, R., & Singh, E. (2018). An efficient approach for dimensionality reduction and classification of high dimensional text documents. In *International Conference on Data Science, E-learning and Information Systems* (pp. 1-5). ACM. 10.1145/3279996.3281364

Kushwaha, N., & Pant, M. (2018). Link based BPSO for feature selection in big data text clustering. *Future Generation Computer Systems*, *82*, 190–199. doi:10.1016/j.future.2017.12.005

Kushwaha, N., & Pant, M. (2020). Textual data dimensionality reduction - a deep learning approach. *Multimedia Tools and Applications*, *79*(15-16), 11039–11050. doi:10.100711042-018-6900-x

Leng, B., Liu, J., Pan, H., Zhou, S., & Niu, Z. (2015). Topic model based behaviour modeling and clustering analysis for wireless network users. In *Asia-Pacific Conference on Communications* (pp. 410-415). IEEE. doi:10.1109/APCC.2015.7412547

Leyli-Abadi, M., Labiod, L., & Nadif, M. (2017). *Denoising Autoencoder as an Effective Dimensionality Reduction and Clustering of Text Data. In Advances in Knowledge Discovery and Data Mining*. Springer. doi:10.1007/978-3-319-57529-2_62

Li, J., Zhu, R., Qu, A., Ye, H., & Sun, Z. (2019). *Semi-orthogonal Non-negative Matrix Factorization with an Application in Text Mining*. Retrieved from https://arxiv.org/abs/1805.02306

Li, K., Ni, T., Xue, J., & Jiang, Y. (2021). Deep soft clustering: Simultaneous deep embedding and soft-partition clustering. *Ambient Intell Human Computing*, *13*. Advance online publication. doi:10.100712652-021-02997-1

Liu, M., Wu, C., & Chen, L. (2015). A vector reconstruction based clustering algorithm particularly for large-scale text collection. *Neural Networks*, *63*, 141–155. doi:10.1016/j.neunet.2014.10.012 PMID:25539500

Lossio-Ventura, J., Gonzales, S., Morzan, J., Alatrista-Salas, H., Hernandez-Boussard, T., & Bian, J. (2021). Evaluation of clustering and topic modeling methods over health-related tweets and emails. *Artificial Intelligence in Medicine*, *18*, 102096. Advance online publication. doi:10.1016/j.artmed.2021.102096 PMID:34127235

Mehta, V., Bawa, S., & Singh, J. (2021). Stamantic clustering: Combining statistical and semantic features for clustering of large text datasets. *Expert Systems with Applications*, *9*, 114710. Advance online publication. doi:10.1016/j.eswa.2021.114710

Mohamed, A. (2020). An effective dimension reduction algorithm for clustering Arabic text. *Egyptian Informatics Journal, 1-5*(1), 1–5. Advance online publication. doi:10.1016/j.eij.2019.05.002

Mustafa, H., Ayob, M., Albashish, D., & Abu-Taleb, S. (2020). Solving text clustering problem using a memetic differential evolution algorithm. *PLoS One, 18*(6), e0232816. Advance online publication. doi:10.1371/journal.pone.0232816 PMID:32525869

Mustafi, D., Mustafi, A., & Sahoo, G. (2022). A novel approach to text clustering using genetic algorithm based on the nearest neighbour heuristic. *International Journal of Computers and Applications, 44*(3), 291–303. doi:10.1080/120621 2X.2020.1735035

Peng, H., Pavlidis, N., Eckley, I., & Tsalamanis, I. (2018). Subspace Clustering of Very Sparse High-Dimensional Data. In *International Conference on Big Data* (p. 4). IEEE. doi:10.1109/BigData.2018.8622472

Praveen, S., & Priya, R. (2020). A unified deep learning framework for text data mining using deep adaptive fuzzy clustering. *European Journal of Molecular & Clinical Medicine*, 2832-2847. Retrieved from https://ejmcm.com/article_7130.html

Purushothaman, R., Rajagopalan, S., & Dhandapani, G. (2020). Hybridizing Gray Wolf Optimization (GWO) with Grasshopper Optimization Algorithm (GOA) for text feature selection and clustering. *Applied Soft Computing, 14*, 106651. Advance online publication. doi:10.1016/j.asoc.2020.106651

Qiang, J., Qian, Z., Li, Y., Yuan, Y., & Wu, X. (2022). Short Text Topic Modeling Techniques, Applications, and Performance: A Survey. *IEEE Transactions on Knowledge and Data Engineering, 34*(3), 1427–1445. doi:10.1109/ TKDE.2020.2992485

Rafi, M., Waqar, M., Ajaz, H., Ayub, U., & Danish, M. (2017). Document Clustering using Self-Organizing Maps: A Multi-Features Layered Approach. *Mendel Soft Computing Journal*, 111-118. doi:10.13164/mendel.2017.1.111

Rakib, M., Zeh, N., & Milios, E. (2020). Short Text Stream Clustering via Frequent Word Pairs and Reassignment of Outliers to Clusters. In *Proceedings of the ACM Symposium on Document Engineering* (pp. 1-4). ACM. 10.1145/3395027.3419589

Rashidi, R., Khamforoosh, K., & Sheikhahmadi, A. (2022). Proposing improved meta-heuristic algorithms for clustering and separating users in the recommender systems. *Electronic Commerce Research, 22*(2), 623–648. doi:10.100710660-021-09478-9

Reddy, G. (2016). Dimensionality reduction approach for high dimensional text documents. In *International Conference on Engineering & MIS* (pp. 1-6). IEEE. 10.1109/ICEMIS.2016.7745364

Rezaee, M., Eshkevari, M., Saberi, M., & Hussain, O. (2021). GBK-means clustering algorithm: An improvement to the K-means algorithm based on the bargaining game. *Knowledge-Based Systems*, *13*. Advance online publication. doi:10.1016/j.knosys.2020.106672

Rui, W., Xing, K., & Jia, Y. (2016). *BOWL: Bag of Word Clusters Text Representation Using Word Embeddings. In Knowledge Science, Engineering and Management.* Springer. doi:10.1007/978-3-319-47650-6_1

Salem, R. (2017). A manifold learning framework for reducing high-dimensional big text data. In *International Conference on Computer Engineering and Systems* (pp. 347-352). IEEE. doi:10.1109/ICCES.2017.8275330

Sangaiah, A., Fakhry, A., Abdel-Basset, M., & El-henawy, I. (2018). Arabic text clustering using improved clustering algorithms with dimensionality reduction. *Cluster Computing*, 4535–4549. doi:10.100710586-018-2084-4

Sarkar, S., Ejaz, N., & Maiti, J. (2018). Application of hybrid clustering technique for pattern extraction of accident at work: A case study of a steel industry. In *International Conference on Recent Advances in Information Technology* (pp. 1-6). IEEE. 10.1109/RAIT.2018.8389052

Schubert, E., & Feher, G. (2021). *Accelerating Spherical k-Means. Similarity Search and Applications.* Springer. doi:10.1007/978-3-030-89657-7_17

Shah, S., & Koltun, V. (2018). *Deep Continuous Clustering.* Advance online publication. doi:10.48550/arXiv.1803.01449

Sreelekshmi, K., & Remya, R. (2018). A Fuzzy Document Clustering Model Based on Relevant Ranked Terms. In P. Sa, S. Bakshi, I. Hatzilygeroudis, & M. Sahoo (Eds.), *Recent Findings in Intelligent Computing Techniques. Advances in Intelligent Systems and Computing* (p. 11). Springer. doi:10.1007/978-981-10-8633-5_11

Sun, Y., & Platos, J. (2020). High-Dimensional Data Clustering Algorithm Based on Stacked-Random Projection. In *International Conference on Intelligent Networking and Collaborative Systems* (pp. 391-401). Springer. doi:10.1007/978-3-030-57796-4_38

Sun, Y., & Platoš, J. (2020). High-Dimensional Text Clustering by Dimensionality Reduction and Improved Density Peak. *Wireless Communications and Mobile Computing, 16*, 1–16. Advance online publication. doi:10.1155/2020/8881112

Suprem, A. (2019). *Concept Drift Detection and Adaptation with Weak Supervision on Streaming Unlabeled Data*. doi:10.48550/arXiv.1910.01064

Tao, Q., Gu, C., Wang, Z., & Jiang, D. (2020). An intelligent clustering algorithm for high-dimensional multiview data in big data applications. *Neurocomputing, 393*, 234–244. doi:10.1016/j.neucom.2018.12.093

Thirumoorthy, K., & Muneeswaran, K. (2021). A hybrid approach for text document clustering using Jaya optimization algorithm. *Expert Systems with Applications, 16*, 115040. Advance online publication. doi:10.1016/j.eswa.2021.115040

Tjøstheim, D., Jullum, M., & Løland, A. (2021). *Statistical embedding: Beyond principal components*. doi:10.48550/arXiv.2106.01858

Trad, R., & Spiliopoulou, M. (2021). A Framework for Authorial Clustering of Shorter Texts in Latent Semantic Spaces. In P. Abreu, P. Rodrigues, A. Fernández, & J. Gama (Eds.), *Advances in Intelligent Data Analysis* (pp. 301–312). Springer. doi:10.1007/978-3-030-74251-5_24

Tseng, S., Lu, Y., Chakraborty, G., & Chen, L. (2019). Comparison of Sentiment Analysis of Review Comments by Unsupervised Clustering of Features Using LSA and LDA. In *International Conference on Awareness Science and Technology* (pp. 1-6). IEEE. doi:10.1109/ICAwST.2019.8923267

Wan, H., Ning, B., Tao, X., & Long, J. (2020). *Research on Chinese Short Text Clustering Ensemble via Convolutional Neural Networks. In Artificial Intelligence in China*. Springer. doi:10.1007/978-981-15-0187-6_74

Wan, H., Ning, B., Tao, X., & Long, J. (2020). Research on Chinese Short Text Clustering Ensemble via Convolutional Neural Networks. In Q. Liang, W. Wang, J. Mu, X. Liu, Z. Na, & B. Chen (Eds.), *Artificial Intelligence in China. Lecture Notes in Electrical Engineering* (p. 7). Springer. doi:10.1007/978-981-15-0187-6_74

Wang, H., Zhou, C., & Li, L. (2019). Design and Application of a Text Clustering Algorithm Based on Parallelized K-Means Clusterin. *Revue d'Intelligence Artificie*, 453-460. doi:10.18280/ria.330608

Wang, X., Liao, Y., Zhu, J., Zhou, B., & Jia, Y. (2020). A Low-Dimensional Representation Learning Method for Text Classification and Clustering. In *International Conference on Data Science in Cyberspace* (p. 4). IEEE. 10.1109/DSC50466.2020.00039

Wankhade, K., Jondhale, K., & Dongre, S. (2021). A clustering and ensemble based classifier for data stream classification. *Applied Soft Computing, 15*, 107076. Advance online publication. doi:10.1016/j.asoc.2020.107076

Wu, D., Yang, R., & Shen, C. (2021). Sentiment word co-occurrence and knowledge pair feature extraction based LDA short text clustering algorithm. *Journal of Intelligent Information Systems, 56*(1), 1–23. doi:10.100710844-020-00597-7

Wu, G., Lin, H., Fu, E., & Wang, L. (2015). An Improved K-means Algorithm for Document Clustering. In *International Conference on Computer Science and Mechanical Automation* (pp. 65-69). IEEE. 10.1109/CSMA.2015.20

Xu, J., Xu, B., Wang, P., Zheng, S., Tian, G., Zhao, J., & Xu, B. (2017). Self-Taught convolutional neural networks for short text clustering. *Neural Networks, 88*, 22–31. doi:10.1016/j.neunet.2016.12.008 PMID:28157556

Yang, B., Fu, X., Sidiropoulos, N., & Hong, M. (2017). Towards K-means-friendly Spaces: Simultaneous Deep Learning and Clustering. *Proceedings of Machine Learning Research*, 3861-3870. Retrieved from http://proceedings.mlr.press/v70/yang17b.html

Zhang, D., Sun, Y., Eriksson, B., & Balzano, L. (2017). *Deep Unsupervised Clustering using mixture of autoencoders.* doi:10.48550/arXiv.1712.07788

Zhang, Y., Lu, J., Liu, F., Liu, Q., Porter, A., Chen, H., & Zhang, G. (2018). Does deep learning help topic extraction? A kernel k-means clustering method with word embedding. *Journal of Informetrics, 12*(4), 1099–1117. doi:10.1016/j.joi.2018.09.004

Zhao, H., Salloum, S., Cai, Y., & Huang, J. (2017). Ensemble subspace clustering of text data using two-level features. *International Journal of Machine Learning and Cybernetics, 8*(6), 1751–1766. doi:10.100713042-016-0556-5

Zhao, Y., Liang, S., Ren, Z., Ma, J., Yilmaz, E., & Rijke, M. (2016). *Explainable User Clustering in Short Text Streams. In International ACM SIGIR conference on Research and Development in Information Retrieval.* ACM., doi:10.1145/2911451.2911522

Zheng, Y., Meng, Z., & Xu, C. (2015). A Short-Text Oriented Clustering Method for Hot Topics Extraction. *International Journal of Software Engineering and Knowledge Engineering, 25*(03), 453–471. doi:10.1142/S0218194015400161

KEY TERMS AND DEFINITIONS

Deep Learning Text Clustering: Deep neural network implementation that combines feature extraction, dimensionality reduction, and clustering to learn representations from text data and to adapt into the clustering module.

Dirichlet Method: Stochastic process used as a prior for mixture models, which is often used in Bayesian inference to describe the prior knowledge about the distribution of random variables. Is a method of clustering that unknown the number of clusters ahead of time.

Evolutionary Text Clustering: Task to find patterns within a set of mapped text data through temporal networks with no fixed instances, but grows as time passes. To define clusters for the next generation of the network is used information available in the history of that network.

Optimization Text Clustering: Evolutionary and nature-inspired techniques that adapt to the changing environment and can learn to do better and explain their decisions to improve the efficiency of document clustering.

Text Streams Clustering: Task to assign a massive amount of text generated from different sources to a new cluster or an existing one in a reasonable time to achieve clustering results through similarity-based or model-based stream methods. A similarity-based use vector space model to represent the documents. Model-based commonly uses Gibbs sampling to estimate the parameters of the mixture model.

Vector Space Model: An algebraic model in NLP that considers the relationship between text (words and documents) and represent similarities as a vector of identifiers. This model assumes two requirements: (1) each term is unique, and (2) the terms have no order. Thus, the relevance of a word or document is equal to the word or document query similarity.

Word Embedding: Document dense vocabulary representation in which similar words have a similar encoding mapping into low d-dimensional distributed real-valued vector. Capture the context of words in a document, semantic and syntactic similarity, relation with other words, etc. The technique often merged into the field of deep learning.

Chapter 4
Community Detection Algorithms:
A Critical Review

Akib Mohi Ud Din Khanday
United Arab Emirates University, Al Ain, UAE

Syed Tanzeel Rabani
Baba Ghulam Shah Badshah University, India

Qamar Rayees Khan
Baba Ghulam Shah Badshah University, India

Fayaz Ahmad Khan
Cluster University of Srinagar, India

ABSTRACT

Modern networks, like social networks, can typically be characterised as a graph structure, and graph theory approaches can be used to address issues like link prediction, community recognition in social network analysis, and social network mining. The community structure or cluster, which is the organisation of vertices with numerous links joining vertices of the same cluster and comparatively few edges joining vertices of different clusters, is one of the most important characteristics of graphs describing real systems. People post content on social media platforms and others comment, share, and like their messages. There are various approaches in finding the communities on online social networks. In this chapter an overview of community structure is provided. A critical analysis is being done on various community detection algorithms.

DOI: 10.4018/978-1-6684-6909-5.ch004

OVERVIEW OF COMMUNITY STRUCTURE

Online social networks, unlike the traditional web, which is mainly driven by content, treat users as first-class citizens. A user joins a network, posts content, creates friendly ties and remains connected with other users in the network. This fundamental user-to-user link structure supports online engagement by offering a framework for organizing real-world and virtual contacts, identifying content and expertise provided or recommended by friends, and discovering other users with similar interests (Wang and Gan, 2017; Orlov and Litvak, 2018). Blogs, content aggregation sites, internet fora, online social networks, and phone data records all real-time data (Ashcroft et al., 2015). New technologies are required to obtain, handle, and evaluate these data.

In recent years, social community research has relied heavily on data gathered from online interactions and explicitly involved linkage in online social community systems such as Facebook, Twitter, LinkedIn, Flickr, Instant Messenger, and Others. Twitter is one of the most popular social media platforms, with millions of active users from almost every country and generating a revenue of more than $3.7 billion[1]. Twitter is a real-time, highly social micro-blogging site that al- lows users to publish short status updates known as tweets, which are displayed on timelines. In their 280-character content, tweets may contain one or more entities and references to one or more places in the actual world. Twitter is a public platform with millions of tweets published daily from millions of user accounts, all of which have academic and commercial value (Kwak et al., 2010; Mendoza et al., 2010). The Twitter API allows developers to access Twitter's data. With successfully using Twitter's API, understanding users, tweets, and timelines is very important. In Twitter, there are three types of API: Search API, Streaming API, and REST API (Mishra et al., 2016; Sharma and Moh, 2016; Bakshy et al., 2011).

Socio-metrics is a method for measuring social relationships and may be used to investigate the structure of a network (Gupta et al., 2013; Ashcroft et al., 2015). The structure of the network is determined by checking the quality of interconnections, role of entities, information flows, network evolution, clusters/communities in a network, nodes in a cluster, the cluster/centre network's node, and nodes on the periphery. The functioning of connected items from network groups is detected based on interaction modules, characteristic values, and the expectation of undetected connections among nodes. In communities, the nodes have various relationships with one another. Identifying a community is a difficult task involving grouping nodes into small communities, and a node in a community structure may belong to several communities simultaneously (Golbeck, 2013).

Clustering algorithms can detect communities but only use node characteristics and ignore the relationship/link among nodes. Some community detection methods fail to describe a community's critical shape. For example, some characteristics may reveal which node in a community has a small number of hyperlinks which otherwise is difficult to detect in a community structure. Even if some nodes have no attribute values, the community provides information about them. The network structure can be balanced using node properties, resulting in reliable community discovery. When both node attributes and network topology are considered, community detection becomes difficult.

LITERATURE REVIEW

Humans have the nature to make communities in the real world, which is reflected in social media. Newman and Girvan (2004) proposed algorithm for detecting group structure. The two major characteristics of the algorithm are: The first step is to remove edges from the network iteratively, forming communities from the networks; the second step is to recalculate the edges after each removal. The algorithms used are more effective at detecting group structure in both machine and real-world network data. Finding a faster version of the algorithm since this algorithm becomes intractable for larger systems. The algorithm has been improved to reduce the computational complexity.

Wan et al. (2008) proposed an algorithm for detecting a network's group structure. The algorithm has two essential functions: the first is to remove edges from the network iteratively so that communities can be created from the networks, and the second is to recalculate the edges after each removal. For both real and real-world network results, the algorithm performed efficiently. This work aims to find a faster version of the algorithm since it becomes intractable for larger systems, and the complexity can be reduced.

Liu et al. (2013) identified the inner circles of government political power under formal work relations and observed how the selected political groups form and change over time. Network Construction, Community Discovery, and Community Evolution Tracking were the three key processes they used to accomplish this. The study's findings could be used to create a political culture observation method that aids public oversight of political power transitions for better checks and balances in democratic societies.

Bhat and Abulaish (2014) developed a novel method for detecting Stealthy accounts in online social networks. Node-level community identification, Features, Classification, and Finding Stealthy Sybils are some of the steps in their approach. The research can be expanded to find new approaches to dealing with malicious accounts based on OSN users' community-based features. Sutaria et al. (2015) proposed a new algorithm for detecting social network groups to obtain useful and relevant data.

According to the findings, the Modularity-based approach outperformed the Eigen Vector-based approach. The authors did not include complex, dense networks with overlapping nodes and cross edges.

Hasanzadeh et al. (2014) proposed new method that employs ontology and clustering algorithms. They perform relation analysis and group detection in each cluster. There are five modules in this method:

1. Preparation of a social network dataset.
2. Text preprocessing and data modelling.
3. Clustering of social objects.
4. Partitioning of social network members.
5. Examine the connections.

They obtained a dataset consisting of 517431 emails from 151 Enron Company employees. As dimensions, they receive 506 keywords. They eliminated terms with similar meanings after using their definition. There are 414 words left after this. There was a higher level of success with their system. Other clustering al- algorithms that work based on weight can be used. The proposed approach is also applicable to dynamic graph datasets.

Rao and Mitra (2014) proposed a new algorithm for detecting communities using Graph mining techniques. They begin by creating a community incidence matrix. The occurrence matrix was then used to determine the number of communities. The group graph can be detected using the community number series.

Isolated groups may also be identified. They tested their algorithm by detecting groups in different villages. This method for detecting communities is easy and efficient. This technique can be used on social media sites with the support of tags, likes, and retweets.

Roy et al. (2015) proposed the Attention Automaton, a probabilistic finite automaton that can estimate a user community's collective attention. The Communities on Twitter are focused on user's geographical proximity or shared interests (such as followers of a specific account). They discovered that the likelihood is determined by two factors:1. The inclination of the user group to change their focus. 2. The categorical affinity of the user community. They coined the term "Volatility" to describe the inclination for people attention to change based on time slots. In addition, different user groups respond to patterns in different categories differently. They used GT-TTL (Graphical Location – Trending Topic List) and BT-TTL (Brand Audience – Trending Topic List) to conduct various experiments. They choose 30 locations around the world at random in GT-TTL. The Attention Automaton performed 44 percent better than ARIMA and 71 percent better than random selection in terms of F-score results. In BT-TTL, 30 consumer groups of brands were chosen at random.

Overall, the Attention Automaton outperformed the random scheme by 38 percent and the ARIMA model by 74 percent in terms of F-score. They used patterns as an attention function, but it would be fascinating to see what other social network assets might be used similarly. It's an intriguing challenge for patterns beyond hashtags, such as multi-word expressions like "America Loves Justin Bieber", which falls into the category (Location + Entertainment). In terms of game theory, it will be interesting to learn how patterns fight to break into the *TjjTL*.

Aylani and Goyal (2017) detected groups based on shared interests, user engagement, and social events. This method necessitates seed user and friend list user data. Various parameters about the seed consumer are extracted, such as the number of tags and general interests. They proposed a formula for calculating the value of tag-like and tag statements. After determining the typical social activity value and number of tags, the data is fed into the k clustering algorithm. Communities are represented by the clusters formed. The dataset of 121 users with their social activities was used as the input data. The equations are applied to the dataset as part of the method. The CSA (Common social activity) parameter is developed. The CSA and number of tags are fed into the K clustering algorithm. The clusters create societies. A semantic-based approach can be used to determine the user's area of interest more accurately.

Khanday et al. (2023) proposed a hybrid approach for identifying community structure on social networks. The authors used leader ranker algorithm and network constraint to identify the main node, the propagandistic network structure. The results generated by there approach were more accurate than other previous work.

COMMUNITY DETECTION IN SOCIAL NETWORKS

Modern networks like the social network can generally be modelled as a graph structure, and the problems like link prediction, community detection in social network analysis and social network mining can be solved using graph theory techniques. One of the most relevant features of graphs representing real systems is community structure or cluster, i.e., the organization of vertices, with many edges joining vertices of the same cluster and comparatively few edges joining vertices of different clusters. Such clusters, or communities, can be measured as fairly independent compartments of a graph, playing a similar role. Detecting communities is important in disciplines where systems are often represented as graphs. This section presents the basic concepts of graph theory and the theoretical background of community detection.

Terminology in Graph Theory

Most social networks are directed graphs with a set of nodes connected by edges, with the edges having a direction associated with them. This section provides the basic terminology and graph theory background that is used throughout the research work.

Graph

A graph usually represents a network. A graph $G = (V, E)$ consists of a set of nodes V and a set of edges $E\ V\ V$ which connect pairs of nodes. The number of nodes in the graph equals $n = V$, and the number of edges $m = E$.

Nodes

All graphs have fundamental building blocks. One significant component of any graph is the set of nodes. In a graph representing friendship, these nodes represent people, and any couple of connected people denotes the company be- tween them. Depending on the perspective, these nodes are called vertices or act ors. For example, in a web graph, nodes represent websites, and th e connections between nodes indicate web links between them. In a social setting, these nodes are called actors. The mathematical repr esentation for a set of nodes is $V = v1, v2, vn.$, where V is the set of nodes and $vi,\ 1in$, is a single node. $V = n$ is called the size of the graph.

Edges

Another important component of any graph is the set of edges. Edges connect nodes. In a social setting, where nodes represent social entities such as people, edges indicate inter-node relationships and are therefore known as relationships or ties. The edge set is usually represented as E, such that $E = e1, e2, em$ where $ei,\ 1im$, is an edge and the set size is commonly shown as $m = E$. Edges are also represented by their endpoints. So $e(v1; v2)$ defines an edge e between nodes $V\ 1$ and $V\ 2$. Edges can contain directions, meaning one node is linked to another but not vice versa. When edges are undirected, nodes are linked both ways. In Figure 1b, edges e (v1, v2) and e (v2, v1) are the same edges because there is no direction stating how nodes get connected. These edges in this graph are called undirected edges, and this kind of graph is an undirected graph. Conversely, when edges include directions, $e(v1, v2)$, is not the same as $e(v2, v1)$.

A graph can be directed or undirected, unipartite or bipartite and the edges may contain weights or not. Directed edges are represented using arrows. In a directed graph, an edge $e(vi, vj)$ is characterized using an arrow that starts at vi and ends at

Figure 1. Directed and undirected graph

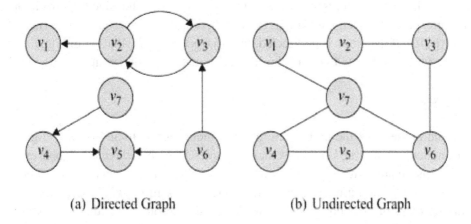

(a) Directed Graph   (b) Undirected Graph

vj. Edges can begin and end at the same node; these edges are called loops or self-links and are represented as *e(vi, vi)*. For any node *vi*, in an undirected graph, the set of nodes connected to via an edge is called its neighborhood and is represented as neighborhood *N (vi)*. *N (Jade) = Jeff, Juan*. In directed graphs, node *vi* has arriving neighbors *Nin(vi)* (nodes that connect to *vi*) and outgoing neighbors *Nout(vi)*. The mathematical definitions are given below. Directed and Undirected Graph: In a directed graph *G = (V, E)*, every edge *(i, j)E* links node *i* to node *j*. An undirected graph *GU = (V, E)* is a directed one where if edge *(i, j)E*, then edge *(j, i)E*.

Bipartite Graph

A graph *GB = (V h, V a, Eb)* is called bipartite if the node set *V* can be partitioned into two dislodge sets *V h* and *V a*, where *V = V hV a*, such that every edge *eEb* connects a node of *V h* to a node of *V a*, i.e., *e = (i, j)EiV h* and *jV a*. In other words, there are no edges between nodes of a similar partition.

Adjacency Matrix

Every graph *G = (V, E)* directed or undirected, weighted or unweighted, can be represented by its adjacency matrix *A*. Matrix *A* has size *V V (ornn)*, where the rows and columns represent the nodes of the graph and the entries indicate the existence of edges.

The adjacency matrix A of a graph *G = (V, E)* is an *|V ||V |* matrix, such that

$A_{ij} = w_{ij}$, *if (i, j)* $\in$ *E*, $\forall i, j \in$ *1, ..., |V |0, otherwise*

1. This definition is suitable for weighted and unweighted graphs. For the former case, each value w_{ij} represents the weight associated with the edge (i, j), while for the latter case of unweighted graphs the weight of each edge is equal to one (i.e., w_{ij} = 1, $(i, j)E$). If the graph is undirected, the adjacency matrix A is symmetric, i.e., $A = AT$, while for directed graphs, the adjacency matrix is non-symmetric.

Degree

A basic property of the nodes in a graph is their degree. In an undirected graph GU, nodes have degree k if it has k incident edges. In case of directed graphs, every node is associated with an in-degree and an out degree. The in-degree k in i of node i V is equal to the number of incoming edges, i.e., k in $i = kj$ $(j, i)Ek$, while the out-degree k out i of node iV equals to the number of outgoing edges, i.e., k out i = kj $(i, j)Ek$. In undirected graphs, the in-degree is equal to the out-degree, i.e., ki = k in i = k out i, iV. The degree matrix is defined as the diagonal nn matrix D, with the degree of each node in the main diagonal. Similarly, in directed graphs the in-degree matrix D_{in} and out-degree matrix D_{out} for the in- and out- degrees can be defined (Diestel, 2006).

Terminology

Edge Betweenness: The betweenness of an edge is the number of shortest paths between vertices that contain the edge.

Random Walks: A Markov chain describes the sequence of nodes visited by a random walker. Random walk is used to calculate the dissimilarity between two nodes in order to identify community.

Centrality: It is a measure indicating the node's importance in the network.

Degree Centrality: Is defined as the ratio of the number of neighbours of a vertex with the total number of neighbours possible.

In Degree: This represents the number of edges incoming to a vertex.

Out Degree: This represents the number of edges outgoing from a vertex.

Clique: A clique is a maximum complete subgraph in which all nodes are adjacent.

Maximum Clique: A maximum clique is the largest clique in a graph, a subset in which all vertices are pair-wise connected by an edge.

Complete Mutuality: It is a measure of tie strength inside the subgroup.

Reachability: It is a low diameter, facilitating fast communication between the group members.

K-Clique: It is a maximal subgraph in which the most significant geodesic distance be- tween any two nodes is no greater than k.

K-Core: The k-core is defined as the most extensive subgraph in which each node has at least k edges. The k-core graph was used to find the maximal subgraph with minimum degree k. kcore is a substructure that connects each node to at least k members.

K-Plex: k-plex of a graph is a maximal subgraph in which each vertex of the induced subgraph is connected to at least n-k other vertices, where n is the number of vertices in the induced subgraph.

Modularity: Modularity measures the excellence of community partitions formed by an algorithm. It is the dissimilarity between the actual density of intra-community edges and the corresponding connections in a random network possessing the same degree of distribution as that of the actual network.

Overlapping: Overlapping communities are possible if a node is a member of more than one community.

COMMUNITY TYPES

Communities can be implicit or explicit. Communities that are not built by their group members but formed by a third party come under an implicit category. For example, yahoo groups come under explicit community, whereas a community in which all the people who use similar or the same programming languages come under implicit. In most social networking sites, in contrast to explicit communities, implicit communities and their members are obscure to many people.

Community structure is defined as the possibility of recognizing within the network, subsets of nodes which are more connected among themselves than to the rest of the network. When detecting communities, there are two possible modes of data (1) the network structure, (2) the features and attributes of nodes. Even though communities form around nodes that have common edges and common attributes, community detection algorithms have only focused any one of these two data modalities. Traditional community detection algorithms concentrate only on the network structure while clustering algorithms mostly consider only node attributes (Zafarani et al., 2014).

Nature of Network Communities

As the complexity of networks increases, the definitions of community also differ. Though there are various definitions of community, many features must be considered in the problem of community identification from complex networks. In this section, some of the important natures of communities are discussed. Directed Network: Some real-world networks are represented with edges and links that are not reciprocal, called directed networks. For example, in the case of web pages, a hyperlink from one page to another is directed and the other carrier may or may not have a hyperlink pointing in the backward direction. In community detection, the direction of edges also plays an important role.

Hierarchy Network

When a node in a network belongs to only one community, the community is said to be separated or disjoint. Most of the disjoint communities are hierarchical. A hierarchy describes the organization of elements in a network. It shows how nodes link to each other to form motifs, how motifs combine to form communities and how communities are joined to form the entire network. In general, a network's community structure encompasses a potentially complicated set of hierarchical and modular components. In this context, the term module is used to refer to a single cluster of nodes. Given a network partitioned into modules, it can be divided in an iterative fashion until each node is in its own singleton community (Raymond, 2002).

Overlapping Network: The complex network models of real-world phenomena exhibit an overlapping community structure, i.e., a node in the network can belong to more than one community. The presence of nodes belonging to several communities occurs naturally from real data. Hence, overlap is one of the peculiar features of the community. The overlap of different communities exists widely in complex real-world networks, particularly in social networks. In complex networks, nodes are typically shared between two or more groups. In such cases, communities are said to be overlapping.

Dense groups in complex networks often overlap with each other. For example, in social networks, human beings have multiple societal roles. These roles make the network members join multiple communities simultaneously, such as colleges, universities, families or relationships, companies, hobby clubs, etc. In a co-authorship network, nodes represent the scientists, and two nodes are connected if they have coauthored one or more articles and the articles are communities. Overlapping considerably increases the complexity of the communities.

Weighted Network

A weighted network is a network where the links among nodes have weights assigned. In many real-world networks, not all links in a network have the same capacity. Links in complex networks are often associated with weights that differentiate them in their strength, intensity, or capacity. In social networks, the strength of social relationships is a function of their duration, emotional intensity, intimacy and exchange of services. For non-social networks, weights often refer to the function performed by links. In weighted networks, a group of vertices can be considered a community only if the weights of their connections are strong enough (Xie et al., 2013).

Dynamic Network

Complex networks are not always static. In reality, networks gradually evolve. Particularly, social networks witness the expansion in size and space as their users continuously increase, changing the network to dynamic. A dynamic network is a special type of evolving complex network where changes are often introduced over time. The set of edges appearing and disappearing in the communities as time evolves has little effect on the network's local structure. But, over a long period, these dynamics may lead to a significant transformation of the network community structure. The study of dynamic communities is an emerging area of interest in complex networks (Seidman and Foster, 1978).

DISCUSSION AND CONCLUSION

Community detection methods can be broadly categorized into Ag- agglomerative and Divisive Methods. In Agglomerative methods, edges are added one by one to a graph which only contains nodes. Edges are added from the stronger edge to the weaker edge. In Divisive methods, edges are removed one by one from a complete graph. There can be any number of communities in a given network and they can be of varying sizes. These characteristics make the detection procedure of communities very hard. However, many different techniques are proposed in community detection. Some popular approaches that are used for detecting communities in a network are Newman-Girvan and Random Walk. The below section discusses these approaches in detail.

Newman and Girvan Algorithm

Newman and Girvan Algorithm is a general approach for locating communities. It divides the vertices without requiring the number of communities to be specified. The algorithm has three distinct features: (1) edges are gradually eliminated from a network; (2) the edges to be deleted are determined by computing betweenness scores; and (3) The betweenness ratings are recalculated once each edge is removed. This algorithm comes under divisive methods in which the number of shortest paths going through the edge determines the edge weight. Edge betweenness is a generalization of central vertex betweenness that determines the influence of a vertex on other vertices in the network. The number of shortest paths passing through the vertex is the number of shortest paths passing through the edge's endpoints. The steps of the Girvan-Newman algorithm are as follows:

1. Compute edge betweenness for every edge in the graph
2. Remove the edge with the highest edge betweenness
3. Calculate edge betweenness for remaining edges
4. Repeat steps 2-4 until all edges are removed

At core, the Girvan Newman algorithm uses the concept of "edge betweenness", the total number of shortest paths passing through an edge in a network. The algorithm starts with one source vertex s in V in a graph, calculates edge weights for pathways that pass through it, and then repeats the process for each vertex in the graph and adding the weights for each edge and implementing this algorithm to a tree which is a form of a graph, with only one shortest path from the source vertex to any other vertex. Starting from the leaf nodes, the edges that connect them to the rest of vertices in a tree are given the value 1, because there is only one shortest path to node (s) travelling through that edge. The edge weight value determines the number of shortest paths in the tree from the source vertex to every other vertex going through a specific edge. The edge betweenness for each edge is obtained by repeating the process for each vertex and computing the sum of weight values for each edge. The algorithm implements two methods for calculating edge betweenness.

(1) The distance from the source vertex is assigned to each vertex using a breadth-first search to identify the shortest paths from the source to the vertices. An abstract data type queue is used to implement this component efficiently the algorithm.

(2) Begins with edge incident to the vertex as the start point and ends with maximum distance covered from the source vertex as the end points. The number of shortest paths travelling through each edge is determined. The (d_i, w_i, b_i) is calculated mathematically for each vertex i in V, where d_i is the distance from the source vertex, w_i is the number of shortest paths from the source vertex to vertex i, and b_i is the number of shortest paths between the source vertex & any vertex in the graph that passes through vertex i. Assume that $Adj(v)$ is the set of all vertices adjacent to v such that v V. The second phase of edge betweenness calculation begins from the last vertex noted in the first phase and works backwards through the vertices visited in the first phase. Only one shortest path passes through the last marked vertex from the source. For all source vertices s, both phases of the algorithm are run, and edge between- ness for each edge is determined as the sum of the edge betweenness calculated in each step. This method component has a computational complexity of $O(mn)$, where m is the number of edges and n is the number of vertices. The edge with the highest edge betweenness is deleted after each edge betweenness

calculation, and the method is repeated until there are no more edges. As a result, the Girvan and Newman algorithm has a complexity of $O(m2n)$ (Fortunato, 2010).

Random Walk

A random walk in the network can be used to capture the network structure and detect communities in a big complicated network. It is based on the idea that a network will tend to stay trapped in a denser region or community for longer. This concept is utilized to bring nodes into the community. In graph theory, random walk is randomly visiting a neighbouring node from the source node and continuing the process throughout the network. The random walk process is analogous to the Markov chain algorithm in which the collection of states corresponds to the visited path's vertices.

Let $G = (V, E)$ be a directed graph and v_0 be the random walk's beginning node mathematically. The random walk is located at node i at the t_{th} step and it moves from node i to node j at the $(t + 1)$th step, with a transition probability of $1/d_i$, where d_i is the degree of node i. The transition matrix Tk represents the chance of reaching all nodes from all other nodes in the network through a k-length random walk. The odds of visiting all other nodes from node i in the k walk length correspond to each tuple in the transition matrix. These probabilities are based on the network's structural information. The following conclusions can be taken from the network's structure:

- If two nodes i and j belong to the same community, the likelihood of accessing node j from i is greater than visiting a node outside the com- munity. Even though the possibility is high, this does not imply they are members of the same community.
- Because the walker tends to visit vertices with high degrees, the probability $Tk_{i,j}$ is dependent on the degree of j.
- Two vertices in the same community tend to see all other vertices in the same way, and $Tk_{i,m} \approx Tk_{j,m}$, $\forall \ i, j \in$ same community and $m \in [1, n]$.

A transition matrix is derived from a random walk through the graph to detect community. The transition matrix describes the probability of visiting each node from every other node in k steps. Tki,j, represents the probability of visiting node j from i in k steps. The random walk transition matrices $T1$, $T2$, $T3$, and Tk correspond to 1, 2, 3, and k walk lengths, respectively. The following equation 2 defines the probability of transitioning from vertex i to vertex j in a one-length random walk:

$$T_{ij}1 = A_{ij}/d_i \qquad (2)$$

where Aj is the adjacency matrix of the network and d_i is the degree of vertex i.

When contrasted to nodes outside the communities, a node belonging to the same community would behave similarly. Any two nodes within a community have the same appearance as the rest of the network's nodes. Based on the walk length k, the transition matrix $Tk_{i,j}$ determines the similarity between two vertices. The likelihood of reaching one node from another would vary for different travel lengths. Figure 2 is the detected community. The Euclidean distance between row vectors corresponding to nodes i and j in matrix can be used to compute the similarity between i and j for k walk length. Equation 3 defines the same:

$$T_k S(i, j) = (T_{ki,l} - T_{kj,l})2dlnl = i \tag{3}$$

The main aim of this community detection method is to calculate node similarity based on a random walk in the network. In the worst scenario, the temporal complexity of this algorithm is $O(mn2)$, where m is the number of edges and n is the number of nodes in the network (Girvan and Newman, 2002). The primary method of community detection focuses on the interactions users frequently have with other network users as well as individual behaviours, resulting in communities with plenty of links inside the community. Basic definitions and terminology that are utilized in identifying communities are discussed in this chapter. This chapter has also covered ideas related to community discovery methods used in social network analysis. Various community detection algorithms like Newman Girvan algorithm, Random Walk were discussed with their advantages and applications.

Figure 2. Community detected

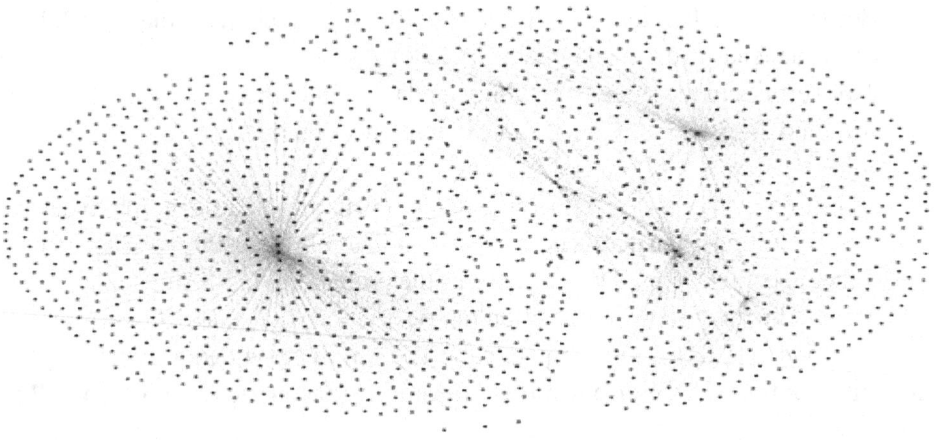

CHALLENGES AND FUTURE DIRECTIONS

Some challenges that may be faced while detecting communities on social networks are the availability of datasets and the required number of nodes and edges. Data set is the main component in every research, and extracting data from social networks like Facebook is difficult. Another challenge is data preprocessing and how to preprocess the data and remove unwanted noise. Some of the future directions in this area are as follows:

- Improving algorithms with a more efficient way of handling overlapping of communities.
- Checking the similarity and degree centrality of the various nodes to form a community structure.
- Identifying malicious community structures on social networks.

REFERENCES

Ashcroft, M., Fisher, A., Kaati, L., Omer, E., & Prucha, N. (2015). *Detecting jihadist messages on twitter. In 2015 European intelligence and security informatics conference*. IEEE.

Aylani, A., & Goyal, N. (2017). Community detection in social network based on useras social activities. In 2017 international conference on I-SMAC (IoT in social, mobile, analytics and cloud) (I-SMAC) (pp. 625–628). IEEE. doi:10.1109/I-SMAC.2017.8058254

Bakshy, Hofman, Mason, & Watts. (2011). Everyone's an influencer: quantifying influence on twitter. *Proceedings of the fourth ACM international conference on Web search and data mining*, 65–74. 10.1145/1935826.1935845

Bhat, S. Y., & Abulaish, M. (2014). Using communities against decep- tion in online social networks. *Computer Fraud & Security, 2014*(2), 8–16. doi:10.1016/S1361-3723(14)70462-2

Diestel. (n.d.). *Graph theory* (3rd ed.). https://sites.math.washington.edu/ billey/classes/562.winter.2018/2006

Fortunato, S. (2010). Community detection in graphs. *Physics Reports, 486*(3-5), 75–174. doi:10.1016/j.physrep.2009.11.002

Gardiner, Raymond, & Rascal. (2002). *Calculation of graph similarity using maximum common edge subgraphs*. https://www.cs.princeton.edu/courses/archive/spring13/cos598C/RASCAL.pdf

Girvan, M., & Mark, E. J. (2002). Newman. Community structure in social and bio-logical networks. *Proceedings of the National Academy of Sciences of the United States of America, 99*(12), 7821–7826. doi:10.1073/pnas.122653799 PMID:12060727

Golbeck, J. (2013). Network structure and measures. Analyzing the social web, 25–44.

Gupta, A., Lamba, H., & Kumaraguru, P. (2013). *1.00perrt#bostonmarathon#pray forboston Analyzing fake content on twitter. In 2013 APWG eCrime*. IEEE.

Hasanzadeh, F., Jalali, M., & Jahan, M. V. (2014). Detecting communities in social networks by techniques of clustering and analysis of communications. In *2014 Iranian Conference on Intelligent Systems (ICIS)* (pp. 1–5). IEEE.

Khanday, A. M. U. D., Wani, M. A., Rabani, S. T., & Khan, Q. R. (2023). Hybrid Approach for Detecting Propagandistic Community and Core Node on Social Networks. *Sustainability (Basel), 15*(2), 1249. doi:10.3390u15021249

Kwak, H., Lee, C., Park, H., & Moon, S. (2010). What is twitter, a social network or a news media? *Proceedings of the 19th international conference on World wide web*, 591–600. 10.1145/1772690.1772751

Liu, J.-S., Ning, K.-C., & Chuang, W.-C. (2013). Discovering and charac- terizing political elite cliques with evolutionary community detection. *Social Network Analysis and Mining, 3*(3), 761–783. doi:10.100713278-013-0125-9

Mendoza, M., Poblete, B., & Castillo, C. (2010). Twitter under crisis: Can we trust what we rt? *Proceedings of the first workshop on social media analytics*, 71–79. 10.1145/1964858.1964869

Mishra, P., Rajnish, R., & Kumar, P. (2016). Sentiment analysis of twitter data: Case study on digital india. In *2016 International Conference on Information Technology (InCITe)-The Next Generation IT Summit on the Theme-Internet of Things: Connect your Worlds* (pp. 148–153). IEEE. 10.1109/INCITE.2016.7857607

Newman, M. E. J., & Girvan, M. (2004). Finding and evaluating community struc-ture in networks. *Physical Review E: Statistical, Nonlinear, and Soft Matter Physics, 69*(2), 026113. doi:10.1103/PhysRevE.69.026113

Orlov, M., & Litvak, M. (2018). Using behavior and text analysis to detect propagandists and misinformers on twitter. In *Annual International Symposium on Information Management and Big Data* (pp. 67–74). Springer.

Rao, B., & Mitra, A. (2014). A new approach for detection of common com- munities in a social network using graph mining techniques. In *2014 Inter- national Conference on High Performance Computing and Applications (ICH-PCA)* (pp. 1–6). IEEE.

Roy, S. D., Lotan, G., & Zeng, W. (2015). The attention automaton: Sensing collective user interests in social network communities. *IEEE Transactions on Network Science and Engineering, 2*(1), 40–52. doi:10.1109/TNSE.2015.2416691

Seidman & Foster. (1978). A graph-theoretic generalization of the clique concept. *The Journal of Mathematical Sociology, 6*(1),139–154. doi:10.1080/002225 0X.1978.9989883

Sharma, P., & Moh, T.-S. (2016). *Prediction of Indian election using sentiment analysis on hindi twitter. In 2016 IEEE international conference on big data (big data)*. IEEE.

Sutaria, K., & Joshi, D. (2015). *An adaptive approximation algorithm for community detection in social network. In 2015 IEEE international conference on computational intelligence & communication technology*. IEEE.

Wan, L., Liao, J., & Zhu, X. (2008). Cdpm: Finding and evaluating com- munity structure in social networks. In *International Conference on Advanced Data Mining and Applications* (pp. 620–627). Springer. 10.1007/978-3-540-88192-6_64

Wang, L., & John, Q. (2017). Gan. Prediction of the 2017 French election based on twitter data analysis. In 2017 9th Computer Science and Electronic Engineering (CEEC) (pp. 89–93). IEEE.

Xie, J., Kelley, S., & Szymanski, B. K. (2013). Overlapping community detection in networks: The state-of-the-art and comparative study. *ACM Comput. Surv., 45*(4). doi:10.1145/2501654.2501657

Zafarani, R., Abbasi, M. A., & Liu, H. (2014). *Social Media Mining: An Introduction*. Cambridge University Press. doi:10.1017/CBO9781139088510

Chapter 5
Emotion Recognition From Text Using Multi-Head Attention-Based Bidirectional Long Short-Term Memory Architecture Using Multi-Level Classification

Vishwanath Pethri Kamath
Samsung R&D Institute, India

Jayantha Gowda Sarapanahalli
Samsung R&D Institute, India

ABSTRACT

Recognition of emotional information is essential in any form of communication. Growing HCI (human-computer interaction) in recent times indicates the importance of understanding of emotions expressed and becomes crucial for improving the system or the interaction itself. In this research work, textual data for emotion recognition is used. The proposal is made for a neural architecture to resolve not less than eight emotions from textual data sources derived from multiple datasets using google pre-trained word2vec word embeddings and a multi-head attention-based bidirectional LSTM model with a one-vs-all multi-level classification. The emotions targeted in this research are anger, disgust, fear, guilt, joy, sadness, shame, and surprise. Textual data from multiple datasets are ingested such as ISEAR, Go Emotions, and Affect dataset. The results show a significant improvement with the modeling architecture with good improvement in recognizing some emotions.

DOI: 10.4018/978-1-6684-6909-5.ch005

INTRODUCTION

Voice Assistants, chatbots, product reviews, or any form of digital conversations that embody users conversing with the digital assistant, include one or the other way of textual communication. Most of the communications surface only if there are appreciations, queries, or concerns. Understanding the emotions of such conversations whether the conversations happening or offline would facilitate tailoring higher solutions on a case-to-case basis. These solutions may be in multiple varied domains and their applications. Conventional methods of machine learning to understand human emotions may hardly help to extract complex, deeper, or indirect emotions, and always appreciate the sequential nature of the language and context, which adds to the complexness, and depth of information. A simple example of this may be, an individual's brain that would perceive the irony in the earlier sentence, it's onerous for a machine to understand.

In emotion recognition systems, the restricted variety of words with robust linguistic relations between them needs special attention. This is because of the involvement of both the language novelty and a wide range of feature prospects. Usually, sentiment analysis looks at the polarity of the text in a document or a sentence. Certainly, the focus would get on whether or not the expressed opinion within the text is positive, negative, or neutral. However advanced sentiment analysis techniques check up on the emotional aspects of the text that are proposed in our approach with the emotional indicators such as anger, surprise, sadness, guilt, shame, disgust, fear, and joy.

Contextual emotion detection in textual communication has been seen as gaining popularity and hence its importance. SemEval-2019 Task 3 Chatterjee et al. (2019) introduces a task to detect contextual emotion in conversational text. Emotion recognition from non-verbal communications such as text becomes more complex due to the usage of non-standard languages. To share a few examples, social/ microblogging language having large usage of contractions (*e.g. I'm gonna bother*), elongations (*e.g. a vacation tooooooo!*), nonstandard use of punctuation (*e.g. gonna explain you later...!*). Moreover, incorrect spelling (*e.g. U r*), emoji's, acronyms, abbreviations, typos, unnecessary spaces, special characters, etc., the text looks more gibberish than more structured if one goes by the book of dictionary. Still, the mass population tenders this data precious considering the volume and usage.

In this paper, the proposal made with a multi-head attention-based deep neural network with bidirectional LSTM for emotion recognition from text.

Main contributions presented or summarized of this work as below:

○ Identification of the data from multiple sources such as ISEAR dataset, Go Emotion dataset, and Affect Data for the 8 emotions 'Anger', 'Joy', 'Sadness', 'Disgust', 'Guilt', 'Shame', 'Fear', 'Surprise'.

○ To build an emotion classifier for the selected emotions text and features extracted from the textual data.

○ Propose the stack of multi-head attention-based bidirectional LSTM with one-vs-all modeling with Google word2vec word embeddings for emotion classifier.

○ Optimize models to improve on the accuracy and f1 scores to reproduce optimal emotion recognition and compared the performance with the state of the art for a comparison study.

In this work, it is shown that, with the consideration of the sequential nature of the text and the context, with multi-head attention and bidirectional LSTM model, is better captured, and emotion recognition performance is also have proven to outperform all the models.

RELATED WORK

Textual emotion recognition is relatively one of the unexplored areas of research as the conventional machine learning techniques are quite not sufficient to capture emotions as the sequential nature of the language adds to the complexity.

One of the works under reference, Emotion Detection in Text, has used bidirectional GRU architecture in the experiment, which is an RNN based approach. Which had tried various word-embedding models but saw little difference in their performance. Moreover, reported the results for two that had the best performance among all, namely ConceptNet Numberbatch by Speer, Chin, and Havasi (2017) and FastText by Mikolov et al. (2018) where both had 300 dimensions. As none of the tweets from the dataset used had more than 35 terms, the embedding layer size used was 35, and padding used for shorter samples. Before transferring its output onward, the output of which then sent to a bidirectional GRU layer that chosen to capture the entirety of each tweet. The global max-pooling and average-pooling layers concatenated (with a window size of two). Then a max-pooling and an average-pooling layer were used above that. Concatenation and then a dense classification layer and final layer used was sigmoid in this research.

From the work, Emotion Recognition from Microblog Managing Emoticon with Text and Classifying using 1D CNN (Habib et al., 2023), the experimental result shows that the model proposed in their paper for emotion recognition scheme outperforms the other existing methods while tested on Twitter data using CNN based approach. An emotion recognition model using CNN is developed here considering emoticons in addition to text.

A survey on deep learning for textual emotion analysis in social networks, after introducing a background for emotion analysis that includes defining emotion, emotion classification methods, and application domains of emotion analysis, they summarize DL technology, and the word/sentence representation learning method (Peng et al., 2020). They then categorize existing TEA methods based on text structures and linguistic types: text-oriented monolingual methods, text conversations-oriented monolingual methods, text-oriented cross-linguistic methods, and emoji-oriented cross-linguistic methods. They discuss emotion analysis challenges and future research trends. This survey assisted in understanding the relationship between TEA and DL methods while also improving TEA development.

Lai et al. (2020) developed an emotion classification model 2020, in which They used syntax based GCN (Graph Convolution Network) model. In this work, diverse grammatical structures were mostly emphasized. The state-of-the-art accuracy of the model enhanced by a percentile-based pooling technique proposed in this work. They experimented with their developed model with their own Chinese microblog dataset.

From Multi-modal Emotion Recognition, the following are the observations in their research with text-based emotion detection. They tried two approaches, First Text Model that uses 1D convolutions of kernel size 3 each, with 256, 128, 64, and 32 filters using ReLU as Activation and Dropout of 0.2 probability, followed by 256 dimensions fully connected layer and ReLU, feeding to 4 output neurons with Softmax. This produced an accuracy of 62.55%. Second, the Text Model uses two stacked LSTM layers with 512 and 256 units followed by a dense layer with 512 units and ReLU Activation. This produced an accuracy of 64.68%. Both of these models initialized with GloVe Embeddings-based word vectors. They also tried Randomized initialization with 128 dimensions in the third Text Model and obtained a similar performance as the second Text Model. This produced an accuracy of 64.78%.

Sayyed M. Zahiri et al. mentioned that RNNs typically perform slower and require more training data to avoid overfitting. In addition, to exploit the sequence information embedded in their corpus and to employ the advantages of CNN, sequenced-based CNN by Yang et al. (2017) proposed along with attention mechanisms, which guide CNN to fuse features from the current state with features from the previous states. They also mentioned that the best model showed accuracies of 37.9% and 54% for fine and coarse-grained emotions, respectively.

In this research work, claim is that the modeling approach consisting of sequential bidirectional classification with Multi-head attention to capturing the context and sequential nature of data and relative importance to the words significantly improves emotion recognition. This research work has shown that a bidirectional LSTM based classifier with Multi-head attention could efficiently capture information from the text of importance. Based on these experiments, this proposal of architecture to detect emotions from the text bearing contextual and sequential information while in prediction with attention to specific words in the text is made. Based on this research, a proposal of architecture to detect significantly improved accuracy in recognizing the text emotions from a combined dataset formed from the ISEAR, Affect Dataset, and GoEmotions datasets for 8 emotions namely 'Anger', 'Joy', 'Sadness', 'Disgust', 'Guilt', 'Shame', 'Fear', 'Surprise' is made.

The word2vec learns the association of words using a neural network model from a huge corpus where vectors represent words and indicate the semantic similarity between them.

In word2vec, when training of skip-gram and continuous bag-of-words (CBOW) models performed on the large corpus with a larger context span, the observations made that resulting vectors bear semantic relationships between words as training performed on high dimensional word vectors with a huge corpus (Mikolov et al., 2013).

For example, Google has used about 100B words for training word2vec algorithms and pre-trained word vectors with 300d released in an update. The resultant word vectors bear semantic and syntactic relationships that can improve many existing NLP applications. Usually, the quality of the representations measured by word

Figure 1. Model architecture

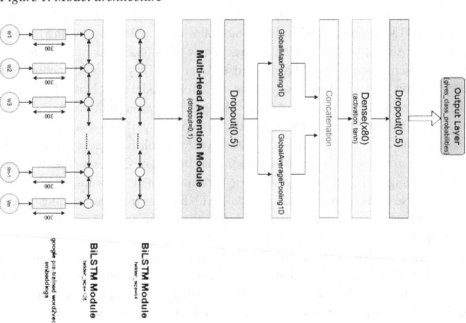

similarity tasks and the results compared to the techniques that show state-of-the-art performance based on different types of neural networks.

As per T. Mikolov et al. (2013), high-quality word vectors could be trained with modeling architectures that are simple enough. Due to the computational complexity being lower, high dimensional very accurate word vectors for a huge corpus computed. In addition, linguistic similarities between the words with the distributed representations are captured in the observations by T. Mikolov et al. (2013) as linear translations.

DATASET

In this research work, various datasets, three datasets specifically, were used, and collation of the text and corresponding emotions into a single dataset containing 2 headers: emotion and corresponding text has been performed. The task is to classify the text into 8 emotions namely, 'Anger' (Figure 3), 'Joy' (Figure 4), 'Surprise' (Figure 5), 'Fear' (Figure 6), 'Disgust' (Figure 7), 'Shame' (Figure 8), 'Guilt' (Figure 9), 'Sadness' (Figure 10). Datasets used to make our final combined corpus are:

1. **ISEAR (International Survey on Emotion Antecedents and Reactions) Dataset:** It contains text corresponding to 7 major emotions ('joy', 'fear', 'anger', 'sadness', 'disgust', 'shame', and 'guilt'). The final dataset thus contains reports on these seven emotions each by close to 3000 respondents in 37 countries on 5 continents.
2. **Affect Data:** Created by Ebba Cecilia Ovesdotter Alm. in 2008, the Affect Dataset is used for the 'surprise' emotion data annotated in the English language. A corpus of 3500 samples created in combination with Go emotions 'surprise' emotion samples.
3. **GoEmotions Dataset:** GoEmotions is a corpus of 58k carefully curated comments extracted from Reddit, with human annotations to 27 emotion categories or Neutral. The number of examples: 58,009.

The number of labels: 27 + Neutral.

Maximum sequence length in training and evaluation datasets: 30.

Table 1 shows the 8 emotions corresponding to data size and the source.

The language structure of the corpus contains many of the features of microblogging language. Constructions such as large use of contractions (*e.g. I'm gonna bother*), elongations (*e.g. a vacation tooooooo!*), non-standard use of punctuation (*e.g. gonna explain you later...!*), incorrect spelling (*e.g. U r*), emojis's, acronyms, abbreviations, typos, unnecessary spaces, special characters, etc., were observed. Since the proposed

Table 1. Statistics of the collated dataset

Emotions	Data Size	From Dataset
Anger	3500	ISEAR and Go-Emotions
Surprise	3500	Affect And Go-Emotions
Sadness	3500	ISEAR and Go-Emotions
Guilt	3500	ISEAR and Go-Emotions
Shame	3500	ISEAR and Go-Emotions
Disgust	3500	ISEAR and Go-Emotions
Fear	3500	ISEAR and Go-Emotions
Joy	3500	ISEAR and Go-Emotions

model depends on terms that appear in the text, the corpus needs to be carefully pre-processed. To handle such language samples, a linguistic review of the selected data performed. And built a pre-processing pipeline consisting of, space addition between words and punctuation, de-emojizing, expanding contractions, lowercasing words, correcting acronyms/typos/abbreviations, replacing elongations with appropriate words, converting emoticons to text, special case handling, removal of special characters/numbers/space or double spaces, removing punctuations/stop-words, lemmatization, tokenization, etc.

WORD EMBEDDINGS

The word embeddings layer is the first layer of the model. Word embeddings, being the dense vector representations of words, capture their semantic and syntactic information. This is a widely used semantic representation of words for almost any neural network based on the text analysis approach. A vector of real numbers used for a single word to represent its distributional semantics in the embedding space. This layer allows the neural network to compute the inputs by transforming the input sentences as a vector of word embeddings of different lengths. To cater to the variable input lengths, a maximum number of terms defined to consider for the computation. The inputs with fewer words added padding to the rest of the text to match the max dimension. Since the space generated by the language model, words that are functionally similar in a certain language are close to each other in the embedding space.

Using the training data, one can also train the word embeddings. By this method, the model built generally fails to provide correct classification to any sentence with new words or sentences provided as inputs. To reduce the computational cost and to cover words from a variety of domains independent of their usage, transfer learning is common in practice in NLP tasks, which helps with the use of vector spaces word embeddings pre-calculated on different domains as per Polignano et al. (2019).

Here, the experimentations done with different types of word embeddings for this research activity. They are as below:

1. **Word2Vec Embedding:** Leverages dataset to train specific word embeddings. The research uses the word2vec algorithm, with the skip-gram model, with a minimum count of one and vector size of 100, using the Word2Vec model from the python gensim library. The resulting vocabulary contained 16000 words and their corresponding 100-dimensional vector representation.

2. **Google's Pre-Trained Word2vec Model:** For constructing vector representations of words, this tool provides an efficient implementation of the continuous bag-of-words and skip-gram designs. These representations then used in a variety of natural language processing applications as well as for additional research. 300-dimensional vectors in the model represent three million words and phrases. The phrases compiled using a straightforward data-driven method.

3. **FastText Pre-Trained Vectors:** These contain 2 million word vectors trained with sub-word information on Common Crawl (600B tokens). All the vectors here are 300 dimensional.

4. **GloVe (Global Vectors for Word Representation):** An unsupervised learning technique for generating word vector representations. The resulting representations highlight intriguing linear substructures of the word vector space, and training based on aggregated global word-word co-occurrence statistics from a corpus. The research work has utilized the variant with 300d vectors with 840B tokens and 2.2M Vocab size.

MODELING ARCHITECTURE

From the very beginning, traditional machine learning approaches to solve Emotion recognition by text analysis had been unsatisfactory. If one looks at the prior works in this domain, the Text-based emotion detection, there were approaches such as keywords-based approach, like Strapparava et al. (2004), they categorized emotions by mapping keywords in the sentences into the lexical representation of affective concepts. Chaumartin et al. (2007) performed emotion detection on news headlines. These approaches did not perform well because the contextual dependency of keyword semantics has significantly affected as not considered as per Shaheen et al. (2014).

There were also approaches observed from supervised and unsupervised learning techniques. Douiji et al. (2016) used YouTube comments and developed an unsupervised learning algorithm to detect emotions from the comments. Their approach gave a comparative performance to supervised approaches such as Chaffar et al. (2011) that support vector machines employed for statistical learning.

Word Embedding

In the current research work, at the word-embeddings stage, an embedding layer generates a 100*300-dimension vector for each text. The embedding layer size is set to 100 since none of our text samples contained more than 100 words. The inputs with fewer words added padding to the rest of the text, which contained fewer words to match the max dimension. Out of the experiments done, observations are that, the pre-trained google word2vec (Figure 2) embedding yielded good accuracy.

The output of this goes to a masking layer, and then propagates over to two-layered Bi-LSTM.

$$X = (x_1, x_2, x_3, x_4, \ldots\ldots\ldots, x_{Tx}) \tag{1}$$

Figure 2. Word2vec model architecture
Source: Mikolov et al. (2013)

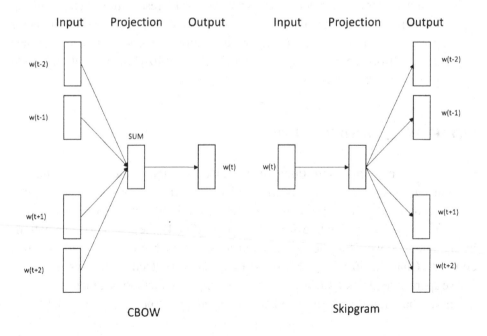

Bidirectional LSTM

Experiments with bidirectional LSTM in this research work with Multi-head attention done in this research work. Recurrent neural networks are widely known to perform well for a variety of tasks in NLP, especially classification tasks. However, RNNs suffer from gradient disappearing. To overcome this problem, Hochreiter and Schmidhuber (1997) proposed LSTM. Different from Recurrent neural networks, LSTM upgrades the hidden layer, introduces a memory unit, and uses the gate control structure to avoid the problem of learning long-term dependencies by the Recurrent Neural Networks. However, whether it is Recurrent neural networks or LSTM, only the information of the previous context at the current moment captured. However, some tasks in NLP, like emotion detection from text, require combining past context with future context. During the course of tackling this problem, observation is that bidirectional LSTM executes forward and backward training separately for each training sequence, then combines the results of forward and backward training as the current time output as in Schuster and Paliwal (1997).

The bidirectional-LSTM layers create an intermediate representation for the text that captures the context of the text and the sequential nature of the data as in Armin Seyeditabari et al. (2019). To prevent overfitting, a dropout of 50% added. Nevertheless, as observed, Bi-LSTM does not give more importance to some input words compared to others while predicting the emotion. To overcome this challenge of assigning importance, Bahdanau et al. (2015) proposed in one of the research papers that not only should all the input words be considered in the context vector, but that relative importance should also be assigned to each one of them.

The LSTM, as shown by Gers et al. (2000) and Chen et al. (2017), uses a gating mechanism to track the state of sequences without using separate memory cells. There are three types of gates: the forget gate f_t, the input gate i_t, and the output o_t. They together control how information is updated to the state. At time t, the LSTM computes the output h_t and the new state C_t as:

$$h_t = o_t * tanh(C_t),$$

$$C_t = f_t * C_{t-1} + i_i * Ć_t,$$

$$Ć_t = tanh (W_C \cdot [h_{t-1}, x_t] + b_C) \tag{2}$$

The output gate o_t decides how much current information C_t is used to the output ht. The current state C_t is a kind of interpolation between the previous state C_{t-1} and the current new state $Ć_t$ computed with new sequence information x_t and the previous output h_{t-1}. The state C_t computed in a way similar to a traditional recurrent neural network (RNN). The forget gate f_t and the input gate controls how much the past state and the current state contribute to the new state. All gates use the sigmoid function with the previous output, the input, and three sets of weights as follows:

$$f_t = \sigma_f (W_f \cdot [h_{t-1}, x_t] + b_f),$$

$$i_t = \sigma_i (W_i \cdot [h_{t-1}, x_t] + b_i),$$

$$o_t = \sigma_o (W_o \cdot [h_{t-1}, x_t] + b_o) \tag{3}$$

The bidirectional LSTM is a combination of forward LSTM h_f, which reads the comment from x_1 to x_N and a backward LSTM h_b, which reads the comment from x_N to x_1:

$$h_f = LSTM_f (w_t, h_{ft-1})$$

$$h_b = LSTM_b (w_t, h_{bt-1}) \tag{4}$$

Concatenation of the forward and backward hidden states to obtain the state representation for each word to capture whole sentence information around every word ($h = [h_f + h_b]$). Such hidden states for all the words represented as:

$$H = (h_1, h_2, h_3, h_4, \dots\dots, h_N) \tag{5}$$

Multi-Head Attention

Although the normal LSTM can learn word order as well as lexical and syntactic information, it overlooks the most significant properties of emotional words when it comes to emotion classification. To solve this problem, in this research work, a multi-head attention layer added, containing 3 heads, to bidirectional LSTM.

Adding a multi-head attention layer will look for the positions where the most relevant information is available in the text. Post Multi-head attention layer, a concatenation performed using global max-pooling and global average-pooling layers. A max pooling to extract the most important features from the Bi-LSTM with attention output and an average-pooling layer used to consider all features to create a representation for the text completely as in Armin Seyeditabari et al., 2019.

$$Y = tanh (W_k H^T) \tag{6}$$

The attention layer takes completely hidden states H as input and multiply it with W_k, the output passed to *tanh* function to get Y.

Concatenation

The emotion classifier built in this research contains 8 binary classifiers, one for each emotion, and each one uses the same architecture for detecting a specific emotion. As seen in the architecture diagram, the first layer is the embedding layer that will not change during training used to convert each word in the text to its corresponding vector. It is verified with different embedding models during the research experiments. The results recorded in Table 2 for different word embeddings, which had the best performance among other experiments. Regarding the word-embeddings used, Google Word2Vec was having 3M words and FastText was having 2M words and 300 dimensions.

Concatenation is at the final hidden representation and for classification, passed to a dense classification layer of 80 nodes along with a dropout layer with 50% to avoid overfitting. A sigmoid layer finally provides the class probability for the emotions as in Armin Seyeditabari et al., 2019.

$$S(x) = 1/(1+e^{-x}) \tag{7}$$

TRAINING PROCEDURES

In this Multi-Level Classification technique, after pre-processing and creating the embedding vectors for each text was fed to the model, since there are 8 binary classifiers for each emotion, was fed to each of the models with validation dataset and have recorded the accuracies and saved the weights for each of 8 binary classifiers. A balanced dataset created by selecting all texts with target emotion as class 1 and a random sample of the same size from other classes as class 0. A random 80% of this balanced data used as training data, 10% as validation data, and 10% as test data, and provided to our model as the training and validation data set and evaluated on test data.

EXPERIMENTS AND RESULTS

When the data is scarce, it has been observed that the bidirectional LSTM model would result fairly with better accuracy according to Al-Amin et al. (2017) and

Lars et al. (2013). However, as the dataset grows, the accuracy declines, showing the model over-fit to the training data. This also contributes to the fact that the increased dataset consists of a larger set of unseen data that the model would not have otherwise seen with the small dataset. Hence, the self-attention mechanism with masking would be one such method to improve the accuracy with increased dataset size as per Tao et al. (2018). Our experiments have shown significantly improved scores using Multi-head attention with bidirectional LSTM.

As shown in Table 2, with the Google word2vec word embeddings better performance as compared to FastText and GloVe. The *tanh* activation in the dense layer is with x80 nodes. Multi-head attention post to 3 heads there was no significant improvement in the accuracy, hence settled with the same. Dropout layers with a 50% dropout rate post the attention layer and dense layer to avoid overfitting. With this research work, prediction on each class using the one-vs-all method and trained 8 binary classifiers, one for each emotion was performed.

Results reported in terms of F1 scores (1: Target Emotion, 0: Other Than Target Emotion). Table 3 explains the scores observed during the experiments. Bidirectional LSTM with multi-head attention has performed better for 6 out of 8 targeted emotions than simple bidirectional LSTM or a bidirectional LSTM with self-attention modeling architectures.

Table 2. F1 scores and comparison

Emotions	One vs All			biGRU	
	Bi-LSTM + Multi-Head Attention			Armin Seyeditabari et al., 2019	Armin Seyeditabari et al., 2019 + Multihead
	Google word2vec	Glove	FastText		
Anger	0.88	0.86	0.85	0.78	0.85
Joy	0.93	0.92	0.89	0.89	0.91
Surprise	0.91	0.89	0.89	0.85	0.88
Fear	0.89	0.89	0.81	0.87	0.88
Disgust	0.84	0.85	0.82	0.78	0.82
Shame	0.86	0.81	0.78	0.74	0.77
Sadness	0.87	0.84	0.82	0.76	0.82
Guilt	0.90	0.88	0.88	0.84	0.90

SAMPLES/EXAMPLES

Following are few of the screenshots for sample sentences and respective predictions by the proposed architecture.

Figure 3. Emotion prediction: Anger

```
#Anger
print(predictEmotions("I was angry when someone stole a magazine which I had borrowed from another friend and locked it in a
                       drawer."))
print(predictEmotions("I sure hope so! Smug bastards!"))
print(predictEmotions("He said he says it on his own but I don't want him to say it at all. I feel like their
                       bio mom hates me"))
print(predictEmotions("A close friend first said he accepted an agreement, but later used that agreement as a reason for
                       attacking me."))
print(predictEmotions("Go away [NAME]...."))

{'anger': 0.999405}
anger
{'anger': 0.999405}
anger
{'anger': 0.999405, 'surprise': 0.98817164, 'shame': 0.6635399}
anger
{'anger': 0.999405, 'sadness': 0.9787729}
anger
{'anger': 0.999405, 'sadness': 0.99952055, 'disgust': 0.9996118}
disgust
```

Figure 4. Emotion prediction: Joy

```
#joy
print(predictEmotions("When the lady who is now my wife accepted my proposal to be my lover and future wife."))
print(predictEmotions("I wrote a difficult Exam at one time while in my Secondary School. When the results were announced
                       on the radio, I came second out of 80 students hence I felt joy."))
print(predictEmotions("When I was selected for the university."))
print(predictEmotions("I was very pleased and happy when my older sister came home from living somewhere out of town
                       and I hadn't seen her for months. We are very close sisters."))
print(predictEmotions("Got in touch with earlier friends after a long absence."))

{'joy': 0.9999695, 'guilt': 0.99941325, 'shame': 0.99969125}
joy
{'joy': 0.9999695}
joy
{'joy': 0.9999695}
joy
{'joy': 0.9999695, 'sadness': 0.9995307}
```

Figure 5. Emotion prediction: Surprise

```
#surprise
print(predictEmotions("Wow that was a roasting... Deserved, but daaaaamn [NAME]"))
print(predictEmotions("Omg like if you read this in 2019Ỹ^,"))
print(predictEmotions("I was wondering if it's Oxford, felt like I walked under that bridge."))
print(predictEmotions("Wow [NAME] is back I hope to see better pain defense when the second unit is out there."))
print(predictEmotions("[NAME] damit you got me! Take your upvote sir!"))

{'surprise': 0.9998493, 'joy': 0.66037464}
surprise
{'surprise': 0.9998493, 'joy': 0.9999695}
joy
{'surprise': 0.9998528, 'shame': 0.99969125}
surprise
```

Figure 6. Emotion prediction: Fear

```
# fear
# print(predictEmotions("when I wanted to go into a house, there was suddenly a big dog standing beside me. It was hardly moving,
print(predictEmotions("When there was a bomb threat in Tolman Hall. This was the first time that I felt my life
                      could be in danger."))
print(predictEmotions("One day, when I realized that I was alone, I felt fear of loneliness."))
print(predictEmotions("I was walking alone along the place where people fear that there are always thieves
                      there and the people who kill their friends during the night two months ago."))
print(predictEmotions("The day the results of the certificate exam came out.  I went to school and at first I did
                      not feel frightened.  By the time I reached the fourth floor ( the results were being given on the
                      fifth floor) I found it difficult to walk and felt that I would die."))
print(predictEmotions("In the traffic with a car, I nearly got crushed between a bus and a tram. |
                      The attention of other drivers saved me at the last moment."))
```

Figure 7. Emotion prediction: Disgust

```
# disgust
print(predictEmotions("*Ugh..* You are 23 and not married - leave."))
print(predictEmotions("I had a quarrel with a friend who lived with me in the same flat. He moved out. Before he went
                      he invited me and some friends for a drink. At last he was totally drunk and smelled disgusting.
                      Besides, he told lies about us and behaved as if he was to be pitied."))
print(predictEmotions("To be fair, the world (especially politics) has been kind of a shit show since 2016"))
print(predictEmotions("Helping older people on the toilet."))
print(predictEmotions("I feel disgust when hearing or seeing other people being treated inhumanely.
                      For example torturing in chili."))

{'sadness': 0.9995301, 'disgust': 0.9996123}
disgust
{'disgust': 0.99963427}
disgust
{'disgust': 0.9996244}
```

Figure 8. Emotion prediction: Shame

```
#shame
print(predictEmotions("when dropping a carton of boiling soup onto a co-worker's leg - causing great pain, and for me,
                      severe embarassment at my own ineptitude, and shame that another person suffered as a result."))
print(predictEmotions("I felt ashamed of myself the first time I drank as nobody in the family drinks.  I felt that I had
                      let down my parents and my friends."))
print(predictEmotions("when I stole a packet of cigarettes from a neighbour  and the next day I owned up and returned it."))
print(predictEmotions("There was a time when my room looked terribly untidy; just at that time my aunt came to see me;
                      fortunately I could prevent her from entering the room."))
print(predictEmotions("This is an event I will never forget.  I am considered a good mimic.  This particular day we were
                      waiting for a professor to take her class.  This  professor had a peculiar accent and a very
                      horrible way of lecturing and to top it all we had this class at the fag end of the day.
                      So this particular day I got into my element and started imitating the professor,
                      and the professor entered the class right in the middle of it .  I was unaware of her presence,
                      some of my friends tried to warn me but it was of no avail as I was too engrossed in mimicing.
                      Then I suddenly noticed the silence and turned around to see her entering the class.
                      I do not know till today if she actually saw what I had been doing or she had completely ignored it.
```

Figure 9. Emotion prediction: Guilt

```
#guilt
print(predictEmotions("While intoxicated I damaged my sister's car in a minor way and someone elses in a minor way."))
print(predictEmotions("My heart broke for him when his wife suddenly passed away. I worried about him with his issues with
                      depression but he seems to be doing okay."))
print(predictEmotions("I lied to my mother in the sixth form she said she would ring to find out and I had to tell her
                      I had lied."))
print(predictEmotions("You're right. Sorry for the poor reply."))
print(predictEmotions("9 to 4. That's pretty sorry."))

{'guilt': 0.9994085, 'shame': 0.99969125, 'fear': 0.99989796, 'disgust': 0.99962425}
fear
{'sadness': 0.9995301, 'guilt': 0.999426, 'fear': 0.99989796}
fear
{'anger': 0.99932086, 'guilt': 0.9994087, 'shame': 0.9997068}
shame
{'anger': 0.99883777, 'sadness': 0.5822625, 'guilt': 0.9993944}
```

Figure 10. Emotion prediction: Sadness

```
#sadness
print(predictEmotions("I was really hoping that I would pass the examination, but I failed and so I felt very sad."))
print(predictEmotions("Getting to know that my uncle in America had a brain tumor."))
print(predictEmotions("Seriously. I had 2 jobs and was in college. I sleep more now!"))
print(predictEmotions("I'd rather take the chance that a kind, helpful comment falls on deaf ears than a snide one
                       ends up hurting someone. "))
print(predictEmotions("When I heard the news that my grandfather had died."))

{'sadness': 0.9995301}
sadness
{'surprise': 0.999853, 'sadness': 0.9995296}
surprise
{'sadness': 0.9995301}
sadness
```

AMODEL PERFORMANCE

With the modeling stack described for this research activity in Figure 1, our model with Google word2vec embeddings outperformed most of the state-of-the-art models.

Research results compared with Armin Seyeditabari et al. (2019), the research dataset was used to run the referenced model and have reported the results. Table 1 illustrates the model performance. Some very good improvements observed in scores because of the usage of attention mechanisms. The attention mechanism was added in the model used with changes and has observed improvements in the score.

The Bi-GRU model with the attention mechanism and FastText embeddings gave comparable results to our model with FastText embeddings though a little better in 'fear' emotion. However, our proposed model with Google word2Vec embeddings outperforms other models with considerably a good margin. In Table 3 comparison was done on simple bidirectional LSTM, bidirectional LSTM with self-attention, and bidirectional LSTM with multi-head attention with 3 heads. It is observed that bidirectional LSTM with multi-head attention is giving better results. With Current

Table 3. Comparison between scores of simple, self-attention, and multi-head attention Bi-LSTM (maximum values are in bold). Embeddings used: Google word2vec.

Emotion	Bi-LSTM	Bi-LSTM + Self Attention	Bi-LSTM + Multi-Head Attention (n_head = 3) (Proposed)
Anger	0.87	0.86	**0.88**
Joy	0.89	0.91	**0.93**
Surprise	0.88	**0.91**	**0.91**
Fear	**0.90**	**0.90**	0.89
Disgust	0.85	**0.86**	0.84
Shame	0.82	0.83	**0.86**
Sadness	0.85	0.84	**0.87**
Guilt	**0.90**	0.89	**0.90**

Table 4. Performance on ISEAR

Emotions	Our Model (f1)
Anger	**0.84**
Joy	**0.89**
Fear	**0.85**
Disgust	**0.86**
Shame	**0.81**
Sadness	**0.85**
Guilt	**0.82**

Table 5. F1 scores and comparison of one-vs-all with different approaches

Emotions	One vs All				
	Bi-LSTM + Multi-Head Attention			biGRU	
				Armin Seyeditabari et al. (2019)	Armin Seyeditabari et al. (2019) + Multi-Head
	Google word2vec	Glove	FastText		
Anger	0.88	0.86	0.85	0.78	0.85
Joy	0.93	0.92	0.89	0.89	0.91
Surprise	0.91	0.89	0.89	0.85	0.88
Fear	0.89	0.89	0.81	0.87	0.88
Disgust	0.84	0.85	0.82	0.78	0.82
Shame	0.86	0.81	0.78	0.74	0.77
Sadness	0.87	0.84	0.82	0.76	0.82
Guilt	0.90	0.88	0.88	0.84	0.90

experiments, the efficacy of bidirectional LSTM with Multi-Head Attention in predicting emotions from the text demonstrated.

FUTURE SCOPE

In this research work, observation is that the designed network could significantly increase the performance of classification.

This research has shown that by considering the nature of the data, modeling and accuracy of emotion prediction can be challenging and sometimes beneficial based on the modeling approach and language under consideration. While working with textual data, it was observed that the task of detecting complex emotions becomes exponentially challenging.

This research work has accomplished the task by experimenting with multiple word-embeddings and bidirectional LSTM with Multi-head attention, and there can be scope for future improvements based on future developments. Improvements such as different word-embeddings, experiment with adding a BERT layer (as on date), use of a nested LSTM instead of bidirectional LSTM, SVM layer for classification (as on date).

REFERENCES

Acheampong, F. A., Wenyu, C., & Nunoo-Mensah, H. (2020). Text-based emotion detection: Advances, challenges, and opportunities. *Engineering Reports*, 2(7). Advance online publication. doi:10.1002/eng2.12189

Ahsan Habib, Md. (2023). *Emotion Recognition from Microblog Managing Emoticon with Text and Classifying using 1D CNN.* https://arxiv.org/ftp/arxiv/papers/2301/2301.02971.pdf

Al-Amin, M., Islam, M. S., & Das Uzzal, S. (2017). Sentiment analysis of Bengali comments with Word2Vec and sentiment information of words. *2017 International Conference on Electrical, Computer and Communication Engineering (ECCE).* 10.1109/ECACE.2017.7912903

Alswaidan, N., & Menai, M. E. (2020). A survey of state-of-the-art approaches for emotion recognition in text. *Knowledge and Information Systems*, 62(8), 2937–2987. Advance online publication. doi:10.100710115-020-01449-0

Armin, S., Narges, T., Shafie, G., & Wlodek, Z. (2019). Emotion Detection in Text: Focusing on Latent Representation. *Computation and Language.*

Attention-based modeling for emotion detection and classification in textual conversations. (n.d.). https://arxiv.org/abs/1906.07020

Attention is all you need. (n.d.). https://doi.org//arXiv.1706.03762 doi:10.48550

Bahdanau, D., Cho, K., & Bengio, Y. (2014). *Neural machine translation by jointly learning to align and translate.* arXiv preprint arXiv:1409.0473.

Basile, A., Franco-Salvador, M., Pawar, N., Štajner, S., Chinea Rios, M., & Benajiba, Y. (2019). SymantoResearch at semeval-2019 task 3: Combined neural models for emotion classification in human-chatbot conversations. *Proceedings of the 13th International Workshop on Semantic Evaluation.* 10.18653/v1/S19-2057

Baziotis, C., Nikolaos, A., Chronopoulou, A., Kolovou, A., Paraskevopoulos, G., Ellinas, N., Narayanan, S., & Potamianos, A. (2018). NTUA-SLP at semeval-2018 task 1: Predicting affective content in tweets with deep attentive RNNs and transfer learning. *Proceedings of the 12th International Workshop on Semantic Evaluation.* 10.18653/v1/S18-1037

Chaffar, S., & Inkpen, D. (2011). Using a heterogeneous dataset for emotion analysis in text. *Lecture Notes in Computer Science*, *6657*, 62–67. doi:10.1007/978-3-642-21043-3_8

Chatterjee, A., Narahari, K. N., Joshi, M., & Agrawal, P. (2019). Semeval-2019 task 3: EmoContext contextual emotion detection in text. *Proceedings of the 13th International Workshop on Semantic Evaluation.* 10.18653/v1/S19-2005

Chen, Q., Zhu, X., Ling, Z., Wei, S., Jiang, H., & Inkpen, D. (2017). Enhanced LSTM for natural language inference. *Proceedings of the 55th Annual Meeting of the Association for Computational Linguistics (*Volume 1*: Long Papers).* 10.18653/v1/P17-1152

Demszky, D., Movshovitz-Attias, D., Ko, J., Cowen, A., Nemade, G., & Ravi, S. (2020). GoEmotions: A dataset of fine-grained emotions. *Proceedings of the 58th Annual Meeting of the Association for Computational Linguistics.* 10.18653/v1/2020.acl-main.372

Du, P., & Nie, J. (2018). Mutux at semeval-2018 task 1: Exploring impacts of context information on emotion detection. *Proceedings of The 12th International Workshop on Semantic Evaluation.* 10.18653/v1/S18-1052

Dzmitry, B., Kyunghyun, C., & Yoshua, B. (2014). Neural Machine Translation by Jointly Learning to Align and Translate. *Computation and Language.*

Ebba & Ovesdotter. (2008). *Affect Data.* http://people.rc.rit.edu/~coagla/affectdata/index.html

Fernández-Gavilanes, M., Àlvarez-López, T., Juncal-Martínez, J., Costa-Montenegro, E., & González-Castaño, F. J. (2015). GTI: An unsupervised approach for sentiment analysis in Twitter. *Proceedings of the 9th International Workshop on Semantic Evaluation (SemEval 2015).* 10.18653/v1/S15-2089

François-Régis, C. (2007). *UPAR7: A knowledge-based system for headline sentiment tagging.* doi:10.3115/1621474.1621568

Gated recurrent neural network approach for Multilabel emotion detection in Microblogs. (n.d.). https://doi.org//arXiv.1907.07653 doi:10.48550

Ge, S., Qi, T., Wu, C., & Huang, Y. (2019). THU_NGN at semeval-2019 task 3: Dialog emotion classification using attentional LSTM-CNN. *Proceedings of the 13th International Workshop on Semantic Evaluation.* 10.18653/v1/S19-2059

Gers, F. A., Schmidhuber, J., & Cummins, F. (2000). Learning to forget: Continual prediction with LSTM. *Neural Computation, 12*(10), 2451–2471. doi:10.1162/089976600300015015 PMID:11032042

Haryadi, D., & Putra, G. (2019). Emotion Detection in Text using Nested Long Short-Term Memory. *International Journal of Advanced Computer Science and Applications, 10*(6). Advance online publication. doi:10.14569/IJACSA.2019.0100645

Hochreiter, S., & Schmidhuber, J. (1997). Long short-term memory. *Neural Computation, 9*(8), 1735–1780. doi:10.1162/neco.1997.9.8.1735 PMID:9377276

Kumar, A., Narapareddy, V. T., Aditya Srikanth, V., Malapati, A., & Neti, L. B. (2020). Sarcasm detection using multi-head attention based bidirectional LSTM. *IEEE Access : Practical Innovations, Open Solutions, 8*, 6388–6397. doi:10.1109/ACCESS.2019.2963630

Nogueira dos Santos, Tan, Xiang, & Zhou. (2016). *Attentive pooling networks.* CoRR, abs/1602.03609.

Pennington, J., Socher, R., & Manning, C. (2014). Glove: Global vectors for word representation. *Proceedings of the 2014 Conference on Empirical Methods in Natural Language Processing (EMNLP).* 10.3115/v1/D14-1162

Polignano, M., Basile, P., De Gemmis, M., & Semeraro, G. (2019). A comparison of word-embeddings in emotion detection from text using BiLSTM, CNN and self-attention. *Adjunct Publication of the 27th Conference on User Modeling, Adaptation and Personalization.* 10.1145/3314183.3324983

Radim & Sojka. (2010). Software Framework for Topic Modelling with Large Corpora. LREC 2010, 46-50.

Ragheb, W., Azé, J., Bringay, S., & Servajean, M. (2019). LIRMM-advanse at semeval-2019 task 3: Attentive conversation modeling for emotion detection and classification. *Proceedings of the 13th International Workshop on Semantic Evaluation.* 10.18653/v1/S19-2042

Rashid, U., Iqbal, M. W., Skiandar, M. A., Raiz, M. Q., Naqvi, M. R., & Shahzad, S. K. (2020). Emotion detection of contextual text using deep learning. *2020 4th International Symposium on Multidisciplinary Studies and Innovative Technologies (ISMSIT).* 10.1109/ISMSIT50672.2020.9255279

Samarth, Homayoon, & Beigi. (2018). Multi-Modal Emotion recognition on IEMOCAP Dataset using Deep Learning. *Artificial Intelligence.*

Sancheng Peng. (2022). *A survey on deep learning for textual emotion analysis in social networks.* doi:10.1016/j.dcan.2021.10.003

Scherer, K. R., & Wallbott, H. G. (1997). *The ISEAR questionnaire and codebook.* Geneva Emotion Research Group.

Schuster, M., & Paliwal, K. (1997). Bidirectional recurrent neural networks. *IEEE Transactions on Signal Processing, 45*(11), 2673–2681. doi:10.1109/78.650093

Shaheen, S., El-Hajj, W., Hajj, H., & Elbassuoni, S. (2014). Emotion recognition from text based on automatically generated rules. *2014 IEEE International Conference on Data Mining Workshop.* 10.1109/ICDMW.2014.80

Speer, R., Chin, J., & Havasi, C. (2017). ConceptNet 5.5: An open multilingual graph of general knowledge. *Proceedings of the AAAI Conference on Artificial Intelligence, 31*(1). Advance online publication. doi:10.1609/aaai.v31i1.11164

Speer, R., & Lowry-Duda, J. (2017). ConceptNet at semeval-2017 task 2: Extending word embeddings with multilingual relational knowledge. *Proceedings of the 11th International Workshop on Semantic Evaluation (SemEval-2017).* 10.18653/v1/S17-2008

Tao, S. Tianyi, Z., Guodong, L., Jing, J., & Chengqi, Z. (2018). Bi-Directional Block Self-Attention for Fast and Memory-Efficient Sequence Modeling. *Computation and Language.*

Tomas, M. (2017). Advances in Pre-Training Distributed Word Representations. Academic Press.

Xiao, J. (2019). Figure eight at semeval-2019 task 3: Ensemble of transfer learning methods for contextual emotion detection. *Proceedings of the 13th International Workshop on Semantic Evaluation.* 10.18653/v1/S19-2036

Yang, H., Yuan, C., Xing, J., & Hu, W. (2017). SCNN: Sequential convolutional neural network for human action recognition in videos. *2017 IEEE International Conference on Image Processing (ICIP).* 10.1109/ICIP.2017.8296302

Yasmina, D., Hajar, M., & Hassan, A. M. (2016). Using YouTube comments for text-based emotion recognition. *Procedia Computer Science, 83,* 292–299. doi:10.1016/j.procs.2016.04.128

Zhang, J., & Tansu, N. (2013). Optical gain and laser characteristics of ingan quantum wells on ternary ingan substrates. *IEEE Photonics Journal, 5*(2), 2600111–2600111. doi:10.1109/JPHOT.2013.2247587

Chapter 6
Learning From Small Samples in the Age of Big Data

Ishfaq Hussain Rather
Jawaharlal Nehru University, India

Shakeel Ahamad
Jawaharlal Nehru University, India

Upasana Dohare
Galgotias University, India

Sushil Kumar
Jawaharlal Nehru University, India

ABSTRACT

Humans learn new concepts from a few observations with strong generalisation ability. Discovering patterns from small samples is complicated and challenging in machine learning (ML) and deep learning (DL). The ability to successfully learn and generalise from relatively short data is a glaring difference between human and artificial intelligence. Because of this difference, artificial intelligence models are impractical for applications where data is scarce and limited. Although small sample learning is challenging, it is crucial and advantageous, particularly for attaining rapid implementation and cheap deployment costs. In this context, this chapter examines recent advancements in small-sample learning. The study discusses data augmentation, transfer learning, generative and discriminative models, and meta-learning techniques for limited data problems. Specifically, a case study of convolutional neural network training on a small dataset for classification is provided. The chapter also highlights recent advances in many extensional small sample learning problems.

DOI: 10.4018/978-1-6684-6909-5.ch006

1. INTRODUCTION

Humans learn new concepts from few observations with strong generalization ability (Świechowski, 2022). The main issue with deep learning models is that they are data-hungry, relying on substantial training samples where data preparation cost is relatively high in many applications (Shu et al., 2018). Second, because data labelling is expensive, it is very challenging to acquire labelled big data for instance to annotate medical scans an experienced radiologist or a doctor is needed to obtain high-quality annotated data (Anwar et al., 2018). Thirdly, there is an imbalance in the data across a wide range of applications, including healthcare, defence, credit card transaction (Tang et al., 2009), etc., where some data classes are more frequently available while others are less frequent. For example, in the case of credit card fraud detection, 99% of the data may be legitimate, and only 1% of transactions may be fraudulent. Due to imbalanced dataset issues, machine learning models become biased towards the classes with enough training data. Fourth, the network stability of deep learning models using small datasets is a concern (Marcus et al., n.d.). The loss and accuracy variation ranges are still quite broad, and significant variances may occur infrequently. Due to the lack of diversity in the generated images and the short number of original samples, it is not easy to fully train deep learning models like convolutional neural networks, even when the data quality is good.

Small sample learning is the new machine learning revolution. Although challenging, it is crucial and advantageous, particularly for attaining rapid implementation and cheap deployment costs. Researchers are working ceaselessly to make machine learning (ML) models generalize well on small datasets. In all types of problems, machine learning based on small datasets can be required, but the academic research on short dataset learning is mainly centred around images such as image classification and image segmentation problems. However, these approaches can be applied directly to other datasets as well. Some key benefits of utilizing small datasets for training deep learning models include (a) In many cases, big datasets are not available especially in the fields such as defence and medicine (Rather et al., 2023), where data collection is expensive and time-consuming. (b) Faster model training due to less computations and utilization of limited resource (c) Privacy preserving can be one more benefit of learning from small datasets as small data often contain less identifying information than larger ones.

Data is the driving force behind machine learning, and deep learning represents the most advanced machine learning technique, which typically needs thousands of instances for every class of the dataset (Wang & Perez, 2017). Deep learning algorithms acquire considerably better accuracy with sufficient training datasets than shallow neural networks and conventional machine learning models (Nagarajan, 2021). The quantity of annotated data needed to train a model varies depending on the dataset and the type of model used; deep learning models with many layers and complicated datasets need large data. The quantity of data necessary to train a model is the main obstacle in applying these models (Lemberger, 2017). These models, therefore, do not provide satisfying results in applications where the data is scarce. Utilizing limited data approaches that typically use small datasets to solve these problems is highly significant. In this context, the chapter of the book examines the effectiveness of deep neural networks in situations where there is not enough data to train them traditionally. Following are the chapter's key contributions:

- Firstly, we examine the techniques that are used to increase the size of the dataset by employing different traditional machine learning and image processing techniques.
- Secondly, generative models used for fake data synthesis are analyzed for the process of data augmentation.
- Thirdly, this paper examines the use of transfer learning in small dataset problems.
- Next, we examine the most recent developments in several freshly developed extensional small sample learning issues.
- Lastly, we draw attention to the significant small sample learning applications encompass various current research areas in computer vision and natural language processing.

The remaining sections of the paper are organized as follows. Section 2 discusses the effectiveness of data augmentation techniques on deep learning models. In Section 3, the chapter Generative Adversarial Network(s) (GAN) based image synthesis techniques for increasing data size to train deep learning models are presented in detail. Section 4 discusses transfer learning-based problem-solving methods. Finally, Section 5 discusses meta-learning approaches for small data problems, and the chapter concludes with discussions on some strategies for solving limited data problems and their limitations.

2. TRADITIONAL DATA AUGMENTATION

The data augmentation method is widely applied in machine learning to increase the variety of the dataset, not simply for problems with small datasets but also for large datasets. Data augmentation uses the invariances in the data to generate new examples from the existing dataset. Simple transformations like reflection, rotation, and translation work well for larger datasets. Additionally, more advanced data augmentation methods, like Generative Adversarial Networks and Style Transfer

Networks, are covered in Section 3. Some applications where data augmentation plays a vital role include medical industry (Panayides et al., 2020), where access to data is heavily restricted due to privacy considerations. For instance, classification of data into cancer and non-cancer types or different cancer grades becomes difficult due to lack of sufficient training data (Vasconcelos & Vasconcelos, 2020). Insufficient training data leads to model overfitting where as data augmentation acts as a regulariser in preventing overfitting and improves the generalization in the model. Other applications where data augmentation plays a vital role are imbalanced dataset problems Tang et al., 2009). In imbalanced datasets there are some classes with more frequent data where as many more classes are those where the data is infrequent. Data augmentation techniques can be used to balance these datasets by augmenting the data of the less data classes. For example, the study carried out by (Chawla et al., n.d.) utilized Synthetic Minority Over-Sampling Technique (SMOTE) in response to the handwritten digit problem, which employed data-warping to lessen class imbalance. However, it was suggested that applying it in feature space would be domain agnostic. As a result, it has subsequently been widely employed in medical research, where datasets with many classes have infrequent data. By choosing a random point in feature space along a line that intersects randomly selected samples of the same class, SMOTE creates a new synthetic sample. The Density Based SMOTE (DBSMOTE) algorithm (Bunkhumpornpat et al., 2012), a more variant of SMOTE, generates fresh synthetic samples within a distance of eps from the cluster centre for the class. One could anticipate that since the DBSMOTE algorithm creates its synthetic samples at the centre of each class, they might not help lessen classifier overfitting. It was discovered that DBSMOTE uses enhanced the rate of overfitting.

Small AI players frequently lack access to large volumes of data. Access to reliable data is the limiting constraint for most AI applications. An ML algorithm is more powerful when it gets access to more data. As long as the model can retrieve information from the original data set, algorithms can perform better even when the data is of poorer quality (Liu & Hu, 2020). As suggested by the authors of (Halevy et al., 2009), text-to-speech and text-based models have greatly improved due to Google's release of a trillion-word corpus. This outcome was obtained despite the data being gathered from unfiltered Web pages and containing numerous inaccuracies. However, with such enormous unstructured data volumes, the challenge is to uncover structure in a sea of unstructured data. The paper (Wong et al., 2016), discusses the performance of Convolutional Neural Networks (CNN), Support Vector Machine (SVM) and Extreme Learning Machine (ELM) on the different amounts of data samples utilized. The most important finding is that by increasing data size from 500 to 5000 samples per class. Overfitting is less apparent as the difference between training and testing errors narrows. However, the performance improvement varies across classifiers. Another exciting observation the paper mentions is that CNN profits the most from extra training examples; the experimental results presented by the article show that increasing the number of samples improves both the *training and test errors*.

This book chapter presents a case study where a convolutional neural network model is trained from scratch on a small image dataset. A small dataset in this context is a dataset of few images to few thousand images. The dataset chosen for study is a binary classification problem that consists of the images of cats and dogs. The dataset consists of 2000 training images (1000 for each class), 1000 images for validation (500 for each class) and 1000 for testing (500 for each class). Figure 1 (a) and (b) set a baseline of training a CNN model from scratch without utilizing any regularisation. Two parameters model accuracy and binary cross entropy loss function, are used to validate the model. Accuracy can be defined as the ratio of the percentage of correctly predicted outputs or labels by the model and actual or expected labels, whereas the binary cross entropy loss function measures the difference between the predicted probabilities of a binary classification model and the actual binary labels.

It can bee seen from the Figure 1(a) that the accuracy achieved by the model is 75%, but the main issue here is overfitting. Overfitting (Power et al., 2022) refers to the performance of the model on unseen data. As a result the model performs well on training data but poorly on the test or validation data, which indicates that the model has failed to generalize beyond the training data (Bousquet & Elisseeff, 2002; Kawaguchi et al., 2022). In other words the model has memorized the training data, that's why it can't accurately predict new data. It can be seen in figure 1(b) that the model overfits after only four epochs.

In order to improve the performance, reduce overfitting and increase the model generalization, the data is then augmenting, which is a powerful computer vision technique to improve the model's accuracy and mitigate the overfitting. After data augmentation is performed the accuracy of the model is improved from 75% to 81.5% as depicted by the Figure 1 (c). Figure 1 (d) shows the training and validation loss of the model and the reduction in model overfitting.

It is partially true that deep learning models only function when they have access to large amounts of data. For instance, it is incorrect to use the convolutional neural network model to solve a complex problem with few data samples, but if the model is modest and properly regularised and the task is simple, a few hundred data samples may be plenty. The Kaggle website[1] offers a free download of the dataset that was used in this study.

Data augmentation must be used cautiously to avoid emphasizing the biases in limited data.

Figure 1. Demonstrates the performance of CNN model. (a), (b) show the training accuracy, validation accuracy, and loss plots of the CNN model on actual data, and (c) and (d) show the training accuracy, validation accuracy, and loss plots of the CNN model on augmented data.

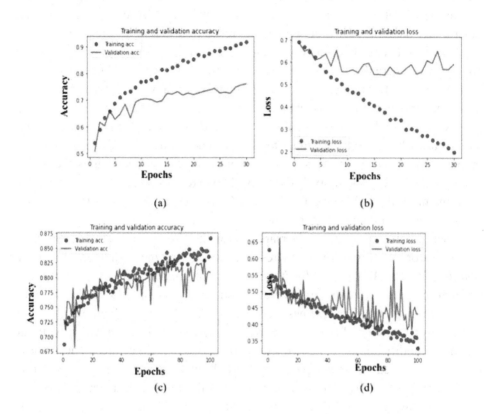

3. GENERATIVE ADVERSARIAL NETWORK(S) (GAN)-BASED DATA AUGMENTATION

Generative modelling is another strategy for data augmentation to solve the limited data problem. GANs generate synthetic examples from a dataset that share the same properties as the original set. The very intriguing and enormously well-liked generative modelling framework known as Generative Adversarial Networks (GANs) was developed using the concepts of adversarial training. GANs are described in Paper (Bowles et al., n.d.) as a means to "unlock" more data from a dataset.

The GAN architecture was proposed by Ian Goodfellow (Goodfellow et al., 2014). The remarkable performance of GANs has drawn more focus to how they may be used for data augmentation (Hulea et al., 2022). These networks can generate new training data that performs better with classification models. Earlier GANs like Vanilla GAN (Zhao et al., 2020) synthesized suitable image datasets like MNIST, which are simple and less challenging. GANs produce potentially decent results when applied on the MNIST dataset. This is because the low intra-class variance and resolution of MNIST images make them much less difficult to analyze than other image datasets. However, with higher resolution, and more complex datasets, it is unable to deliver high-quality results. Thus, Vanilla GAN had poor results in applications where the complex datasets need to be augmented. Numerous studies have been published that alter the GAN framework using various network designs, loss functions, evolutionary techniques, and other techniques. This research has greatly increased the quality of samples produced by GANs. Numerous additional architectures have been developed to broaden the scope of GANs and generate output images with improved resolution. Amongst these new architectures, DCGANs (Geng et al., 2022), Progressively Growing GANs (Karras et al., 2017), CycleGANs (Hammami et al., 2020), and Conditional GANs (Gauthier & 2014(5), n.d.) are primarily used for data augmentation.

When training generative adversarial networks (GAN) with insufficient data, discriminator overfitting frequently results, causing training to diverge. The study (*Data-Efficient GANs with Adaptive Discriminator Augmentation*, n.d.) propose an adaptive discriminator augmentation strategy that significantly stabilizes training in restricted data regimes(Karras et al., 2020). The method may be used to start from scratch and fine-tune an existing GAN on a different dataset without requiring modifications to loss functions or network architectures. The authors have demonstrated this technique with several limited data problems and obtained significant results. Thus, in applications where the limited data synthesis seems producing low-quality synthetic images. This technique can be used to augment the data.

4. TRANSFER LEARNING IN SMALL DATA PROBLEMS

Transfer Learning Will Be the Next Machine Learning Success (Andrew Ng NIPS 2016 Tutorial)

Transfer learning is a technique that utilizes the knowledge obtained by solving a problem on a sufficient dataset such as ImageNet and applying it to a different but related problem (Romero et al., 2019). The feature extraction phase of the neural networks is quite similar for issues on comparable datasets. Transfer learning attempts to lower the quantity of training data needed to learn a task by reusing the feature extraction layers developed on other datasets. To improve the performance of these models, transfer learning can be employed in conjunction with methods for learning from small amounts of data (Hulea et al., 2022). There are two approaches to transfer learning a) Fine tuning and b) Domain Adaptation.

Using a deep learning model that has been trained on a sizable dataset with a distribution similar to the target problem, one method of transfer learning is to fine-tune or replace the final few layers of the neural network and train it on the target problem (Neyshabur et al., 2020). It is commonly accepted that a neural network's initial layers conduct generic feature extraction while its final levels specialize in solving particular problems (Raghu et al., 2019). Heuristics and guessing are typically used to determine how many layers need to be fine-tuned or retrained.

Domain Adaptation is the other type of transfer learning approach. This type of transfer learning has also undergone extensive research (Plested & Gedeon, 2022). Transfer learning is called domain adaptation when the sample and label spaces are kept constant, but the instances come from various probability distributions. For example, in defence, we could train a vehicle classifier using data from a ground-based camera and then move this classifier to overhead imagery using domain adaptation.

An efficient transfer learning method for image classification uses pre-training and fine-tuning (Han et al., n.d.). The accuracy of all fine-tuned networks on the original dataset demonstrated their ability to quickly reach the highest accuracy levels. Using pre-trained networks is a popular and very efficient method for applying deep learning to situations with tiny datasets. This method of leveraging trained networks for feature extraction across many challenges is a crucial improvement of deep learning models for applications with few datasets. We consider a sizable CNN model in Figures 2(a) and 2(b) that was trained on the ImageNet dataset, consisting of 1.4 million annotated images divided into 1000 different classes. To extract features from this dataset, a pre-trained VGG16 is used. Feature extraction can leverage other pre-trained models like ResNet, Inception, and Xception.

We use pretrained models by two ways a) feature extraction b) fine tuning as explained early in this section. In our case study on dog vs cat dataset we utilize whole base of the VGG16 model that's pretrained on ImageNet, we extract only features by this network. We then train a classifier utilizing cat vs dog dataset on top of these extracted features. By employing simple feature extraction technique with VGG16 model, the validation accuracy of 90% is achieved as depicted in Figure 2(a), but the gap between training and validation loss increases after only 8 epochs. Which is the sign of model overfitting.

To reduce overfitting, we have employed the process of data augmentation same way as was done in the previous example in Figure 1. We utilize the same data augmentation to reduce the overfitting of the model. The plot presented in Figure 3 displays the results after the data augmentation. It can be seen the model achieves

Figure 2. Simple feature extraction: (a) training and validation accuracy, (b) shows training and validation loss

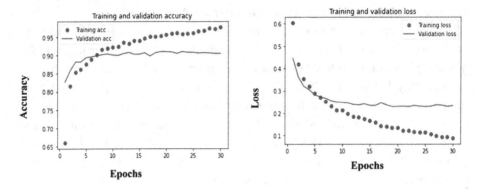

Figure 3. Feature extraction and data augmentation: (a) training and validation accuracy, (b) training and validation loss

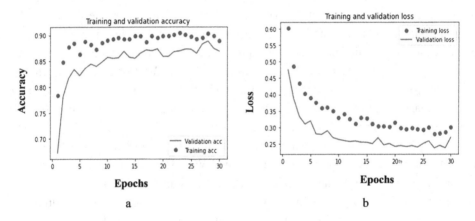

a   b

an accuracy of 96% which is higher than the earlier model trained from scratch shown in Figure 1.

To fine-tune the model, we unfreeze a portion of the top layers of a model base that was frozen and used for feature extraction. We then jointly train the top layers and the newly added model component, in this case, the fully connected classifier as shown in Figure 5. This process, known as fine-tuning, modifies the more abstract model representations being reused just enough to make them more pertinent to the current issue. In our case, we fine-tune the last three layers of the convolutional model. Thus, all the model layers up to the last three layers are non-trainable; only

Figure 4. Fine tuning: (a) training and validation accuracy, (b) training and validation loss

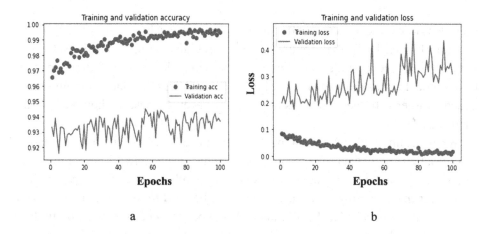

a   b

Figure 5. Shows classifier swap while keeping the convolution base as same

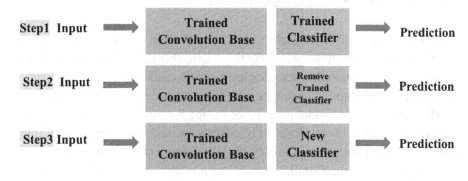

the last three layers of the model are trainable. The performance of this model is depicted in Figure 3.

As depicted in the Figure 4 (a) the model achieves validation accuracy of 94%. This accuracy is obtained when we only used 2k images out of 20k total images which is 10% of the original dataset. Thus, it can be said that by using only a small fraction of training dataset modern deep learning techniques can reach a good performance accuracy.

When a big dataset is available that is similar to the task problem, transfer learning can be utilized to enhance the performance of machine learning models on limited data challenges. Transfer learning can sometimes outperform methodologies for machine learning with low data, such as few-shot learning.

5. META-LEARNING FOR LIMITED DATA "LEARNING ABOUT LEARNING"

Meta-learning is the term most often used to describe machine learning approaches that draw knowledge from the output of other machine learning algorithms. In order to train a machine learning model more quickly, meta-learning aims to understand how a model learns (Huisman et al., 2021). On a variety of related learning tasks, a meta-learner is trained. As a result, it can discover the best method for learning a new task.

When dealing with small data, meta-learning can be utilized to quickly adapt to new situations and generalize to previously undiscovered tasks. As a data-driven methodology, meta-learning necessitates a sizable number of tasks from a comparable dataset for meta-training. The meta-model can be used to learn an unknown task with little input once it has been trained. The model can be supported by lifelong learning through meta-learning. For the model to continue to evolve while employed, meta-learning encourages lifelong learning.

5.1. Few-Shot Learning Classification

When there are few samples in each class, a classification method called few-shot learning is used. In N-way k-shot problems, where there are N classes, and each class includes labelled samples, few-shot learning is considered. To quickly adapt to a new task, few-shot learning leverages meta-learning across various classification tasks. The meta-learning model is developed using a similar dataset and a sizable number of -way -shot tasks. To quickly adapt to a new task, few-shot learning leverages meta-learning across a variety of classification tasks. The meta-learning model is developed using a similar dataset and a sizable number of N-way k-shot tasks. The most accurate models at the moment achieve about 80% accuracy on 5-way 5-shot tasks and 60% on 5-way 1-shot tasks on the miniImageNet dataset (Vinyals et al., 2016).

5.2. Few-Shot Segmentation and Object Detection

Image segmentation and object detection issues can be solved using many of the few-shot learning and meta-learning strategies. In few-shot segmentation, we attempt to divide the image's pixels into classes, with examples for each class. Using examples for each class, few-shot object detection attempts to identify different classes of objects. The -way -shot problems used for few-shot classification use structures similar to these problem models. State-of-art object identification and segmentation models significantly improve mean IOU (Intersection over Union) compared to fine-tuning methods.

Some challenges with Few-Shot Segmentation and object detection in small datasets are a) they are immature and have been utilized for elementary research problems. Segmentation models are complex, which makes training meta-learners difficult and computationally expensive. Hyperparameter optimization can be complicated.

6. CONCLUSION AND FUTURE RESEARCH DIRECTIONS

Today's standard deep learning algorithms can produce excellent performance with little to no adjusting if enough data is available. On the other hand, diligent training and proper source dataset selection result in small datasets' most significant performance improvement. This paper has examined the most recent developments in small-sample learning models. We discussed data augmentation, transfer learning, generative and discriminative models, and meta-learning approaches for solving small dataset problems.

Data augmentation has a highly promising future. Although similar approaches and principles can be applied to other applications, this chapter focused on applications that use image data. Access to vast data generally makes overfitting less of a problem. Data augmentation transforms small datasets into big data to prevent overfitting. But once a certain amount of data augmentation is attained, the quality of the augmented data stagnates or stalls. Finding the appropriate data augmentation level for a given issue is challenging and requires investigation. Class imbalance in datasets can be effectively addressed with GAN-based data augmentation. For instance, imbalance datasets are common in medical industry. In medical applications, where datasets are frequently both tiny and skewed, GAN-based data augmentation techniques are notably effective throughout low-data regimes and demonstrate promising outcomes for rectifying class imbalance. However, the fundamental problem is the GANs' difficult and unstable training procedure. Using conventional and GAN-based data augmentation techniques for low data regime issues would be ideal. Small dataset problems are also solved with the help of transfer learning, although they are vulnerable to negative transfer.

The issue of small datasets in deep learning requires much study to solve. In addition to the techniques mentioned in this chapter bayesian deep learning and active learning approaches can also be used. Bayesian deep Learning approaches include uncertainty estimates into deep learning models, which are another way to use deep learning models. Uncertainty estimation can reduce overfitting and enhance model performance with minimal datasets. Active learning entails randomly selecting the most instructive examples repeatedly and labelling them before adding them to the training dataset. Active learning can lessen the demand for a lot of labelled data and enhance model performance with limited datasets.

Small data are expected to remain a crucial part of research projects. However, they are in the process of assuming new forms, which will impact how we see and apply such data. While we have made an initial effort to describe some of these shifts, further critical reflection and normative thinking are necessary to understand the changes occurring and their ramifications.

REFERENCES

Anwar, S. M., Majid, M., Qayyum, A., Awais, M., Alnowami, M., & Khan, M. K. (2018). Medical Image Analysis using Convolutional Neural Networks: A Review. Journal of Medical Systems, 42(11). doi:10.100710916-018-1088-1

Bousquet, O., & Elisseeff, A. (2002). Stability and Generalization. *Journal of Machine Learning Research*, 2(3), 499–526. doi:10.1162/153244302760200704

Bowles, C., Chen, L., & Guerrero, R. (n.d.). *Gan augmentation: Augmenting training data using generative adversarial networks*. Retrieved September 19, 2022, from https://arxiv.org/abs/1810.10863

Bunkhumpornpat, C., Sinapiromsaran, K., & Lursinsap, C. (2012). DBSMOTE: Density-based synthetic minority over-sampling technique. *Applied Intelligence*, *36*(3), 664–684. doi:10.100710489-011-0287-y

Chawla, N., & Bowyer, K. (n.d.). *SMOTE: Synthetic minority over-sampling technique*. Retrieved September 19, 2022, from https://www.jair.org/index.php/jair/article/view/10302

Data-efficient GANs with Adaptive Discriminator Augmentation. (n.d.). Retrieved March 30, 2023, from https://keras.io/examples/generative/gan_ada/

Gauthier, J. C. (n.d.). *Conditional generative adversarial nets for convolutional face generation.* foldl.me.

Geng, Z., Shi, C., & Han, Y. (2022). Intelligent Small Sample Defect Detection of Water Walls in Power Plants Using Novel Deep Learning Integrating Deep Convolutional GAN. *IEEE Transactions on Industrial Informatics*, 1. Advance online publication. doi:10.1109/TII.2022.3159817

Goodfellow, I. J., Pouget-Abadie, J., Mirza, M., Xu, B., Warde-Farley, D., Ozair, S., Courville, A., & Bengio, Y. (2014). Generative Adversarial Nets. *Advances in Neural Information Processing Systems, 27.* https://www.github.com/goodfeli/adversarial

Halevy, A., Norvig, P., & Pereira, F. (2009). The unreasonable effectiveness of data. *IEEE Intelligent Systems*, *24*(2), 8–12. doi:10.1109/MIS.2009.36

Hammami, M., Friboulet, D., & Kechichian, R. (2020). Cycle GAN-based data augmentation for multi-organ detection in CT images via Yolo. *2020 IEEE International Conference on Image Processing (ICIP)*, 390–393. 10.1109/ICIP40778.2020.9191127

Han, D., & Liu, Q. (n.d.). *A new image classification method using CNN transfer learning and web data augmentation*. Elsevier. Retrieved September 20, 2022, from https://www.sciencedirect.com/science/article/pii/S095741741 7307844

Huisman, M., van Rijn, J. N., & Plaat, A. (2021). A survey of deep meta-learning. *Artificial Intelligence Review*, *54*(6), 4483–4541. doi:10.100710462-021-10004-4

Hulea, M., Gavrilescu, M., de Marchi, S., Chatterjee, S., Hazra, D., Byun, Y.-C., & Kim, Y.-W. (2022). Enhancement of Image Classification Using Transfer Learning and GAN-Based Synthetic Data Augmentation. *Mathematics, 10*(9), 1541.

Karras, T., Aila, T., Laine, S., & Lehtinen, J. (2017). Progressive Growing of GANs for Improved Quality, Stability, and Variation. *6th International Conference on Learning Representations, ICLR 2018 - Conference Track Proceedings.* 10.48550/arxiv.1710.10196

Karras, T., Aittala, M., Hellsten, J., Laine, S., Lehtinen, J., & Aila, T. (2020). styleGAN_with Limited data. *Conference on Neural Information Processing Systems (NeurIPS 2020),* 12104–12114.

Kawaguchi, K., Bengio, Y., & Kaelbling, L. (2022). Generalization in Deep Learning. *Mathematical Aspects of Deep Learning*, 112–148. doi:10.1017/9781009025096.003

Ker, J., Wang, L., Rao, J., & Lim, T. (2017). Deep learning applications in medical image analysis. *IEEE Access : Practical Innovations, Open Solutions*, *6*, 9375–9389. doi:10.1109/ACCESS.2017.2788044

Lemberger, P. (2017). *On Generalization and Regularization in Deep Learning.* https://arxiv.org/abs/1704.01312

Liu, D., & Hu, N. (2020). *GAN-Based Image Data Augmentation*. Stanford CS229 Final Project: Computer Vision.

Marcus, G. (n.d.). *Deep Learning: A Critical Appraisal.* https://www.nytimes.com/2012/11/24/science/scientists-see-advances-in-deep-learning-a-part-of-artificial-

Nagarajan, V. (2021). *Explaining generalization in deep learning: progress and fundamental limits.* https://arxiv.org/abs/2110.08922

Neyshabur, B. Sedghi, H., & Zhang, C. (2020). What is being transferred in transfer learning? Advances in Neural Information Processing Systems, 33, 512–523.

Panayides, A. S., Amini, A., Filipovic, N. D., Sharma, A., Tsaftaris, S. A., Young, A., Foran, D., Do, N., Golemati, S., Kurc, T., Huang, K., Nikita, K. S., Veasey, B. P., Zervakis, M., Saltz, J. H., & Pattichis, C. S. (2020). AI in Medical Imaging Informatics: Current Challenges and Future Directions. IEEE Journal of Biomedical and Health Informatics, 24(7), 1837–1857. doi:10.1109/JBHI.2020.2991043

Plested, J., & Gedeon, T. (2022). *Deep transfer learning for image classification: A survey.* https://arxiv.org/abs/2205.09904

Power, A., Burda, Y., Edwards, H., Babuschkin, I., & Misra, V. (2022). *Grokking: Generalization Beyond Overfitting on Small Algorithmic Datasets.* https://doi.org/doi:10.48550/arxiv.2201.02177

Raghu, M., Zhang, C., Kleinberg, J., & Bengio, S. (2019). Transfusion: Understanding Transfer Learning for Medical Imaging. *Advances in Neural Information Processing Systems, 32.* Advance online publication. doi:10.48550/arxiv.1902.07208

Rather, I. H., Minz, S., & Kumar, S. (2023). *Hybrid Texture-Based Feature Extraction Model for Brain Tumour Classification Using Machine Learning.* doi:10.1007/978-981-19-4676-9_38

Romero, M., Interian, Y., Solberg, T., & Valdes, G. (2019). *Targeted transfer learning to improve performance in small medical physics datasets.* doi:10.1002/mp.14507

Shu, J., Xu, Z., & Meng, D. (2018). *Small Sample Learning in Big Data Era.* https://arxiv.org/abs/1808.04572

Świechowski, M. (2022). *Deep Learning and Artificial General Intelligence: Still a Long Way to Go.* https://arxiv.org/abs/2203.14963

Tang, Y., Zhang, Y. Q., & Chawla, N. V. (2009). SVMs modeling for highly imbalanced classification. *IEEE Transactions on Systems, Man, and Cybernetics. Part B, Cybernetics, 39*(1), 281–288. doi:10.1109/TSMCB.2008.2002909 PMID:19068445

Vasconcelos, C. N., & Vasconcelos, B. N. (2020). Experiments using deep learning for dermoscopy image analysis. *Pattern Recognition Letters*, *139*, 95–103. doi:10.1016/j.patrec.2017.11.005

Vinyals, O., Blundell, C., Lillicrap, T., Kavukcuoglu, K., & Wierstra, D. (2016). Matching Networks for One Shot Learning. Advances in Neural Information Processing Systems, 29.

Wang, J., & Perez, L. (2017). *The Effectiveness of Data Augmentation in Image Classification using Deep Learning*. https://arxiv.org/abs/1712.04621

Wong, S. C., Gatt, A., Stamatescu, V., & McDonnell, M. D. (2016). Understanding data augmentation for classification: when to warp? *2016 International Conference on Digital Image Computing: Techniques and Applications, DICTA 2016*. 10.1109/DICTA.2016.7797091

Zhao, Z., Zhang, Z., Chen, T., Singh, S., & Zhang, H. (2020). *Image Augmentations for GAN Training*. https://doi.org/ doi:10.48550/arxiv.2006.02595

ENDNOTE

[1]   Dogs vs. Cats | Kaggle.

Chapter 7

LSTM Network:
A Deep Learning Approach and Applications

Anil Kumar
RD Engineering College, India

Abhay Bhatia
Roorkee Institute of Technology, India

Arun Kashyap
GL Bajaj Institute of Technology and Management, India

Manish Kumar
Ajay Kumar Garg Engineering College, India

ABSTRACT

The world wide web (WWW) is an advanced system with an unmatched amount of digital data. Today's internet usage is accessible through common search engines like Google and Yahoo. Cybercriminals have become more assertive on social media. As a result, numerous commercial and trade websites are hacked, leading to forced trafficking of women and children as well as a number of other cybercrimes. Due to this, it is important to identify social media crimes as soon as possible in order to avoid them. To do this, a machine learning technique to detect crimes early must be proposed. Long short-term memory networks are a type of recurrent neural network that can pick up order dependency in problems involving prediction of sequence.

DOI: 10.4018/978-1-6684-6909-5.ch007

INTRODUCTION

Sequence prediction problems have been around for a while. They are regarded as one of the most difficult challenges to address in the community of data science. These cover a wide range of issues, from data prediction and pattern recognition to understanding movie storylines and speech recognition, from language translations to word prediction on your phone's keypad. LSTM networks have been determined to be the most widely solution for practically all of these prediction of sequence problems thanks to recent advancements in data science.

During the past several years DL algorithms have been well developed and used frequently to extract information from many types of data. They are taking into account various aspects of the input data, and there are various DL architecture types, including RNN, CNN, and deep neural networks. The temporal information of incoming data is typically for CNN and DNN, too complex to handle. Therefore, RNNs are prevalent in study fields and deal with sequential data, like text, audio, and video. The RNNs unfortunately are unable to connect the pertinent data when there is a significant gaping between relevant data input. Hochreiteret al. (1997) advocated lengthy short-term memory to address "long-term dependency" (LSTM). Since, LSTM has produced all intriguing RNN-based outcomesnearly; it has taken centre stage in deep learning. LSTMs perform incredibly well and have been extensively employed in a variety of tasks, including speech recognition, acoustic modelling, trajectory prediction, phrase embedding, and correlation analysis. This is mostly due to their powerful learning ability. We examine these LSTM networks in this review, which focuses on developments of the LSTM network cell and topologies of LSTM network. Here, the recurrent unit of LSTM networks is referred to as the LSTM cell.

Background: Recurrent Neural Networks (RNN)

RNNsfor sequential data and the most advanced techniques are used for Google's voice search and Apple's Siri. Basically, it is the 1stalgorithm with memory with internal that keeps records of its input, making it ideal for required machine learning issues of sequential data. Although recurrent neural networks were initially created in the round of 1980s, it wasn't until recently became clear that their full potential. RNNs have truly risen to the fore because to the introduction of LSTM in round of 1990s, as well as improvements in computing power and the various volumes of data we now have to deal with. In the AI domains, machine learning, deep learning and neural networks simulate how the human brain functions, enabling computer systems to discover patterns and resolve challenges. The neural network style is known as RNNs may used to model sequence data. The feed-forward networks are used built behavior of RNNs, which is comparable to that of human brains.

Figure 1. Simple recurrent neural network

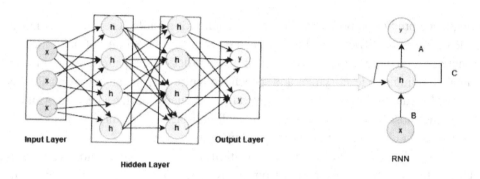

In CNNs, all inputs and outputs are independent of each other. However, there are times when past words are needed, like as when we predicting the next word in a sentence and it is an important to remembering the prior words. As a consequence, the RNN was developed and it solve the issue by employed a Hidden Layer to it. The particular information is retain in Hidden state about a sequence, and is the most crucial part of an RNN. The RNNs have a memory unit where they keep records of all computations data. Since, it generates the similar result by carrying out the similar operations on all inputs or hidden layers ;for each input, it uses the same parameters.

RNN vs. Feed-Forward Neural Networks

The Internet of Things framework necessitates near-edge better memories and information processing due to the volume, veracity, and velocity of data coming from edge devices. Recurrent neural networks are effective instruments for real-time contextual information (RNN). Although employing neural networks to handle data is not a novel concept, it is quickly becoming a reality thanks to rapid device scaling and cutting-edge technologies like in-memory computing and neuromorphic circuits.

RNNs, in contrast to feed-forward neural networks, handle input sequences of any length thanks to feedback connections between nodes and layers. However, training the simplistic RNN can be tough process. The creation of "Long Short-Term Memory" has been shown to be able to solve the vanishing or ballooning gradient difficulties caused by the techniques employed for weight updating in RNNs (LSTM). An RNN with multiplicative gates and an internal memory is known as an LSTM. Since the initial LSTM announcement in 1997, a variety of LSTM cell configurations have been developed.

The thing that RNNs and channel information gives them their identity using feed-forward neural networks. In a feed-forward neural network, information only flows in one direction from the input to the output, via the hidden layers. The network receives the information without any delays. Therefore, making the predictions of Feed-forward neural networks is poor because they have little recall of the information they receive. There is no concept of time order in feed-forward network since it simply takes into account the current input. It just isn't able to recall anything from the past outside its schooling.

The RNN information loops back on itself. It takes into account both the current input and what it has discovered from the inputs it has received while making decisions.

The RNN information loops back on itself. It takes into account both the current input and when making a decision the lessons it has learnt from prior inputs.

The flow of information between an RNN and a feed-forward neural network is shown in the two pictures below.

Figure 2. RNN vs. feed-forward neural network

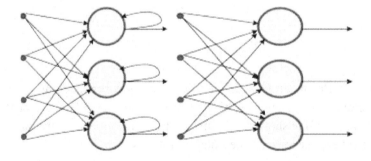

Issues of Standard RNNs

Vanishing Gradients: The model stops learning or takes an unusually long time to train when the gradient values are too small. This was a major issue in the 1990s, and it was far more difficult to resolve than the gradient explosion issue. Thankfully, Sepp Hochreiter and Juergen Schmidhuber's LSTM concept offered the answer.

Standard Recurrent Cell

Recurrent cells in RNNs' recurrent layers or hidden layers contain feedback connections, and both historical and current input have an impact on how they are now behaving. To create different RNNs, the recurrent layers can be arranged in a variety of ways. As a result, they might be recognized using RNNs' network and recurrent cell designs. RNNs are capable of having a range of functions due to their various cells and internal connections. This section provides an overview of the LSTM cell and its modifications before discussing how LSTM networks have evolved.

Figure 3. Standard recurrent sigma cell

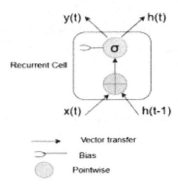

Traditional Recurrent Cell, RNNs are often networks made up of sigma cells and tanh cells, two common types of recurrent cells. A schematic of the typical recurrent sigma cell is shown in Figure 3. The conventional recurrent sigma cell's mathematical expressions are presented as follows:

$$h_t = \sigma\left(W_h.h_{t-1} + W_x.x_t + b\right),$$

$$y_t = h_t,$$

Where $y_t = h_t$ are the weights; bias denoted by b; and output of the cell at time t and W_x and W_h and x_t, h_t stand for the input, recurrent information, respectively.

Some challenges have seen some progress using standard recurrent cells (Karpathy, et al, 2015; Li et al, 2018). Standard recurrent networks of cells-based, on the other hand, are unable to manage long-term dependencies because it becomes more challenging to acquire the link information as the distance between related inputs widens. Bengio et al. (1994) and Hochreiter (1991) examined the underlying causes for dependency issue for duration of long-term. Error messages that go back in time generally burst or disappear.

LSTM

Hochreiteret al. (1997) suggested the LSTM network cell as a solution to the issue of "long-term dependency." By adding a "gate" to the typical recurrent cell, they were able to increase its memory capacity. Since this groundbreaking breakthrough, several researchers have modified and popularized LSTMs (Gers, 2001; Gers et al, 2000). There are LSTM variants with and with no forget gates as well as LSTM connection with a peephole. An LSTM with a forget gate is referred to as a "LSTM cell" often. We start by introducing the fundamental LSTM model, which is made up only of input and output gates.

No Forget Gate Exists in LSTM

Figure 4. No forget gate LSTM

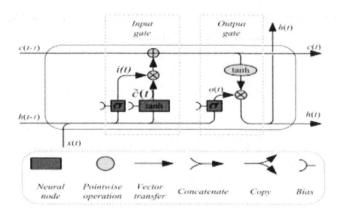

The LSTM architecture is shown in Figure 4 with simply input and output gates. The LSTM in fig 4mathematically may be expressed as followings:

$$y_t = i_t),$$

$$\sigma(W_{i.h}.h_{t-1} + W_{i.x} \cdot x_t + b_i$$

$$o_t = \sigma\left(W_{o.h}.h_{t-1} + W_{o.x}.x_t + b_o\right),$$

$$h_t = o_t.\tanh\left(c_t\right),,$$

$$c_t = c_{t-1} + i_t - \overline{c}_t,$$

where the LSTM's cell state is referred to as c_t. The point-by-point multiplication of two vectors is denoted by the operator "•," and the weights are Wi, Wc, and Wo. Contingent upon the cell express, the result entryway concludes what data might be produced; In contrast, the cell's state is decided by the input gate, which new data can be maintained.

Forget Gate Exists in LSTM

In original LSTM, a forget gate was added to the cell by Gers et al. (2000). Figure 5 shows the inner connections of this modified LSTM cell, from which one may derive its mathematical expressions. According to the connections in Figure 5, the LSTM cell may be mathematically described as follows:

$$\overline{c}_t = \tanh\left(W_{\overline{c}.h} \cdot h_{t-1} + W_{\overline{c}.x} \cdot x_t + b_{\overline{c}}\right)$$

$$f_t = \sigma\left(W_{f.h} \cdot h_{t-1} + W_{f.x}.x_t + b_f\right),,$$

$$\overline{c} = \tanh\left(W_{\overline{c}h}.h_{t-1} + W_{\overline{c}.x}.x_t + b_{\overline{c}}\right)$$

$$i_t = \sigma\left(W_{i.h}.h_{t-1} + W_{i.x}.x_t + b_i\right),$$

$$o_t = \sigma\left(W_{o.h}.h_{t-1} + W_{o.x}.x_t + b_o\right),$$

$$h_t = o_t.\tanh\left(c_t\right),$$

What data from the cell state will be erased depends on the forget gate. This information is kept when the forget gate's $c_t = f_t.c_{t-1} + i_t.\overline{c}_t$, value is 1, but a value

Figure 5. Forget gate

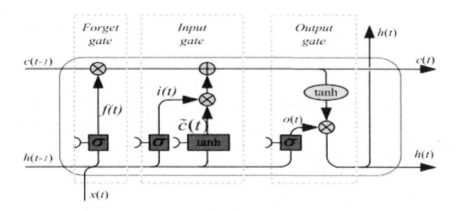

of 0 signifies that all of the information is deleted. Jozefowicz et al. (2015) discovered that LSTM network often improved the performance when the bias of the forget gate, f_t, was increased. Additionally, it was suggested by Schmidhuber et al. (2007) that LSTM sometimes might be taught more effectively using evolutionary algorithms mixed with various methods as opposed to only gradient descent.

With a Peephole Connection LSTM

Because the gates of the LSTM cells listed above don't have direct connections to the cell state, performance of network will hurt due to crucial information is absent from them. Gers et al. (2000) have added a peephole connection by extended the LSTM cell and for solving this problem, as seen in Figure 6.

The following mathematical formulas may be generated based on the relationships in Figure 6:

b_f

$$f_t = \sigma\left(W_{f.h}.h_{t-1} + W_{f.x}.x_t + P_f.c_{t-1} + b_f\right),$$

$$i_t = \sigma\left(W_{i.h}.h_{t-1} + W_{i.x}x_t + P_i.c_{t-1} + b_i\right),,$$

$$\overline{c}_t = \tanh\left(W_{\overline{c}.h}.h_{t-1} + W_{\overline{c}.x}.x_t + b_{\overline{c}}\right)$$

$$c_t = f_t.c_{t-1} + i_t.\overline{c}_t,$$

$$o_t = \sigma\left(W_{o.h}.h_{t-1} + W_{o.x}.x_t + P_o.\ c_t + b_o\right),$$

where $h_t = o_t.\tanh\left(c_t\right), , P_f$, and P_i , respectively, are the peephole weights for the forget gate, input gate, and output gate. Because the peephole connections allow the LSTM cell to monitor its current internal states, the LSTM with a peephole connection may learn stable and precise timing algorithms without the aid of a teacher (Gers et al., 2001).

Figure 6. LSTM peephole architecture.

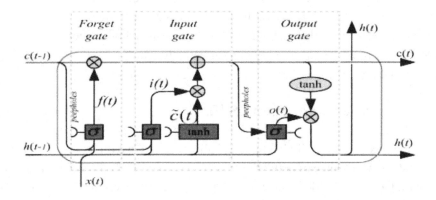

Greff et al. (2016) investigated, the performance of eight versions: linked input and forget gate (CIFG), no peepholes, no output gate, no input gate, and no output gate and in order to fully study a peephole connection with the LSTM. Each model's addition of a peephole connection only slightly differs from the original LSTM. The output and forget gates were found to be the most important components, and it is obvious that removing any one of them will lower network performance. Moreover, the new connected input and neglect door might bring about a decrease in the quantity of boundaries and computational costs without fundamentally compromising organization execution. LSTM has taken control of deep learning and been applied to a wide range of issues as a result of this potent capability.

Gated Recurrent Unit

The LSTM cell has a greater ability for learning than a typical recurrent cell. The extra parameters do, however, add to the computing load. Cho et al. as a result created the GRU (2014). The linkages and specifics of the GRU cell's architecture are depicted in detail in Figure 7. The math's formulations of the GRU cell are as:

$$P_0$$

$$r_t = \sigma\left(W_{r.h}.h_{t-1} + W_{r.x}.x_t + b_r\right),$$

$$z_t = \sigma\left(W_{z.h}.h_{t-1} + W_{z.x}.x_t + b_z\right),,$$

$$\bar{h}_t = \tanh\left(W_{\bar{h}.h}(r_t.\ h_{t-1}) + W_{\bar{h}.x}.x_t + b_z\right)$$

Figure 7. GRU cell architecture

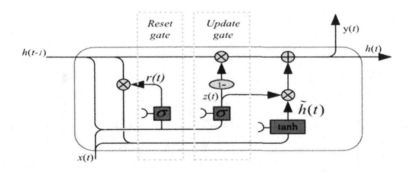

The GRU cell incorporates the input gate and forget gate of the LSTM cell as an update gate in order to decrease the number of parameters. Only an update gate and a reset gate are present in the GRU cell. As a result, it may conserve a single gating signal and its related properties. The GRU is just a forget gate-equipped version of the standard LSTM. Since, one gate is missing; the single GRU cell performs less well compare to the original LSTM. The GRU cannot be trained to count or to answer the context-free language problems, nor does it work for translation. Weiss et al, 2018), Britz et al. (2017), Chung et al. (2014) found that, given that each network had about the same number of parameters, the LSTM cell and GRU cell beat the traditional tanh unit in an empirical comparison of the performance of the LSTM network, GRU network, and conventional tanh-RNN. Dey et al. (2017) modified the original GRU and evaluated the effectiveness of three GRU iterations using data from the IMDB and MNIST. The results showed that these three changes may still retain the original GRU cell's performance parity.

Minimal Gated Unit

The smallest gated unit, which contains just one gate, was recommended by Zhou et al. (2016) to further reduce the number of cell parameters. The schematic MGUis described in Figure 8, basically having a base of the relationships in the image, the mathematics used as formulations of MGU is to be represented as follows:

$$h_t = (1 - z_t). \ h_{t-1} + z_t.\bar{h}_t.$$

$$f_t = \sigma\left(W_{f.h}.h_{t-1} + W_{f.x}.x_t + b_f\right),,$$

Figure 8. MGU

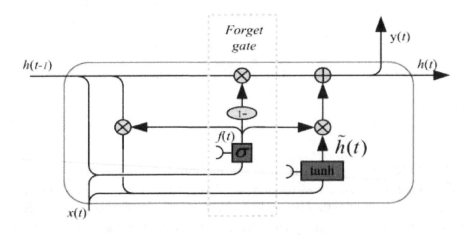

$$\bar{h}_t = \tanh\left(W_{\bar{h}.h}(f_t.\quad h_{t-1}) + W_{\bar{h}x}.x_t + b_{\bar{h}}\right)$$

The cells of MGU contains simply one forget gate. As a result, this form of cell has fewer parameters and a simpler structure than LSTM and GRU. According to evaluation findings (Zhou et al., 2016), the MGU's performance is comparable to the GRU's based on a variety of sequence data. Heck et al. (2017) Simplify the MGU, created three model versions, MGU-1, MGU-2, and MGU-3, which have reduced the number of parameters in the forget gate. They establish that the exhibitions of these alterations were equivalent to such of the MGU in the assignments utilizing the informational indexes MNIST and the Reuters Newswire Points.

CATEGORIES OF LSTM NETWORKS

When processing real-world data, LSTM cells must be arranged into particular network architecture because to the single LSTM cell's has limited ability to handling engineering problems. All RNNs can be transform to LSTM networks by swapping out the conventional recurrent cell with an LSTM cell, however only are included the validated LSTM networks in this review. We categorize LSTM networks into two groups: integrated LSTM networks and LSTM-dominated networks. The term LSTM cells are used to construct neural networks that are referred regarded as

Figure 9. Simplified schematic diagram of the LSTM cell

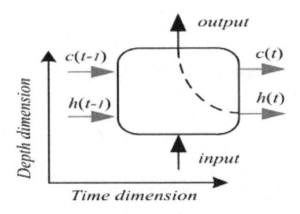

"LSTM-dominated networks". To enhance the properties of the network, these networks place a high priority on enhancing the connections between the core LSTM cells (Nie et al., 2016; Zhao et al., 2016). LSTM layers are joined with other components like a CNN and an external memory unit in integrated LSTM networks. The integrated LSTM networks concentrate mostly on integrating the advantageous qualities of several components while solving the target task.

In Figure 9, we deconstruct the LSTM cell design before introducing the LSTM networks. Identity changes are depicted in the figure by the dashed line. As a consequence, the LSTM cell transmits the h(t) along the depth dimension without any time delay while only broadcasting the c(t) along the time dimension with a one-unit-interval delay.

Dominated Neural Networks

Stacked LSTM

In the typical application, stacking the LSTM layers is the simplest technique to increase the capacity and depth of the network. Consequently, the stacked LSTM

Figure 10. The stacked LSTM network

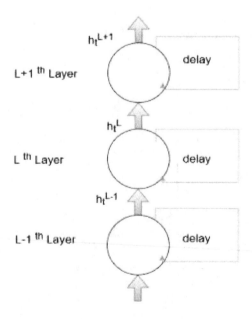

network is the most basic and uncomplicated LSTM network structure (Fernandez, et al. 2007). You may also picture it as a series of interconnected layers. Figure 10 shows a block with three recurring levels. Because of its simple and efficient design, the stacked LSTM network has received widespread support from researchers. Vehicle-to-vehicle communication is a problem that Du, Zhang et al. (2017) employed the stacked LSTM network to solve and discovered that it was substantially more efficient than logistic regression. Sutskever et al. (2014) have used with four layers a stacked LSTM network and 1000 cells each to solve the translation problem of English-to-French.

Bidirectional LSTM Network

Only a previous context may be used by conventional RNNs. Schuster and Paliwal created the bidirectional RNN to address this drawback (1997). With distinct hidden layers, this architecture might be educated simultaneously in both temporal directions i.e., forward and backward layers. In 2005, Graves and Schmidhuber proposed the bidirectional LSTM by combining the BRNN with the LSTM cell. Due to its exceptional qualities, bidirectional LSTM networks have been frequently used by researchers (Han, et al. 2017; Yu, et al. 2018). This design was used by Thireou et al. (2007) to predict protein localization using sequence data. The results show that the bidirectional LSTM network outperforms the feed-forward network and CNN. Wu, Zhang, et al. (2016) investigated the various skip connections in the network and found that adding skip connections to the cell outputs for a gated identity to function may enhance the part-of-speech performance tagging of a stacked bidirectional LSTM network. The suffix bidirectional LSTM (SuBiLSTM), developed by Brahma (2018), improves the bidirectional LSTM network using suffix encoding of the each sequence.

Multi-Dimensional LSTM Network

Only one-dimensional data can be handled by the conventional RNNs. However, the capabilities of RNNs the capacity to acquire contextual data and resistance to input warping are also needed in sectors involving multidimensional data, such as video processing. Graves et al. (2007) created multidimensional LSTM to increase the potential application domains for RNNs. To build as many recurrent connections as there were data dimensions was the primary objective of MDLSTM.

Graph LSTM Network

The graph LSTM network, based on the graph RNN network, was presented by Liang et al. in 2016 and expanded the fixed topologies (Goller & Kuchler, 1996). When process current pixel-wise LSTM designs frequently make the assumption that each pixel is influenced by fixed neighboring pixels when working with graph-structured data. Some of these designs are the row LSTM (Oord et al. 2016), the diagonal BiLSTM (Shabanian et al., 2017), and the local-global LSTM (Liang et al. 2016). Usually, these planned recurrent patterns result in unneeded processing overhead. Liang et al. (2016) graph LSTM network showed the superiority on four distinct data sets: the Fashionista type data set (Yamaguchi, 2012), PASCAL-Person-Part type data set (Chen et al., 2014), ATR type data set (Liang et al., 2015), and Horse-Cow Parsing type data set (Wang & Yuille, 2015).

Grid LSTM Network.

Kalchbrenner et al. (2015) developed the Grid LSTM network might also be used to manage multi-dimensional data. In this arrangement, the cells of LSTM are organized in a grid of one or more dimensions. In contrast to other networks, the grid LSTM network has recurrent connections along the depth axis. The one-dimensional (1D) grid LSTM network, according to Kalchbrenner et al. (2015), is the design that replaces the transfer functions of the feed-forward network (such as tanh and ReLU; Nair & Hinton, 2010) with the 1D grid LSTM block. According to Graves (2012), the MDLSTM is comparable to the grid LSTM with three or more dimensions, with the exception that the N-way recurrent interactions exit along every dimension. Kalchbrenner et al. (2015) found that when it comes to recalling numerical sequences, the 2D grid LSTM performed better than the stacked LSTM (Zaremba & Sutskever, 2014). The intermittent organization associations alongside the profundity aspect might further develop learning limit of the Framework LSTM. Li and Sainath (2017) evaluated four Grid LSTM variants with the intention of lowering the network's computational complexity. On a 12,500-hour voice search workload, they discovered that the frequency-block grid LSTM achieved this without compromising accuracy.

ConvLSTM

The fully connected LSTM layer's redundant spatial data is too abundant (Sainath et al., 2015; Shi et al., 2015). So, to address the spatiotemporal sequence forecasting issue, convolutional LSTM, which featured convolutional features in the recurrent connections, was presented. The future state of a cell is calculated by the ConvLSTM network using the convolution operator, and is then determined by the inputs and previous states of its close neighbours. Wei et al. (2018) employed the ConvLSTM network to address the spatiotemporal sequence forecasting problem of tweet count prediction. Studies on the city of Seattle have shown that the proposed network consistently outperforms the three competing baseline methods, the autoregressive integrated moving average model, ST-ResNet (Zhang, Zheng, & Qi, 2016), and Eyewitness (Krumm & Horvitz, 2015). Zhu, Zhang, et al. (2017) used the 3D CNN and ConvLSTM to provide a multimodal gesture recognition model. The ConvLSTMand 3D CNN, respectively, learned the long-term and short-term spatiotemporal features of the gestures. If evaluate on Sheffield Kinect Gesture data set and ChaLearn LAP large-scale isolated gesture data set, the findings revealed that the recommended technique outperformed earlier models. Liu, Zhou, Hang, and Yuan (2017) enhanced both the ConvLSTM and bidirectional LSTM and presented architecture of the bidirectional-ConvLSTM to learn properties of spectrum-spatial from hyper-spectral images.

Depth-Gated LSTM

By using layered LSTM networks, creating a DNN is the simplest process. Yao et al. (2015) noted that the error signals in the stacked LSTM network may be either decreased or enlarged since the error signals from the top must be back propagated via many layers of nonlinear transformations. To solve such problem, they developed the depth-gated LSTM, in that a depth gate was used to link memory cells in neighboring LSTM layers. The DPLSTM design was inspired by the highway network (Kim, et al. 2017; Srivastava, et al. 2015) and grid LSTM (Kalchbrenner et al., 2015). Yao et al. (2015) used the variable depth of DGLSTMs to finish the Chinese to English machine translation challenge. The results showed that, in terms of performance, the DGLSTM network regularly outperforms the stacked LSTM network. Zhang, et al. (2015) proposed efficient methods to train the DGLSTM network and achieved even better results using both frame and sequence discriminative criteria.

Gated-Feedback LSTM Network

Chung, Gulcehre, Cho, and Bengio (2015) introduced the gated-feedback RNN (GF-RNN) and the gated-feedback LSTM (GF-LSTM) network to address the issue of learning various adaptive timescales. The GF-RNN employs a global gating unit for each pair of layers to enable and regulate signals flowing from upper recurrent levels to lower layers, or gated-feedback connections. On the job of evaluating a Python program, the suggested GF-RNN was compared to the traditional stacked RNN. The findings revealed that the GF-RNN performs better than the stacked RNN.

LSTM Network With Tree-Structured

Chain-structured LSTM networks make up the majority of current implementations. Speech recognition and machine translation are two areas where these networks excel. However, when it comes to merging words and phrases in natural language processing, these chain-structured networks have poor properties (Li, Luong, et al. 2015; Zhang, et al. 2015). Therefore, Zhu et al. (2015) and Tai et al. (2015) enlarged the chain-structured LSTM networks to tree-structured networks based on the original tree-structured recursive models (Goller & Kuchler, 1996; Sperduti & Starita, 1997; Francesconi et al., 1997; Frasconi, Gori, & Sperduti, 1998). Zhu et al. (2015) showed that the tree-structured LSTM network outperformed other recursive models while learning distributed sentiment representations for texts.

Coupled LSTM Network

Liu, et al. (2016) developed two coupled LSTMs designs, the loosely coupled LSTM and the tightly coupled LSTM, to represent the interactions of phrase pairs. The multidimensional RNN and the grid LSTM served as inspiration for these architectural designs. To imitate the robust interactions of two phrases, these two connected LSTM networks exploit connections between hidden states.

Deep Fusion LSTM Networks

Using a deep fusion network for LSTM, Liu et al. (2016) was able to extract the strong interaction between text pairs. In this network, there were two LSTMs that were linked together. The memory capacity of the LSTMs was later increased by the authors using external memory, allowing them more complex matching patterns to store. They offered a qualitative evaluation of the model's capabilities and demonstrated its efficacy using data from the Corpus to Stanford Natural Language Inference.

Multiplicative Types LSTM Network

For various inputs, the weighted matrices of conventional LSTM networks are fixed. Those organizations need expressiveness while the managing assortments of unmistakable, shared restrictive parts. The multiplicative LSTM was created by combining the LSTM and the multiplicative type RNN architecture to produce adjustable input dependent weighted matrices. This model outperformed the stacked LSTM in some character-level language modeling experiments.

Integrated Level LSTM Networks

In some cases, a single LSTM network capacity cannot always satisfy the actual engineering needs. In these cases, integrated LSTM networks combine an LSTM layer with other components, such as a CNN and a unit of external memory.

Neural Turing Machine

The RNN's memory capacity is a crucial component since it must update the current cell states based on inputs and past states. Neural networks have been used to learn to regulate end-to-end differentiable stack machines so as to increase the memory capacity of networks (Sun, 1990; Mozer, & Das, 1993). The structure was expanded by Schmidhuber (1993), Schlag and Schmidhuber (2017), and end-to-end-differentiable rapid weight memory was learned and managed by the RNN. Graves, et al. (2014) further provided the neural Turing machine with an LSTM controller, which took design inspirations from both biological memory models and digital computer architecture.

DBN-LSTM Network

This network, which combines LSTM with a deep belief network, was first introduced by Vohra, Goel, and Sahoo (2015). It advances from the RNN-DBN (Goel et al. 2014). The multilayer DBN helps with high-level data representation when the DBN and LSTM networks are coupled, while the LSTM network provides temporal information. The key difference between the DBN-LSTM and the RNN-DBN is that the DBN-LSTM uses the LSTM cell in place of the standard recurrent cell to increase the model's time-to-event handling capacity.

Multi-Scale LSTM Network

Cheng et al. (2016) combined an LSTM network with a preprocessing block to construct the multi-scale LSTM network. The preprocessing block assists in selecting a suitable period for the incoming data, and the LSTM layer are utilised to model the processed sequential data. This approach was used by Cheng et al. (2016) to handle dynamic Internet traffic while learning the Internet traffic pattern across a variable time window. By combining the MS-LSTM and a CNN, Peng, et al. (2016) created a recurrent architecture for geometric scene parsing.

CFCC-LSTM Network

To forecast sea surface temperature, Yang et al. (2017) proposed a CFCC-LSTM network that incorporated a fully connected LSTM and a CNN. They initially developed a 3D grid to preprocess the data before forecasting the temporal information in the 3D grid. They then used a convolution operation to handle the temporal data and an FC-LSTM layer to handle the spatial data. This strategy's effectiveness was proved by the results on two datasets, the China Ocean dataset and the Bohai Sea dataset.

C-LSTM Network

The C-LSTM network is made by joining the CNN and LSTM organizations. The suggestion was made by Zhou, Wu, Zhang, and Zhou (2016). A number of higher-level phrase representations may be extracted by this network using CNN, which is then fed into the LSTM network to obtain the sentence representation required for the task of sentence and document modeling.

LSTM-Inside-LSTM Network

Song, et al. (2016) used a Deep-CNN network with an LSTM-in-LSTM architecture to provide in-depth, fine-grained textual descriptions of images. The LSTM-in-LSTM design contains an inner type LSTM cell and an outer type LSTM cell. Using such architecture, which can learn about the contextual links between visual data, long sentence descriptions may be anticipated.

LSTM Applications

With LSTM neural networks, it is possible to accomplish a wide range of tasks, including prediction, pattern classification, various types of recognition, analysis, and even sequence creation. Due to its ability to comprehend sequential data, LSTM is a useful tool in a variety of fields, including statistics, linguistics, health, transportation, computer science, and others. Long-term memory networks are a type of recurrent neural network (RNN). LSTMs are often used to learn, interpret, and categories sequential data due to their ability to learn long-term relationships between input time steps. Common LSTM applications include speech recognition, sentiment analysis, video analysis, and language modeling.

1. Speech Recognition (Output is text whereas Input is audio) - as done by Google Assistant, Microsoft Cortana, Apple Siri.
2. Machine Translation (Input is text and output is also text) - as done by Google Translate.
3. Image Captioning (Input is image and output is text).
4. Sentiment Analysis (Input is text and output is rating).
5. Music Generation/Synthesis (input music notes and output is music).
6. Video Activity Recognition (input is video and output is type of activity)
7. Moreover it can be used for all time dependent activities with good efficiency.

CONCLUSION

The distribution system of the human brain memory is where information is stored and processed. Modern tools like LSTM can handle a variety of sequential and temporal input, that including audio, video, market data, and mores. The internal memory of LSTM enables the maintenance for long-term dependence. The most common LSTM setups, as well as its capability and promise, were covered in this study. LSTM neural networks are sluggish despite their benefits because of their extensive parallelism and sequential nature. Hopefully, a trustworthy hardware accelerator will be introduced soon to address this issue. Utilizing memory might help current computers overcome a "bottleneck" that prevents them from implementing vector-matrix multiplication and achieving improved non-linearity for a variety of calculation workloads.

REFERENCES

Altché, F., & Fortelle, A. D. L. (2017). An LSTM network for highway trajectory prediction. In *Proceedings of the IEEE 20th International Conference on Intelligent Transportation Systems*. IEEE. 10.1109/ITSC.2017.8317913

Bhatia, Kumar, Jain, Kumar, Verma, Illes, Aschilean, & Raboaca. (2022). Networked Control System with MANET Communication and AODV Routing. *SCI Journal*. doi:10.1016/j.heliyon.2022.e11678

Bhatia, A., Kumar, A., Khan, I., & Kumar, V. (2011). Analysis of Pattern Recognition (text mining) with Web Crawler. In *International Transactions in Applied Sciences*. ITAS.

Cheng, M., Xu, Q., Lv, J., Liu, W., Li, Q., & Wang, J. (2016). MS-LSTM: A multi-scale LSTM model for BGP anomaly detection. In *Proceedings of the IEEE 24th International Conference on Network Protocols*. IEEE. 10.1109/ICNP.2016.7785326

Chung, J., Gulcehre, C., Cho, K., & Bengio, Y. (2015). *Gated feedback recurrent neural networks*. arXiv:1502.02367v1.

Deng, L. (2013). Three classes of deep learning architectures and their applications: A tutorial survey. In *APSIPA transactions on signal and information processing*. Cambridge University Press.

Dey, R., & Salemt, F. M. (2017). Gate-variants of gated recurrent unit (GRU) neural networks. In *Proceedings of the IEEE International Midwest Symposium on Circuits and Systems*. IEEE. 10.1109/MWSCAS.2017.8053243

Gers, Schmidhuber, & Cummins. (1999). *Learning to forget: Continual prediction with LSTM*. Academic Press.

Hochreiter, S., & Schmidhuber, J. (1997). Long Short-term Memory. *Neural Computation*, *9*(8), 1735–1780. doi:10.1162/neco.1997.9.8.1735 PMID:9377276

Kumar, A., & Gupta, T. (2012). Genetic Algorithm for Dynamic Capacitated Minimum Spanning Tree. International Journal of Computational Engineering and Management, 28-35.

Li, C., Wang, Z., Rao, M., Belkin, D., Song, W., Jiang, H., Yan, P., Li, Y., Lin, P., Hu, M., Ge, N., Strachan, J. P., Barnell, M., Wu, Q., Williams, R. S., Yang, J. J., & Xia, Q. (2019). Long short-term memory networks in memristor crossbar arrays. *Nature Machine Intelligence*, *1*(1), 49–57. doi:10.103842256-018-0001-4

Lipton, Berkowitz, & Elkan. (2015). *A critical review of recurrent neural networks for sequence learning*. arXiv preprint arXiv:1506.00019.

Olah. (2015). *Understanding LSTM networks*. Academic Press.

Oparin, I., Sundermeyer, M., Ney, H., & Gauvain, J. (2012). Performance analysis of Neural Networks in combination with n-gram language models. ICASSP.

Sundermeyer, M., Schlüter, R., & Ney, H. (2012). LSTM Neural Networks for Language Modeling. INTERSPEECH. doi:10.21437/Interspeech.2012-65

Sutskever, Vinyals, & Le. (2014). Sequence to sequence learning with neural networks. *Advances in Neural Information Processing Systems*, 3104-3112.

Zhao, Srivastava, Peng, & Chen. (2019). Long short-term memory network design for analog computing. ACM Journal on Emerging Technologies. *Computing Systems*, *15*(1), 13.

Chapter 8

Machine Learning–Based Prediction of Users' Involvement on Social Media

Vibhor Sharma
Swami Rama Himalayan University, India

Lokesh Kumar
Roorkee Institute of Technology, India

Deepak Srivastava
ⓘ https://orcid.org/0000-0002-7440-8311
Swami Rama Himalayan University, India

ABSTRACT

Useful information can be extracted through the analysis of Facebook posts. Text analysis and image analysis can play a vital role towards this. To predict the users' involvement, text data and image data can be incorporated using some machine learning models. These models can be used to perform testing on advertisements that are posted on Facebook for users' involvement prediction. Count of share and comments with sentiment analysis are included as users' involvement. This chapter contributes to understand the users' involvement on social media along with finding out the best machine learning model for prediction of users' involvement. The procedure of prediction with both text data and image data by suitable models is also discussed. This chapter produces a predictive model for posts of Facebook to predict users' involvement that will be based on the number of shares and comments on the post. The best models are obtained by using the combination of image data and text data. Further, it demonstrated that random models are surpassed by the models that are integrated for prediction.

DOI: 10.4018/978-1-6684-6909-5.ch008

INTRODUCTION

Social media platform acts like an interface for advertisers. Multiple organizations post their ads on social media platform by paying very less amount. This makes beneficial impact on consumers as well as business (Azizian et al., 2017). Nowadays, this kind of marketing is on peak due to its tremendous benefits. All the organizations want to make a good reach to their customers by selling their products on social media platform that is becoming effective medium to reach most of the customers (Fisher, 2009). It becomes a challenge for social media platforms to make an efficient and effective way for companies to reach their customers. This kind of marketing on social media platform is new, where platforms are required to justify their worth by providing best services to advertisers. After displaying the advertisement, effectiveness can be judged easily. But, requirement is to analyze these things before investing in advertisement that makes sense for advertisers in context of return on investment. Solution for this may be to find out users' involvement. This chapter provides a solution in form of a machine learning model to predict users' involvement in advertisements posted on social media platform. Multiple machine learning models are used to check the required prediction in order to find out the best model for prediction so that advertisements posted on social media platform could perform better. These models are used to identify the best suited advertisement in the perspective of performance.

Multiple algorithms have already been implemented which are used to act as an interface with social media. Most of the advertisements on social media contain text data with image data. When an advertisement appears in front of user, he/she is only concerned about the content. For prediction of users' involvement, these kinds of advertisement data are required. Prediction can be done more effectively if image data is also used for analysis along with text data. A kind of new analysis is required that contains both text data and image data. On social media, image data analysis is not addressed that much. Because an image may contain text, color, any object with different projections etc. However, an image represents meaning of that but from the image data perspective, it contains large amount of variability. That is the reason; an image data analysis is more difficult. In the last decade, many application programming interfaces and tools have been developed that are used to identify an object and features of an image. There are many algorithms have been implemented for object identification and finding similarity in multiple images. Sentiment analysis has also been done on images so far (Wang et al., 2015). This kind of approach to identify objects in images, find similarity in images along with sentiment analysis may be useful for social media data analysis.

The number of machine learning libraries is being increased that shows the implementation of algorithms which are based on image data. Some libraries like

TensorFlow provide easy access of convolutional neural networks. Users can do better image analysis using these convolutional neural networks most probably in an image classification, image clustering along with synthesis of text data. Through this, social media data analysis can be done in more efficient way if image data analysis is added. Maximum of data is available through social media platform application programming interfaces for analysis purpose that provides greater opportunity to implement new approaches and feature selection for analysis of social media data. This chapter focuses on this under addressed thing to predict users' involvement on social media.

BACKGROUND

According to Li et al., Twitter click-through rates are expected to increase in the future (Li, Fang, Yang, Wang, Lu, & Yang, 2017). Predicting whether a person will click on advertising is known as click-through prediction. To give you an idea, let's say you go to Amazon and look at various products. When the user returns to Amazon, Amazon places a cookie on their browser. Amazon will later pay Twitter to re-display this product on the user's Twitter feed when they are on the social media network's site. Advertisement click rates on user feeds may be predicted using data from this study. Since there are so few clicks, it is difficult to estimate this probability. An ad's click-through rate is often less than one percent. Modeling the likelihood of a user's actions is the purpose of the project. The results of the study were predicted by establishing a link between the interests of users and the relevancy of relevant advertisements. In addition, the study used Twitter sessions as a model.

Stranton et al. employ post, text, and time data to forecast user involvement on Facebook (Straton et al., 2015). This data was used to forecast the number of page likes, shares, and comments. All postings were divided into three levels of engagement: low, medium, and high, based on the results of the study. This data was used to train a neural network. The research was able to accurately forecast low levels of user involvement. However, when it came to forecasting higher degrees of involvement, the neural network did not do very well. Public health data was used in this particular research. 100k posts were included in the study's sample size. Images and comments were not included in the study's projections.

Predicting Facebook page user activity was the subject of an investigation by authors in Ohsawa and Matsuo (2013). Based on the page's description, the research estimated how many people would enjoy it. Page entities are used to build a neural network of pages for this research. This projection is based upon the amount of likes on other sites that are like your own. For its forecast, the model used Wikipedia page count likes. The final algorithm was able to accurately forecast how many people would like a Facebook page.

Numerous studies have examined how people feel about text they read on social media. Liu is an expert in social media sentiment analysis (Liu, 2012). Opinion mining uses terms that indicate a person's feelings. Predicting the sentiment of a given text may be done using existing sentiment lexicons. Wang et al. concentrate on the analysis of picture sentiment through the grouping of images based on emotion (Wang et al., 2015). Clustered pictures are used to train an unsupervised model. Sentiment banks are also used to classify image sentiment. Images of objects can be categorized using an existing model. The set of picture objects in a sentiment bank is used to categorize the emotional content of an image.

Mandhyani et al. investigate image classification methods (Wang et al., 2017). The program identifies things in the picture using an algorithmic process. Feature detection and key point clusters are used to identify items in the data. Databases of object features can be mapped to the features. Classifying objects is done by comparing their features to a database of other items. Classification is carried out on this collection of items by the algorithm. Once an item is discovered, it may be mapped to a set of keywords. To categorize the image, the system makes use of this jumble of words. Image vectors are clustered using k-means clustering in the process.

Sophisticated outcomes in texture generation have been achieved using generative modeling techniques (Li, Fang, Yang, Wang, Lu, & Yang, 2017). Efficiency and universality are sometimes at odds with one another. The pictures produced by efficient algorithms are generally identical and non-diverse. It is hoped that one generative model can be used to synthesize a variety of textures. Both non-parametric and parametric texture generation is available. When the picture statistics match, it is assumed that two photographs are aesthetically comparable. Random noise is used as the starting point for synthesis.

It is possible to analyze images using Convolutional Neural Networks. They've become the norm in the social media world. Authors utilize CNNs to categorize people based on age and gender (Levi & Hassncer, 2015). Visual sentiment classifiers with CNNs are developed by Chen et al. and Xu et al. (Xu, 2014). You et al. used CNNs to identify picture polarity (You, 2015). Sarcasm was found on Twitter with CNNs by Poria et al. (Sarsam et al., 2020). Using CNN photos, Lin et al. discovered the presence of stress in social media photographs (Lin et al., 2014). With CNN's help, authors conducted social profiling (Segalin et al., 2017). It was determined that CNN was the most popular social media platform by Gelli et al. (2015). Unlike previous studies, this one focuses on a variety of social media measures.

PROBLEM STATEMENT

A study says that around 70% of adults are using Facebook nowadays (Gramlich, 2021). This becomes too expensive to operate a website with a large number of users. There is no amount that is being paid by users for Facebook. Google is also providing free of cost services to its users as Facebook is doing. The reason behind the free service is the earning from the advertisements posted on the platform. Around 80% of revenue is being generated by Facebook through advertisements. On the other hand, Google is generating around 70% of its earning through advertisements. But this is also the fact that users don't like advertisements and due to this users' involvement also gets less (Shi, 2016). If the users' involvement will get lesser, it will directly make a negative impact of company's revenue generation. This will also float a negative message that company is not able to reach people effectively. In this regard, we can say that advertisements are making adverse effects on social media platform and advertisers as well. So, it becomes a challenge to find out the relevant content for user that may relate to interests and preference of users. If advertisement will be related to users' interest, that will be beneficial for advertisers and platform. The content will be bought by users (Smith & Anderson, 2018). Thus, this chapter focuses on predicting users' involvement based on their interests and preferences that will help the company to manage their advertisements to make money. The confidence of advertisers will be increased in platform and they will invest more appropriately. It will become possible by analyzing the Facebook posts along with text data and image data as an input. Computation is performed on the data using proposed machine learning models to predict the users' involvement based on their interests that required the thousands of Facebook posts on to which the machine learning model are trained. The posts include advertisements with number of shares and comments.

RESEARCH METHODOLOGY

Data Context

An online post and its associated information comprise the data context. Online posts are the most common kind of user-generated contents. The majority of posts are made up of text, but they may also include a picture. Metadata can also be found in these posts. Post metadata includes likes, shares and responses as well as tag and time stamp data. For example, users can leave comments, like, and reply to a post by hand, or share it with their Facebook friends, which all contribute to the post's meta-data (Azizian et al., 2017). Ads from Facebook pages were used to compile the post information we have. Ratings, followers, and the amount of people actively conversing about a page are all included in these pages. For the study, the page data, its postings, the post data, and the comments were all gathered.

Source of Data

It is possible to handle social media advertising campaigns with AdEspresso's online interface. Marketers can use it to develop and disseminate advertising. These advertising are shared across different social media channels by the website. For marketers, this means that all of their advertising needs may be met in one place: An advertising consultancy service is also available on the website. Over one lack sample Facebook ads may be viewed on the website.

Figure 1. Data fetching

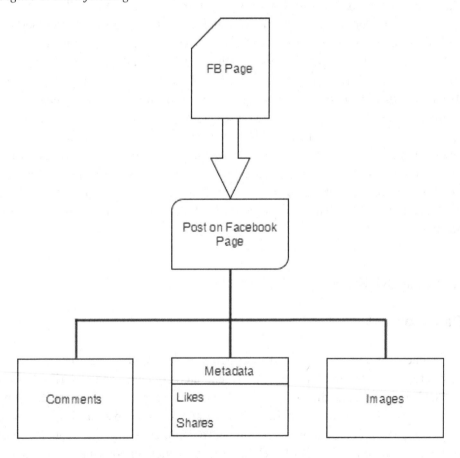

Data Fetching

A Python web scraper was used to crawl through these Facebook pages as part of the research. This crawler was done using the Facebook graph API, which is open to all users. There were ranged from a few hundred to several thousand posts on each Facebook page. Each page had a maximum of 1200 posts scraped from it. To avoid bias in machine learning due to a single Facebook page, a limit of 1200 posts was set. We went with the maximum since Facebook has a daily API request restriction of just a certain number of requests per Facebook page. There is a limit to the number of posts and comments that can be requested. A total of almost 30,000 posts were gathered in total. To save space, the URLs for the images are kept rather than downloaded. A database is used to store the text data. Figure 1 depicts the complete data fetching process and Figure 2 displays a graph of the posts gathered from each Facebook page.

Figure 2. Facebook per page scraping

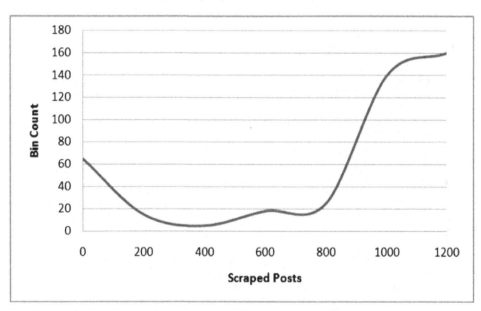

As a result, the URL may be used as a database primary key. The sample size for share and comment counts is around 350k, while the sentiment of comments is approximately 50k. For this investigation, the user engagement metrics are depicted in Figures 3-4.

Figure 3. Comment count graph

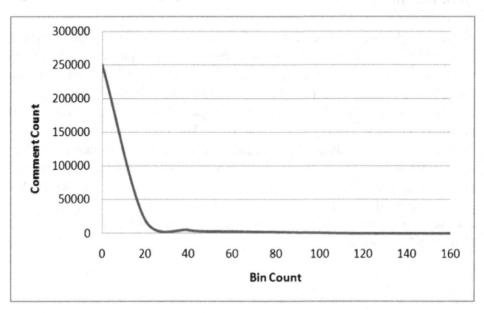

Figure 4. Share count graph

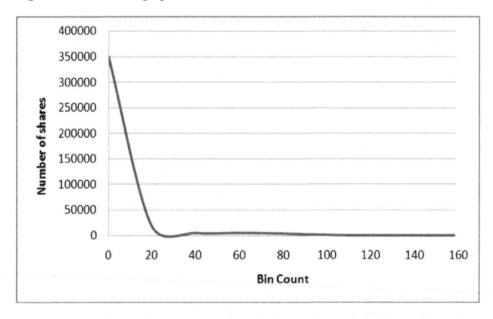

Analysis Approaches

Image processing was part of the data gathering procedure. Images are de-noised as a part of the image processing process in order to draw attention to specific aspects of the image. Each de-noising algorithm has its own set of properties that it considers relevant. Edges, gradient contrasts, and curves are generally emphasized by the de-noising techniques (Sánchez et al., 2018). De-noising can reduce the quantity of picture data, freeing up storage space on the computer. The smaller picture size makes it easier to save all of the photographs on a computer. The ultimate aim is not to reduce the size of the image, but rather to reduce the amount of data that must be sent. Ultimately, the aim is to eliminate visual noise that can interfere with image-based model training. De-noising allows the models to focus on the image's most important elements by removing background noise.

Processing of Plain Text

Feature vectors are input to neural networks. The neural network, on the other hand, is unable to handle plain text data. In order to use a neural network, researchers need to turn the text data into vectors. Examples from "Deep Learning with Keras" are used to illustrate how text data is transformed into a word vector (Antonio & Sujit, 2017). Whitespace was used as a delimiter to separate the text data into words. Split strings are used to construct word tokens. Tokens were turned into whole sentences by the algorithm. The stop words are then eliminated and the text is lowercased. Words less than three letters are discarded. All of the words' stems are generated using a port stemmer. To tag parts of speech, a POS tag library was used.

MODEL ANALYSIS

Validation of Data

As soon as the necessary data has been gathered, the research team may begin creating the machine learning models. In this study, the obtained data was employed as a model parameter. Text and picture data have been converted for use as input features. The word vectors and processed pictures are the altered text data. To train the machine learning models, we plan to employ word vectors and processed photos as model features.

This study examined input qualities that may be used to improve training outcomes. Text-based NNs have been used to assess word vector lengths ranging from 100k to 100k. The least amount of data was lost when using 10,000-word vectors. The term "vector size" is used frequently in the research. Images ranging in size from 30 to 360 pixels have been tested. For 60x60 pictures, CNNs suffer similar training losses as for bigger images. For this reason, all CNN models employ a resolution of 60 pixels or less. Data sets of between 20k and 50k photos were used to evaluate each characteristic. Because they are easier to train with, smaller training sets were employed. The model's size and attributes can then be trained after the features have been specified. What we call "hyper parameters" are the properties of a particular model (Casari, 2017). Badly calibrated hyper parameters may lead to models that are unable to train effectively (Casari, 2017). Some models may be hindered by high learning rates or momentum that prevents them from convergent to the answer. If there are too many hidden layers, training and performance may suffer. Model over fitting or a strange weight distribution inside the neural network, as well as linked inputs, might be caused by a lack of regularization. The inability to recover picture details can be caused by a convolutional neural network filter with a big size.

In addition to page metrics, each Facebook page contains auxiliary page metrics that represent the page's popularity and the number of people who are following it. In this study, linear models were employed to evaluate the practicality of these characteristics. The advantage of linear models is that they can be trained significantly more quickly. The model's performance will improve as a result of greater features. Quick feedback is important in detecting performance characteristics. However, there was no clear correlation between the Facebook page stats and user involvement. Facebook page analytics were omitted from the input process due to their minimal association with user interaction.

Methodology

Scaling, standardization, and classification of data are all part of this application. Creating basic models is achievable following data processing. They can be linear, random, or convolutional neural networks. A certain model is better suited to processing a particular type of data (Krizhevsky et al., 2012). Convolutional neural networks, for example, are good at analyzing pictures. Text can be represented by a bag-of-words or tf-IDF text-based model. Predicting with Naive Bayes may be done by using word vectors. It is expected that basic features would be the main focus of the project. Machine learning models are likely to be used to create new features. It is possible to generate basic features using this model stacking technique. These characteristics can be included into other models. Models and data should be kept as basic as possible. It is simpler to understand and interpret basic data, and simple models handle data more quickly. Better features may be produced and tested using the methods outlined in this chapter.

Data Mining Process

Data mining was carried out using the Facebook API. Creating a Facebook app, getting tokens, and querying the data were all necessary steps in this data mining process. Tokens are Facebook's way of verifying a user's identity. For all Facebook questions, the token is required. This gives Facebook the ability to manage the flow of content. The application requests are throttled on an hourly and daily basis in order to limit the number of API calls that may be made at one time. Based on the amount of users in your application, your API throttles as well. Due to the fact that this program was not intended for general distribution, it was subject to more stricter API restrictions.

Selenium is used to gather AdEspresso URLs in the app. New pages were found by executing JavaScript to go across the web-site. Advertisement URLs were gathered by the Selenium program. No URLs may be used to access the website, and all requests must include an authentication token in order to proceed. One thousand pages of AdEspresso were manually accessed by the program. When the program failed, the list of previously viewed sites was automatically skipped. It was possible to run up to 20 Selenium instances at the same time by storing these page numbers in a shared file. In the database, only unique ad links are stored, therefore the data is unaffected by the presence of several urls. Pickle files with the.pkl file extension can be found on GitHub.

Figure 5. Data extraction and integration

From Espresso, the next app aggregated all of the Facebook links it could find. In the initial application, Facebook links were collected from Espresso pages. The Facebook page URLs were retrieved from those pages by this program. JavaScript was not used in this application. Rather, the data was acquired using the urllib module provided by the Python programming language. The page data is returned in response to Python queries. The HTML data is parsed by the Python software. The application was able to extract the URLs from the HTML. The researchers threaded the application because requesting is mostly I/O-intensive. This software was consistent and could keep running for days on end. A total of 281,090 different Facebook page connections were collected by the program. The data extraction and integration process is depicted in Figure 5.

Figure 6. Input of integrated model

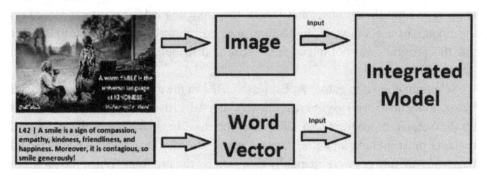

Scraping Facebook pages is possible once the software has obtained Facebook connections. As the third app, we crawled all of the Facebook URLs and harvested their posts. The post's content, picture, share count, and number of comments were all included in the data gathered. The information is kept in a database by the application. A large portion of the application's data comes from this section. Only the Facebook comments for each post were not included in the analysis. The latest Facebook post data gathering software gathered comment data for each post on the social networking site. Each Facebook post's comment data was obtained by the program. After that, the feedback was entered into a database. This data was utilized to train the machine learning models. Machine learning integrated model inputs are depicted in Figure 6.

Users' interactions were recorded and kept in a SQLite database. Posts and comments from Facebook were among the data sets analyzed. This study compiled all of the Facebook posts into a single table. The URL, UUID, and content of the post were included in this post. Additionally, the data in the Facebook post table includes other supporting information, making it simple to feed into a machine learning model without the need for joins. The number of fans, the number of page ratings, the general average page rating, and the number of people discussing about the page are some of the auxiliary data included in the report. Besides the number of comments, the post's text subjectivity is also taken into account in the metrics listed. Using Python's Vader package, this study developed sentiment measures. This is what the library did on social media. Comment data was saved in a basic database that just included the comment's content and its Facebook post ID. This data was used to train the models.

User interaction data underwent a first round of statistical analysis. Analysis of data distribution was carried out using R programming. The number of comments and shares closely resembles a gamma or Weibull curve. Comment counts and the gamma distribution may be analyzed using simple statistical models depicted in the figure. Figure 7 shows a distribution of comment sentiment that resembles a normal distribution.

Figure 7. Distribution of comment sentiment

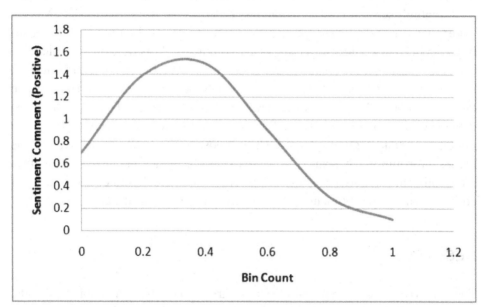

Existing technologies for sentiment analysis were employed in this study to gauge the sentiment of posts and comments. Initially, authors used Python's Blob library, but then quickly moved to the VADER Python library for study. Using a lexicon and a set of rules, the VADER (Valence Aware Dictionary and Sentiment Reasoner) program analyses text for emotional content and is well-suited to social media (Bodhi et al., 2021). Post and comment data were given polarity scores. The polarity scores from the comment data were used to train the sentiment model.

EXPERIMENTAL SETUP

There are a total of thirteen experiments in this study. Users' actions will be predicted by the experiments. Share counts, comment numbers, and comment sentiment are all expected user involvement metrics. What we're looking at here is the combination of a text and image-based convolutional neural network as well as a decision tree model, Word2Vec models, and Word2Vec models. The user engagement metric is predicted by four of the models. To test each of the three models, we run twelve experiments in each one. Finally, three Word2Vec models are used to estimate the emotion of the comments. One Word2Vec model to predict comment sentiment and four other models to predict user interaction totals five models and thirteen trials.

An entirely separate configuration was needed for the Word2Vec models. Models were trained on posts with supportive comments in order to discover fresh sentences by the model that would also get supportive comments. Posts were divided into three categories based on the results of the research. A favorable ($x >= 0.7$) group was separated from the neutral ($0.7 > x >= 0.3$) and the negative comment-making group ($x < 0.3$). A Word2Vec model was developed for each group. This study used test data to evaluate the model's score. Each model estimated how likely a post was to fall into a certain emotion category. The test post is assigned to the model with the highest probability. An evaluation of the model's accuracy in classifying postings into sentiment categories was made. The final score is determined by the ratio of correctly classified sentiments to incorrectly classified sentiments.

RESULTS

There are five different types of machine learning models examined in this study. As a result, there are five distinct models to choose from: Word2Vec, decision trees, and a combination of text-based neural networks with convolutional neural networks (NN/CNN). Models learn to anticipate how users will interact with them. The number of comments, the number of shares, and the frequency with which people leave comments are all measures of how much involvement users have with a post. Data sets of various sizes are used in the tests. 350k articles were used in training and testing for comment and share count analytics. Experiments on the sentiment of commenters have used data from more than 50,000 postings. These are the experimental sizes that the code defines. There is less data on comment sentiment since it is more complicated. The number of times and requests needed to collect post comments is increasing. API queries are limited to a certain number of times per Facebook page. The Python gensim package is used to create Word2Vec models (Řehůřek & Sojka, 2010). The Word2Vec models could not be trained on the 50k comment sentiment data set since it was too small. Because there was not enough data to train the algorithms on, they anticipated that all new phrases would have a 0% similarity.

The remaining twelve models were trained using the Keras package in Python. Models can't make predictions about discrete variables; instead, they must use regression. The regression models are evaluated using a loss function. The loss function is a means of describing how well the model matches the data it is trying to predict. The mean squared error is the loss value utilized to train these models. Other loss functions were also documented by Keras. Mean absolute error and cosine closeness are examples of these functions. There are twelve experiments depicted in Table-1. The variance is included in the results. Assuming that each anticipated value is average, the variance is the mean squared error. Models are more accurate when they are forecasting the mean squared error rather than constantly predicting the mean.

Table 1. Loss-to-gain ratio

Metrics	Variability	Integrated Neural Network Model Mean Square Error			
		Neural Network (Text Based)	Convolutional Neural Network (Image Based)	Integrated Decision Tree	Integrated Neural Network Model
Share	1.08	3.48	1.05	2.62	1
Sentiments	4.01	1.46	1.18	4.24	1
Comment	1.17	1.06	1.05	1.33	1

Using a loss-to-gain ratio, we can see the outcomes in Table-1. That's why we have a mean squared error of 1 in the integrated model (the last column). Due of the huge and difficult-to-compare mean squared errors, this is done. A simple ratio makes it easy to compare two columns of numbers. Across the board, the integrated model outperformed the competition. The integrated model had a loss that was smaller than its standard deviation. The integrated model beat the NN and CNN on a wide range of measures. Comment sentiment was best predicted by a mixed model. The integrated model was the weakest at estimating the number of shares in the market. On every parameter, the merged decision tree failed miserably. It's noteworthy to see that the CNN outperformed the NN across the board in every statistic. Performance on more difficult-to-predict indicators was given particular weight in the models' calculations.

Figure 8. Comparison of actual comment count and prediction

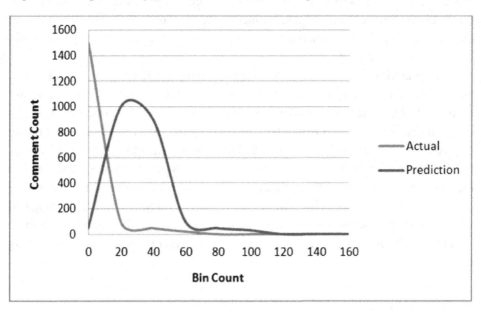

Figure 9. Comparison of actual share count and prediction

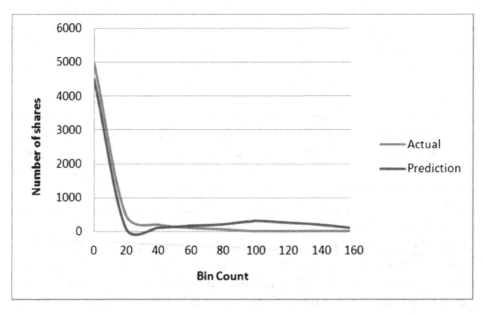

The integrated model outperformed the other machine learning models. Graph showing the integrated model's predictions in the chapter. Initial machine learning algorithms' predictions raised questions. Zero or one is a common outcome in the first models the left skew of the distribution is to blame for this. Predictions were strongly biased left as a result of this bias. Fortunately, this issue was not encountered while using the integrated modeling approach. As a result, the integrated model had a wider distribution of data. For the integrated model, the distributions in Figures 8-9 are shown.

FUTURE RESEARCH DIRECTIONS

In the future, this study's findings will be included into a single model. It's possible that each model learns something unique from the data. Especially in more complex models like the decision tree, this is the case. Each model has the potential to predict user behavior. This is expected to lead to improved precision. A coefficient of correlation of more than 0.4 may be found between share count and comment sentiment. This suggests that a share count model may be used to forecast the emotion of a community. If an ad does well in one statistic, it will also perform well in others. As a result, all 15 models can accurately predict the performance of a generic Facebook ad. Content suggestion might be a function of the new models. Filters, transformations, and rotations could all be applied by the software. As a result of this study, it is possible to predict user behavior. Predicting which alteration would result in an image that performs well on social media might be a result of this.

CONCLUSION

Research on anticipating user engagement is a growing field, and this study contributes to that body of work. Various machine learning models were examined in this study. The findings of this study were presented in a report. Using image and text-based models, this study developed two new models. A comparison was then made between the combined models and the text-based NN and the image-based CNN models. Text-based and image-based models were individually surpassed by the integrated model. CNN's social media data performance was also examined in this study. The text-based models were always surpassed by the image-based ones. The integrated model was applied to a real-world application in this study. Two advertisements were used as input for the model. Each advertisement's user engagement projections were then created by the program. For each post, the model predicted the number of comments, the number of shares, and the emotion of the comments. The actual user engagement numbers were compared to these forecasts. 50% of the time, the random model was right on the money. More than half the time the combination was true for comment count (59%) and share (55%) of the time. For future studies, the model's performance can be used as a standard.

REFERENCES

Antonio, G., & Sujit, P. (2017) *Deep Learning With Keras*. Packt Publishing.

Azizian, S., Rastegari, E., Ricks, B., & Hall, M. (2017). Identifying Personal Messages: A Step towards Product/Service Review and Opinion Mining. *2017 International Conference on Computational Science and Computational Intelligence (CSCI),* 876-881. 10.1109/CSCI.2017.152

Bodhi, R., Singh, T., & Rahman, S. (2021). Recent themes in social media research: A systematic review. *International Journal of Business Information Systems, 37*(3), 287. Advance online publication. doi:10.1504/IJBIS.2021.116081

Casari, A. (2017). *Mastering Feature Engineering Principles and Techniques for Data Scientists*. Oreilly Associates Inc.

Fisher, T. (2009). ROI in social media: A look at the arguments. *J Database Mark Cust Strategy Manag, 16*(3), 189–195. doi:10.1057/dbm.2009.16

Gelli, F., Uricchio, T., Bertini, M., Del Bimbo, A., & Chang, S.-F. (2015). *Image Popularity Prediction in Social Media Using Sentiment and Context Features.* Advance online publication. doi:10.1145/2733373.2806361

Gramlich, J. (2021, June). *10 Facts about Americans and Facebook*. Pew Research Center. https://www.pewresearch.org/fact-tank/2021/06/01/facts-about -americans-and-facebook

Krizhevsky, A., Sutskever, I., & Hinton, G. E. (2012). ImageNet Classification with Deep Convolutional Neural Networks. *Advances in Neural Information Processing Systems, 25,* 1097–1105.

Levi, G., & Hassncer, T. (2015). *Age and gender classification using convolutional neural networks*. . doi:10.1109/CVPRW.2015.7301352

Li, Y., Fang, C., Yang, J., Wang, Z., Lu, X., & Yang, M.-H. (2017). Diversified Texture Synthesis with Feed-Forward Networks. *2017 IEEE Conference on Computer Vision and Pattern Recognition (CVPR),* 266-274. 10.1109/CVPR.2017.36

Lin, H., Jia, J., Guo, Q., Xue, Y., Li, Q., Huang, J., Cai, L., & Feng, L. (2014). User-level psychological stress detection from social media using deep neural network. *MM 2014 - Proceedings of the 2014 ACM Conference on Multimedia*, 507-516. 10.1145/2647868.2654945

Liu, B. (2012). Sentiment Analysis and Opinion Mining. *Sentiment Analysis and Opinion Mining*, 5(May), 1–108. doi:10.2200/S00416ED1V01Y201204HLT016

Ohsawa, S., & Matsuo, Y. (2013). Like Prediction: Modeling Like Counts by Bridging Facebook Pages with Linked Data. *Proceedings of the 22Nd International Conference on World Wide Web Companion*, 541–548. 10.1145/2487788.2487992

Řehůřek, R., & Sojka, P. (2010). *Software Framework for Topic Modelling with Large Corpora*. doi:10.13140/2.1.2393.1847

Sánchez, J., Monzón, N., & Salgado, A. (2018). An Analysis and Implementation of the Harris Corner Detector. *Image Processing On Line.*, 8, 305–328. doi:10.5201/ipol.2018.229

Sarsam, S., Al-Samarraie, H., Alzahrani, A., & Wright, B. (2020). Sarcasm detection using machine learning algorithms in Twitter: A systematic review. *International Journal of Market Research*, 62(5), 578–598. Advance online publication. doi:10.1177/1470785320921779

Segalin, C., Cheng, D. S., & Cristani, M. (2017). Social profiling through image understanding: Personality inference using convolutional neural networks. *Computer Vision and Image Understanding*, 156, 34-50. doi:10.1016/j.cviu.2016.10.013

Shi, X. (2016). A Study on Factors Influencing the Click Through Rate, CTR, of Internet Ads by the Charging Mode of CPM (Cost per Mile) Based on Information Transfer. *International Journal of Simulation Systems, Science and Technology, 17*, 35.1-35.5. doi:10.5013/IJSSST.a.17.32.35

Smith, A., & Anderson, M. (2018). *Social Media Use 2018: Demographics and Statistics*. Pew Research Center. https://www.pewresearch.org/internet/2018/03/01/social-media-use-in-2018/

Straton, N., Mukkamala, R. R., & Vatrapu, R. (2015). *Big Social Data Analytics for Public Health: Predicting Facebook Post Performance using Artificial Neural Networks and Deep Learning*. Academic Press.

Wang, L., Zhang, K., Liu, X., Long, E., Jiang, J., An, Y., Zhang, J., Liu, Z., Lin, Z., Li, X., Chen, J., Cao, Q., Li, J., Wu, X., Wang, D., Li, W., & Lin, H. (2017). Comparative analysis of image classification methods for automatic diagnosis of ophthalmic images. *Scientific Reports*, 7(1), 41545. doi:10.1038rep41545 PMID:28139688

Wang, Y., Wang, S., Tang, J., Liu, H., & Li, B. (2015). Unsupervised sentiment analysis for social media images. In *IJCAI International Joint Conference on Artificial Intelligence* (pp. 2378-2379). International Joint Conferences on Artificial Intelligence.

Xu, C. (2014). *Visual Sentiment Prediction with Deep Convolutional Neural Networks*. Available at: https://arxiv.org/abs/1411.5731

You, Q. (2015). *Robust Image Sentiment Analysis Using Progressively Trained and Domain Transferred Deep Networks*. AAAI. doi:10.1609/aaai.v29i1.9179

Chapter 9

NLP Techniques and Challenges to Process Social Media Data

Tawseef Ahmad Mir
Baba Ghulam Shah Badshah University, India

Aadil Ahmad Lawaye
 https://orcid.org/0000-0003-4072-2043
Baba Ghulam Shah Badshah University, India

Akib Mohi Ud Din Khanday
United Arab Emirates University, Al Ain, UAE

ABSTRACT

Social media, a buzz term in the modern world, refers to various online platforms like social networks, forums, blogs and blog comments, microblogs, wikis, media sharing platforms, social bookmarks through which communication between individuals, communities, or groups takes place. People over social media do not only share their ideas and opinions, but it has become an important source through which businesses promote their products. Analyzing huge data generated over social media is useful in various tasks like analyzing customer trends, forecast sales, understanding opinions of people on different hot topics, views of customers about services/products, and many more. Different natural language processing (NLP) techniques are used for crawling and processing social media data to get useful insights out of this. In this chapter, the focus is on various NLP techniques used to process the social media data. Challenges faced by NLP techniques to process social media data are also put forward in this chapter.

DOI: 10.4018/978-1-6684-6909-5.ch009

INTRODUCTION

The use of social media has grown exponentially in the last few years and it has changed the scenario of how communication takes between individuals, groups, and communities (Hallock et al., 2019; Shahbaznezhad et al., 2021; Khanday et al., 2021). Social media means the use of electronic and internet tools with the aim of sharing and discussing ideas and opinions with other people in a productive way (Durgam, 2018). Information shared over various social media platforms can be in textual form or in the form of audio, pictures, videos, etc. Various social media platforms that are commonly used in the present era can be broadly classified into four types, viz. content-sharing sites, blogs, forums, and microblogs (Farzindar & Inkpen, 2020). Content-sharing sites provide users with the facility to share information in different forms like text, photos, audio, and videos. Commonly used online content-sharing sites with a large user base are Facebook, Flickr, Instagram, TikTok, WeChat, YouTube, and Foursquare (Kinsella et al., 2009; Zuo et al., 2021). Web user forums are used by users to post specialized information, queries, or solutions to queries. Some of the forums include Apple Support, Imgur, Final Thoughts, GamesSpot, Quora, phpBB, Stack Overflow, and CNET forums (Hoogeveen et al., 2018). A blog is a type of online platform that allows a user to self-description and interact with others (Miura & Yamashita, 2007; Hain & Back, 2008). Blogs allow individuals to put their ideas and opinions online or make comments on the ideas shared by others (Mansouri & Piki, 2016). On blogs posts appear in chronological order i.e., recent posts about a topic appear at the top. Examples of popular blogs include A Cup of Jo[1], Lifehacker[2], Hot Air[3], Gizmodo[4], Mashable[5] and many others. Microblogs (like Sina Weibo, Twitter, Pinterest, Tumblr, Plurk, and Reddit) on the other hand are used to share information and opinions with limited length (Zhang et al., 2014; Garg & Pahuja, 2021; Khanday et al., 2023).

With the increase in the population of the world, the number of social media users is also growing at a rapid pace. This is due to the wide coverage of social media platforms and their user-friendliness. Social media has become an integral part of life and a wide range of information is available on it in different forms (Pekkala & van Zoonen, 2022; Borah et al., 2022). During its initial phase young population was mainly active on social media but with time the trend changed and now people belonging to all age groups make use of different social media platforms. It has transformed the way people communicate and express their ideas and opinions. People use social media platforms for different purposes like socializing, business, politics, entertainment, dating, day-to-day communication, and education. According to Statista[6], the largest portal for statistics, 63% (5 billion) of the total world population make use of the internet as of April 2022. Out of this 93% (4.65 billion) were using

Table 1. Ten most popular social media platforms

S. No	Social Media Platform	Purpose
1	Facebook[7]	Launched in 2004 is currently the most popular social network with the largest user base. Allows users to create a profile and connect with people from any part of the world and share their thoughts and expressions in the form of text, audio, pictures, and videos.
2	YouTube[8]	A popular video-sharing platform where a user can upload, share, watch, like, dislike, download videos, and also post comments on the videos shared. To upload videos a user has to create a channel and create a playlist to organize the content uploaded. A user can also subscribe to channels created by other people.
3	WhatsApp[9]	It is a popular messaging application where people communicate with one another via messages, audio, and video calls. A user can also create a group and add members to it. Also used by businesses to deliver customer services and provide the latest updates regarding their services.
4	Instagram[10].	Social-networking platform found in 2010 and is used for sharing photos and videos. The media shared is organized using hashtags and geographical tags. Users can apply various filters to the images they upload on Instagram.
5	WeChat[11]	Chinese application used for texting, voice messaging, audio & video calling, photo and video sharing, and location sharing. By creating a public account, it allows a user to interact with subscribers and communicate with them. It has also the facility to make payments and transfer money to other users.
6	TikTok[12]	It is a video hosting service that allows users to create short-duration videos with music in the background. Videos of different types like pranks, dance, stunts, jokes, and tricks are shared on this platform. Users are also able to comment on specific videos. A user can store a video in a draft and post it later.
7	Facebook Messenger[13]	Instant messaging application used for one-to-one or group chats. Users can also share pictures, voice, and videos with their phone contacts or Facebook friends. Users can also share their location in messages.
8	Douyin[14]	It is a multimedia app used in China with same features as TikTok. Allows users to create, share, edit short duration videos. It also has features like live Q&A and live stream which makes it suitable marketing tool.
9	QQ[15]	Web portal and messaging platform which offers services for group and voice chat, shopping, social games, microblogging, movies and music.
10	Sina Weibo[16]	Is one of the most popular microblogging websites in China. Users can view most popular posts, send text messages share pictures or videos, follow others, receive rewards and can also comment on the content available on it.

social media platforms. The ten most popular used social media platforms that have a wide user base are given in Table 1.

Other important social media platforms include Kuaishou, Snapchat, Telegram, Pinterest, Twitter, Reddit, and Quora. The number of social media users is increasing at a very high rate and Facebook has the highest number of monthly active users. As per Statista, there were about 2.93 billion monthly active users on Facebook in the second quarter of 2022. In January 2022 India was having highest (330 million)

Figure 1. Number of monthly active facebook users worldwide as of 2nd quarter 2022 (in millions)
Source: Provided by Statista

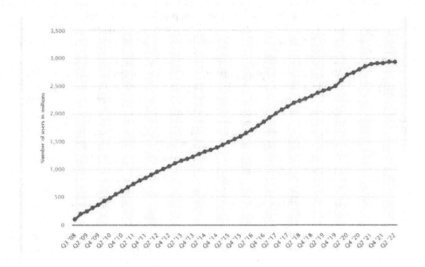

Figure 2. Distribution of Facebook users belonging to different age groups as of Jan 2022
Source: Provided by Statista

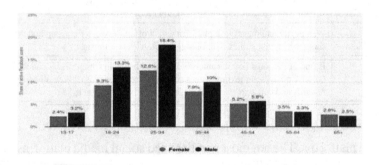

number of monthly active Facebook users followed by the USA with about 179 million monthly active users. Indonesia and Brazil also have more than 100 million Facebook users. As of the second quarter of 2022 Figure 1. gives the number of monthly active Facebook users worldwide in millions.

Even though Facebook is popular among people of all groups but users within the age group 25-34 form the major part of the total users. Figure 2 depicts the monthly active Facebook users belonging to different age groups as per the January 2022 report of Statista.

Not only Facebook people in the world use other social media networks on a great scale. Figure 3 provides the statistics provided by Statista of monthly active social media users on different platforms as of January 2022.

Due to the rapid increase in the number of social media users, the data generated on these platforms is very huge and has different forms. This data is useful from various aspects making its analysis very important. Insights obtained from social media analysis help businesses to enhance their customer satisfaction (Ramanathan et al., 2017), communicate with customers, promote employee collaborations (Bharati et al., 2015; Chui et al., 2012), protect brand health, promote tourism (Gebreel & Shuayb, 2022), understand the opinions of people about topics of interest, crisis management (Saroj & Pal. 2020), enlarge product launches, maintain law and order, etc. As a result of this, it necessitates developing tools and techniques to process this data. Research on creating tools and techniques to handle social media data has gained popularity during the past few years. Natural Language Processing (NLP) techniques used to process the data from a natural language have been explored to process the data coming out of social media platforms. But the traditional NLP techniques do not show better results when applied to social media data (Hu & Liu, 2012; Hasbullah et al., 2016). This is mainly due to the difference in the language used by social media users.

Although communication over social media takes various forms a large content is available in the form of text. People at large scale post their ideas or opinions, express emotions, post comments, etc. in textual form. Much of the research work that has been conducted over the last many years focuses on processing textual data. The use of NLP for social media data processing is a relatively new area of study, and both conventional and novel NLP methods are being developed to carry out this task. As conventional NLP techniques are developed with the aim to process data coming from natural languages which follow the formal syntax rules their performance on social media is not good enough if applied directly to social media data. They need to be adapted to tackle the issues associated with social media data so as to give reasonable results when used on social media data. The main motive of this chapter is to contribute to the literature on various NLP techniques that are used to process social media data. The main objectives of this chapter are:

- Discuss various challenges to process social media data.
- Discuss important preprocessing techniques used in NLP with their adaptation to process social media data and recent research works in this regard.
- Discuss recent NLP methods for social media applications that are meant to infer useful insights from social media data.

Figure 3. Number of monthly active users (in millions) on most popular social media platforms as of January 2022
Source: Provided by Statista

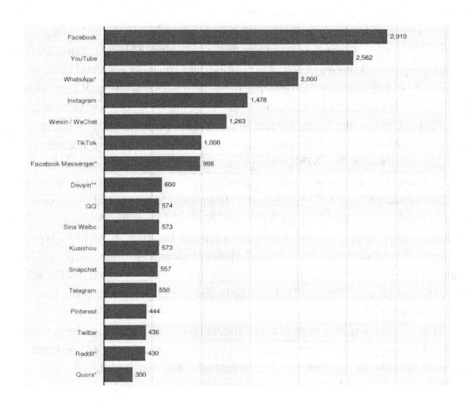

NLP AND SOCIAL MEDIA

NLP is the sub-field of Artificial Intelligence that enables computers to understand and generate natural language as human beings do (Cambria & White, 2014). With the help of NLP, computers can read, analyze and interpret natural language. It combines statistical, machine learning, and deep learning models to make computer systems capable to understand and interpret the way humans communicate (Kiela et al., 2021). Research in NLP started more than 50 years back and has been an area of interest for researchers for so long. It has applications in many fields like machine translation, speech recognition, sentiment analysis, document classification, information extraction and retrieval, question answering, spam filtering, chatbots and voice assistants, automatic summarization, search autocorrect, and autocompletes targeted advertising, management research, construction (Jusoh, 2018; Kang et al., 2020; Ding et al., 2022). Huge research work exists in all these NLP applications and the research is still going on smoothly. Nowadays the use of social media is very common and huge data get generated on daily basis from different social media platforms this needs to be processed so as to extract useful information from it. But data generated from social media platforms is different from that of natural languages and it poses great challenges to the researchers. Various challenges that make the processing of data generated from social media platforms difficult are discussed below.

Challenges to Process Social Media Data

Data generated from various social media platforms like Facebook, YouTube, Instagram, Twitter, etc. is highly dynamic and is generated by people living across the globe belonging to different cultures, religions, castes, regions, etc. Standard NLP techniques when applied to social media data are confronted with various problems due to the nature of the content in social media data. Text generated on different social media platforms is generally informal and contains a huge number of spelling variations, foreign languages, grammatical negligence, filled with dialects, noise, etc. making processing it very difficult (Zarnoufi et al., 2020).

Everyone has now become a potential user of social media, not just well-educated individuals who are familiar with the grammatical conventions of a language. Social media users utilize language that is more comfortable for them rather than utilizing the proper language. Tweets or comments posted by users or status updated by them are more informal and are usually written in a conversational fashion rather than following proper rules of natural language. Grammatical errors and frequent use of fragments as actual sentences complicate the syntactic analysis of social media texts. The presence of these problems makes the automatic processing of social media data for various applications very difficult.

Social media users make use of multiple languages instead of sticking to a single language in the same conversation. Writing or speaking in multilingual instead of monolingual is termed as code-mixing (Thara & Poornachandran, 2018). The use of code-mixing has become a common practice on social media and people use it frequently (Shafie & Nayan, 2013; Barman et al., 2014; Tarihoran & Sumirat, 2022). Code mixing can be intra-sentential or inter-sentential. Intra-sentential code mixing means when the words belonging to different languages are present in the same sentence. Inter-sentential code mixing means when different languages are used in different sentences and it is also termed as code-switching. The use of intra-sentential code-mixing is more common in a social media text. Insertion, alternation, and congruent lexicalization are common patterns used in code-mixing. Insertion means when a code belonging to a different language is inserted into a text written in some other language. For example,

mujhe *clear* batao hua kya.

In this sentence written in Hindi language word *clear* is English.

In alternation, different phrases in a sentence belong to a different language. For example,

tum mujhe dara rahe ho, I don't care.

In this sentence, the first phrase *tum mujhe dara rahe ho* is written in Hindi whereas the second phrase *I don't care* is written in English.

In congruent lexicalizations, tokens from different languages are used randomly in the same sentence. Using code mixing poses a great challenge to traditional NLP techniques when employed on social media data.

Another trend that has been quite famous in social media is the use of non-standard abbreviations (Hilte et al., 2019). People on social media make use of various non-standard abbreviations quite often like *gm* is used by some people to express good morning. Some other abbreviations include *loml* (love of my life), *oomm* (out of my mind), *gnt/gn8* (good night), *lol* (laugh out loudly). The use of non-standard abbreviations and variations in words depends on the user. Using traditional NLP techniques need to handle such non-standard abbreviations while processing social media data. These non-standard abbreviations or variations in them can be transformed to the original form by considering commonly used abbreviations.

Another issue that traditional NLP techniques face while processing social media data is the detection of sentence boundaries and tokenization. Natural languages have a proper way of ending a sentence and detecting sentence boundaries is a straightforward process whereas in social media data processing this process is also complex. Social media users make use of discrepant practices to specify sentence boundaries, like different punctuation marks (e.g., '????' and '!!!!'), mixing different punctuation marks (such as '!?' or '...?'), emoticons (such as ':(', ':D', ':)', '♥', etc.), multiple periods (such as ., ..., ...). In social media data, proper punction marks are missing at times and may also contain improper use of capitalization complicating the process of tokenization and sentence boundary detection. (Rudrapal et al., 2015) proposed a rule-based as well as machine-learning approach to cope up with the problem of sentence boundary detection in social media. In (Kaur & Singh, 2019) deep neural network approach is proposed for sentence boundary marking and suggesting relevant punctuation marks in code mixed data from social media.

In social media, people use different languages in the same sentence and often make use of phonetic typing. Some words have the same surface form like the word "to" is written in Punjabi as "ਤ" whereas in Hindi it is written as "तो". While processing such words resolving ambiguity is a challenging task.

While writing in a natural language users type carefully and many mistakes committed are corrected automatically by the auto-spelling checking feature available on word processing applications whereas on social media due to the use of phonetic typing many words are typed falsely and the auto-spelling correction feature is not of much use.

While writing posts or comments on different social media platforms users make use of the repetition of characters to make emphasis on the actual word (Vijay et al., 2018). For example, in the comment #*Sooooo nice....* the character *o* is repeated five times. Traditional NLP methods need to be adapted to process such character repetitions existing in the words used in social media comments or posts.

Features of a social media platform used to communicate and the way it is used also impacts the summarization process. For example, on Twitter, a user post can have a maximum length of 280 characters making the individual posts contextually poor in comparison to traditional documents (Metzler et al., 2012;). Retweeting the posts on the other hand results in data redundancy making it another challenge for the summarization process. It has been a major challenge to extract useful information from Twitter streams while removing dull and polluted text from the posts for the purpose of detecting hot topics. Other issues that are common in Twitter posts include data sparseness, syntax errors, mixed usage of languages, variations in sentence structure, and diversity in the usage of vocabulary (Atefeh & Khreich, 2015; Alsaeedi et al., 2019). All these issues pose a great challenge to traditional text analysis techniques and make them less fruitful for the analysis of Twitter data.

Another feature that is prominent in social media data is topic drift due to the continuity in the generation of new data. In comparison to traditional data which is mostly static and self-contained social media data is highly dynamic and new data is generated at a very high pace from various social media platforms and various actors are involved in the communication (Sapountzi & Psannis, 2018). On one side this sort of dynamicity in the data is a challenge to the conventional summarization techniques whereas, on the other side it adds to the context which aids in the summarization process and paves ways to explore new summarization techniques.

Social media data also contains cognitive errors due to the unfamiliarity of the users with the proper usage of language. The cognitive error takes place when a user makes use of an incorrect word instead of the correct word as per the context. The sense of the used incorrect word is not as per the sentence context however the spelling of the word is correct. For example, in the sentence *"hey are you their"* the word *there is* used instead of *there*. Such errors can be tackled with the help of the bigram corpus. Similarly, while writing comments or posts using phonetic typing on social media users do the phonetic mis-spellings which can be easily understood by humans but these things are a challenge when the data needs to be processed using NLP techniques. For example, in the sentence *"mujhe tum se baat nhi karni"* the actual spelling for the word "नह□" is n*ahi* instead of n*hi*.

The use of multiword tokens has become a trend among users on different social media platforms (Manjunath, 2022). People on WhatsApp, Twitter, Instagram, and Facebook make use of shortcuts like *asap* for "as soon as possible" *gbu* for "God Bless You" etc. Also, words that do not belong to any language are used on social media like hahaha (used to express amusement). Emoticons are also common on social media and are used to express emotions like:- | which signifies disappointed and:-) which shows happiness.

In short, the conventional NLP methods face numerous challenges while analyzing social media data to get useful information from it. In order to process data generated over various social media platforms some NLP techniques like Normalization, noise reduction, term expansion, and improved feature selection have been put forward to enhance the clustering performance in Twitter (Beverungen & Kalita, 2011). Locating named entities like person names, time expressions, organizations, monetary values medical codes, and locations in the social media data would require sophisticated named-entity recognition techniques. Language detection techniques are required to detect the language used in social media. Options to develop socially aware systems and understand the social behavior of social media users are being explored with the aim to analyze language and its significance in various fields like sociolinguistics, psycholinguistics, etc.

NLP PRE-PROCESSING TECHNIQUES

In this section NLP preprocessing techniques with their adaptation to process social media data are discussed. The performance of the tools used by various researchers to carry out preprocessing is also highlighted.

In order to develop tools and applications that aim to interpret and extract the applicative information from the text the raw text need to go through various pre-processing stages. Various NLP techniques are used to pre-process the text and make it usable for analysis purposes. However, the conventional NLP tools used to pre-process the text are trained on the text that is carefully edited and has a formal structure. Due to the informal and ungrammatical nature of social media text conventional NLP tools do not show the performance that is required hence need to be adapted to give a well-founded performance on these social media texts (Mireshghallah et al., 2022). Two approaches are being used to make NLP tools perform reasonably on social media text namely; a) text normalization and b) Re-training NLP tools using social media data (Farzindar & Inkpen, 2015).

Text Normalization

The aim of text normalization is to make social media data as similar as possible to formal text on which the NLP model is trained. Normalization enhances the performance of many NLP tasks like Named Entity Recognition (NER), Part of Speech (POS) tagging, machine translation, etc. (Ariffin & Tiun, 2020). It is carried out in two phases; in the first phase various differences that pose challenges to conventional NLP tools to process social media data are detected and in the second phase these difficulties are resolved. In normalization, the misspelled words are corrected by consulting a dictionary consisting of known rightly spelled words. With the help of this dictionary out of vocabulary words can be easily filtered out. However due to its conversational nature social media data cannot become fully formal and the basic normalization procedure is not of much use for tasks like named entity recognition in the case of Twitter data (Derczynski et al., 2013). Also, Twitter text normalization to formal English results in lossy translation (Han and Baldwin, 2011).

(Demir, 2016) have used context-tailored text normalization in this research work. In this noise is reduced by comparing the non-standard and standard terms contextually and lexically. If there is a context match between non-standard terms and standard text then the non-standard terms are tailored into a direct match. The model is evaluated on a Turkish dataset containing formal Turkish text and Turkish tweets and yielded state-of-art accuracy. (Maitama et al., 2014) proposed an automatic text normalization algorithm for Facebook chats posted in the Hausa Language. In this study, a manually created dictionary is used to map non-standard terms to their corresponding standard terms. They evaluated the proposed model on 129 non-standard terms and the model normalized all the non-standard terms accurately. (Tiwari and Naskar, 2017) proposed text normalization technique for social media based on Deep Neural Networks. The model is implemented using Recurrent Neural Network based Encoder-Decoder architecture. For training and evaluation purposes WNUT[17] shared task dataset and Synthetic datasets developed were used. The model showed state of art performance (F1 score of 0.9098) with an improvement of 7% than previous works on the WNUT test dataset. (Khan & Lee, 2021) proposed a hybrid normalization technique for social media data. They integrated the deep learning text-analysis models with Textual Variations Handler (TVH) to enhance the model performance. (Vehomäki, 2022) used bidirectional recurrent neural networks (BRNN) and ByT5 (Xue et al., 2022) foundation model for normalization of social media text in Finnish language. From the experiments it was observed that ByT5 models outperform BRNN models.

Normalization can be basic or advanced. Basic normalization takes care of errors like spelling mistakes, errors related to the part of speech (POS) tagging, detecting unknown words, etc. whereas advanced normalization which is more flexible makes use of an automatic supervised approach where the model is trained with the help of annotated dataset.

Re-Training NLP Tools Using Social Media Data

This is the second approach to adapt the conventional NLP tools to show good performance on social media text. This method is easy to implement in comparison to the first approach if the training dataset is available. In order to train the model for a specific task we need annotated dataset related to the task. However, annotated datasets for social media tasks are rare which hinders the usage of this approach and it is a hard and time-consuming task to develop the annotated manually.

Although some annotated social media datasets have been created, their size is not sufficiently vast in order to effectively train NLP models. NLP tools are re-trained using these available annotated social media datasets along with the already available training datasets so that the size of the training dataset becomes large enough. Also, the small annotated dataset is used in addition to some untagged datasets to train the NLP model. Another issue that needs to be taken into consideration while choosing the social media data for developing annotated datasets is to select the platform from which the data is to be used for developing training datasets. In comparison to posts posted on other forums and blogs tweets have a maximum length of 280 characters only which forces the users to make use of shortened forms of words and abbreviations more frequently. As a result of this, Twitter data is more difficult to process than the data coming out from blogs and forums. Therefore, the data for training the NLP models need to be carefully selected.

Cirqueira et al. (2018) have categorized various preprocessing methods that are employed on social media data for sentiment analysis into seven different categories. These include Transformation, Deletion, Expansion and Replacement, Correction and Replacement, Content Extraction, Identifier Replacement, and Polarity Computation. Various pre-processing techniques that are employed on the text to make it usable for various applications along with their adaptation to social media data are discussed below.

Tokenization

Tokenization is the first pre-processing technique applied to the given data with the aim to split the given data into individual lexical items. The NLP tool that deals with the tokenization of the given input data is called a tokenizer. Here the first question arises how we can detect the individual tokens from the given input. White space usually indicates the token boundary in most natural languages with the exception of some languages like Chinese and Japanese. Using white spaces only as the indicator of token boundary is however not sufficient, we need to take into consideration many other issues related to tokenization. We have to decide what a word is. Even though the word is a string of characters but at times it is not apparent whether a string is a word or not. Also, the text contains various punction marks that need to be separated from the words in most cases but on some occasions, punction marks are part of a word. For example, in the sentence *"Tokenization, stemming, lemmatization, part of speech tagging, etc. are some NLP tasks."* the words *"tokenization"* *"stemming"* and *"lemmatization"* have comma appended but it is not part of these words, and need to be removed, however punctuation mark dot *"."* is a part of the abbreviation *"etc."*. Contractions like *I'll, don't,* etc. are also found in the text data which needs to be expanded to full words i.e. *I'll* to I will and *don't* to do not. The use of commas is also common with numbers like 10,000 in these cases the commas need not to be removed.

Tokenization involves detecting sentence boundaries and token boundaries. The absence of white spaces in text complicates the tokenization process. Tokenization is not constrained to tokens or punctuation marks in some cases tokenization may be required to split the text into syllables. The type of tokenization that is required depends on the type of task. Character tokenization is suited for tasks like spell checking, word tokenization is used in most of the applications, whereas Bert models make use of subword tokenization. Some words need to be grouped so that they give proper meaning like "New York". Combining more than one word and treating them as a single token is called n-grams.

In order to tokenize the given input text different tokenizers are already available; NLTK (Natural Language Toolkit) a Python library provides different tokenizers to tokenize the data. Some tokenizers available are dedicated to specific tasks like WordPunctTokenizer handles the punctuation whereas TweerTokenizer performs the tweet tokenization. While developing the tokenization algorithms different issues that need to be dealt with include the language of the text that is to be tokenized and the character set used to encode the text, the application for which tokenized text is to be used, and the characteristics of the corpus that is to be processed (Palmer, 2000).

(Toleu et al., 2017) addressed various issues related to the tokenization and segmentation of sentences. In this study, researchers have proposed character-based deep learning models to perform tokenization and sentence segmentation. These are independent of rule and feature engineering. A training set is used in which each character is tagged with an Inside-Outside-Beginning (IOB) label. IOB or like annotation treats tokenization and segmentation as a single sequence-labeling task. Three neural network-based models are designed for the experimentation purpose namely; (a) fully connected feed-forward network; (b) bidirectional Long Short Term Memory (BiLSTM) and (c) Long Short Term Memory (LSTM). Evaluation of the proposed models is carried out on datasets for three different languages namely Italian, English, and Kazakh, and the results obtained are contrasted to the results reported in the research work presented by (Evang et al., 2013). The findings demonstrated that applying character-based deep learning techniques produced better results for token boundary detection as well as competitive outcomes for sentence segmentation.

When we talk of tokenization of social media text it is more complicated and needs to take care of various issues in addition to those present in regular text. Presence of emoticons, hashtags, and usernames in Twitter (identified by # and @ respectively), URLs need to be treated as tokens without excluding punctuation symbols. In the research work of (Derczynski et al., 2013) tokenizer for Twitter is evaluated giving an F-score measure of about 80%. When regular expressions specific to Twitter messages were used the F-score enhanced to 96%.

Stop Word Removal

Stop word removal is a common preprocessing step in natural language processing, including social media data analysis. Stop words are words that are commonly used in language but do not provide much meaning to the text, such as "the," "a," "an," "and," etc. Removing stop words from social media data can help to reduce the size of the data, make it easier to process, and improve the accuracy of the analysis.

However, stop word removal should be used with caution when dealing with social media data, as these platforms often have their own unique language patterns and abbreviations that may be considered stop words but are actually important to understanding the meaning of the text. For example, in Twitter data, hashtags and mentions should not be removed as they provide important context to the tweet.

Stemming

Stemming is a natural language processing technique that involves reducing words to their root or base form, which can help with information retrieval and analysis (Jivani, 2011). In social media data, stemming can be particularly useful for tasks such as sentiment analysis and topic modeling. In social media data, people often use a variety of slang, abbreviations, and misspellings, which can make it difficult to accurately identify the underlying sentiment or topic. By using stemming, these variations can be reduced to their base form, making it easier to identify patterns and trends in the data. For example, if someone uses the word "running" in a tweet, stemming would reduce it to its base form "run". There are two types of stemming techniques. One is the rule-based technique which acts according to the specific rules of a natural language. The second one is the statistical stemming technique which is based on lexical analysis, discovering the co-occurrence of terms in the corpus, and unsupervised learning of the language. A systematic survey of both these stemming techniques is presented in (Singh & Gupta, 2017).

(Maylawati et al., 2018) proposed a novel stemming algorithm for Indonesian social media data with slang. The proposed stemming algorithm showed better performance than other research works existing. However, the proposed algorithm is memory expensive comparatively. (Pradana & Hayaty, 2019) analyzed the role of stemming and stop word removal on the performance of sentiment analysis. The experiments were carried out on tweets in Indonesian language. (Rizki et al., 2019) evaluated the performance of different stemming algorithms on Twitter data. (Cyril et al., 2021) analyzed the impact of stemming on text classification. Machine learning approach based on SVM is used to carry out text classification on data taken from Twitter. The results show that the proposed stemming algorithm enhanced the accuracy of text classification algorithm.

Part of Speech (POS) Tagging

Part of Speech (POS) tagging means associating with each token extracted from the given input text its lexical category (Lawaye & Purkayastha, 2013; Lawaye & Purkayastha, 2014). Some important lexical categories that are tagged to the tokens are nouns, pronouns, verbs, adverbs, interjections, adjectives, conjunctions, etc. In order to assign a POS category to a given token different tag sets are available notably the Penn Treebank tagset (Marcus et al., 1993). Tagsets for various Indian languages and their performance in POS tagging is reported in (Chandra et al.,

2014). While developing a tagset for POS tagging important issues that need to be kept in view include coarseness vs fineness, syntactic vs lexical category, and new tags vs already available standard tags. Due to the ambiguity, a word can have more than one tag and to solve this problem the context in which the word exists is used to assign an appropriate POS tag to it instead of considering the individual word.

Techniques that are used for POS tagging are of three types; (i) rule-based POS tagging approach (Sadredini et al., 2018), (ii) statistical POS tagging approach (Rathod & Govilkar, 2015), and (iii) hybrid POS tagging approach (Hadni et al., 2013). In the rule-based approach, a token is assigned a POS tag according to a set of handwritten linguistic rules and information present in the context. The main drawback faced by these approaches is that they don't work on the unknown text. Statistical based POS tagging approach work on the basis of probability and frequency. In its simplest form, the statistical-based POS approach assigns a POS tag to a token on the basis of the probability of its occurrence with a specific POS tag. This approach faces with the problem that the tag sequence generated by the tagger may be incorrect according to the language syntax rules. A hybrid approach for POS tagging performs tagging using features of both rule-based and statistical-based POS tagging approaches. To develop the efficient POS tagger researchers are currently working on machine learning and deep learning techniques. In (Chiche & Yitagesu, 2022) machine learning and deep learning techniques used for POS tagging are reviewed. It discusses the strengths and weaknesses and evaluation metrics of POS approaches proposed by different researchers in recent years. It also provides directions and recommendations to enhance the existing POS models based on machine learning and deep learning.

Using POS taggers developed for formal text need to be retrained in order to make them applicable to the social media data. To be useful for tagging social media data the existing POS tagsets need to be extended. (Ritter et al., 2011) have used the Penn Treebank tagset to annotate the Twitter data consisting of 800 tweets. For Twitter-specific features like @usernames, URLs, and #hashtags new tags are added. These types of words can be tagged with high accuracy by using regular expressions but need to be added to features for retraining the model. (Neunerdt et al., 2013) introduced annotated social media dataset and retrained four different state-of-art POS taggers on it. The results reported on evaluation showed domain-specific training data enhances the performance of all state-of-art taggers by a significant margin. In (Gupta et al., 2017) supervised POS tagger based on a Conditional Random Field classifier for mixed Indian social media data is proposed. In this study, three language pairs (English-Hindi, English-Telugu, and English-Bengali) are taken into consideration for three social media platforms namely Facebook, WhatsApp, and Twitter. The model successfully tagged the data with both coarse-grained POS tags as well as fine-grained POS tags. The system shows good performance in all domains for all three language pairs and is generic in nature.

As recent approaches in NLP are based on deep neural networks researchers have explored these approaches in POS task. (Meftah & Semmar, 2018) proposed Convolutional Neural Networks based model for social media POS tagging. Transfer Learning is implemented to overcome the annotated dataset scarcity. The proposed model is evaluated on social media data in five different languages (French, English, Spanish, German, and Italian).

(Bharti et al., 2022) proposed heuristic based for Hindi POS tagging. Forward and backward bigram sequences are created using the context-based bigram model to predict the POS of the target word. The researchers compared the results of the proposed model with existing state-of-art techniques like conditional random fields, the Hidden Markov Model, neural networks, Decision Trees, and recurrent neural networks and showed that it outperforms all these existing models.

Chunking and Parsing

Chunking is the process of analyzing the text to detect its various constituents (noun phrases, adjectival phrases, verb phrases, and adverbial phases) (Arora et al., 2013). An NLP tool called chunker is used to perform chunking and it performs so by identifying the boundaries of various constituents present in the given text. Chunker does not connect different constituents of the sentence to check its syntactic structure. On the other hand, in parsing the text is analyzed for its conformity with the syntax of the language. The parse trees derived as a result of parsing are useful in extracting useful information from the text. Like POS taggers parsers are also developed based on rule-based approaches, statistical approaches, and deep neural networks. A parser employing neural-network is proposed in the study presented by Chen and Manning (2014). The dependency parser presented is trained using a dataset extracted from a newspaper. Comparative analysis of different parsing strategies is presented in Kaur et al. (2019). The study analyzes the LR parsing, its development and implementation. Comparative analysis of the different parsing strategies showed that LR parsing is efficient than other parsing strategies.

Li et al. (2022) proposed a semantic dependency parser based on Graphical Neural Networks. The proposed model has been evaluated on SemEval 2015 Task 18 datasets for three languages namely; Czech, Chinese, and English. The results shown by the proposed model showed improvement from the previous research works. The experiments also showed that higher-order information encoded by Graphical Neural Networks is very beneficial for semantic parsing.

Parsers developed for formal text show poor performance when applied to social media text. In Foster et al. (2011) four dependency parsers when evaluated using newspaper text showed an F-score of about 90%, and the performance degraded by 10-20% when applied to social media data extracted from Twitter and discussion forums. However, the parsers showed an improvement in performance when retrained on small annotated social media text along with large unannotated social media data.

Sharma et al. (2016) presented a shallow-parsing technique to parse English-Hindi social media data. In this study, a dataset comprising of 858 posts extracted from social media is annotated out of which about 70% of the posts contain mixed English-Hindi language. The system first identifies the language of the given input, normalizes it, assigns POS labels to the tokens, and finally divides it into chunks.

In Singkul et al. (2019) a suitable dependency parser is identified for Thai social data. To identify the suitable parser six models out of which four graph-based models and two transition-based models are analyzed and the social dataset from the financial domain is obtained from Facebook, Pantip, and Twitter. The dataset collected from various social media platforms is divided into Elementary Discourse Units (EDUs) and contains a sum of 219,585 EDUs. On analyzing the various models, it is found that transform-based models perform better than graph-based models, and among the various models tested improved Elaref dependency parser (Kiperwasser & Goldberg., 2016) showed the best performance with an accuracy of 79.84%. In Van der Goot (2019) impact of normalization on parsing is analyzed. Impact of manual and automatic lexical normalization on lexical dependency parsing is analyzed. It showed that automatic normalization shows comparative results to that of manual lexical normalization.

NLP TECHNIQUES FOR SOCIAL MEDIA DATA ANALYSIS

In this section, a brief discussion of various NLP techniques used in different social media applications that aim to extract meaningful information from social media data is provided. In order to carry out different NLP tasks the text needs to be represented into feature vectors. Different text representation techniques have been used in different NLP techniques and performance of NLP tasks vary based on the feature extraction technique used. Bag of Words (BoW), word embeddings (Almeida & Xexéo, 2019), and pre-trained language models (Edunov et al., 2019) are commonly used text representation schemes.

Bag of Words Model

The Bag-of-Words (BoW) model is a technique for representing text data as a collection of word counts or frequencies (Yan et al., 2020). The preprocessed data is tokenized and converted into a set of unique terms, which make up the vocabulary of the BoW model. Once the vocabulary is defined, each document in the corpus is represented as a vector of term frequencies. The length of the vector is equal to the size of the vocabulary, and each element of the vector corresponds to the frequency of a particular term in the document. One advantage of the BoW model is that it is simple and computationally efficient, making it suitable for large-scale social media data analysis. However, it also has limitations, such as losing the order and context of words in the original text, and not capturing the semantic relationships between terms.

Word Embeddings

In word embedding, each word is represented by a vector that captures its semantic meaning and context within a given corpus of text (Wang et al., 2019). This means that words that are similar in meaning will have similar vector representations, while words that are dissimilar will have more different vector representations. There are many different methods for generating word embeddings, but one of the most popular is the Word2Vec algorithm (Church, 2017). This algorithm takes a large corpus of text and learns to represent each word as a vector based on the context in which it appears. By representing words as dense vectors, word embedding allows machine learning algorithms to better understand the meaning and context of text data, even when it is short and informal.

Pre-Trained Language Models

In the recent years use of pre-trained language models for different NLP applications has increased. Pre-training language models involves training a large neural network on a vast corpus of text data. This training process is unsupervised, meaning that the model is not given any explicit labels or targets. Instead, it learns to predict the next word in a sentence, given the preceding words. Pre-trained language models can be used for a variety of tasks related to social media, such as sentiment analysis, topic modeling, and language translation, cyberbullying detection, text classification, Recommendation systems (Guo et al., 2018; Guo et al., 2020; Yadav et al., 2020). One example of a pre-trained language model that is specifically designed for social media is RoBERTa-MMLM (Multilingual Masked Language Model) (Goyal et al., 2021), which was trained on a massive dataset of multilingual social media text. This model is designed to handle the challenges of noisy and informal language commonly found in social media data.

Named Entity Recognition (NER)

Also called named entity identification is a subtask of information extraction that aims at identifying and classifying the named entities present in unstructured text into a set of pre-defined categories like person names, locations, organizations, time expressions, percentages, quantities, monetary values, etc. (Shelke & Vanjale, 2022). Named Entity Recognizer performs the task of NER by detecting the boundaries of the entities present in the data. For example, *Rahul is working at Microsoft Corporation and gets an annual package of $50000.* In this sentence *Rahul* is the name of a person and has a single token, *'Microsoft Corporation'* is the name of an organization consisting of two tokens and *$50000* is the monetary value. Methods that are used for NER are either based on linguistic grammar or statistical methods. Systems implemented using hand-crafted grammar show better precision but lower recall and are time-consuming Currently supervised machine learning approaches are being used on the available annotated datasets like CoNLL 2002 (Malouf, 2002), CoNLL 2003 English NER dataset (Tjong Kim Sang & De Meulder, 2003), Few-NERD (Ding et al., 2021).

Mikheev (1999) proposed a NER system by combining linguistic-based grammar and statistical models. The system is tested on MUC-7(Marsh & Perzanowski, 1998) dataset and shows that instead of using large gazetteers of common names it is enough to use small gazetteers of popular names. The system shows good performance on evaluation and is domain independent.

In Florian (2003) a framework for NER is proposed in which four classifiers (robust linear classifier, transformation-based learning, maximum entropy, and hidden Markov model) are combined under different environments. The combined framework gives an F-score of 91.6 on English data without using gazetteers or additional training resources. The F-score however drops by 15-21% when the name, person, and location gazetteers are integrated along with additional training data.

In Yadav and Bethard (2019) a survey of NER systems based on deep neural networks is carried out and contrasted with other NER systems based on feature engineering, supervised or supervised technique. The survey concluded that incorporating the lessons from NER methods based on feature-engineering in the NER methods utilizing neural networks can improve the results. In (Liu et al., 2022) comprehensive survey of the recent progress of NER research work in Chinese is provided. The paper also provides an overview of resources available for Chinese NER and future directions for NER research.

NER systems show a performance measure of 70-80% when evaluated on the formal text but the performance decreases to 30-50% when social media data is used (Li et al., 2022b, Gerguis et al., 2016). A NER tool can either detect all named entities in the given input or just only one type of entity. For example, in Derczynski and Bontcheva (2014) the NER tool presented detects only the person entities.

In addition to identifying entities the NER tool also resolves entity ambiguity and co-references. Once the named entities are identified in the soil media data these are disambiguated using linked data resources. Some important data sources that are used for this purpose include DBpedia, BabelNet, and YAGO. NERSO a tool that identifies and disambiguates named entities using DBpedia is developed by Hakimov et al. (2012). Several research attempts have been made to map microblog posts to some linked data or Wikipedia articles most of which make use of semantic networks obtained from linked data. Meij et al. (2012) linked named entities extracted from microblog posts to encyclopedic resources on the basis of graph-based centrality scoring.

Shen et al. (2014) provides a survey of various methods used for entity linking. It also discusses the challenges, applications, evaluation mechanisms, and future directions in the research of entity linking. In Ali et al. (2020) survey of NER works is carried out on Arabic social media data and various challenges specific to Arabic in NER task. Liu et. (2022a) investigated the recent developments carried out on NER task in Chinese social media data.

Automatic Summarization

The process of analyzing the document and extracting the summary from it by retaining the important points from it is called automatic summarization (Sotudeh et al., 2021). It is one of the important tasks in NLP and there exists a lot of research on this topic. The main focus of automatic summarization is to extract the part of the data that represents the whole data and is useful in applications like classification and clustering. Instead of providing the users with the whole data, it is better to present them only the summary of the data and that is the main motive behind automatic summarization.

Automatic summarization methods have been classified into two sub-categories namely; (i) Extractive summarization and (ii) abstractive summarization (Moussan et al., 2018). In the extractive summarization technique, a subset of tokens, phrases, or sentences from the whole data is extracted to create the summary. In abstractive summarization, the task is carried out in three phases namely, data analysis, data transformation, and realization. In the analysis phase, a concise summary of the most important information is produced out of the given data. Here the input data need to be modified, reorganized, and merged. In the transformation phase, the internal representation of the text is modified to create the ordered text. The final summary is generated in the realization phase by considering the scores in the transformation phase.

191

Verma et al. (2022) proposed an extractive summarization model based on clustering and fuzzy evolutionary algorithms. Significant sentences from different clusters obtained using the clustering algorithm are extracted on the basis of their text feature scores. Optimal weights for the text features are then obtained using the teaching-learning optimization technique and the final score of the sentences is obtained with the help of a fuzzy inference system. The summarization problem is also tackled in this study as an Integer Linear Programming problem. The proposed system showed better performance than the previously proposed models.

Alomari et al. (2022) gives a review of recent research works based on deep reinforcement and transfer learning approaches for abstractive summarization. It also highlights the weakness and strengths of the research works reviewed and provides the possible solution to the challenges faced by these research works. Notable research works in abstractive summarization are also compared and future directions are also proposed in this study.

A large volume of data gets generated on social media platforms and is usually in an informal structure and has a number of issues associated which are discussed above. The quantity of data that is useful from this huge volume of data generated to various users is less as the data generated contains large irrelevant data. So, in order to extract the data that is required for a particular purpose needs to be extracted and provided to the users in summarized form. Research work in this regard is going on and various research works already exist in this domain. Judd and Kalita (2013) produced exhaustive summaries from a dataset extracted from Twitter. Utilizing a dependency parser, the summaries created are parsed to eliminate noise and provide better summaries. Zhoa et al. (2011) used the key phrases to derive the summary from the tweets. In order to rank the key phrases context-sensitive topical PageRank algorithm is used and then the relevance of the key phrases is calculated using a probabilistic weighting function.

Nichols et al. (2012) used the status updates from the tweeter to generate a summary of the sports events. To generate the summary temporal cues are used to extract significant moments associated with the event and then relevant status updates are extracted from the status dataset using the sentence ranking algorithm. The system is evaluated by comparing the summaries produced by the system with the human-generated summaries and the previous research work results. The results produced by the proposed system are better than the results reported by previous works.

Kim and Monroy-Hernandez (2016) used narrative theory to deduce the links between the social media content. The summaries of the content are generated on the basis of narrative templates which are commonly used.

In Amato et al. (2018) summarization technique for multimedia content on online social networks is presented. With the use of a hypergraph-based technique, the objects that are the most pertinent to a certain topic of interest are found. In order to get the summaries of the list of candidate multimedia objects with priorities a summarization technique with heuristics is employed. The model presented is evaluated using the Flickr dataset YFCC100M [18]. In order to produce a summary of 50 elements using 5000 candidate objects having five topic levels on average the model requires a few minutes.

Fung et al. (2022) presented a mobile application that summarizes the news content from news media Facebook pages using sentiment analysis.

Machine Translation

Machine Translation an important task in NLP means the automatic conversion of data from one language to another language using machines (Kenny, 2019). It has been an important topic among researchers for a quite long time and a lot of research work exists to tackle this problem. Developing efficient and resilient machine translation systems is still a hot topic for researchers in academic and corporate domains. Hundreds of human languages are currently supported by social media platforms like Twitter & Facebook (Cunliffe, 2019). Automatic Machine translation of data extracted from social media platforms is a challenging task and research lacks far behind in this domain.

One of the important techniques used for machine translation is Neural Machine Translation (NMT) (Stahlberg, 2020). Social media platforms are often used by people from different linguistic backgrounds, and NMT can be a powerful tool to help bridge the language barrier and facilitate communication between individuals (Wu et al., 2016). NMT shows better results in comparison to traditional machine learning techniques (Koehn & Knowles, 2017). There are several ways in which NMT can be used in social media. One common approach is to integrate NMT directly into social media platforms, allowing users to translate posts, comments, and messages in real-time. Facebook, Instagram, and LinkedIn make use of NMT that allows users to convert posts into the language of interest. YouTube also supports the multilingual feature and uses automatic speech recognition to generate the subtitles which are then translated using the NMT feature. Another approach is to use NMT to train chatbots or virtual assistants to provide multilingual support on social media platforms. This can be particularly useful for businesses that want to engage with customers from different linguistic backgrounds. By using NMT to translate customer queries and respond in the appropriate language, businesses can improve customer satisfaction and build stronger relationships with their customers.

In Jehl (2010) a machine translation model to translate tweets from English to German is proposed. The study is carried out on an English-German (bilingual) corpus of 1000 tweets. Translation of unknown words gives a tough challenge in this study and translation is limited up to 140 characters.

Researchers in Vathsala and Ganga (2020) analyzed the machine translation and transliteration of Twitter data using the LSTM network which is a kind of Recurrent Neural Network (RNN). In this study, one million tweets are used for analysis purposes. It shows using RNN-LSTM is performing better than the traditional statistical machine-translation models.

Zakaryia et al. (2021) evaluated the Facebook Translation Service for the translation of posts related to COVID-19 from English to Arabic. The translation is evaluated on the basis of fluency and adequacy. Even though the translation service showed good results in terms of adequacy and fluency but the research is not generic and covers only posts related to COVID-19.

Facebook Artificial Intelligence has introduced the multilingual translation model, M2M-100 (Fan et al., 2021), having the machine translation capability between any pair of 100 human languages independent of the English language. The M2M-100 model is trained on 2200 language directions. Tran et al. (2021) showed that multilingual translation models show better performance than bilingual translation models.

Hashtags are an important component of social media data and translating these from one language to another is pose a great challenge. Users use hashtags within tweets to relate them to a particular topic and this can be a way to categorize tweets topic-wise. A simple method to translate hashtags would be to simply use statistical translation methods where hashtags from the source language would be translated to hashtags in the target language. However, there arises two problems in this approach; (a) hashtags are not necessarily proper words (b) hashtags from the source language may get translated into their equivalent hashtag in the target language. Carter et al. (2011) proposed a solution for hashtag translation which resolves both these issues. The words present along with the hashtags in the source language are obtained and the words expressing the same topic in the target language are obtained. Hashtags existing with the words in the target language are used to find out the equivalent hashtags of the hashtags present in the source language.

Keyphrase Extraction

An important task in NLP is keyword extraction which automatically extracts the most significant words or phrases from the given input text that gives the overview of the given input (Papagiannopoulou, 2020). With Automatic Keyphrase Extraction (AKPE) most relevant, descriptive, and expressive information is obtained from a given document or a set of documents. The importance of AKPE cannot be underestimated as it has implications in many NLP applications like Information Retrieval, Text Mining & automatic summarization and helps a lot to reduce the difficulties faced in extracting valuable information from the vast data available.

Keyphrase extraction can be helpful in browsing, clustering, categorizing, indexing, classifying, and managing a given collection of documents. With Keyphrase extraction a reader can easily identify and decide whether a given document is of interest or not.

In the keyphrase extraction process, the prior identified candidate phrases are checked for relevance and then ranked on the basis of specified criteria. The techniques used are of three types namely (a) supervised techniques, (b) unsupervised techniques, and (c) deep learning techniques. Turney (2000) and Jiang et al. (2009) used supervised techniques for AKPE. Unsupervised techniques used for AKPE can be either statistical-based or graph-based. In statistical-based approaches, words extracted from the input text are ranked using statistical measures like tf-idf. Frikh et al. (2011) used a statistical-based approach for AKPE whereas Frantzi et al. (1998) used statistical along with linguistic information for extracting the Keyphrases.

In graph-based AKPE methods, a graph is built for a document in which words/phrases are represented as nodes and the edges between these nodes are drawn on the basis of semantic/lexical relations that exist between the words/phrases. The node vertices are ranked based on some metric like PageRank or its variants. Mihalcea and Tarau (2004), Smatana and Butka (2016), and Yang et al. (2017) used unsupervised techniques for AKPE. Deep Learning based APKE methods are more famous nowadays and are very efficient. Zhang et al. (2016) and Meng et al. (2017) used deep-learning based approaches for AKPE task. A comprehensive survey of AKPE methods used by various researchers along with strengths and limitations is given by Merrouni et al. (2020).

Research works cited above for AKPE were meant for scientific documents and most of the research works conducted so far in AKPE are applicable to scientific documents as authors provide keywords with these documents manually that simplifies the AKPE task. As far as AKPE for social media data is concerned less work exists and it is still a great challenge. Due to the unstructured nature of data and the presence of a large number of short terms, symbols, URLs, and emoticons AKPE is more challenging in social media data than formal text.

Yang et al. (2018) proposed an AKPE model for extracting keyphrases from social media data on a particular topic. In this study, a weak supervised model is used to extract candidate keyphrases, and the extracted keyphrases are made specific to the user requirements. A sequence-to-sequence-based neural keyphrase extraction model is proposed in Wang et al. (2019). To overcome the data scarcity problem in social media data the model allows joint modeling of dataset-level latent topic representation. The system is evaluated on three datasets obtained from Twitter, Weibo, and StackExchange. The research concluded that the system outperforms the models not taking into account latent topics.

In Ray Chowdhury et al. (2019) Recurrent Neural Network based approach is used to identify and extract tweets related to disaster so as to enhance situational awareness. The model used features based on POS tags, phonology, word embeddings, and phonetics so as to enhance the performance of the already existing models. Instead of using the F1 measure to measure the system performance embedding-based metrics are used. The system is evaluated on both general Twitter data and data related to disaster and showed better performance in both cases.

Jayasiriwardene and Ganegoda (2020) proposed a keyword extraction framework for extracting the relevant news from Twitter so as to check the authenticity of the news. The model proposed in this study is generic in nature and is based on WordNet, a Standard NLP toolkit and statistical-based method. The system is evaluated using the Turing test and gives 67.6% accuracy. Devika et al. (2021) proposed an AKPE model for social media data based on BERT and sentence transformer. Due to the preservation of syntactic and semantic interconnections between tweets the accuracy of the model gets enhanced. On evaluation, the model outperforms the previous research works and shows an accuracy of 86%.

Opinion Mining and Emotion Analysis

People share their opinions and ideas on different social media platforms like Twitter, Facebook, and Social Blogs and it has become a common practice among users. A huge amount of data gets generated on daily basis and it is very essential to have efficient tools to process such a huge quantity of data and extract meaningful information from it. The opinions shared by users are very helpful for different people to make decisions and shape policies. The decisions can be as simple as choosing the right place for shopping or complex as making policies for public security and safety.

The process of identifying, extracting, and enumerating the opinions and ideas shared by users on social media platforms is known as opinion mining or sentiment analysis. The opinions and sentiments shared by different users can be positive, neutral, or negative. A number of research efforts so far aimed at developing automatic opinion and sentiment analysis tools to interpret opinions. The aim of opinion analysis is to deduce the contrariety from the given text. (Wankhade et al., 2022) carries out the analysis of challenges, applications, methodologies and algorithms in sentiment analysis.

Analyzing the sentiments and opinions is a great challenge as humans differ on the opinions expressed over social media and the length of text expressing opinions is smaller, detecting sentiments at different text granularities, and detection of semantic roles of sentiments complicate the process further (Mohammad, 2017; Hussein, 2018). Users may express different opinions on the different aspects of the same entity. For instance, users may like an actor for his personality but may not be satisfied by his acting skills. So, it is also a challenging task to extract not only opinions but also the aspects of the object about which the opinions are expressed.

There are various other challenges that need to be handled when analyzing the sentiments of the users expressed on social media. Mohammad (2017) and Devi and Kamalakkannan (2020) gives an overview of the challenges faced by researchers while the sentiment analysis process.

Sentiment analysis is an emerging research trend and is used to interpret the opinions of social media users in various situations. Khanbhai et al. (2021) surveyed the research work using NLP and machine learning techniques about the analysis of the feedback of the patients shared on social media. It showed most researchers used NLP techniques based on supervised machine learning, followed by unsupervised techniques and then semi-supervised techniques to process the sentiments present in the feedback given by patients. Conway et al. (2019) also reviewed the recent advances in handling health-related research questions using NLP techniques on social media.

Solangi et al. (2018) gives an overview of NLP techniques used for opinion mining and sentiment analysis. In addition to the review of the NLP techniques for sentiment analysis, the study also discusses pre-processing steps involved in the sentiment analysis process and also proposes recommendations for future work in sentiment analysis and opinion mining.

Babu and Kanaga (2022) surveyed the research work aimed at sentiment analysis for the purpose of depression detection. The study revealed that the use of multi-class classification models in conjunction with deep learning techniques yields higher precision. Zhao et al. (2021) analyzed the use of pre-trained language models for identifying toxic comments. Three language models BERT, RoBERT, and XLM are used on four datasets extracted from Twitter, Wikipedia, and Facebook. The authors concluded from the analysis that BERT and RoBERT show better performance than the XLM model in toxic comment classification.

Emotion analysis a more clear-cut form of opinion analysis aims at analyzing subjective information from the text and interpreting the emotions behind it. Although opinion analysis and emotion analysis are not the same but share a large in common. Emotion analysis is carried out in different fields like sociology, political science, philosophy, biology, and psychology. The key player in shaping opinions or emotions at the local level or internationally are news sites working day and night (Ahmad, 2011). Blogs are found to be the most important and informative storehouse for emotion-related content.

Emotion analysis has become an important research area and the research work to identify emotions started with Holzman and Pottenger (2003). When we talk about NLP emotion analysis is treated as a sub-task at the crossroads of computational linguistics (Wiebe et al. 2005) and information retrieval (Sood & Vasserman 2009). Approaches related to emotion analysis are categorized into two classes: rule-based and corpus-based (Das & Bandyopadhyay, 2014). Rule-based approaches demarcate markers and grammatical rules so as to deduce emotions from the text. In corpus-based approaches emotions are interpreted and analyzed on the knowledge acquired from an annotated corpus.

In Kramer (2012) study is carried out to know how emotions get spread over social media networks. The study is carried out to find out the emotion contagion through Facebook status updates. As per this study, the emotions get spread not only via communication over social networks directly but are spread through indirect communication media also. Vo and Collier (2013) performed the emotion analysis of the tweets related to earthquakes posted by users in Japan which can help in the better management of the situation. In this study Multinominal Naïve Bayes model with n-grams showed the best results out of the various models tested. The people showed fear and anxiety after the occurrence of earthquakes of high intensity and after the passage of time, there was a sort of calmness in their emotions.

Mores et al. (2018) proposed one of the first complete architectures for evaluating emotion analysis techniques used for extracting emotions from Facebook posts. It showed that incorporating bootstrapping approach with the neural recurrent neural networks and convolutional networks enhances their performance. Rodriguez et al. (2019) used emotion and sentiment analysis in order to detect hate speech propagation on sensitive topics via Facebook pages. The research work proposed a novel framework to detect the Facebook pages that spread hate speech in comments on sensitive issues.

In Sampath et al. (2022) findings of the shared task for emotion analysis in the Tamil posts on social media at DravidianLangTech-ACL 2022 are presented. The emotion analysis is divided into two categories; Task A and Task B. in Task A emotions in Tamil comments are to be classified into 11 categories whereas Task B categorizes the emotions into 31 classes.

Geolocation Detection

Finding out the geolocation of the content posted on different social media platforms is one of the new challenges for NLP. Predicting the geolocation of users on social media platforms is important not only for marketing purposes but also from the perspective of public health (Dredze et al., 2013; Madleňák, 2021). Geolocation analysis is also used for tasks like tourism analysis and traffic analysis. But the posts on different social networking sites containing geolocation information are very limited. Out of the total social media content only 0.87% to 3% has geolocation information tagged with it (Utomo et al., 2018). Geolocation of social media users may be extracted from their profiles directly but due to some privacy and security reasons, users do not disclose their real location on their profiles or give incorrect location details. So, in order to get the correct and precise information about the locations of the social media users we need some other approaches like deducing the location from the social network of the users or the content posted by them in conjunction with the geolocation content visible in some messages. Research aimed at geolocation prediction has used different methods and parameters for predicting the location at which the content is posted on social media platforms. Various research approaches used for location prediction can be classified into two types; (a) content-based geolocation prediction and (b) user-profile based geolocation prediction (Utomo et al., 2018).

Using location information available in the content posted by a user on the social media platform to predict the exact location of the user is a challenging task as the location available in the content may be ambiguous. This is due to the reason that many places on the globe have the same names, like "Ottawa" is the name of a city in Canada, USA, Ivory Coast, and many other places have this name also. So, this ambiguity needs to be resolved for correct location prediction. Also, there is ambiguity at times whether a word present in the content placed on social media refers to a person or a location. For example, the word Georgia may be a person or may refer to the state of USA, or country. Resolving such issues are more difficult in social media data as text contained on social media does not follow the formal writing procedures. Han et al. (2012) used location-indicative words (LIWs) to predict the geolocation of the content posted on social media. The result showed that using LIWs as features improves the accuracy as well as efficiency of the geolocation prediction model to a large extent. Lourentzou et al. (2017) used neural networks for geolocation prediction from Twitter posts. Carrying out experiments on three Twitter datasets results showed that using a proper architecture with appropriate activation function and batch normalization boosts the system performance.

A number of devices have installed GPS systems entrenched and it is easier to tag the data with geolocation information. Users prefer to provide their geolocation information at the city level mostly followed by information provided at the state level (Hecht et al., 2011).

Using the social network of the people is also an important method to predict their location as people use to interact with friends living in their vicinity. McGee et al. (2013) proposed a model which finds out the location of the social media users on the basis of the strength of their social ties. Tie strength between each user pair along with the distance between them is taken into account to find out the location of the users. However, it's not true that friends on the social network may be living in close vicinity, so assuming that the social network of a user lives in close proximity is not true always. To address this issue (Yamaguchi et al., 2013) put forward a novel approach to detect the location of social media users based on the concept of landmarks. Landmarks are users with large friend circles living in a small region. The model showed an improvement of 27% than previous state-of-art works when tested on Twitter data. Jurgens et al. (2015) surveys the research work aimed at geolocation prediction using social networks. In this study, nine-state-of-art works are analyzed and various evaluation metrics used in these research works are also reviewed. As per this study, there exists a great dissimilarity between the reported results and the real-world scenario exhibits.

Zheng et al. (2020) proposed the Hybrib-Attentive User Geolocation (HUG) model which combines the context of the text and features of the social networks to predict the geolocation of social media users. As most of the previous works used either text context or social networks as features to predict the geolocation leading to sub-optimal performance and also does not consider the importance of these two features for different users this research addressed this challenge. The experiments carried out on Twitter data showed that the HUG model performed better than previous baselines and is robust.

Mahajan and Mansotra (2021) used convolutional neural networks (CNN) and BiLSTM for geolocation prediction from tweets obtained for 30 days from Twitter. In this study, both features which are within tweets or affiliated with tweets are used for the prediction process. The prediction is made not only at the city level but latitudinal and longitudinal coordinates of the tweets are also predicted. The results produced by the system showed that the system showed better performance (accuracy of 92.6% with a median error of 22.4 km at city-level prediction) than the previous baselines.

Tang et al. (2022) proposed a Multilayer Recognition Model (MRM) for the geolocation prediction of Twitter users at the city level. The tweets extracted from Twitter are passed through different optimization techniques like spatial clustering, entity selection and outlier filtering and then the Multinominal Naïve Bayes classifier is used for location prediction. The model showed better performance than the already models.

SUMMARY

In this chapter, a brief description of the social media platforms is provided and the growing trend of using different social media platforms is given. Then we presented an overview of NLP and the differences that exist between the text from a natural language and text present in social media platforms. Various challenges that conventional NLP tools designed and developed for processing text from a formal natural language face while processing social media data. Various pre-processing techniques that are employed on natural language text to make it useful for various NLP tasks are discussed along with their adaptation to process social media data. Notable preprocessing techniques that are discussed are tokenization, chunking, parsing, and POS tagging with their application on social media data. An overview of the research work that aimed at preprocessing social media data is also presented. As social media data is different than the data of a natural language and preprocessing tools are developed to process natural language data. Two important techniques, normalization, and re-training of NLP tools using social media data, that are employed to make these tools suitable to preprocess the social media data are also discussed. At last, we discussed various techniques used in different NLP applications for social media data. Important NLP tasks that are discussed are NER, Automatic Summarization, Keyphrase extraction, Machine Translation, Opinion mining and emotion analysis, and geolocation prediction. Computational linguistics tools have an important role to extract useful information from social media data which is also discussed.

In this chapter, we discussed social media data analysis in various NLP applications but the discussion mainly focused on the textual data. This is mainly due to the scarcity of the literature on other forms of data hence there needs an improvement in this area. Availability of the metadata for other forms of data will boost the progress in this field by concatenating the information from both these sources.

REFERENCES

Ahmad, K. (Ed.). (2011). *Affective computing and sentiment analysis: Emotion, metaphor and terminology* (Vol. 45). Springer Science & Business Media. doi:10.1007/978-94-007-1757-2_8

Alami Merrouni, Z., Frikh, B., & Ouhbi, B. (2020). Automatic keyphrase extraction: A survey and trends. *Journal of Intelligent Information Systems*, *54*(2), 391–424. doi:10.100710844-019-00558-9

Ali, B. A. B., Mihi, S., El Bazi, I., & Laachfoubi, N. (2020). A Recent Survey of Arabic Named Entity Recognition on Social Media. *Rev. d'Intelligence Artif.*, *34*(2), 125-135.

Almeida, F., & Xexéo, G. (2019). *Word embeddings: A survey.* arXiv preprint arXiv:1901.09069

Alomari, A., Idris, N., Sabri, A. Q. M., & Alsmadi, I. (2022). Deep reinforcement and transfer learning for abstractive text summarization: A review. *Computer Speech & Language*, *71*, 101276. doi:10.1016/j.csl.2021.101276

Alsaeedi, A., & Khan, M. Z. (2019). A study on sentiment analysis techniques of Twitter data. *International Journal of Advanced Computer Science and Applications*, *10*(2). Advance online publication. doi:10.14569/IJACSA.2019.0100248

Amato, F., Castiglione, A., Moscato, V., Picariello, A., & Sperlì, G. (2018). Multimedia summarization using social media content. *Multimedia Tools and Applications*, *77*(14), 17803–17827. doi:10.100711042-017-5556-2

Ariffin, S. N. A. N., & Tiun, S. (2020). Rule-based text normalization for Malay social media texts. *International Journal of Advanced Computer Science and Applications*, *11*(10). Advance online publication. doi:10.14569/IJACSA.2020.0111021

Arora, C., Sabetzadeh, M., Briand, L., Zimmer, F., & Gnaga, R. (2013, October). Automatic checking of conformance to requirement boilerplates via text chunking: An industrial case study. In *2013 ACM/IEEE International Symposium on Empirical Software Engineering and Measurement* (pp. 35-44). IEEE.

Atefeh, F., & Khreich, W. (2015). A survey of techniques for event detection in twitter. *Computational Intelligence*, *31*(1), 132–164. doi:10.1111/coin.12017

Babu, N. V., & Kanaga, E. (2022). Sentiment analysis in social media data for depression detection using artificial intelligence: A review. *SN Computer Science*, *3*(1), 1–20. doi:10.100742979-021-00958-1 PMID:34816124

Barman, U., Das, A., Wagner, J., & Foster, J. (2014, October). Code mixing: A challenge for language identification in the language of social media. In *Proceedings of the first workshop on computational approaches to code switching* (pp. 13-23). 10.3115/v1/W14-3902

Beverungen, G., & Kalita, J. (2011). Evaluating methods for summarizing twitter posts. *Proceedings of the 5th AAAI ICWSM*.

Bharati, P., Zhang, W., & Chaudhury, A. (2015). Better knowledge with social media? Exploring the roles of social capital and organizational knowledge management. *Journal of Knowledge Management*, *19*(3), 1–39. doi:10.1108/JKM-11-2014-0467

Bharti, S. K., Gupta, R. K., Patel, S., & Shah, M. (2022). Context-Based Bigram Model for POS Tagging in Hindi: A Heuristic Approach. *Annals of Data Science*, 1-32.

Borah, P. S., Iqbal, S., & Akhtar, S. (2022). Linking social media usage and SME's sustainable performance: The role of digital leadership and innovation capabilities. *Technology in Society*, *68*, 101900. doi:10.1016/j.techsoc.2022.101900

Cambria, E., & White, B. (2014). Jumping NLP curves: A review of natural language processing research. *IEEE Computational Intelligence Magazine, 9*(2), 48–57. doi:10.1109/MCI.2014.2307227

Carter, S., Tsagkias, M., & Weerkamp, W. (2011). *Twitter hashtags: Joint translation and clustering*. Academic Press.

Chandra, N., Kumawat, S., & Srivastava, V. (2014). Various tagsets for indian languages and their performance in part of speech tagging. *Proceedings of 5th IRF International Conference.*

Chen, D., & Manning, C. D. (2014, October). A fast and accurate dependency parser using neural networks. In *Proceedings of the 2014 conference on empirical methods in natural language processing (EMNLP)* (pp. 740-750). 10.3115/v1/D14-1082

Chiche, A., & Yitagesu, B. (2022). Part of speech tagging: A systematic review of deep learning and machine learning approaches. *Journal of Big Data, 9*(1), 1–25. doi:10.118640537-022-00561-y

Chui, M., Manyika, J., Bughin, J., Dobbs, R., Roxburgh, C., Sarrazin, H., Sands, G. & Westergren, M. (2012). *The Social Economy: Unlocking Value and Productivity through Social Technologies*. McKinsey Global Institute.

Church, K. W. (2017). Word2Vec. *Natural Language Engineering, 23*(1), 155–162. doi:10.1017/S1351324916000334

Cirqueira, D., Pinheiro, M. F., Jacob, A., Lobato, F., & Santana, A. (2018, December). A literature review in preprocessing for sentiment analysis for Brazilian Portuguese social media. In *2018 IEEE/WIC/ACM International Conference on Web Intelligence (WI)* (pp. 746-749). IEEE. 10.1109/WI.2018.00008

Conway, M., Hu, M., & Chapman, W. W. (2019). Recent advances in using natural language processing to address public health research questions using social media and consumergenerated data. *Yearbook of Medical Informatics, 28*(01), 208–217. doi:10.1055-0039-1677918 PMID:31419834

Cunliffe, D. (2019). Minority languages and social media. The Palgrave handbook of minority languages and communities, 451-480.

Cyril, C. P. D., Beulah, J. R., Subramani, N., Mohan, P., Harshavardhan, A., & Sivabalaselvamani, D. (2021). An automated learning model for sentiment analysis and data classification of Twitter data using balanced CA-SVM. *Concurrent Engineering, Research and Applications, 29*(4), 386–395. doi:10.1177/1063293X211031485

Das, D., & Bandyopadhyay, S. (2014). Emotion analysis on social media: natural language processing approaches and applications. In *Online Collective Action* (pp. 19–37). Springer. doi:10.1007/978-3-7091-1340-0_2

Demir, S. (2016, June). Context tailoring for text normalization. In *Proceedings of TextGraphs-10: the Workshop on Graph-based Methods for Natural Language Processing* (pp. 6-14). Academic Press.

Derczynski, L., & Bontcheva, K. (2014). Passive-aggressive sequence labeling with discriminative post-editing for recognising person entities in tweets. *Proceedings of the 14th Conference of the European Chapter of the Association for Computational Linguistics, 2,* 69–73. 10.3115/v1/E14-4014

Derczynski, L., Maynard, D., Rizzo, G., Van Erp, M., Gorrell, G., Troncy, R., Petrak, J., & Bontcheva, K. (2015). Analysis of named entity recognition and linking for tweets. *Information Processing & Management, 51*(2), 32–49. doi:10.1016/j.ipm.2014.10.006

Derczynski, L., Ritter, A., Clark, S., & Bontcheva, K. (2013, September). Twitter part-of-speech tagging for all: Overcoming sparse and noisy data. In *Proceedings of the international conference recent advances in natural language processing ranlp 2013* (pp. 198-206). Academic Press.

Devi, G. D., & Kamalakkannan, S. (2020). Literature Review on Sentiment Analysis in Social Media: Open Challenges toward Applications. *Test Eng. Manag, 83*(7), 2466–2474.

Devika, R., Vairavasundaram, S., Mahenthar, C. S. J., Varadarajan, V., & Kotecha, K. (2021). A Deep Learning Model Based on BERT and Sentence Transformer for Semantic Keyphrase Extraction on Big Social Data. *IEEE Access : Practical Innovations, Open Solutions, 9,* 165252–165261. doi:10.1109/ACCESS.2021.3133651

Ding, N., Xu, G., Chen, Y., Wang, X., Han, X., Xie, P., . . . Liu, Z. (2021). *Few-nerd: A few-shot named entity recognition dataset.* doi:10.18653/v1/2021.acl-long.248

Ding, Y., Ma, J., & Luo, X. (2022). Applications of natural language processing in construction. *Automation in Construction, 136,* 104169. doi:10.1016/j.autcon.2022.104169

Dredze, M., Paul, M. J., Bergsma, S., & Tran, H. (2013, July). Carmen: A twitter geolocation system with applications to public health. In AAAI workshop on expanding the boundaries of health informatics using AI (HIAI) (Vol. 23, p. 45). Citeseer.

Durgam, V. (2018). Social media and its role in marketing. *International Journal of Advanced Research in Management, 9*(2), 1-10.

Edunov, S., Baevski, A., & Auli, M. (2019). *Pre-trained language model representations for language generation.* doi:10.18653/v1/N19-1409

Evang, K., Basile, V., Chrupała, G., & Bos, J. (2013, October). Elephant: Sequence labeling for word and sentence segmentation. EMNLP 2013.

Fan, A., Bhosale, S., Schwenk, H., Ma, Z., El-Kishky, A., Goyal, S., ... Joulin, A. (2021). Beyond English-Centric Multilingual Machine Translation. *Journal of Machine Learning Research, 22*(107), 1–48.

Farzindar, A. A., & Inkpen, D. (2015). Linguistic Pre-processing of Social Media Texts. In *Natural Language Processing for Social Media* (pp. 15–41). Springer International Publishing. doi:10.1007/978-3-031-02157-2_2

Farzindar, A. A., & Inkpen, D. (2020). Natural language processing for social media. *Synthesis Lectures on Human Language Technologies, 13*(2), 1–219. doi:10.1007/978-3-031-02175-6

Florian, R., Ittycheriah, A., Jing, H., & Zhang, T. (2003). Named entity recognition through classifier combination. In *Proceedings of the seventh conference on Natural language learning at HLT-NAACL 2003* (pp. 168-171). 10.3115/1119176.1119201

Foster, J., Cetinoglu, O., Wagner, J., Le Roux, J., Nivre, J., Hogan, D., & Van Genabith, J. (2011). *From news to comment: Resources and benchmarks for parsing the language of web 2.0.* Academic Press.

Frantzi, K. T., Ananiadou, S., & Tsujii, J. (1998). The C-VALUE/NC-VALUE method of automatic recognition for multi-word terms. In *International conference on theory and practice of digital libraries* (pp. 585–604). Springer. 10.1007/3-540-49653-X_35

Frikh, B., Djaanfar, A. S., & Ouhbi, B. (2011). A new methodology for domain ontology construction from the Web. *International Journal of Artificial Intelligence Tools, 20*(6), 1157–1170. doi:10.1142/S0218213011000565

Fung, Y. C., Lee, L. K., Chui, K. T., Cheung, G. H. K., Tang, C. H., & Wong, S. M. (2022). Sentiment Analysis and Summarization of Facebook Posts on News Media. In *Data Mining Approaches for Big Data and Sentiment Analysis in Social Media* (pp. 142–154). IGI Global. doi:10.4018/978-1-7998-8413-2.ch006

Garg, P., & Pahuja, S. (2020). Social media: Concept, role, categories, trends, social media and AI, impact on youth, careers, recommendations. In *Managing social media practices in the digital economy* (pp. 172–192). IGI Global. doi:10.4018/978-1-7998-2185-4.ch008

Gebreel, O. S. S., & Shuayb, A. (2022). Contribution of social media platforms in tourism promotion. *International Journal of Social Science, Education Communist Economies, 1*(2), 189–198.

Gerguis, M. N., Salama, C., & El-Kharashi, M. W. (2016, December). ASU: An Experimental Study on Applying Deep Learning in Twitter Named Entity Recognition. In *Proceedings of the 2nd Workshop on Noisy User-generated Text (WNUT)* (pp. 188-196). Academic Press.

Goyal, N., Du, J., Ott, M., Anantharaman, G., & Conneau, A. (2021). *Larger-scale transformers for multilingual masked language modeling.* doi:10.18653/v1/2021.repl4nlp-1.4

Guo, L., Wen, Y. F., & Wang, X. H. (2018). Exploiting pre-trained network embeddings for recommendations in social networks. *Journal of Computer Science and Technology, 33*(4), 682–696. doi:10.100711390-018-1849-9

Guo, Y., Dong, X., Al-Garadi, M. A., Sarker, A., Paris, C., & Aliod, D. M. (2020, December). Benchmarking of transformer-based pre-trained models on social media text classification datasets. In *Proceedings of the The 18th Annual Workshop of the Australasian Language Technology Association* (pp. 86-91). Academic Press.

Gupta, D., Tripathi, S., Ekbal, A., & Bhattacharyya, P. (2017). *SMPOST: parts of speech tagger for code-mixed indic social media text.* arXiv preprint arXiv:1702.00167.

Hadni, M., Ouatik, S. A., Lachkar, A., & Meknassi, M. (2013). Hybrid part-of-speech tagger for non-vocalized Arabic text. *Int. J. Nat. Lang. Comput, 2*(6), 1–15. doi:10.5121/ijnlc.2013.2601

Hain, S., & Back, A. (2008). Personal Learning Journal â€" Course Design for Using Weblogs in Higher Education. *Electronic Journal of e-Learning, 6*(3), 189–196.

Hakimov, S., Oto, S. A., & Dogdu, E. (2012, May). Named entity recognition and disambiguation using linked data and graph-based centrality scoring. In *Proceedings of the 4th international workshop on semantic web information management* (pp. 1-7). 10.1145/2237867.2237871

Hallock, W., Roggeveen, A., & Crittenden, V. (2019). Firm-level perspectives on social media engagement: An exploratory study. *Qualitative Market Research, 22*(2), 217–226. Advance online publication. doi:10.1108/QMR-01-2017-0025

Han, B., & Baldwin, T. (2011, June). Lexical normalisation of short text messages: Makn sens a# twitter. In *Proceedings of the 49th annual meeting of the association for computational linguistics: Human language technologies* (pp. 368-378). Academic Press.

Han, B., Cook, P., & Baldwin, T. (2012, December). Geolocation prediction in social media data by finding location indicative words. *Proceedings of COLING, 2012*, 1045–1062.

Hasbullah, S. S., Maynard, D., Chik, R. Z. W., Mohd, F., & Noor, M. (2016, January). Automated content analysis: A sentiment analysis on Malaysian government social media. In *Proceedings of the 10th International Conference on Ubiquitous Information Management and Communication* (pp. 1-6). 10.1145/2857546.2857577

Hecht, B., Hong, L., Suh, B., & Chi, E. H. (2011, May). Tweets from Justin Bieber's heart: the dynamics of the location field in user profiles. In *Proceedings of the SIGCHI conference on human factors in computing systems* (pp. 237-246). 10.1145/1978942.1978976

Hilte, L., Vandekerckhove, R., & Daelemans, W. (2019). Adolescents' perceptions of social media writing: Has non-standard become the new standard? *European Journal of Applied Linguistics, 7*(2), 189-224.

Holzman, L. E., & Pottenger, W. M. (2003). *Classification of emotions in internet chat: An application of machine learning using speech phonemes.* Academic Press.

Hoogeveen, D., Wang, L., Baldwin, T., & Verspoor, K. M. (2018). Web forum retrieval and text analytics: A survey. *Foundations and Trends® in Information Retrieval, 12*(1), 1-163.

Hu, X., & Liu, H. (2012). Text analytics in social media. *Mining Text Data,* 385-414.

Hussein, D. M. E. D. M. (2018). A survey on sentiment analysis challenges. *Journal of King Saud University. Engineering Sciences, 30*(4), 330–338. doi:10.1016/j.jksues.2016.04.002

Jayasiriwardene, T. D., & Ganegoda, G. U. (2020, September). Keyword extraction from Tweets using NLP tools for collecting relevant news. In *2020 International Research Conference on Smart Computing and Systems Engineering (SCSE)* (pp. 129-135). IEEE. 10.1109/SCSE49731.2020.9313024

Jehl, L. E. (2010). *Machine translation for Twitter* [Master's thesis]. The University of Edinburgh.

Jiang, X., Hu, Y., & Li, H. (2009). A ranking approach to keyphrase extraction. In *Proceedings of the 32nd international ACM SIGIR conference on research and development in information retrieval*, SIGIR '09.

Jivani, A. G. (2011). A comparative study of stemming algorithms. *Int. J. Comp. Tech. Appl, 2*(6), 1930–1938.

Judd, J., & Kalita, J. (2013, June). Better twitter summaries? In *Proceedings of the 2013 Conference of the North American Chapter of the Association for Computational Linguistics: Human Language Technologies* (pp. 445-449). Academic Press.

Jurgens, D., Finethy, T., McCorriston, J., Xu, Y., & Ruths, D. (2015). Geolocation prediction in twitter using social networks: A critical analysis and review of current practice. In *Proceedings of the International AAAI Conference on Web and Social Media* (*Vol. 9*, No. 1, pp. 188-197). AAAI.

Jusoh, S. (2018). A study on NLP applications and ambiguity problems. *Journal of Theoretical and Applied Information Technology, 96*(6).

Kang, Y., Cai, Z., Tan, C. W., Huang, Q., & Liu, H. (2020). Natural language processing (NLP) in management research: A literature review. *Journal of Management Analytics, 7*(2), 139–172. doi:10.1080/23270012.2020.1756939

Kaur, J., & Singh, J. (2019, October). Deep neural network based sentence boundary detection and end marker suggestion for social media text. In *2019 International Conference on Computing, Communication, and Intelligent Systems (ICCCIS)* (pp. 292-295). IEEE. 10.1109/ICCCIS48478.2019.8974495

Kenny, D. (2019). Machine translation. In *Routledge encyclopedia of translation studies* (pp. 305–310). Routledge. doi:10.4324/9781315678627-65

Khan, J., & Lee, S. (2021). Enhancement of Text Analysis Using Context-Aware Normalization of Social Media Informal Text. *Applied Sciences (Basel, Switzerland), 11*(17), 8172. doi:10.3390/app11178172

Khanbhai, M., Anyadi, P., Symons, J., Flott, K., Darzi, A., & Mayer, E. (2021). Applying natural language processing and machine learning techniques to patient experience feedback: A systematic review. *BMJ Health & Care Informatics, 28*(1), e100262. doi:10.1136/bmjhci-2020-100262 PMID:33653690

Khanday, A. M. U. D., Khan, Q. R., & Rabani, S. T. (2021). Detecting textual propaganda using machine learning techniques. *Baghdad Sci. J*, *18*(1), 199–209. doi:10.21123/bsj.2021.18.1.0199

Khanday, A. M. U. D., Wani, M. A., Rabani, S. T., & Khan, Q. R. (2023). Hybrid Approach for Detecting Propagandistic Community and Core Node on Social Networks. *Sustainability (Basel)*, *15*(2), 1249. doi:10.3390u15021249

Kiela, D., Bartolo, M., Nie, Y., Kaushik, D., Geiger, A., Wu, Z., . . . Williams, A. (2021). *Dynabench: Rethinking benchmarking in NLP*. doi:10.18653/v1/2021. naacl-main.324

Kim, J., & Monroy-Hernandez, A. (2016, February). Storia: Summarizing social media content based on narrative theory using crowdsourcing. In *Proceedings of the 19th ACM Conference on Computer-Supported Cooperative Work & Social Computing* (pp. 1018-1027). 10.1145/2818048.2820072

Kinsella, S., Passant, A., Breslin, J. G., Decker, S., & Jaokar, A. (2009). The future of social web sites: Sharing data and trusted applications with semantics. *Advances in Computers*, *76*, 121–175. doi:10.1016/S0065-2458(09)01004-3

Kiperwasser, E., & Goldberg, Y. (2016). Simple and accurate dependency parsing using bidirectional LSTM feature representations. *Transactions of the Association for Computational Linguistics*, *4*, 313–327. doi:10.1162/tacl_a_00101

Kiran, S., Sai, C. R. S., & Pooja, M. R. (2019, March). A comparative study on parsing in natural language processing. In *2019 3rd International Conference on Computing Methodologies and Communication (ICCMC)* (pp. 785-788). IEEE. 10.1109/ICCMC.2019.8819687

Koehn, P., & Knowles, R. (2017). *Six challenges for neural machine translation*. doi:10.18653/v1/W17-3204

Lawaye, A. A., & Purkayastha, B. S. (2013). Towards Developing a Hierarchical Part of Speech Tagger for Kashmiri: Hybrid Approach. In *Proceedings of the 2nd National Conference on Advancement in the Era of Multidisciplinary Systems* (pp. 187-192). Academic Press.

Lawaye, A. A., & Purkayastha, B. S. (2014). Kashmir part of speech tagger using CRF. *Computer Science*, *3*(3), 3.

Li, B., Fan, Y., Sataer, Y., Gao, Z., & Gui, Y. (2022). Improving Semantic Dependency Parsing with Higher-Order Information Encoded by Graph Neural Networks. *Applied Sciences (Basel, Switzerland)*, *12*(8), 4089. doi:10.3390/app12084089

Li, C., Weng, J., He, Q., Yao, Y., Datta, A., Sun, A., & Lee, B. S. (2012, August). Twiner: named entity recognition in targeted twitter stream. In *Proceedings of the 35th international ACM SIGIR conference on Research and development in information retrieval* (pp. 721-730). 10.1145/2348283.2348380

Liu, J., Cheng, J., Wang, Z., Lou, C., Shen, C., & Sheng, V. S. (2022a). A Survey of Deep Learning for Named Entity Recognition in Chinese Social Media. In *International Conference on Adaptive and Intelligent Systems* (pp. 573-582). Springer. 10.1007/978-3-031-06794-5_46

Liu, P., Guo, Y., Wang, F., & Li, G. (2022b). Chinese named entity recognition: The state of the art. *Neurocomputing*, *473*, 37–53. doi:10.1016/j.neucom.2021.10.101

Lourentzou, I., Morales, A., & Zhai, C. (2017, December). Text-based geolocation prediction of social media users with neural networks. In *2017 IEEE International Conference on Big Data (Big Data)* (pp. 696-705). IEEE. 10.1109/BigData.2017.8257985

Madlcňák, A. (2021). Geolocation Services and Marketing Communication from a Global Point of View. In *SHS Web of Conferences* (Vol. 92, p. 02040). EDP Sciences.

Maitama, J. Z., Haruna, U., Gambo, A. Y. U., Thomas, B. A., Idris, N. B., Gital, A. Y. U., & Abubakar, A. I. (2014, November). Text normalization algorithm for Facebook chats in Hausa language. In *The 5th International Conference on Information and Communication Technology for The Muslim World (ICT4M)* (pp. 1-4). IEEE. 10.1109/ICT4M.2014.7020605

Malouf, R. (2002). Markov models for language-independent named entity recognition. In *COLING-02: The 6th Conference on Natural Language Learning 2002 (CoNLL-2002)*. 10.3115/1118853.1118872

Manjunath, V. (2022, November). Mining Twitter Multi-word Product Opinions with Most Frequent Sequences of Aspect Terms. In *Information Integration and Web Intelligence: 24th International Conference, iiWAS 2022, Virtual Event, November 28–30, 2022 Proceedings, 13635*, 126.

Mansouri, S. A., & Piki, A. (2016). An exploration into the impact of blogs on students' learning: Case studies in postgraduate business education. *Innovations in Education and Teaching International*, *53*(3), 260–273. doi:10.1080/1470329 7.2014.997777

Marcus, M., Santorini, B., & Marcinkiewicz, M. A. (1994). Building a large annotated corpus of English: The Penn Treebank. *Computational Linguistics*, *19*(2), 313–330.

Marsh, E., & Perzanowski, D. (1998). MUC-7 evaluation of IE technology: Overview of results. *Seventh Message Understanding Conference (MUC-7): Proceedings of a Conference.*

Maylawati, D. S. A., Zulfikar, W. B., Slamet, C., Ramdhani, M. A., & Gerhana, Y. A. (2018, August). An improved of stemming algorithm for mining indonesian text with slang on social media. In *2018 6th International Conference on Cyber and IT Service Management* (CITSM) (pp. 1-6). IEEE. 10.1109/CITSM.2018.8674054

McGee, J., Caverlee, J., & Cheng, Z. (2013, October). Location prediction in social media based on tie strength. In *Proceedings of the 22nd ACM international conference on Information & Knowledge Management* (pp. 459-468). 10.1145/2505515.2505544

Meftah, S., & Semmar, N. (2018, May). A neural network model for part-of-speech tagging of social media texts. In *Proceedings of the eleventh international Conference on Language Resources and Evaluation (LREC 2018)*. Academic Press.

Meng, R., Zhao, S., Han, S., He, D., Brusilovsky, P., & Chi, Y. (2017). *Deep keyphrase generation.* doi:10.18653/v1/P17-1054

Metzler, D., Cai, C., & Hovy, E. (2012, June). Structured event retrieval over microblog archives. In *Proceedings of the 2012 Conference of the North American Chapter of the Association for Computational Linguistics: Human Language Technologies* (pp. 646-655). Academic Press.

Mihalcea, R., & Tarau, P. (2004). TEXTRANK: Bringing order into text. *Proceedings of the 2004 conference on empirical methods in natural language processing.*

Mikheev, A., Moens, M., & Grover, C. (1999, June). Named entity recognition without gazetteers. In *Ninth Conference of the European Chapter of the Association for Computational Linguistics* (pp. 1-8). Academic Press.

Mireshghallah, F., Vogler, N., He, J., Florez, O., El-Kishky, A., & Berg-Kirkpatrick, T. (2022). *Non-parametric temporal adaptation for social media topic classification.* arXiv preprint arXiv:2209.05706.

Miura, A., & Yamashita, K. (2007). Psychological and social influences on blog writing: An online survey of blog authors in Japan. *Journal of Computer-Mediated Communication, 12*(4), 1452–1471. doi:10.1111/j.1083-6101.2007.00381.x

Moers, T., Krebs, F., & Spanakis, G. (2018, January). SEMTec: social emotion mining techniques for analysis and prediction of facebook post reactions. In *International Conference on Agents and Artificial Intelligence* (pp. 361-382). Springer.

Mohammad, S. M. (2017). Challenges in sentiment analysis. In *A practical guide to sentiment analysis* (pp. 61–83). Springer. doi:10.1007/978-3-319-55394-8_4

Moussa, M. E., Mohamed, E. H., & Haggag, M. H. (2018). A survey on opinion summarization techniques for social media. *Future Computing and Informatics Journal*, *3*(1), 82–109. doi:10.1016/j.fcij.2017.12.002

Neunerdt, M., Trevisan, B., Reyer, M., & Mathar, R. (2013). Part-of-speech tagging for social media texts. In *Language Processing and Knowledge in the Web* (pp. 139–150). Springer. doi:10.1007/978-3-642-40722-2_15

Nichols, J., Mahmud, J., & Drews, C. (2012, February). Summarizing sporting events using twitter. In *Proceedings of the 2012 ACM international conference on Intelligent User Interfaces* (pp. 189-198). ACM.

Palmer, D. D. (2000). Tokenisation and sentence segmentation. Handbook of natural language processing, 11-35.

Papagiannopoulou, E., & Tsoumakas, G. (2020). A review of keyphrase extraction. *Wiley Interdisciplinary Reviews. Data Mining and Knowledge Discovery*, *10*(2), e1339. doi:10.1002/widm.1339

Pekkala, K., & van Zoonen, W. (2022). Work-related social media use: The mediating role of social media communication self-efficacy. *European Management Journal*, *40*(1), 67–76. doi:10.1016/j.emj.2021.03.004

Pradana, A. W., & Hayaty, M. (2019). The effect of stemming and removal of stopwords on the accuracy of sentiment analysis on indonesian-language texts. *Kinetik: Game Technology, Information System, Computer Network, Computing, Electronics, and Control*, 375-380.

Ramanathan, U., Subramanian, N., & Parrott, G. (2017). Role of social media in retail network operations and marketing to enhance customer satisfaction. *International Journal of Operations & Production Management*, *37*(1), 105–123. doi:10.1108/IJOPM-03-2015-0153

Rathod, S., & Govilkar, S. (2015). Survey of various POS tagging techniques for Indian regional languages. *International Journal of Computer Science and Information Technologies*, *6*(3), 2525–2529.

Ray Chowdhury, J., Caragea, C., & Caragea, D. (2019, May). Keyphrase extraction from disaster-related tweets. In The world wide web conference (pp. 1555-1566). doi:10.1145/3308558.3313696

Rizki, A. S., Tjahyanto, A., & Trialih, R. (2019). Comparison of stemming algorithms on Indonesian text processing. *TELKOMNIKA*, *17*(1), 95–102. doi:10.12928/telkomnika.v17i1.10183

Rodriguez, A., Argueta, C., & Chen, Y. L. (2019, February). Automatic detection of hate speech on facebook using sentiment and emotion analysis. In 2019 international conference on artificial intelligence in information and communication (ICAIIC) (pp. 169-174). IEEE. doi:10.1109/ICAIIC.2019.8669073

Rudrapal, D., Jamatia, A., Chakma, K., Das, A., & Gambäck, B. (2015, December). Sentence boundary detection for social media text. In *Proceedings of the 12th International Conference on Natural Language Processing* (pp. 254-260). Academic Press.

Sadredini, E., Guo, D., Bo, C., Rahimi, R., Skadron, K., & Wang, H. (2018, July). A scalable solution for rule-based part-of-speech tagging on novel hardware accelerators. In *Proceedings of the 24th ACM SIGKDD international conference on knowledge discovery & data mining* (pp. 665-674). ACM.

Sampath, A., Durairaj, T., Chakravarthi, B. R., Priyadharshini, R., Cn, S., Shanmugavadivel, K., ... Pandiyan, S. (2022, May). Findings of the shared task on Emotion Analysis in Tamil. In *Proceedings of the Second Workshop on Speech and Language Technologies for Dravidian Languages* (pp. 279-285). 10.18653/v1/2022.dravidianlangtech-1.42

Sang, E. F., & De Meulder, F. (2003). *Introduction to the CoNLL-2003 shared task: Language-independent named entity recognition.* arXiv preprint cs/0306050.

Sapountzi, A., & Psannis, K. E. (2018). Social networking data analysis tools & challenges. *Future Generation Computer Systems*, *86*, 893–913. doi:10.1016/j.future.2016.10.019

Saroj, A., & Pal, S. (2020). Use of social media in crisis management: A survey. *International Journal of Disaster Risk Reduction*, *48*, 101584. doi:10.1016/j.ijdrr.2020.101584

Shafie, L. A., & Nayan, S. (2013). Languages, code-switching practice and primary functions of Facebook among university students. *Study in English Language Teaching*, *1*(1), 187–199. doi:10.22158elt.v1n1p187

Shahbaznezhad, H., Dolan, R., & Rashidirad, M. (2021). The role of social media content format and platform in users' engagement behavior. *Journal of Interactive Marketing*, *53*(1), 47–65. doi:10.1016/j.intmar.2020.05.001

Sharma, A., Gupta, S., Motlani, R., Bansal, P., Srivastava, M., Mamidi, R., & Sharma, D. M. (2016). *Shallow parsing pipeline for hindi-english code-mixed social media text*. doi:10.18653/v1/N16-1159

Shelke, R., & Vanjale, S. (2022). Recursive LSTM for the Classification of Named Entity Recognition for Hindi Language. *Journal, 27*(4), 679–684. doi:10.18280/isi.270420

Shen, W., Wang, J., & Han, J. (2014). Entity linking with a knowledge base: Issues, techniques, and solutions. *IEEE Transactions on Knowledge and Data Engineering, 27*(2), 443–460. doi:10.1109/TKDE.2014.2327028

Singh, J., & Gupta, V. (2017). A systematic review of text stemming techniques. *Artificial Intelligence Review, 48*(2), 157–217. doi:10.100710462-016-9498-2

Singkul, S., Khampingyot, B., Maharattamalai, N., Taerungruang, S., & Chalothorn, T. (2019). Parsing thai social data: A new challenge for thai nlp. In *2019 14th International Joint Symposium on Artificial Intelligence and Natural Language Processing (iSAI-NLP)* (pp. 1-7). IEEE. 10.1109/iSAI-NLP48611.2019.9045639

Smatana, M., & Butka, P. (2016). Extraction of keyphrases from single document based on hierarchical concepts. In *IEEE 14th international symposium on applied machine intelligence and informatics (SAMI)* (pp. 93–98). IEEE. 10.1109/SAMI.2016.7422988

Solangi, Y. A., Solangi, Z. A., Aarain, S., Abro, A., Mallah, G. A., & Shah, A. (2018, November). Review on natural language processing (NLP) and its toolkits for opinion mining and sentiment analysis. In *2018 IEEE 5th International Conference on Engineering Technologies and Applied Sciences (ICETAS)* (pp. 1-4). IEEE.

Sood, S., & Vasserman, L. (2009). ESSE: Exploring mood on the web. *Proceedings of the 3rd international AAAI conference on weblogs and social media (ICWSM)*.

Sotudeh, S., Deilamsalehy, H., Dernoncourt, F., & Goharian, N. (2021). *TLDR9+: A large scale resource for extreme summarization of social media posts*. doi:10.18653/v1/2021.newsum-1.15

Stahlberg, F. (2020). Neural machine translation: A review. *Journal of Artificial Intelligence Research, 69*, 343–418. doi:10.1613/jair.1.12007

Tang, H., Zhao, X., & Ren, Y. (2022). A multilayer recognition model for twitter user geolocation. *Wireless Networks, 28*(3), 1–6. doi:10.100711276-018-01897-1

Tarihoran, N. A., & Sumirat, I. R. (2022). The impact of social media on the use of code mixing by generation Z. *International Journal of Interactive Mobile Technologies, 16*(7), 54–69. doi:10.3991/ijim.v16i07.27659

Thara, S., & Poornachandran, P. (2018, September). Code-mixing: A brief survey. In *2018 International conference on advances in computing, communications and informatics (ICACCI)* (pp. 2382-2388). IEEE.

Tiwari, A. S., & Naskar, S. K. (2017, December). Normalization of social media text using deep neural networks. In *Proceedings of the 14th International Conference on Natural Language Processing (ICON-2017)* (pp. 312-321). Academic Press.

Toleu, A., Tolegen, G., & Makazhanov, A. (2017). *Character-based deep learning models for token and sentence segmentation.* Academic Press.

Tran, C., Bhosale, S., Cross, J., Koehn, P., Edunov, S., & Fan, A. (2021). *Facebook ai wmt21 news translation task submission.* arXiv preprint arXiv:2108.03265.

Turney, P. D. (2000). Learning algorithms for keyphrase extraction. *Information Retrieval*, 2(4), 303–336. doi:10.1023/A:1009976227802

Utomo, M. N. Y., Adji, T. B., & Ardiyanto, I. (2018, March). Geolocation prediction in social media data using text analysis: A review. In *2018 International Conference on Information and Communications Technology (ICOIACT)* (pp. 84-89). IEEE. 10.1109/ICOIACT.2018.8350674

Van der Goot, R. (2019, October). An in-depth analysis of the effect of lexical normalization on the dependency parsing of social media. In *Proceedings of the 5th Workshop on Noisy User-generated Text* (pp. 115-120). Association for Computational Linguistics. 10.18653/v1/D19-5515

Vathsala, M. K., & Holi, G. (2020). RNN based machine translation and transliteration for Twitter data. *International Journal of Speech Technology*, 23(3), 499–504. doi:10.100710772-020-09724-9

Verma, P., Verma, A., & Pal, S. (2022). An approach for extractive text summarization using fuzzy evolutionary and clustering algorithms. *Applied Soft Computing*, 120, 108670. doi:10.1016/j.asoc.2022.108670

Vijay, D., Bohra, A., Singh, V., Akhtar, S. S., & Shrivastava, M. (2018, June). Corpus creation and emotion prediction for Hindi-English code-mixed social media text. In *Proceedings of the 2018 conference of the North American chapter of the Association for Computational Linguistics: student research workshop* (pp. 128-135). 10.18653/v1/N18-4018

Vo, B. K. H., & Collier, N. (2013). Twitter emotion analysis in earthquake situations. *Int. J. Comput. Linguistics Appl.*, 4(1), 159–173.

Wang, B., Wang, A., Chen, F., Wang, Y., & Kuo, C. C. J. (2019). Evaluating word embedding models: Methods and experimental results. *APSIPA Transactions on Signal and Information Processing*, *8*(1), e19. doi:10.1017/ATSIP.2019.12

Wang, Y., Li, J., Chan, H. P., King, I., Lyu, M. R., & Shi, S. (2019). *Topic-aware neural keyphrase generation for social media language.* doi:10.18653/v1/P19-1240

Wankhade, M., Rao, A. C. S., & Kulkarni, C. (2022). A survey on sentiment analysis methods, applications, and challenges. *Artificial Intelligence Review*, *55*(7), 5731–5780. doi:10.100710462-022-10144-1

Wiebe, J., Wilson, T., & Cardie, C. (2005). Annotating expressions of opinions and emotions in language. *Language Resources and Evaluation*, *39*(2), 165–210. doi:10.100710579-005-7880-9

Wu, Y., Schuster, M., Chen, Z., Le, Q. V., Norouzi, M., Macherey, W., . . . Dean, J. (2016). *Google's neural machine translation system: Bridging the gap between human and machine translation.* arXiv preprint arXiv:1609.08144.

Xue, L., Barua, A., Constant, N., Al-Rfou, R., Narang, S., Kale, M., Roberts, A., & Raffel, C. (2022). Byt5: Towards a token-free future with pre-trained byte-to-byte models. *Transactions of the Association for Computational Linguistics*, *10*, 291–306. doi:10.1162/tacl_a_00461

Yadav, J., Kumar, D., & Chauhan, D. (2020, July). Cyberbullying detection using pre-trained bert model. In *2020 International Conference on Electronics and Sustainable Communication Systems (ICESC)* (pp. 1096-1100). IEEE. 10.1109/ICESC48915.2020.9155700

Yadav, V., & Bethard, S. (2019). *A survey on recent advances in named entity recognition from deep learning models.* arXiv preprint arXiv:1910.11470.

Yamaguchi, Y., Amagasa, T., & Kitagawa, H. (2013, October). Landmark-based user location inference in social media. In *Proceedings of the first ACM conference on Online social networks* (pp. 223-234). 10.1145/2512938.2512941

Yan, D., Li, K., Gu, S., & Yang, L. (2020). Network-based bag-of-words model for text classification. *IEEE Access : Practical Innovations, Open Solutions*, *8*, 82641–82652. doi:10.1109/ACCESS.2020.2991074

Yang, M., Liang, Y., Zhao, W., Xu, W., Zhu, J., & Qu, Q. (2018). Task-oriented keyphrase extraction from social media. *Multimedia Tools and Applications*, *77*(3), 3171–3187. doi:10.100711042-017-5041-y

Yang, S., Lu, W., Yang, D., Li, X., Wu, C., & Wei, B. (2017). KEYPHRASEDS: Automatic generation of survey by exploiting keyphrase information. *Neurocomputing, 224*, 58–70. doi:10.1016/j.neucom.2016.10.052

Zakaryia, A., Mohammad, A. T., & Jaccomard, H. (n.d.). *Evaluation of Facebook Translation Service (FTS) in Translating Facebook Posts from English into Arabic in Terms of TAUS Adequacy and Fluency during Covid-19*. Academic Press.

Zarnoufi, R., Jaafar, H., & Abik, M. (2020). Machine normalization: Bringing social media text from non-standard to standard form. *ACM Transactions on Asian and Low-Resource Language Information Processing, 19*(4), 1–30. doi:10.1145/3378414

Zhang, L., Peng, T. Q., Zhang, Y. P., Wang, X. H., & Zhu, J. J. (2014). Content or context: Which matters more in information processing on microblogging sites. *Computers in Human Behavior, 31*, 242–249. doi:10.1016/j.chb.2013.10.031

Zhang, Q., Wang, Y., Gong, Y., & Huang, X. (2016). Keyphrase extraction using deep recurrent neural networks on Twitter. *Proceedings of the 2016 conference on empirical methods in natural language processing*, 836–845. 10.18653/v1/D16-1080

Zhao, W. X., Jiang, J., He, J., Song, Y., Achanauparp, P., Lim, E. P., & Li, X. (2011, June). Topical keyphrase extraction from twitter. In *Proceedings of the 49th annual meeting of the association for computational linguistics: Human language technologies* (pp. 379-388). Academic Press.

Zhao, Z., Zhang, Z., & Hopfgartner, F. (2021, April). A comparative study of using pre-trained language models for toxic comment classification. In *Companion Proceedings of the Web Conference 2021* (pp. 500-507). 10.1145/3442442.3452313

Zheng, C., Jiang, J. Y., Zhou, Y., Young, S. D., & Wang, W. (2020, July). Social media user geolocation via hybrid attention. In *Proceedings of the 43rd International ACM SIGIR Conference on Research and Development in Information Retrieval* (pp. 1641-1644). 10.1145/3397271.3401329

Zuo, Y., Ma, Y., Zhang, M., Wu, X., & Ren, Z. (2021). The impact of sharing physical activity experience on social network sites on residents' social connectedness: A cross-sectional survey during COVID-19 social quarantine. *Globalization and Health, 17*(1), 1–12. doi:10.118612992-021-00661-z PMID:33430894

KEY TERMS AND DEFINITIONS

Automatic Summarization: The process of extracting the important information from a document or set of documents and presenting it in a concise form so that the viewer gets the idea of what about the document actually is.

Machine Translation: Machine Translation is an application of NLP that performs the translation of text encoded in one language to some other language.

Natural Language Processing: Natural Language Processing is a discipline of Artificial Intelligence that deals with how computers can be made capable of automatically manipulating, understanding, and generating natural languages like text, and speech.

Opinion Mining: Opinion mining is an approach in NLP that tries to infer information about the emotions embedded in the text.

Social Media: Social media is an online platform that allows users to find friends, and communicate their ideas and expressions to them and the rest of the world in a way that suits them without the need to follow the linguistic rules of the language they use to communicate.

ENDNOTES

1   https://cupofjo.com/
2   https://lifehacker.com/
3   https://hotair.com/
4   https://gizmodo.com/
5   https://in.mashable.com/
6   https://statista.com
7   https://facebook.com
8   https://youtube.com
9   https://whatsapp.com
10 https://instagram.com
11 https://wechat.com
12 https://tiktok.com
13 https://messanger.com
14 https://douyin.com
15 https://qq-messenger.en.softonic.com/
16 https://weibo.com
17 https://noisy-text.github.io/2015/norm-shared-task.html
18 https://webscope.sandbox.yahoo.com.

Chapter 10
Trolling, Cyber–Stalking, Cyber–Bullying, and Identity Theft in OSNs:
Methods, Issues, and Challenges

Ovais Bashir Gashroo
Jamia Millia Islamia, India

Saima Saleem
Jamia Millia Islamia, India

Monica Mehrotra
Jamia Millia Islamia, India

ABSTRACT

Before the development of information and communication technology, social connections were confined by narrow cultural borders. User-generated multimodal information, online social networks, and rich data related to human behavior have all undergone a revolution as a result of these social technologies. However, the abuse of social technology, such as social media platforms, has given rise to a brand-new type of cyber-crimes such as cyberbullying, cyberstalking, cyber trolling, identity theft, etc. Such crimes result in a breach of privacy, a security lapse, financial fraud, and harm to public mental health and property. This chapter discusses various automated methods and systems driven by machine learning, deep learning, and fuzzy-logic-based algorithms for tackling various types of cybercrimes on various social media platforms. It then highlights various issues and challenges pertaining to the existing methods, which offer new study avenues for researchers to investigate.

DOI: 10.4018/978-1-6684-6909-5.ch010

INTRODUCTION

With the development of the Internet, the usage of communication technologies such as social media platforms have increased dramatically over time and has emerged as the most powerful networking tool of the twenty-first century. Moreover, 4.26 billion individuals utilized social media globally in 2021, with that figure likely to climb to around six billion by 2027 as can be seen in Figure 1. (S. Dixon, 2022). Communication technologies have completely altered the communicational landscape which has resulted in replacing traditional forms of crime with technological ones called Cybercrimes. Cybercrime can be committed utilizing computers or other communication devices to terrorize victims, inflict harm on them, or destroy their property. Cybercrime damages the world economy between US$375 billion and $575 billion per year, according to one estimate[1]. Broadly, a cyber-criminal can commit a crime either using a computer as a target or using a computer as a tool (Al-Khater et al., 2020).

Figure 1. Global social network user numbers from 2018 to 2022, with estimations for 2023 to 2027
Source: S. Dixon (2022)

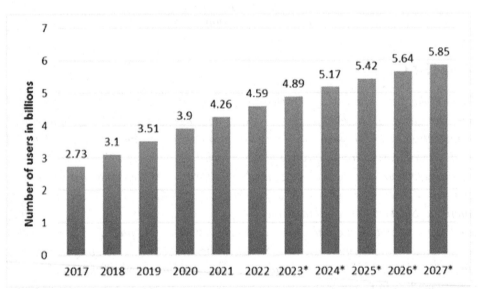

Figure 2. Types of cybercrime

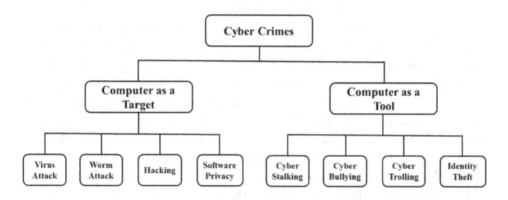

Some examples of cybercrimes where computers are targets and computers are used as a tool to commit crimes are shown in Figure 2. In this chapter, we will be discussing the crimes where computers are used as a tool to conduct crimes that include cyberstalking, cyberbullying, cyber trolling, and identity theft.

Cybercrime, such as cyber trolling, cyberstalking, cyberbullying, and identity theft, can have a negative influence on a victim's physical, emotional, or educational progress. Cyber victims are more prone to experience depression and anxiety, along with school avoidance and poor academic performance. Additionally, the victims of cybercrime have been observed to report psychosomatic ailments such as headaches, stomachaches, bedwetting, and other issues more frequently. In cases of trolling and bullying, computer-based comments are more permanent than vocal ones since comments are saved on websites, internet archives, search engine caches, and user devices. It is easier Because of the difficulty in finding and identifying the offending party's misbehaviour, it is simpler to make nasty, embarrassing, or threatening comments on the Internet. It is also difficult to prove or authenticate the act of wrongdoing and impose a meaningful legal consequence. The global threat of cyber trolling, cyber-stalking, cyber-bullying, and identity theft is serious, and its assessment and prevention have become even more critical. This is because technology is becoming more universally available, internet subscriptions are getting more affordable, and politicians are pursuing and pushing the dream of a "Digital World" with zeal. Currently, most people have Internet access through a computer, tablet, or mobile device. Children and teenagers are the most vulnerable users because they are thrown into cyberspace before they have the mental capacity to comprehend it.

With the recent rise in stories concerning trolling, cyber-stalking, cyber-bullying, and identity theft including severe issues like self-harm and suicide and the frequent appearance of horrific newspaper headlines, these crimes have gained attention on a global scale. More than one-fifth of youth who experience online harassment admit to participating in it themselves, and two-thirds of those who observe others engaging in it also report seeing it themselves (Lenhart et al., 2011). In addition to children, adults frequently experience internet bullying. Trolls on the internet, also known as cyberbullies, have the power to harass and abuse a person without worrying about the consequences of their behaviour. Politicians, actors, and athletes frequently experience cyberbullying and acknowledge the distress it brings. However, there are no definite laws or regulations to deal with this complicated subject. The relevance of this topic in the contemporary context is being acknowledged by mainstream national TV networks, who are developing campaigns and shows like "Troll Police."[2]

Cybercrimes including cyberstalking, cyberbullying, cyber trolling, and identity theft are illegal activities conducted using technology or the internet. While each of these crimes involves the use of technology or the internet, they differ in their methods and their intended targets. Table 1 shows the comparison of these 4 different cybercrimes.

Table 1. Comparison of types of cybercrime

Cyber Stalking	Cyberbullying	Cyber Trolling	Identity Theft
The aim is to harass, threaten, or intimidate an individual.	The aim is to harm or harass someone.	The aim is to elicit a strong emotional response from other users.	The aim is to misuse the personal information of the victim to open credit cards, take out loans, or make fraudulent purchases.
Use of social media, email, or other forms to make unwanted contact with the victim.	Involvement of threats, insults, or spreading rumours or false information about the victim.	Involvement in posting inflammatory or offensive comments on social media, forums, or other platforms.	Involves stealing someone's personal information, such as their name, address, or bank account information.
Can control or frighten the victim, leading to serious psychological and emotional consequences.	Typically targeted at young people, and causes severe consequences for victims, including depression, anxiety, and even suicide.	Disrupts the normal functioning of online communities.	Poses serious financial consequences that take months or even years to fully resolve, and never in some cases.

To interpret, evaluate, and model online abusive, or unpleasant content in text messages, comments, or photos, advanced computational approaches are required. As manually tracking such content is impracticable. Thus, researchers from around the world have been creating automated methods and systems for the automatic identification of several types of cybercrime on various social media platforms. However, there are still various challenges and issues in the existing methods that need to be addressed to offer efficient solutions to tackle and control such online crimes.

The remaining portions of the chapter are arranged as Section 2 offers an outline of several types of cybercrimes. Section 3 discusses various methods for cybercrime detection. Section 4 highlights various challenges and issues related to the existing cybercrime detection methods. Finally, this chapter is concluded in section 5.

TYPES OF CYBERCRIME

Cyberbullying

Cyberbullying is defined as an "aggressive, intentional act carried out by a group or individual, using electronic forms of contact, repeatedly and over time against a victim who cannot easily defend himself or herself" (Bauman et al., 2012). Bullying, long limited to the school or neighbourhood, has now entered the digital sphere as a result of the widespread use of digital social technologies like social media platforms by teenagers and adults (Smith et al., 2008). The range of ways in which cyberbullying can emerge poses a major risk to the victim's mental and physical health, including personal attacks, harassment, discriminatory behaviour, etc. The trauma resulting from bullying can also promote suicidal and self-destructive thoughts in victims (Fisher et al., 2012). The nature of social media sites has made it possible for cyberbullying to transcend physical boundaries. Numerous incidents of young people being subjected to life-threatening cyberbullying have been reported globally. A recent study (NEWALL, 2018) from Ipsos 2018 surveyed parents globally to determine the prevalence of cyberbullying. It found that almost one in five parents globally reported that their child has at least once been the victim of cyberbullying. The issue is particularly severe in India, where parents confirmed cases of cyberbullying at the greatest rate. Cyberbullying differs from traditional bullying in that the bully can remain anonymous and the victim might be difficult to identify. This, along with the clear absence of monitoring and control in cyberspace, makes the problem more complicated to handle.

Cyberstalking

Cyberstalking is a "course of actions that involves more than one incident perpetrated through or utilizing electronic means that cause distress, fear or alarm" (Maple et al., 2012). Sometimes this problem is related to people's obsession or their feeling

Figure 3. Prevalence of cyberbullying
Source: https://www.statista.com/chart/15926/the-share-of-parents-wh
o-say-their-child-has-experienced-cyberbullying/

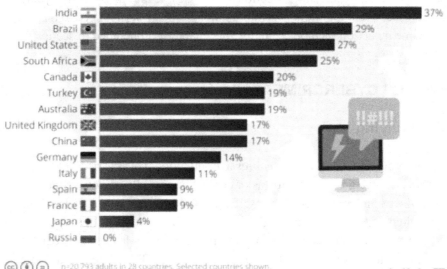

of insecurity to track their close ones. Still, there are reported cases where such acts led to violence and harm to people. The first case of cyberstalking was registered in India in 2009 according to the BBC report (Roy, 2015). Nearly 20% of people have experienced cyberstalking while using online applications (Jurgens et al., 2012). A cyber stalker can quickly find confidential information about a potential victim given a large amount of personal information available through social media platforms. Cyberstalking is routinely underestimated by the public, researchers, and the government. It is a rising global cybercrime that is responsible for creating a virtual fear world, and it requires significant attention.

Cyber Trolling

Trolling is considered an antisocial behaviour that disrupts a constructive discussion on a social media platform (J. Cheng et al., 2017). Before the inception of social media platforms, trolling was present usually in the form of verbal communication or physical actions. But online platforms give access to everyone to join a discussion and contribute to it the way they want without any prior moderation to the content they share. From trolling famous personalities present on online social media platforms to normal people sharing their thoughts and opinions over some issue, everyone can become a target of trolling. This can have effects on the person's emotional state, it can also lead to physical threats and offline harassment for users. Due to its negative impacts on the well-being of a person to the collective impact on society, trolling content must be detected on time and taken proper measures to stop its spread. A 'Troll' can be sometimes a single user, sometimes a group of users, and sometimes a whole community against another community based on their gender, religion, ethnicity, race etc. As can be seen, trolling as a behaviour can be disruptive to the peace and harmony of the overall community and society, we live in. Even if the target is a single or a whole community, the negative effects range from emotional distress, chaos, a threat to life and property, harassment, and people feeling unsafe.

Since trolls actively disseminate hoaxes and false information during important events like elections or referendums, trolling becomes critical. These days, new content is being created every day for a wide range of internet channels, including social media status updates, videos, photos, and applications. Social media, e-commerce websites, mobile platforms, and applications, among other types of media, are used by people to share information and to express their suggestions and viewpoints on goods and services as well as social issues. Trolling can hamper the progress of various business enterprises that are dealing in e-commerce platforms, as trolls can write bogus reviews for products just to confuse the consumers purchasing decisions, which can be seen in today's market are driven and influenced by online product reviews.

The need of the hour is systems that can automatically detect and remove such content present in text, image, or video form. Researchers have developed machine learning and deep learning-based methods to curb the menace and devised techniques that can be leveraged to detect such content on these online social media platforms. Some of them are discussed in the forthcoming section to get an insight into the current progress of the research and various limitations and challenges will also be discussed.

Identity Theft

As per Wang et al. (2022), online identity theft is a common online crime that involves the intentional use of another person's account (Egele et al., 2017), typically to gain a financial benefit or acquire credit for other benefits in another person's name. In reality, hacked accounts are frequently used as entry points for most cybercrimes (Onaolapo et al., 2016), such as blackmail (Bilge et al., 2009), fraud (Pratt et al.,

2010), and spam (Thomas et al., 2011), (H. Li et al., 2017). As a result, detecting identity theft is critical to ensuring users' safety in the cyber world.

As per Golladay (2020), there are both financial and reputation losses associated with the victims of identity theft. Following their victimization, victims stated that they needed to take further measures or alter their lifestyles. Victims may borrow money or make changes to their lifestyle or finances. A lot of victims were forced to use credit cards they had not intended to use, borrow money from friends and relatives, take out bank loans, and borrow money from retirement funds. Lifestyle changes included moving, liquidating goods, requesting government assistance, switching careers, and devoting time away from friends, family, and interests. Authors (Sharp et al., 2004) stated victims suffered from a variety of mental and physical side effects, including gastrointestinal issues, trepidation, anxiety, insomnia, and rage.

Online identity theft allows the criminal and victim to traverse jurisdictional lines, particularly international borders. When people are in danger of being harmed by an offender on the other side of the world, in a nation with distinct laws, rules, and procedures, policy and research should concentrate on how to safeguard them as effectively as possible.

Cybercrime is a problem that has arisen from the usage of the internet and the increased use of social media platforms. Amongst all types of cybercrime, identity theft occurs when an unauthorized person uses information that is specific to a person such as a name, photograph, or other personal information without any proper permission. Identity theft intends to commit fraud or other crimes under the blanket of someone else's identity. As has been reported in past incidents of identity theft, the information that was stolen constituted personal details like name, date of birth, credit/debit card details, bank account details, and personal photos. One of the biggest misuses of such data has been money-related. Cybercriminals stole personal information from victims, and they misused that information to get access to bank accounts and withdraw their money without his/her knowledge. Identity theft incidents have also led to cases where considerable damage was caused to a person's reputation by getting access to the list of social media friends/ followers and sharing obscene content on those platforms through accounts that were created using the stolen information. We can say those cybercriminals who steal personal information usually have different motivations to do so. Some limit themselves to impersonating the user's account, while others go ahead and use the information for extortion, fraud, stealing money, and spam using different online services.

Different authentication methods to establish a user's identity have been developed by developers to prevent and detect identity theft in online services. The need of the hour is systems that can automatically detect and remove such content present in text, image, or video form. Researchers have developed machine learning, deep learning-based and fuzzy-based methods to curb the menace and devised techniques that can be leveraged to detect such content on these online social media platforms. Some of them are discussed here to get an insight into the current progress of the research and various limitations and challenges will be also discussed.

AUTOMATED DETECTION OF CYBERBULLYING, STALKING, TROLLING, AND IDENTITY THEFT

Due to the generation of a massive volume of content (text and images) from various social media sites like Facebook, Instagram, Twitter, etc., manually detecting cybercrimes like Cyberbullying, Cyberstalking, Cyber trolling, and Identity Theft is impossible. Moreover, using conventional methods like statistical methods is challenging in terms of accuracy and scale.

Advanced computational methods are imperative to process, analyze and model such bitter, taunting, abusive or negative content in text messages, comments, or images efficiently. Researchers globally have been working to build automated methods and systems powered by machine learning, deep learning, natural language processing and fuzzy logic-based systems for the detection of several types of cybercrimes on various social media platforms. Figure 4 shows various classical machine learning, deep learning, and fuzzy logic-based algorithms that have been used to build methods for detecting cyberbullying, cyberstalking, cyber trolling, and identity theft from online social media.

Machine Learning Methods

This subsection covers the methods based on machine learning algorithms that have been developed to detect various cyber crimes on online social networks.

Machine Learning comprises a set of techniques that provides a machine with the capability to learn automatically with no human programming (Navamani & Kannammal, 2015). The machine can learn either in a supervised or unsupervised way. In the supervised learning method, the machine learns on labelled training data to mean the correct output is already known. The machine tries to learn how inputs are mapped to outputs to make its predictions later. In unsupervised learning methods, the machine learns from unlabeled and acts on that data to predict output with no supervision (Shalev-Shwartz & Ben-David, 2013). Machine learning involves supervised learning algorithms including Naïve Bayes (NB), K-Nearest Neighbor (KNN), Decision Tree (DT), Random Forest (RF), Support Vector Machine (SVM), etc. as well as unsupervised learning algorithms like self-organizing maps and, k-means, etc.

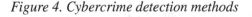

Figure 4. Cybercrime detection methods

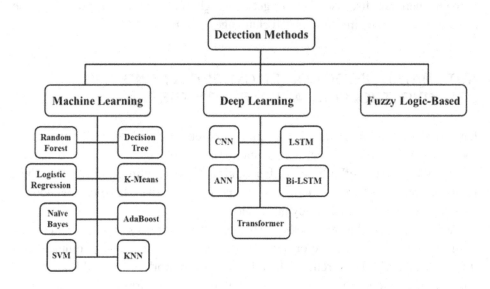

One of the early research projects on NLP cyberbullying detection was conducted by the Massachusetts Institute of Technology. For this job, the authors explored the predictive strength of n-grams, part-of-speech information, and sentiment information based on profane lexicons. They employed various supervised machine learning algorithms to detect sensitive topics from some controversial YouTube comments such as "race & culture," "sexuality," and "intelligence." However, their system produced a low accuracy of 66.7% (Dinakar et al., 2011).

The biggest social media sites that have ingrained themselves into users' lives are Facebook and Twitter. As a result, these websites are now the most often used venues for cyberbullying victimization. To detect cyberbullying on Twitter, (Sanchez & Kumar, 2011) were among the first researchers to propose a cyberbullying tweet detection method. They employed an NB classifier and identified tweets that contained offensive language targeted at a particular gender. Another study by Al-Garadi et al. (2016) presented a cyberbullying tweets detection tool. They proposed several types of features derived from each tweet to be utilized in several machine learning classifiers such as SVM, NB, KNN and DT to detect cyberbullying.

Saravanaraj et al. (2016) proposed a general framework for identifying rumours and cyberbullying tweets. Machine learning algorithms like NB and RF were utilized for classification and used wor2vec for representing textual content. Furthermore, they asserted that their framework could extract demographic information about the perpetrators, such as name, gender, and age. Identifying the Bully is also equally imperative as identifying cyberbullying. To this end, Sri Nandhini and Sheeba (2015) presented a system for detecting cyber bully and cyberbullying using the Levenshtein algorithm and NB method respectively using FormSpring.me question and answer website posts. To categorize the tweets based on user behaviour (Balakrishnan et al., 2020) presented a machine learning-based ensemble method. They categorized the tweets into bully, spammer, aggressor, and normal.

An unsupervised machine learning approach is proposed by Di Capua et al. (2016) for the detection of bullying behaviour in social networks. Their approach is based on a Growing hierarchical Self-organizing map. Frommholz et al. (2016) proposed a framework, "Anti cyberstalking Text-Based System (ACTS)" for Textual Analysis and cyberstalking detection using machine learning algorithms. It determines whether a text message is valid, or undesirable based on user profiles, content, and author identification. Ganesan and Mayilvahanan (2017) proposed an approach based on supervised and unsupervised algorithms such as SVM, DT, NB, ANN, and K-means to analyze the cybercrime textual data from different web pages. The authors asserted that their approach will be able to distinguish between violent and non-violent cybercrime offences as well as between different sorts of cybercrimes, such as cyberterrorism, cyberstalking, cyber-fraud, and cyber theft.

For enhancing cyberbullying and cyberstalking detection on social media networks, Islam et al. (2020) presented an approach utilizing supervised machine learning algorithms. The authors evaluated their suggested approach using various classifiers such as DT, RF, NB, and SVM. They used Bag-of-Words (BoW) and TF-IDF (Term Frequency- Inverse Document Frequency) for extracting features. Email is one of the most often-used ways of cyberstalking, and the availability of email's anonymous character combined with its protocol flaws has helped to significantly increase the number of email crimes (Roberts, 2008). To automate the detection and documentation of email-based cyberstalking evidence (Ghasem et al., 2015) proposed the "Anti-Cyberstalking Email System" (ACES) framework. They integrated text categorization, statistical analysis, and supervised machine learning for finding, filtering, and saving evidence of cyberstalking emails. Dughyala et al. (2021) proposed an automated solution for online stalker identification using Machine Learning and Natural Language Processing techniques. Machine learning techniques such as Decision Trees and SGD regressors have been used for the task. Gautama and Bansal (2022) used an SVM machine learning algorithm based on Bag of Word with unigram, bigram, and trigram features for detecting cyberstalking from tweet texts. Gautam and Bansal (2022) reviewed various supervised machine learning algorithms to determine the largely used effective algorithm for cyberstalking, and cyberbullying detection on Facebook and Twitter. They found that LR and SVM performed the best with the highest accuracy.

As there are very fewer data available for identity theft detection and the data related to identifying a particular user is also not available, the authors (Villar-Rodríguez et al.,

2016) produced synthetic data of connection time traces of users. The dataset created includes actual social network user behaviour from people who maintain frequent connection behaviour. They employed a support vector machine with a synthetically created feature set to represent any non-observable behaviour in the user connection record that appears to be an imitation attack. This study offered an early-warning system that would provide an alert if the user signed into the account's connection behaviour changes. The technique uses the user's behaviour to train the SVM model and determine whether the user's activity matches its activity behaviour on social media platforms. An investigation of Facebook wall posts produced by 46,952 individuals was performed to validate the expected connection time behavioural regularity.

The authors (Wang et al., 2022) looked into the viability of developing a user identification system for OSNs that uses a behavioural model that performs well starting with low-quality behavioural data. Through the incorporation of online and offline activities, they propose a joint probabilistic generative model. Extensive evaluations of real-world OSN datasets support the designed joint model's comprehensive performance in terms of detection efficacy, response latency, and robustness when used for identity theft detection in OSNs. The joint model surpasses the conventional fused model significantly. Their proposed model outperforms the existing ones, with area under the receiver operating characteristic curve (AUC) values of 0.956 in Foursquare and 0.947 in Yelp, respectively.

The authors (Wang et al., 2019) analyze the viability of creating a fusion behavioural model for tailored identity theft detection in OSNs by starting with a variety of behavioural projection models and working their way up to a high-quality, comprehensive model. In Wang et al. (2017), they used a probabilistic generative model to detect identity theft in mobile social networks. They experimented on two datasets namely Foursquare and yelp. Semantic & spatial features were used in experimentation and semantic features showed to achieve better performance in identity theft detection than spatial features.

Deep Learning Methods

This subsection covers the methods based on deep learning that have been developed to detect hostile behaviours on online social networks.

Deep Learning is a sub-branch of machine learning that includes algorithms that are motivated by the structure and operation of the brain called Artificial neural networks (Al-Sarem et al., 2019). Deep learning techniques are proven effective and produce cutting-edge outcomes with end-to-end training and representation learning capabilities (Kumar & Jaiswal, 2021; Young et al., 2018). The DL paradigm has several benefits over traditional machine learning, including a noticeable increase in performance and the removal of the laborious feature extraction procedure.

Additionally, neural networks are thought to be superior to machine learning algorithms because of their great fault tolerance against noisy input data (KRIESEL, 2007). Deep learning algorithms include Convolutional Neural Networks (CNN), Recurrent Neural Networks (RNN) Long Short-Term memory neural Networks (LSTM), Bidirectional Long Short-Term memory neural networks (Bi-LSTM), etc.

A methodology for detecting cyberbullying was given by Agrawal and Awekar (2018). They argued that their method circumvents some drawbacks of currently existing systems, which confine the detection to a single type of cyberbullying and rely on handmade features that standard machine learning algorithms must give. To get over these restrictions, the authors investigated four deep learning architectures: CNN, LSTM, BiLSTM, and BiLSTM with an attention layer. Bullying, racism, sexism, and attack were the four categories the authors used to categorize hate speech on social media platforms. They also used transfer learning to apply the information gained from deep learning on one dataset to another similar dataset. The examined architectures underwent tests on various datasets including Twitter, Wikipedia, and Formspring.

Sadiq et al. (2021) investigated different deep architectures such as MLP, CNN-LSTM and CNN-BiLSTM for detecting cyberbullying presented on Twitter comments. Both deep learning approaches (CNN-LSTM and CNN-BiLSTM) achieved great detection performance with an accuracy of 92%. Gambäck and Sikdar (2017) presented a system based on CNN for classifying the comments on Twitter into multiple categories such as sexism, racism, both (i.e., sexism and racism), and non-offensive comments. Pradhan et al. (2020) investigated the efficacy of self-attention models that attained cutting-edge outcomes in a variety of machine translation tasks. Three data sources from Formspring, Wikipedia, and Twitter were used by the authors to examine the utility of the self-attention model known as the transformer architecture for cyberbullying detection.

A few studies (Haidar et al., 2017; Plaza-del-Arco et al., 2021; Van Hee et al., 2018) have proposed methods for cyberbullying detection from non-English texts. Haidar et al. (2017, 2018) have focused on Arabic language tweets. Van Hee et al. (2018) implemented a system to automatically detect signals of cyberbullying content from social media posts and applied the proposed system to texts in Dutch in addition to English posts. Plaza-del-Arco et al. (2021) proposed an approach to detect cyberbullying in social media that is related to Spanish content by utilizing deep learning techniques.

The use of image and video content for cyberbullying has significantly increased (Seiler & Navarro, 2014). Moreover, it has been asserted that "cyberbullying grows more vicious with images and videos" (Janet Kornblum, 2008). However, only a few Works have been done where pictures are utilized for the discovery of cyberbullying utilizing deep learning models like CNN, and RNN or where semantic image features are utilized for identifying bullying (L. Cheng et al., 2019). Although the significance of comprehending multimodal content for cyberbullying identification has been widely recognized, the accuracy of cyberbullying detection methods is still limited because they are still primarily focused on (advanced) text analysis. Few initiatives (Kumar & Sachdeva, 2021; Singh et al., 2017) have been made thus far to use visual cues to detect cyberbullying. Multimodal approaches must be created immediately since audio and video characteristics may enhance text features for earlier and more precise cyberbullying identification.

For identifying trolls in online chats, Al-Adhaileh et al. (2022) suggested a deep learning model (CNN-BiLSTM) in their article. The research work included two independent experiments. Consequently, when trained and tested on numerical data, the CNN-BiLSTM model outperformed text data. This is because the first set of data was numerical, and the second set was text. The model produced satisfactory results for both experiments.

The work of Saeed et al. (2022) presented TROLLMAGNFIER, a troll detection system for troll accounts. The system effectively distinguished normal and troll accounts on the Reddit dataset with precision and recall scores up to 97.8%. They used various machine learning models on their dataset and their results showed random forest outperforming KNN, Linear support vector machine and decision tree in four evaluated performance metrics. Of all the detected accounts as troll accounts by the TROLLMAGNIFIER system, they validated it by performing further analysis over the detected troll accounts on Reddit, some of the accounts had been suspended by Reddit, and some had deleted the comments that caused the system to detect the account as troll account. They used nine features that demonstrate the distinguishable behaviour of troll accounts like total comments posted by accounts, total submissions, the age of the account, etc., all of which are relatable and somehow are responsible for distinguishing the behaviour of normal from a troll account.

Ting Li et al. proposed a hierarchical cyber troll detection method with text and user behaviour. They constructed a new cyber troll dataset from the social media platform Weibo. Through their analysis, they conclude that there are differences at the behavioural level among users who have commented on a post multiple times or have commented once only. Based on the number of comments by a user, they divided the users into two categories namely, inactive, and active. The degree of user participation, the influence of users, the popularity of comments, and the popularity of posts commented on by users are the behavioural features they constructed based on the statistical features of the dataset. They also extracted text features from the dataset using TF-IDF and used feature selection methods to select the top features among the ranked lists. Their model has achieved better detection performance results in terms of accuracy, precision, recall and F1 score than the baseline models like Naïve Bayes (NB), Logistic Regression (LR), Decision Tree (DT), and Support Vector Machine (SVM).

Table 2. Automated methods for detecting cyber crimes

Ref	Cyber Crime	Content-Type	Dataset	Methods	Language
(Sri Nandhini & Sheeba, 2015)	Cyberbullying	Text	FormSpring.me, MySpace.com	Levenshtein distance algorithm and naïve bayes	English
(Dinakar et al., 2011)	Cyberbullying	Text	YouTube comments	Naive Bayes, JRIP, J48, SVM	English
(Al-Garadi et al., 2016)	Cyberbullying	Text	Twitter	SVM, Naïve bayes, KNN and Decision Trees	English
(Haidar et al., 2017)	Cyberbullying	Text	Facebook, Twitter	Naïve Bayes and SVM	Arabic
(Van Hee et al., 2018)	Cyberbullying	Text	ASKfm posts	Binary classifier and linear SVM classifier	English, Dutch
(Haidar et al., 2018)	Cyberbullying	Text	Twitter	FFNN	Arabic
(L. Cheng et al., 2019)	Cyberbullying	Images	Instagram	CNN, RNN	
(Sanchez & Kumar, 2011)	Cyberbullying	Text	Twitter	Naïve Bayes	English
(Saravanaraj et al., 2016)	Cyberbullying	Text	Twitter	NB and RF	English
(Balakrishnan et al., 2020)	Cyberbullying	Text	Twitter	Random Forest	English
(Gambäck & Sikdar, 2017)	Cyberbullying	Text	Twitter	CNN	English
(Sadiq et al., 2021)	Cyberbullying	Text	Twitter	CNN-LSTM, CNN-BiLSTM	English
(Pradhan et al., 2020)	Cyberbullying	Text	Twitter, Wikipedia, Formsping	Transformer	English
(Agrawal & Awekar, 2018)	Cyberbullying	Text	Twitter, Wikipedia, Formsping.me	CNN, LSTM, Bi-LSTM with Attention	English
(Plaza-del-Arco et al., 2021)	Cyberbullying	Text	Twitter	CNN, LSTM, BILSTM, BERT	Spanish
(Singh et al., 2017)	Cyberbullying	Text, Image	Instagram	Bagging Algorithm	English
(Kumar & Sachdeva, 2021)	Cyberbullying	Text, Image, Infographic	YouTube, Instagram, Twitter.	Deep CNN	English
(Di Capua et al., 2016)	Cyberbullying	Text	Twitter, YouTube, FormSpring	Growing hierarchical Self-organizing map	English
(Ganesan & Mayilvahanan, 2017)	Cyber Stalking	Text	Web pages	SVM, DT, NB, ANN, and K-means	English

continued on following page

Table 2. Continued

Ref	Cyber Crime	Content-Type	Dataset	Methods	Language
(Islam et al., 2020)	Cyber Stalking, Cyber Bullying	Text	Facebook, Twitter	NB, SVM, DT, RF	English
(Ghasem et al., 2015)	Cyber Stalking	Text	Email	NN, SVM	English
(Gautama & Bansal, 2022)	Cyber Stalking	Text	Twitter	SVM	English
(Gautam & Bansal, 2022)	Cyber Stalking	Text	Twitter	LR, SVM, RF, DT, KNN, NB	English
(Dughyala et al., 2021)	Cyber Stalking	Text	Twitter	SGDRegressor, DT	English
(Wang et al., 2022)	Identity Theft	Text	Foursquare & yelp	Composite Behavioral Modelling	English
(Wang et al., 2019)	Identity Theft	Text	Foursquare & Yelp	Behavioral Projection Models	English
(Villar-Rodríguez et al., 2016)	Identity Theft	Text	Facebook	Support Vector Machine (SVM)	English
(Wang et al., 2017)	Identity Theft	Text	Foursquare & Yelp	Probabilistic Generative Model	English
(Al-Adhaileh et al., 2022)	Troll Detection	Text	Reddit	CNN-BiLSTM	English
(Saeed et al., 2022)	Troll Account Detection	Text	Reddit	KNN, Linear SVM, Decision Tree (DT), Random Forest (RF)	English
(T. Li et al., 2021)	Troll Detection	text	Weibo	XGBoost	Chinese

Fuzzy-Logic Methods

To detect identity theft, a research study (Concepción-Sánchez et al., 2018) proposes the use of a text-mining and fuzzy logic-based system to decide if a person is being victimized by this problem. To do so, the natural language of each user is considered, considering values such as the total frequency of appearance of words and expressions they do not frequently use. Other factors such as the location from which users log on or the number of messages sent in a brief period are also considered to make the final decision.

ISSUES AND CHALLENGES

1. **Language:** Particularly among the younger population, language is changing swiftly. The language culture is constantly incorporating new slang. As a result, researchers are encouraged to suggest dynamic algorithms to monitor for new slang and acronyms associated with aggressive behaviour on SM websites and to constantly upgrade the training processes of ML algorithms using recently introduced phrases.

2. **Lack of Labelled Benchmark Cybercrime Datasets:** The lack of benchmark datasets is because there is an absence of collaboration between researchers and law enforcement in terms of data collection on cyber criminals.

3. To get over the problem of a lack of availability of cybercrime datasets, it is advised to develop cyber criminal profiling that researchers can utilize as cybercrime datasets to get over the problem of the lack of availability of such datasets. However, developing cyber criminal profiling necessitates a significant collaboration between law enforcement, researchers, and governmental authorities. The legality of disclosing this information is debatable because the data that can be used in cybercriminal profiling is primarily crucial, sensitive, and private. The data of cybercriminals provided by law enforcement can be used by researchers for research while also safeguarding their privacy if they can discover a way to secure data privacy (Al-Khater et al., 2020). The variety of cybercrimes, which can occur on many platforms like Twitter, YouTube, Instagram, or through networks, including various dataset types, is another challenge. Existing research datasets, however, are frequently skewed toward the platform of interest.

4. **Cultural Variance:** There is a cultural variance regarding how victims and observers both perceive harassment and aggression. Due to the advent of OSNs, for example, what was once regarded as cyberbullying may no longer be regarded as such today. Given that cultural influences also have an impact on deviant behaviours online. It is crucial to consider how aggressive behaviour is conveyed in social media terminology when annotating the data. A multinational culture permeates OSNs. Machine learning, however, always picks up the latest information from examples. As a result, it is still unclear how to build examples that accurately depict many cultures and solid work from various fields is needed. Cross-disciplinary coordination is particularly desirable for this reason.

5. **Anonymous Identifications:** Various social networks support anonymous user interactions which makes them hard to trace and is one of the main factors contributing to increased cyber aggression (Nakano et al., 2016). For example, according to the report (Patchin, 2022), less than half of kids who have been

cyberbullied are aware of who is responsible. Effective methods need to be developed to monitor, detect and control the behaviour of such users.

6. **Low-Resource Language Content:** Users posting content in low-resource languages is a big challenge for the research community. The resources available for such languages are extremely low and developing automatic systems to detect offensive remarks from the content will be a challenge. Also, the content posted in the form of slang and symbols that are known to a particular group or community is a challenge that needs more attention.

7. **OSN Platform Policies and Regulations:** If social media companies give more emphasis on privacy and do not let users share anything related to their identity, which will violate the nature of social networks and will eventually lead them to become "non-social" networks.

8. Many organizations have produced features that help users to decide what to share and what not to, giving the control users hands to be the guardians of their privacy. This helps in solving the problem to some extent, but this method has its limitations. The default privacy settings are the same for every new user for a particular platform. And most of the users are not so familiar with the platform's features, and many inexperienced users are not aware of the kind of cybercrimes that happen over these platforms. So, giving the control to users to decide for themselves is also not a kind of solution that will solve the problem completely. The organizations too must come forward with policies, regulations and new and improved methods that can curb these issues on a bigger level.

9. Social media platforms have become an easy target to get those details of a victim that are usually not available through other ways. Suppose a user is using some banking application or other financial platform where some personal information is stored, it is very unlikely that the attacker will try to get information like personal photographs, addresses, and date of birth like personal information from these platforms. Social media on the other side are popular for this very thing only that they allow users to share their photos, and other personal information and let that content be visible and accessible to other connected or non-connected users. It makes these platforms a favourite place for cybercriminals, as all that is required to steal information related to someone's identity is available at a commonplace. It becomes easy for anyone to see the photos of their friends or someone they know on a social media platform profile and not believe that it can be a fake profile created to attack the victim's identity or cause any damage to his reputation or revenge.

CONCLUSION

In this chapter, a variety of cybercrimes were broadly classified, and it was highlighted how social media platforms can be exploited by individuals with malicious intentions who are located remotely using devices like laptops, tablets, or mobile phones equipped with an internet connection. The research community has developed advanced computational approaches to comprehend, evaluate and model harmful content in online communications such as text messages, comments, or photos. Due to the impracticality of manual tracking and moderation for vast amounts of generated content which would incur substantial monetary costs for social network organizations; accurate automatic detection techniques utilizing deep learning methods along with knowledge from other fields including psychology and sociology have become necessary at present times.

As discussed in the chapter, there are still various challenges and issues in the existing methods that need to be addressed to offer efficient solutions to tackle and control such online crimes. With every passing day, social media platforms are growing at a very fast rate, and their decision of including more languages in their platforms so that users from any part of the world know any language can use these platforms has posed a great challenge to the research community with very little information available for low resource languages, to be able to tackle such offensive content posted on social media. Going through the available literature, offensive English language content has been detected with promising results by using deep learning methods. This chapter highlighted some of the works conducted on Arabic, and Chinese datasets too, and the work in these languages is progressing at an excellent rate. The future work of this work will be to highlight and address the challenges present in the content shared using low-resource languages like Hindi, Urdu, Bengali, etc. and how can machine learning be used to lessen the effects of this content on the victim's life.

REFERENCES

Agrawal, S., & Awekar, A. (2018). Deep learning for detecting cyberbullying across multiple social media platforms. Lecture Notes in Computer Science, 10772. doi:10.1007/978-3-319-76941-7_11

Al-Adhaileh, M. H., Aldhyani, T. H. H., & Alghamdi, A. D. (2022). Online Troll Reviewer Detection Using Deep Learning Techniques. *Applied Bionics and Biomechanics, 2022*, 2022. doi:10.1155/2022/4637594 PMID:35747397

Al-Garadi, M. A., Varathan, K. D., & Ravana, S. D. (2016). Cybercrime detection in online communications: The experimental case of cyberbullying detection in the Twitter network. *Computers in Human Behavior*, *63*, 433–443. Advance online publication. doi:10.1016/j.chb.2016.05.051

Al-Khater, W. A., Al-Maadeed, S., Ahmed, A. A., Sadiq, A. S., & Khan, M. K. (2020). Comprehensive review of cybercrime detection techniques. *IEEE Access : Practical Innovations, Open Solutions*, *8*, 137293–137311. Advance online publication. doi:10.1109/ACCESS.2020.3011259

Al-Sarem, M., Boulila, W., Al-Harby, M., Qadir, J., & Alsaeedi, A. (2019). Deep learning-based rumor detection on microblogging platforms: A systematic review. In IEEE Access (Vol. 7). doi:10.1109/ACCESS.2019.2947855

Balakrishnan, V., Khan, S., & Arabnia, H. R. (2020). Improving cyberbullying detection using Twitter users' psychological features and machine learning. *Computers & Security*, *90*, 101710. Advance online publication. doi:10.1016/j.cose.2019.101710

Bauman, S., Cross, D., & Walker, J. (2012). Principles of Cyberbullying Research: Definitions, Measures, and Methodology. In *Principles of Cyberbullying Research. Definitions, Measures, and Methodology*. doi:10.4324/9780203084601

Bilge, L., Strufe, T., Balzarotti, D., & Kirda, E. (2009). All your contacts are belong to us: Automated identity theft attacks on social networks. *WWW'09 - Proceedings of the 18th International World Wide Web Conference*. 10.1145/1526709.1526784

Cheng, J., Bernstein, M., Danescu-Niculescu-mizil, C., & Leskovec, J. (2017). Anyone can become a troll: Causes of trolling behavior in online discussions. *Proceedings of the ACM Conference on Computer Supported Cooperative Work, CSCW*. 10.1145/2998181.2998213

Cheng, L., Guo, R., Silva, Y., Hall, D., & Liu, H. (2019). Hierarchical attention networks for cyberbullying detection on the instagram social network. *SIAM International Conference on Data Mining, SDM 2019*. 10.1137/1.9781611975673.27

Concepción-Sánchez, J., Molina-Gil, J., Caballero-Gil, P., & Santos-González, I. (2018). Fuzzy logic system for identity theft detection in social networks. *Proceedings - 2018 International Conference on Big Data Innovations and Applications, Innovate-Data 2018*. 10.1109/Innovate-Data.2018.00017

Di Capua, M., Di Nardo, E., & Petrosino, A. (2016). Unsupervised cyber bullying detection in social networks. *Proceedings - International Conference on Pattern Recognition, 0*. 10.1109/ICPR.2016.7899672

Dinakar, K., Reichart, R., & Lieberman, H. (2011). Modeling the detection of textual cyberbullying. *AAAI Workshop - Technical Report, WS-11-02.*

Dixon, S. (2022). *Number of global social network users 2018-2022, with forecasts up until 2027.* https://www.statista.com/statistics/278414/number-of-worldwi de-social-network-users/#statisticContainer

Dughyala, N., Potluri, S., Sumesh, K. J., & Pavithran, V. (2021). Automating the Detection of Cyberstalking. *Proceedings of the 2nd International Conference on Electronics and Sustainable Communication Systems, ICESC 2021.* 10.1109/ICESC51422.2021.9532858

Egele, M., Stringhini, G., Kruegel, C., & Vigna, G. (2017). Towards Detecting Compromised Accounts on Social Networks. *IEEE Transactions on Dependable and Secure Computing, 14*(4), 447–460. Advance online publication. doi:10.1109/TDSC.2015.2479616

Fisher, H. L., Moffitt, T. E., Houts, R. M., Belsky, D. W., Arseneault, L., & Caspi, A. (2012). Bullying victimisation and risk of self harm in early adolescence: Longitudinal cohort study. *BMJ (Clinical Research Ed.), 344*(7855), e2683. Advance online publication. doi:10.1136/bmj.e2683 PMID:22539176

Frommholz, I., al-Khateeb, H. M., Potthast, M., Ghasem, Z., Shukla, M., & Short, E. (2016). On Textual Analysis and Machine Learning for Cyberstalking Detection. *Datenbank-Spektrum: Zeitschrift fur Datenbanktechnologie: Organ der Fachgruppe Datenbanken der Gesellschaft fur Informatik e.V, 16*(2), 127–135. Advance online publication. doi:10.100713222-016-0221-x PMID:29368749

Gambäck, B., & Sikdar, U. K. (2017). *Using Convolutional Neural Networks to Classify Hate-Speech.* doi:10.18653/v1/W17-3013

Ganesan, M., & Mayilvahanan, P. (2017). Cyber Crime Analysis in Social Media Using Data Mining Technique. *International Journal of Pure and Applied Mathematics, 116*(22).

Gautam, A. K., & Bansal, A. (2022). Performance analysis of supervised machine learning techniques for cyberstalking detection in social media. *Journal of Theoretical and Applied Information Technology, 100*(2).

Gautama, A. K., & Bansal, A. (2022). A Predictive Model for Cyberstalking Detection on Twitter Using Support Vector Machine (Svm). *AIJR Abstracts,* 12.

Ghasem, Z., Frommholz, I., & Maple, C. (2015). Machine Learning Solutions for controlling Cyberbullying and Cyberstalking. *Journal of Information Security Research*, *6*(2).

Golladay, K. A. (2020). Identity theft: Nature, extent, and global response. In The Palgrave Handbook of International Cybercrime and Cyberdeviance. doi:10.1007/978-3-319-78440-3_40

Haidar, B., Chamoun, M., & Serrhrouchni, A. (2017). A multilingual system for cyberbullying detection: Arabic content detection using machine learning. *Advances in Science. Technology and Engineering Systems*, *2*(6), 275–284. Advance online publication. doi:10.25046/aj020634

Haidar, B., Chamoun, M., & Serrhrouchni, A. (2018). Arabic Cyberbullying Detection: Using Deep Learning. *Proceedings of the 2018 7th International Conference on Computer and Communication Engineering, ICCCE 2018*. 10.1109/ICCCE.2018.8539303

Islam, M. M., Uddin, M. A., Islam, L., Akter, A., Sharmin, S., & Acharjee, U. K. (2020). Cyberbullying Detection on Social Networks Using Machine Learning Approaches. *2020 IEEE Asia-Pacific Conference on Computer Science and Data Engineering, CSDE 2020*. 10.1109/CSDE50874.2020.9411601

Jurgens, D. A., Mohammad, S. M., Turney, P. D., & Holyoak, K. J. (2012). SemEval-2012 Task 2: Measuring degrees of relational similarity. **SEM 2012 - 1st Joint Conference on Lexical and Computational Semantics, 2*.

Kornblum. (2008). *Cyberbullying grows bigger and meaner with photos, video*. https://abcnews.go.com/Technology/AheadoftheCurve/story?id=5376341&page=1

Kriesel, D. (2007). *A Brief Introduction to Neural Networks*. https://www.dkriesel.com/en/science/neural_networks

Kumar, A., & Jaiswal, A. (2021). A Deep Swarm-Optimized Model for Leveraging Industrial Data Analytics in Cognitive Manufacturing. *IEEE Transactions on Industrial Informatics*, *17*(4), 2938–2946. Advance online publication. doi:10.1109/TII.2020.3005532

Kumar, A., & Sachdeva, N. (2021). Multimodal cyberbullying detection using capsule network with dynamic routing and deep convolutional neural network. *Multimedia Systems*. Advance online publication. doi:10.100700530-020-00747-5

Lenhart, A., Madden, M., Smith, A., Purcell, K., Zickuhr, K., Rainie, L., & Project, A. L. (2011). *Teens, Kindness and Cruelty on Social Network Sites.* PewResearchCenter.

Li, H., Fei, G., Wang, S., Liu, B., Shao, W., Mukherjee, A., & Shao, J. (2017). Bimodal distribution and co-bursting in review spam detection. *26th International World Wide Web Conference, WWW 2017.* 10.1145/3038912.3052582

Li, T., Yu, K., & Wu, X. (2021). Hierarchical Cyber Troll Detection with Text and User Behavior. *Proceedings of 2021 7th IEEE International Conference on Network Intelligence and Digital Content, IC-NIDC 2021.* 10.1109/IC-NIDC54101.2021.9660415

Maple, C., Short, E., Brown, A., Bryden, C., & Salter, M. (2012). Cyberstalking in the UK: Analysis and recommendations. *International Journal of Distributed Systems and Technologies, 3*(4), 34–51. Advance online publication. doi:10.4018/jdst.2012100104

Nakano, T., Suda, T., Okaie, Y., & Moore, M. J. (2016). Analysis of Cyber Aggression and Cyber-Bullying in Social Networking. *Proceedings - 2016 IEEE 10th International Conference on Semantic Computing, ICSC 2016.* 10.1109/ICSC.2016.111

Navamani, J. M. A., & Kannammal, A. (2015). Predicting performance of schools by applying data mining techniques on public examination results. *Research Journal of Applied Sciences, Engineering and Technology, 9*(4), 262–271. Advance online publication. doi:10.19026/rjaset.9.1403

Newall, M. (2018). *Cyberbullying: A Global Advisor Survey.* https://www.ipsos.com/sites/default/files/ct/news/documents/2018-06/cyberbullying_june2018.pdf

Onaolapo, J., Mariconti, E., & Stringhini, G. (2016). What happens after you are Pwnd: Understanding the use of leaked webmail credentials in the wild. *Proceedings of the ACM SIGCOMM Internet Measurement Conference, IMC, 14-16-November-2016.* 10.1145/2987443.2987475

Patchin, J. W. (2022). *Summary of Our Cyberbullying Research (2007-2021).* https://cyberbullying.org/summary-of-our-cyberbullying-research

Plaza-del-Arco, F. M., Molina-González, M. D., Ureña-López, L. A., & Martín-Valdivia, M. T. (2021). Comparing pre-trained language models for Spanish hate speech detection. *Expert Systems with Applications, 166,* 114120. Advance online publication. doi:10.1016/j.eswa.2020.114120

Pradhan, A., Yatam, V. M., & Bera, P. (2020). Self-Attention for Cyberbullying Detection. *2020 International Conference on Cyber Situational Awareness, Data Analytics and Assessment.* 10.1109/CyberSA49311.2020.9139711

Pratt, T. C., Holtfreter, K., & Reisig, M. D. (2010). Routine online activity and internet fraud targeting: Extending the generality of routine activity theory. *Journal of Research in Crime and Delinquency, 47*(3), 267–296. Advance online publication. doi:10.1177/0022427810365903

Roberts, L. (2008). Jurisdictional and definitional concerns with computer-mediated interpersonal crimes : An Analysis on Cyber Stalking. *International Journal of Cyber Criminology, 2*(1).

Roy, P. K. (2015). *Why online harassment goes unpunished in India.* https://www.bbc.com/news/world-asia-india-33532706

Sadiq, S., Mehmood, A., Ullah, S., Ahmad, M., Choi, G. S., & On, B. W. (2021). Aggression detection through deep neural model on Twitter. *Future Generation Computer Systems, 114*, 120–129. Advance online publication. doi:10.1016/j.future.2020.07.050

Saeed, M. H., Ali, S., Blackburn, J., De Cristofaro, E., Zannettou, S., & Stringhini, G. (2022). TrollMagnifier: Detecting State-Sponsored Troll Accounts on Reddit. *2022 IEEE Symposium on Security and Privacy (SP)*, 2161–2175. 10.1109/SP46214.2022.9833706

Sanchez, H., & Kumar, S. (2011). Twitter bullying detection. *Ser. NSDI, 12*, 15.

Saravanaraj, A., Sheeba, J. I., & Devaneyan, S. P. (2016). *Automatic detection of cyberbullying from twitter. International Journal of Computer Science and Information Technology & Security.*

Seiler, S. J., & Navarro, J. N. (2014). Bullying on the pixel playground: Investigating risk factors of cyberbullying at the intersection of children's online–offline social lives. *Cyberpsychology (Brno), 8*(4). Advance online publication. doi:10.5817/CP2014-4-6

Shalev-Shwartz, S., & Ben-David, S. (2013). Understanding machine learning: From theory to algorithms. Understanding Machine Learning: From Theory to Algorithms. doi:10.1017/CBO9781107298019

Sharp, T., Shreve-Neiger, A., Fremouw, W., Kane, J., & Hutton, S. (2004). Exploring the Psychological and Somatic Impact of Identity Theft. *Journal of Forensic Sciences, 49*(1). Advance online publication. doi:10.1520/JFS2003178 PMID:14979359

Singh, V. K., Ghosh, S., & Jose, C. (2017). Toward multimodal cyberbullying detection. *Conference on Human Factors in Computing Systems - Proceedings, Part F127655.* 10.1145/3027063.3053169

Smith, P. K., Mahdavi, J., Carvalho, M., Fisher, S., Russell, S., & Tippett, N. (2008). Cyberbullying: Its nature and impact in secondary school pupils. *Journal of Child Psychology and Psychiatry, and Allied Disciplines, 49*(4), 376–385. Advance online publication. doi:10.1111/j.1469-7610.2007.01846.x PMID:18363945

Sri Nandhini, B., & Sheeba, J. I. (2015). Cyberbullying detection and classification using information retrieval algorithm. *ACM International Conference Proceeding Series, 06-07-March-2015.* 10.1145/2743065.2743085

Thomas, K., Grier, C., Ma, J., Paxson, V., & Song, D. (2011). Design and evaluation of a real-time URL spam filtering service. *Proceedings - IEEE Symposium on Security and Privacy.* 10.1109/SP.2011.25

Van Hee, C., Jacobs, G., Emmery, C., DeSmet, B., Lefever, E., Verhoeven, B., De Pauw, G., Daelemans, W., & Hoste, V. (2018). Automatic detection of cyberbullying in social media text. *PLoS One, 13*(10), e0203794. Advance online publication. doi:10.1371/journal.pone.0203794 PMID:30296299

Villar-Rodríguez, E., Del Ser, J., Torre-Bastida, A. I., Bilbao, M. N., & Salcedo-Sanz, S. (2016). A novel machine learning approach to the detection of identity theft in social networks based on emulated attack instances and support vector machines. *Concurrency and Computation, 28*(4), 1385–1395. Advance online publication. doi:10.1002/cpe.3633

Wang, C., Yang, B., Cui, J., & Wang, C. (2019). Fusing Behavioral Projection Models for Identity Theft Detection in Online Social Networks. *IEEE Transactions on Computational Social Systems, 6*(4), 637–648. Advance online publication. doi:10.1109/TCSS.2019.2917003

Wang, C., Yang, B., & Luo, J. (2017). Identity Theft Detection in Mobile Social Networks Using Behavioral Semantics. *2017 IEEE International Conference on Smart Computing, SMARTCOMP 2017.* 10.1109/SMARTCOMP.2017.7947016

Wang, C., Zhu, H., & Yang, B. (2022). Composite Behavioral Modeling for Identity Theft Detection in Online Social Networks. *IEEE Transactions on Computational Social Systems, 9*(2), 428–439. Advance online publication. doi:10.1109/TCSS.2021.3092007

Young, T., Hazarika, D., Poria, S., & Cambria, E. (2018). Recent trends in deep learning based natural language processing. IEEE Computational Intelligence Magazine, 13(3). doi:10.1109/MCI.2018.2840738

ENDNOTES

[1]   **Net Losses:** Estimating the Global Cost of Cybercrime: https://www.csis.org/analysis/net-losses-estimating-global-cost-cybercrime

[2]   **Troll Police:** A Reality Show That Addresses the Issue of Cyber Bullying: https://www.mid-day.com/entertainment/television-news/article/troll-police-a-reality-show-that-addresses-the-issue-of-cyber-bullying-18916156

Chapter 11
Uncertainty Quantification in Advanced Machine Learning Approaches

Shakeel Ahamad
Jawaharlal Nehru University, India

Ishfaq Hussain Rather
Jawaharlal Nehru University, India

Ratneshwer Gupta
Jawaharlal Nehru University, India

ABSTRACT

Artificial intelligence (AI) systems perform critical tasks in various safety-critical (e.g., medical devices, mission-control systems, and nuclear power plants). Uncertainty in the system may be caused by various reasons. Uncertainty quantification (UQ) approaches are essential for minimising the influence of uncertainties on optimisation and decision-making processes. Estimating the uncertainty is a challenging issue. Various machine-learning approaches are used for uncertainty quantification. This chapter comprehensively views uncertainty quantification approaches in machine learning (ML) techniques. Various factors cause uncertainty, and their possible solutions are presented. The uncertainty analysing approaches of the different machine learning methods, such as regression, classification, and segmentation, are discussed. The uncertainty optimisation process is broadly categorised into backward and forward approaches. The subsequent sections further classify and explain these backward and forward uncertainty approaches.

DOI: 10.4018/978-1-6684-6909-5.ch011

INTRODUCTION

Machine learning (ML) has become a popular methodology for data analysis and prediction due to the availability of data and computational technology in the modern world (Siddique et al., 2022). Although the potential of ML, limitations brought on by uncertainty mean that the outcomes of such models are not entirely unreliable. A machine-learning model creates an ideal answer based on its training set of data. However, such ideal solutions run a significant risk of failure when implemented in the real world if the uncertainty in the data and the model parameters are not considered. Artificial Intelligent (AI) based systems are very beneficial for the various business domain and provide competent and intelligent assistants to carry out complex tasks (Yang & Li, 2023).

On the other hand, AI techniques are based on data validation training and testing. The outcome of AI is also used to decide and take decisions (Ahmad et al., 2020). In many cases, the result of the machine learning outcome is uncertain because uncertainty in the input data and model parameters is not considered. Various limitations and a lack of data lead to deviation from the actual result. The deviation of the result caused uncertainty in the AI model's outcome (Abdar et al., 2021a). AI technology has various steps to reach the inferences for the learning model. Each step has some uncertainty.

Predictive uncertainty consists of two parts: epistemic uncertainty and aleatoric uncertainty (Mishra et al., 2021). The aleatory uncertainty is due to the probabilistic variation in the experiment. This uncertainty is present in each model. It is almost impossible to reduce ultimately, but some actions may take to reduce it. So, it is called fundamental (Irreducible) uncertainty. The scientific error causes epistemic uncertainty in the model process. Data limitations and lack of knowledge cause this uncertainty. These uncertainties may exist simultaneously in the system. The machine learning model presents aleatory and epistemic uncertainty (Peterson et al., 2017).

Uncertainty modelling is essential to achieve optimum decision-making. There are various approaches to optimise the uncertainty of the system. E.g., A better representation process can reduce the uncertainty in the data, but the model uncertainty can be improved by collecting more data. The selection of the uncertainty model depends on many factors, like the model type and the machine learning approach. An uncertainty model may lead to poor estimation to cause mislead the user. Or highly accurate model may be misleading if poorly communicated (Ståhl et al., 2020; Zhan & Kitchin, 2022).

This chapter studies the available approaches for uncertainty quantification in machine learning. Further, the source of the uncertainty and the factor affecting the uncertainty in the model is characterised. The main focus is the uncertainty approaches used in the different machine learning tasks. The uncertainty approach is broadly divided into two categories: forward and backward.

The rest of the chapter is organised as follows: in section 2, various factors of the uncertainty at the various level of machine learning is surmised. Section 3 of the chapter presents the various approaches for uncertainty quantification in machine learning. Finally, section 4 concludes the chapter.

LITERATURE REVIEW

When it comes to minimising the impact of uncertainties on the optimisation and decision-making processes, uncertainty quantification (UQ) methodologies are crucial. They have been used to address various contemporary issues in engineering and research. Uncertainty quantification (UQ) techniques include Bayesian approximation and ensemble learning techniques, which are often utilised. Regarding this, researchers have put forth various UQ methods and evaluated their effectiveness in various applications, including computer vision (X. Wang & Peng, 2014). So, various approaches regarding uncertainty quantification are used nowadays, like the Method of Moments, Reliability of The Output, PDF of The Output, etc., which are summarised and explained in detail in section 4.

Koh et al. (2021) assess deep learning uncertainty quantification (UQ) approaches for physics analytical tasks in the liquid argon time projection chamber (LArTPC). In a simulated 3D LArTPC point cloud dataset, applying a few deep-learning UQ algorithms to particle classification has been evaluated. It is also concluded that the basic ensemble techniques are sufficient in the majority of scenarios for getting properly calibrated classification probabilities and typically achieving superior overall accuracy. Zhan and Kitchin (2022) provide examples of using the regression technique's uncertainty strategy in molecular simulation and neural network applications. This technique can be used to spot extrapolation, as well as to help choose training data or evaluate model reliability. Convolutional neural networks (CNN) are extremely popular, yet its uncertainty quantification (UQ) issue has largely gone unnoticed. In some fields, like medicine, where prediction uncertainty is crucial, the deployment of CNN is severely constrained by the lack of effective UQ methods. To solve this problem, Du and Barut (2021) suggest a brand-new bootstrap-based approach for estimating prediction uncertainty.

BACKGROUND OF AI AND UNCERTAINTY

One of the hottest buzzwords in technology right now is artificial intelligence (AI), and for a good reason. But it is not a new word because it was coined in 1956 by John McCarthy. Many inventions and developments previously only found in science fiction have begun to materialise over the past several years. AI further have two parts machine learning and deep learning (Polužanski et al., 2022). AI can learn because of machine learning. In order to achieve this, algorithms are used to mine the data they are exposed to for patterns and insights. AI can imitate the neural network of the human brain with the help of deep learning (Loftus et al., 2022). It can make sense of the data's patterns, noise, and sources of confusion. AI-based applications are used in various domains. It has various pros and cons. Some of the pros of AI in the various application are:

- Human mistake is decreased.
- It is always accessible because it never sleeps.
- It never gets bored, so it can do monotonous chores with ease.
- Fast-paced

Some cons make AI use complex. Those are listed below.

- It requires a lot of money to implement, and technology can't replace creativity.
- Unemployment will result since some jobs will undoubtedly be replaced.
- It can cause people to become too dependent.

AI make the decision based on the machine learning algorithm and deep learning based on the dataset training. There is a variation in the actual value of the model's output and the calculated value due to the errors in the data and the various assumption in the modelling of the algorithm. Uncertainty is present in almost all AI models (Woodward et al., 2021). The purpose of the uncertainty quantification in the AI model is to take care of those variables in the decision-making of the AI model. the measurement of the uncertainty is very significant in the system where AI perform the critical functionality. Because minor variations in the actual and calculated value may cause a huge loss. Such application domain is listed in Table 1.

So, uncertainty in the AI-based system should be measured and minimised to increase the degree of trust in the AI-based system.

Table 1. Application of AI in the various applications and implications of uncertainty

AI Applications	Uncertainty Implications
Public policy decisions (Nordström, 2022)	Because the outcomes of AI implementations are unpredictable, public policy decisions on AI are uncertain. Decisions regarding the implementation of such applications are particularly challenging because many potential uses of AI in the public sector involve responsibilities that are fundamental to the public domain
The navigation system in the mission-critical systems (Hüllermeier & Waegeman, 2021)	Uncertainty may cause the loss of trajectory of the mission-critical system.
Autonomous Vehicles (Bloise & Orlandelli, 2018)	A self-driving automobile must use reasoning to account for the unpredictable and ever-changing traffic situation, road conditions, weather, and other drivers' and pedestrians' intents.
AI-based healthcare devices (Begoli et al., 2019)	AI is used in various PCA devices. And various critical operation (like retinal operation and spinal cord operation) is done by a robotic machine. Uncertainty in the measurement may cause the death of the patient.
AI in Architectural, Engineering and Construction (AEC) (An et al., 2021)	Due to the lack of a thorough knowledge of the fundamental and mathematical aspects of the inherent uncertainty, many AI applications are subject to various restrictions and limits, and as a result, the use of AI has not progressed to a suitable level.
Digital Economy (Boukherouaa et al., 2021)	Uncertainty may cause a loss of the integrity and safety of the financial system. Concrete policy solutions will be needed in response to the rapid deployment of AI/ML technologies in banking.

UNCERTAINTY AT THE VARIOUS LEVELS OF THE ML

The uncertainty in the output of the machine learning approaches is the sum of the various levels of uncertainty. Table 2 shows the various levels of uncertainty and the corresponding causes for the uncertainty.

The first step of machine learning is data collection. The data collection is the hard step. The data collection is based on machine learning output and inference. The wrong collection of data leads to the wrong output. Some challenges during the data collection are given in Table 1.

UNCERTAINTY APPROACH

The available approaches to uncertainty modelling are analysed in this section. The uncertainty approaches are classified. Figure 1 shows the classification of the available approaches for uncertainty quantification in machine learning.

Table 2. Factors of uncertainty caused at the different levels of machine learning

Level	Uncertainty Factors
Data Collection	Information Loss Sample Frame Error Selection Error Non-Responsive Error Measurement (Observational) Error Inability To Collect Not Represent Real-World Data Accurately
Pre-Processing	Missing Anonymization Regional Formats Wrong Data Types Missing Data Data Inconsistency Numerical Units File Manipulation
Model Selection	Lack Of Knowledge Insufficient Model Structures Bias Variance A Lousy Coverage of Training Data Set Underfitting Overfitting
Learning Algorithm	Mistake In Categorisation of the Input and Output of the Model
Result in Inference	Inferential Uncertainties

Even though many successful research efforts in modelling and predicting the uncertainty of machine learning techniques over the past decades remain an unresolved scientific problem. A few recurring challenges to the model's accuracy and precision include the assimilation of noise and data gaps, lowering computational costs, especially for high-dimensional systems, and resolving poorly posed problems, like those with unknown parameters and boundary conditions (Psaros et al., 2022). The uncertainty approaches are broadly divided into two categories, forward and backward. These are discussed in detail in the following subsections.

Forward Approaches

The forward approaches of uncertainty quantification start with the input of the machine learning approach and end with the model's output (Du et al., 2021). In these approaches, the classification task of data and model, distributional uncertainty in the classification task, and regression uncertainty in the data and model are measured from input to output through the learning model.

Figure 1. uncertainty quantification approaches classification

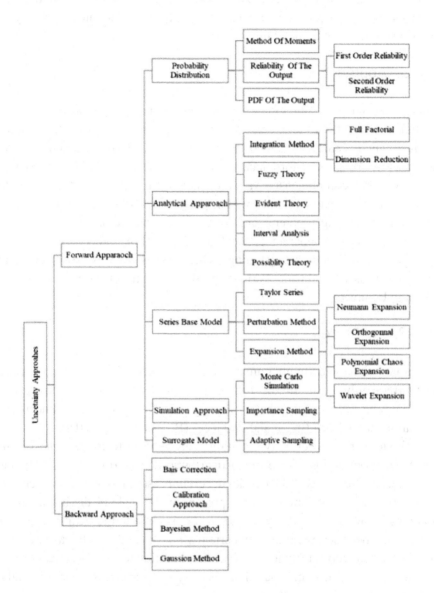

Probability Distributions

Typically, Probabilistic models are employed for estimation and diagnostics. For instance, the uncertainty model may include extra noise components introduced to the data and the process model. The uncertainty in empirically produced models, like regression models, is typically present due to the regression or other techniques used. The method of moments estimates the mean and the variance from the mean value that shows the uncertainty of the model's output. The output's reliability and PDF are also used for the uncertainty modelling.

Analytical Approach

The analytical technique validation's goal is to ensure that every measurement made in the future during the routine analysis will be sufficiently close to the sample's true value, which is currently unknown (Abdar et al., 2021b). Traditional ways to validate merely compare performance to reference values, which does not consider consumer wants. A comprehensive validation method also considers the anticipated percentage of acceptable outcomes within predetermined acceptability intervals. Systems for diagnosing problems are, by their very nature, uncertain. The only mystery is whether it is apparent, concealed by "black box" procedures, or simply due to technical judgment during tuning. When models don't express uncertainty, we refer to them as deterministic. Various approaches for the uncertainty calculation are given in Figure 1.

Series-Based Model

The assumption that uncertainties are constant or a linear function of the measured value is frequently false. In the presence of nonlinear, time-varying errors, conventional uncertainty approaches are inappropriate for calculating the uncertainty of measurement statistics (mean and variance) (B. Wang et al., 2019). It is shown that the Taylor-series uncertainty equations can be used to model time-varying systematic, random, and asymmetric error distributions. When there are uncertainties regarding the mean quantity, Taylor-series uncertainty estimations are always correct. Suppose asymmetric random errors are present or the scale of the instantaneous fluctuations in the random and systematic errors is close to the 'real' variance. In that case, the Taylor-series variance uncertainty is comparable to the Monte-Carlo results. The Taylor-series technique, however, overestimates the variance's level of uncertainty since the instantaneous changes of systematic errors are substantial or of a size comparable to the variance's 'real' variance.

Simulation Approach

The uncertainty distribution for each variable and a model for calculating the desired quantity is the sources for Monte Carlo simulations of uncertainty propagation. The target quantity is then calculated by selecting at random from the input variable's chosen uncertainty distributions. Then, this calculation is performed numerous times, using new random draws each time. The numerous random trials directly yield the resultant uncertainty distribution of the estimated value. The advantage of Monte Carlo uncertainty propagation is that it supports a wide range of uncertainty distributions and is straightforward to understand (D. Wang et al., 2021).

Surrogate Model

Numerous disciplines, many inputs, and lengthy computation timeframes are frequently used in the complicated numerical simulation models that assist decision- and policy-making processes. Such models' inputs are inevitably uncertain, which causes uncertainty in the model's outputs. However, the enormous number of model evaluations necessary to sample the uncertainty space (for example, via Monte Carlo sampling) presents an immense computational burden. Characterising, propagating, and analysing this uncertainty is crucial to model development and successfully applying model results in decision-making (Wen & Tadmor, 2020). The fundamentals of low-rank tensor approximations and polynomial chaos expansions are presented, along with tips on estimating the relevant statistics, such as moments, sensitivity indices, or failure probability (Koh, 2021).

BACKWARD APPROACH

In the backward approach, the uncertainty is minimised using various methods. These methods use the reversed methods from output to input. Some of the common approaches are given in the following subsections.

Bias Correction

Recently, several bias correction strategies have been presented using machine learning algorithms. Machine learning techniques are generally quite complex, and describing how machine learning corrects model biases is pretty challenging. As a result, scientists are constantly trying to test the validity of machine learning techniques by applying them to various scenarios. Here, we assumed a relationship between actual and simulated precipitation matching weather conditions and created a machine-learning algorithm utilising simple input data (Chan & Elsheikh, 2017). This straightforward approach can determine the ideal relationship without dimension reduction, making it easier to understand precipitation properties. A validation experiment revealed that this straightforward method could estimate the characteristics of the local precipitation distribution and correct the precipitation frequency corresponding to the orography, producing values consistent with the observed data even when forecasted more than 24 hours in advance (Musil et al., 2019).

Calibration

Knowing the degree of uncertainty in a neural network's predictions is essential for many applications. To estimate uncertainty, several neural network parameters estimate techniques have been put forth; however, they have not been thoroughly evaluated across different uncertainty metrics (Palmer et al., 2022). Using four alternative uncertainty measures—entropy, mutual information, aleatoric uncertainty, and epistemic uncertainty, Using the anticipated calibration error, we assess the calibration of various parameter estimate techniques.

Bayesian

Bayesian learning of neural networks (NN) enables the incorporation of epistemic and aleatoric uncertainties, which account for the intrinsic stochasticity of the data-generating process and arise from the analysis of tiny amounts of data (Brnabic & Hess, 2021). The research goes into more detail about the GPR and BNN for UQ in classical ML and DL. Both methods can be used to solve PDEs and SPDEs with physics as a basis because they both have their roots in Bayesian inference.

Gaussian

The Gaussian Process in machine learning can be used for regression and classification with uncertainty quantification. As a Bayesian approach, the Gaussian Process makes predictions subject to error (Sabharwal & Miah, 2022). For instance, it will forecast a stock price of $100 with a standard deviation of $30 for tomorrow. For applications like algorithmic trading, understanding uncertainty is crucial. I have created successful trading plans and those that were unsuccessful. I know first-hand the damage that uncertainty can do. I decided to investigate the inner workings of the Gaussian Process.

CONCLUSION

When it comes to minimising the impact of uncertainties on decision-making and the optimisation processes, uncertainty quantification (UQ) in critical infrastructure plays a crucial role. They have been used to address various contemporary issues in engineering and research. Uncertainty quantification (UQ) techniques include various approaches. As time has passed, more researchers have proposed more UQ strategies and assessed their efficacy in various applications, such as computer vision, image processing, medical image analysis, natural language processing, bioinformatics, etc. The usage of UQ techniques in deep learning is examined in this work. Further, determine important research issues and UQ-related directions.

This paper summarises the many methods for quantifying uncertainty in machine learning. Uncertainty has various dimensions, and it can be conceived of as either a forward propagation problem or an inverse propagation problem when it spreads throughout a model. Uncertainty quantification is the essential part of the AI system that carries out the critical task. Minor variations in the actual result may lead to the system's failure and loss of time and money. Applying machine learning to critical functionality makes uncertainty inseparable from machine learning techniques and tools. This Study also presented the factors that caused the uncertainty in machine learning.

REFERENCES

Abdar, M., Pourpanah, F., Hussain, S., Rezazadegan, D., Liu, L., Ghavamzadeh, M., Fieguth, P., Cao, X., Khosravi, A., Acharya, U. R., Makarenkov, V., & Nahavandi, S. (2021a). A review of uncertainty quantification in deep learning: Techniques, applications and challenges. *Information Fusion*, *76*, 243–297. doi:10.1016/j. inffus.2021.05.008

Abdar, M., Pourpanah, F., Hussain, S., Rezazadegan, D., Liu, L., Ghavamzadeh, M., Fieguth, P., Cao, X., Khosravi, A., Acharya, U. R., Makarenkov, V., & Nahavandi, S. (2021b). A review of uncertainty quantification in deep learning: Techniques, applications and challenges. *Information Fusion*, *76*, 243–297. doi:10.1016/j. inffus.2021.05.008

Ahmad, A., Feng, C., Khan, M., Khan, A., Ullah, A., Nazir, S., & Tahir, A. (2020). A Systematic Literature Review on Using Machine Learning Algorithms for Software Requirements Identification on Stack Overflow. *Security and Communication Networks*, *2020*, 1–19. Advance online publication. doi:10.1155/2020/8830683

An, Y., Li, H., Su, T., & Wang, Y. (2021). Determining Uncertainties in AI Applications in AEC Sector and their Corresponding Mitigation Strategies. *Automation in Construction*, *131*, 103883. Advance online publication. doi:10.1016/j. autcon.2021.103883

Begoli, E., Bhattacharya, T., & Kusnezov, D. (2019). The need for uncertainty quantification in machine-assisted medical decision making. *Nature Machine Intelligence, 1*(1), 20–23. doi:10.103842256-018-0004-1

Bloise, I., & Orlandelli, M. (2018). *A Deep Learning Approach To Autonomous.* Academic Press.

Boukherouaa, E. B., AlAjmi, K., Deodoro, J., Farias, A., & Ravikumar, R. (2021). Powering the Digital Economy: Opportunities and Risks of Artificial Intelligence in Finance. *Departmental Papers, 2021*(24). https://doi.org/ doi:10.5089/9781589063952.087.A001

Brnabic, A., & Hess, L. M. (2021). Systematic literature review of machine learning methods used in the analysis of real-world data for patient-provider decision making. *BMC Medical Informatics and Decision Making, 21*(1), 1–19. doi:10.118612911-021-01403-2 PMID:33588830

Chan, S., & Elsheikh, A. H. (2017). A machine learning approach for efficient uncertainty quantification using multiscale methods. *Journal of Computational Physics, 354*, 493–511. doi:10.1016/j.jcp.2017.10.034

Du, H., Barut, E., & Jin, F. (2021). Uncertainty Quantification in CNN Through the Bootstrap of Convex Neural Networks. *35th AAAI Conference on Artificial Intelligence, AAAI 2021, 13B*, 12078–12085. 10.1609/aaai.v35i13.17434

Hüllermeier, E., & Waegeman, W. (2021). Aleatoric and epistemic uncertainty in machine learning: An introduction to concepts and methods. *Machine Learning, 110*(3), 457–506. doi:10.100710994-021-05946-3

Koh, D. H. (2021). Evaluating Deep Learning Uncertainty Quantification Methods for Neutrino Physics Applications. *6th Workshop on Byesian Deep Learning, NeurIPS.*

Loftus, T. J., Shickel, B., Ruppert, M. M., Balch, J. A., Ozrazgat-Baslanti, T., Tighe, P. J., Efron, P. A., Hogan, W. R., Rashidi, P. Jr, Upchurch, G. R., & Bihorac, A. (2022). Uncertainty-aware deep learning in healthcare: A scoping review. *PLOS Digital Health, 1*(8), e0000085. doi:10.1371/journal.pdig.0000085 PMID:36590140

Mishra, A. A., Edelen, A., Hanuka, A., & Mayes, C. (2021). Uncertainty quantification for deep learning in particle accelerator applications. *Physical Review. Accelerators and Beams, 24*(11), 114601. Advance online publication. doi:10.1103/PhysRevAccelBeams.24.114601

Musil, F., Willatt, M. J., Langovoy, M. A., & Ceriotti, M. (2019). Fast and Accurate Uncertainty Estimation in Chemical Machine Learning. *Journal of Chemical Theory and Computation, 15*(2), 906–915. doi:10.1021/acs.jctc.8b00959 PMID:30605342

Nordström, M. (2022). *AI under great uncertainty: Implications and decision strategies for public policy.* doi:10.1007/s00146-021-01263-4

Palmer, G., Du, S., Politowicz, A., Emory, J. P., Yang, X., Gautam, A., Gupta, G., Li, Z., Jacobs, R., & Morgan, D. (2022). Calibration after bootstrap for accurate uncertainty quantification in regression models. In NPJ Computational Materials (Vol. 8, Issue 1). doi:10.103841524-022-00794-8

Peterson, A. A., Christensen, R., & Khorshidi, A. (2017). Addressing uncertainty in atomistic machine learning. *Physical Chemistry Chemical Physics, 19*(18), 10978–10985. doi:10.1039/C7CP00375G PMID:28418054

Polužanski, V., Kovacevic, U., Bacanin, N., Rashid, T. A., Stojanovic, S., & Nikolic, B. (2022). Application of Machine Learning to Express Measurement Uncertainty. *Applied Sciences, 12*(17), 8581. doi:10.3390/app12178581

Psaros A. F. Meng X. Zou Z. Guo L. Karniadakis G. E. (2022). *Uncertainty Quantification in Scientific Machine Learning: Methods, Metrics, and Comparisons.* https://arxiv.org/abs/2201.07766

Sabharwal, R., & Miah, S. J. (2022). An intelligent literature review: Adopting inductive approach to define machine learning applications in the clinical domain. *Journal of Big Data, 9*(1), 1–18. doi:10.118640537-022-00605-3

Siddique, T., Mahmud, M. S., Keesee, A. M., Ngwira, C. M., & Connor, H. (2022). A Survey of Uncertainty Quantification in Machine Learning for Space Weather Prediction. *Geosciences, 12*(1), 27. doi:10.3390/geosciences12010027

Ståhl, N., Falkman, G., Karlsson, A., & Mathiason, G. (2020). Evaluation of Uncertainty Quantification in Deep Learning. *Communications in Computer and Information Science, 1237*, 556–568. https://doi.org/ doi:10.1007/978-3-030-50146-4_41/FIGURES/4

Wang, B., Luo, H., Lu, J., Li, T., Zhang, G., Yan, Z., & Zheng, Y. (2019). Deep uncertainty quantification: A machine learning approach for weather forecasting. *Proceedings of the ACM SIGKDD International Conference on Knowledge Discovery and Data Mining*, 2087–2095. 10.1145/3292500.3330704

Wang, D., Yu, J., Chen, L., Li, X., Jiang, H., Chen, K., Zheng, M., & Luo, X. (2021). A hybrid framework for improving uncertainty quantification in deep learning-based QSAR regression modeling. *Journal of Cheminformatics*, *13*(1), 1–17. doi:10.118613321-021-00551-x PMID:34544485

Wang, X., & Peng, Z. (2014). Method of moments for estimating uncertainty distributions. *Journal of Uncertainty Analysis and Applications*, *2*(1), 5. doi:10.1186/2195-5468-2-5

Wen, M., & Tadmor, E. B. (2020). Uncertainty quantification in molecular simulations with dropout neural network potentials. *npj Computational Materials*, *6*(1), 124. Advance online publication. doi:10.103841524-020-00390-8

Woodward, D., Hobbs, M., Gilbertson, J. A., & Cohen, N. (2021). Uncertainty Quantification for Trusted Machine Learning in Space System Cyber Security. *Proceedings - 8th IEEE International Conference on Space Mission Challenges for Information Technology, SMC-IT 2021*, 38–43. 10.1109/SMC-IT51442.2021.00012

Yang, C. I., & Li, Y. P. (2023). Explainable uncertainty quantifications for deep learning-based molecular property prediction. *Journal of Cheminformatics*, *15*(1), 1–14. doi:10.118613321-023-00682-3 PMID:36737786

Zhan, N., & Kitchin, J. R. (2022). Uncertainty quantification in machine learning and nonlinear least squares regression models. *AIChE Journal. American Institute of Chemical Engineers*, *68*(6), e17516. doi:10.1002/aic.17516

Compilation of References

Abdar, M., Pourpanah, F., Hussain, S., Rezazadegan, D., Liu, L., Ghavamzadeh, M., Fieguth, P., Cao, X., Khosravi, A., Acharya, U. R., Makarenkov, V., & Nahavandi, S. (2021a). A review of uncertainty quantification in deep learning: Techniques, applications and challenges. *Information Fusion*, *76*, 243–297. doi:10.1016/j.inffus.2021.05.008

Acheampong, F. A., Wenyu, C., & Nunoo-Mensah, H. (2020). Text-based emotion detection: Advances, challenges, and opportunities. *Engineering Reports*, *2*(7). Advance online publication. doi:10.1002/eng2.12189

Adiga, A., Chen, J., Marathe, M., Mortveit, H., Venkatramanan, S., & Vullikanti, A. (2020). Data-driven modeling for different stages of pandemic response. *Journal of the Indian Institute of Science*, *100*(4), 901–915. doi:10.100741745-020-00206-0 PMID:33223629

Agrawal, S., & Awekar, A. (2018). Deep learning for detecting cyberbullying across multiple social media platforms. Lecture Notes in Computer Science, 10772. doi:10.1007/978-3-319-76941-7_11

Ahmad, A., Feng, C., Khan, M., Khan, A., Ullah, A., Nazir, S., & Tahir, A. (2020). A Systematic Literature Review on Using Machine Learning Algorithms for Software Requirements Identification on Stack Overflow. *Security and Communication Networks*, *2020*, 1–19. Advance online publication. doi:10.1155/2020/8830683

Ahmad, K. (Ed.). (2011). *Affective computing and sentiment analysis: Emotion, metaphor and terminology* (Vol. 45). Springer Science & Business Media. doi:10.1007/978-94-007-1757-2_8

Ahmed, F., & Abulaish, M. (2013). A generic statistical approach for spam detection in Online Social Networks. *Computer Communications*, *36*(10–11), 1120–1129. doi:10.1016/j.comcom.2013.04.004

Ahsan Habib, Md. (2023). *Emotion Recognition from Microblog Managing Emoticon with Text and Classifying using 1D CNN.* https://arxiv.org/ftp/arxiv/papers/2301/2301.02971.pdf

Al-Adhaileh, M. H., Aldhyani, T. H. H., & Alghamdi, A. D. (2022). Online Troll Reviewer Detection Using Deep Learning Techniques. *Applied Bionics and Biomechanics*, *2022*, 2022. doi:10.1155/2022/4637594 PMID:35747397

Alami Merrouni, Z., Frikh, B., & Ouhbi, B. (2020). Automatic keyphrase extraction: A survey and trends. *Journal of Intelligent Information Systems, 54*(2), 391–424. doi:10.100710844-019-00558-9

Al-Amin, M., Islam, M. S., & Das Uzzal, S. (2017). Sentiment analysis of Bengali comments with Word2Vec and sentiment information of words. *2017 International Conference on Electrical, Computer and Communication Engineering (ECCE)*. 10.1109/ECACE.2017.7912903

Al-Garadi, M. A., Varathan, K. D., & Ravana, S. D. (2016). Cybercrime detection in online communications: The experimental case of cyberbullying detection in the Twitter network. *Computers in Human Behavior, 63*, 433–443. Advance online publication. doi:10.1016/j. chb.2016.05.051

Ali, B. A. B., Mihi, S., El Bazi, I., & Laachfoubi, N. (2020). A Recent Survey of Arabic Named Entity Recognition on Social Media. *Rev. d'Intelligence Artif., 34*(2), 125-135.

Al-Khater, W. A., Al-Maadeed, S., Ahmed, A. A., Sadiq, A. S., & Khan, M. K. (2020). Comprehensive review of cybercrime detection techniques. *IEEE Access : Practical Innovations, Open Solutions, 8*, 137293–137311. Advance online publication. doi:10.1109/ACCESS.2020.3011259

AlMahmoud, A., Damiani, E., Otrok, H., & Al-Hammadi, Y. (2017). Spamdoop: A privacy-preserving Big Data platform for collaborative spam detection. *IEEE Transactions on Big Data, 7790*, 1–1. doi:10.1109/TBDATA.2017.2716409

Almeida, F., & Xexéo, G. (2019). *Word embeddings: A survey.* arXiv preprint arXiv:1901.09069

Alomari, A., Idris, N., Sabri, A. Q. M., & Alsmadi, I. (2022). Deep reinforcement and transfer learning for abstractive text summarization: A review. *Computer Speech & Language, 71*, 101276. doi:10.1016/j.csl.2021.101276

Alsaeedi, A., & Khan, M. Z. (2019). A study on sentiment analysis techniques of Twitter data. *International Journal of Advanced Computer Science and Applications, 10*(2). Advance online publication. doi:10.14569/IJACSA.2019.0100248

Al-Sarem, M., Boulila, W., Al-Harby, M., Qadir, J., & Alsaeedi, A. (2019). Deep learning-based rumor detection on microblogging platforms: A systematic review. In IEEE Access (Vol. 7). doi:10.1109/ACCESS.2019.2947855

Alswaidan, N., & Menai, M. E. (2020). A survey of state-of-the-art approaches for emotion recognition in text. *Knowledge and Information Systems, 62*(8), 2937–2987. Advance online publication. doi:10.100710115-020-01449-0

Altché, F., & Fortelle, A. D. L. (2017). An LSTM network for highway trajectory prediction. In *Proceedings of the IEEE 20th International Conference on Intelligent Transportation Systems*. IEEE. 10.1109/ITSC.2017.8317913

Amato, F., Castiglione, A., Moscato, V., Picariello, A., & Sperlì, G. (2018). Multimedia summarization using social media content. *Multimedia Tools and Applications, 77*(14), 17803–17827. doi:10.100711042-017-5556-2

Compilation of References

Anderson, D. S., Fleizach, C., Savage, S., & Voelker, G. M. (2006). *Spamscatter : Characterizing Internet Scam Hosting Infrastructure.* Academic Press.

Antonakaki, D., Polakis, I., Athanasopoulos, E., Ioannidis, S., & Fragopoulou, P. (2016). Exploiting abused trending topics to identify spam campaigns in Twitter. *Social Network Analysis and Mining, 6*(1), 1–11. doi:10.100713278-016-0354-9

Antonio, G., & Sujit, P. (2017) *Deep Learning With Keras.* Packt Publishing.

Anwar, S. M., Majid, M., Qayyum, A., Awais, M., Alnowami, M., & Khan, M. K. (2018). Medical Image Analysis using Convolutional Neural Networks: A Review. Journal of Medical Systems, 42(11). doi:10.100710916-018-1088-1

An, Y., Li, H., Su, T., & Wang, Y. (2021). Determining Uncertainties in AI Applications in AEC Sector and their Corresponding Mitigation Strategies. *Automation in Construction, 131,* 103883. Advance online publication. doi:10.1016/j.autcon.2021.103883

Ariffin, S. N. A. N., & Tiun, S. (2020). Rule-based text normalization for Malay social media texts. *International Journal of Advanced Computer Science and Applications, 11*(10). Advance online publication. doi:10.14569/IJACSA.2020.0111021

Armin, S., Narges, T., Shafie, G., & Wlodek, Z. (2019). Emotion Detection in Text: Focusing on Latent Representation. *Computation and Language.*

Arora, C., Sabetzadeh, M., Briand, L., Zimmer, F., & Gnaga, R. (2013, October). Automatic checking of conformance to requirement boilerplates via text chunking: An industrial case study. In *2013 ACM/IEEE International Symposium on Empirical Software Engineering and Measurement* (pp. 35-44). IEEE.

Ashcroft, M., Fisher, A., Kaati, L., Omer, E., & Prucha, N. (2015). *Detecting jihadist messages on twitter. In 2015 European intelligence and security informatics conference.* IEEE.

Atefeh, F., & Khreich, W. (2015). A survey of techniques for event detection in twitter. *Computational Intelligence, 31*(1), 132–164. doi:10.1111/coin.12017

Attention is all you need. (n.d.). https://doi.org//arXiv.1706.03762 doi:10.48550

Attention-based modeling for emotion detection and classification in textual conversations. (n.d.). https://arxiv.org/abs/1906.07020

Aylani, A., & Goyal, N. (2017). Community detection in social network based on useras social activities. In 2017 international conference on I-SMAC (IoT in social, mobile, analytics and cloud) (I-SMAC) (pp. 625–628). IEEE. doi:10.1109/I-SMAC.2017.8058254

Azizian, S., Rastegari, E., Ricks, B., & Hall, M. (2017). Identifying Personal Messages: A Step towards Product/Service Review and Opinion Mining. *2017 International Conference on Computational Science and Computational Intelligence (CSCI),* 876-881. 10.1109/CSCI.2017.152

Babu, N. V., & Kanaga, E. (2022). Sentiment analysis in social media data for depression detection using artificial intelligence: A review. *SN Computer Science*, *3*(1), 1–20. doi:10.100742979-021-00958-1 PMID:34816124

Bahdanau, D., Cho, K., & Bengio, Y. (2014). *Neural machine translation by jointly learning to align and translate*. arXiv preprint arXiv:1409.0473.

Bakshy, Hofman, Mason, & Watts. (2011). Everyone's an influencer: quantifying influence on twitter. *Proceedings of the fourth ACM international conference on Web search and data mining*, 65–74. 10.1145/1935826.1935845

Balakrishnan, V., Khan, S., & Arabnia, H. R. (2020). Improving cyberbullying detection using Twitter users' psychological features and machine learning. *Computers & Security*, *90*, 101710. Advance online publication. doi:10.1016/j.cose.2019.101710

Barman, U., Das, A., Wagner, J., & Foster, J. (2014, October). Code mixing: A challenge for language identification in the language of social media. In *Proceedings of the first workshop on computational approaches to code switching* (pp. 13-23). 10.3115/v1/W14-3902

Basile, A., Franco-Salvador, M., Pawar, N., Štajner, S., Chinea Rios, M., & Benajiba, Y. (2019). SymantoResearch at semeval-2019 task 3: Combined neural models for emotion classification in human-chatbot conversations. *Proceedings of the 13th International Workshop on Semantic Evaluation*. 10.18653/v1/S19-2057

Bauman, S., Cross, D., & Walker, J. (2012). Principles of Cyberbullying Research: Definitions, Measures, and Methodology. In *Principles of Cyberbullying Research*. Definitions, Measures, and Methodology. doi:10.4324/9780203084601

Baziotis, C., Nikolaos, A., Chronopoulou, A., Kolovou, A., Paraskevopoulos, G., Ellinas, N., Narayanan, S., & Potamianos, A. (2018). NTUA-SLP at semeval-2018 task 1: Predicting affective content in tweets with deep attentive RNNs and transfer learning. *Proceedings of the 12th International Workshop on Semantic Evaluation*. 10.18653/v1/S18-1037

Begoli, E., Bhattacharya, T., & Kusnezov, D. (2019). The need for uncertainty quantification in machine-assisted medical decision making. *Nature Machine Intelligence*, *1*(1), 20–23. doi:10.103842256-018-0004-1

Beverungen, G., & Kalita, J. (2011). Evaluating methods for summarizing twitter posts. *Proceedings of the 5th AAAI ICWSM*.

Bharati, P., Zhang, W., & Chaudhury, A. (2015). Better knowledge with social media? Exploring the roles of social capital and organizational knowledge management. *Journal of Knowledge Management*, *19*(3), 1–39. doi:10.1108/JKM-11-2014-0467

Bharti, S. K., Gupta, R. K., Patel, S., & Shah, M. (2022). Context-Based Bigram Model for POS Tagging in Hindi: A Heuristic Approach. *Annals of Data Science*, 1-32.

Bhatia, Kumar, Jain, Kumar, Verma, Illes, Aschilean, & Raboaca. (2022). Networked Control System with MANET Communication and AODV Routing. *SCI Journal*. doi:10.1016/j.heliyon.2022.e11678

Bhatia, A., Kumar, A., Khan, I., & Kumar, V. (2011). Analysis of Pattern Recognition (text mining) with Web Crawler. In *International Transactions in Applied Sciences*. ITAS.

Bhat, S. Y., & Abulaish, M. (2014). Using communities against decep- tion in online social networks. *Computer Fraud & Security*, *2014*(2), 8–16. doi:10.1016/S1361-3723(14)70462-2

Bilge, L., Strufe, T., Balzarotti, D., & Kirda, E. (2009). All your contacts are belong to us: Automated identity theft attacks on social networks. *WWW'09 - Proceedings of the 18th International World Wide Web Conference*. 10.1145/1526709.1526784

Bloise, I., & Orlandelli, M. (2018). *A Deep Learning Approach To Autonomous*. Academic Press.

Bodhi, R., Singh, T., & Rahman, S. (2021). Recent themes in social media research: A systematic review. *International Journal of Business Information Systems*, *37*(3), 287. Advance online publication. doi:10.1504/IJBIS.2021.116081

Borah, P. S., Iqbal, S., & Akhtar, S. (2022). Linking social media usage and SME's sustainable performance: The role of digital leadership and innovation capabilities. *Technology in Society*, *68*, 101900. doi:10.1016/j.techsoc.2022.101900

Boukherouaa, E. B., AlAjmi, K., Deodoro, J., Farias, A., & Ravikumar, R. (2021). Powering the Digital Economy: Opportunities and Risks of Artificial Intelligence in Finance. *Departmental Papers, 2021*(24). https://doi.org/ doi:10.5089/9781589063952.087.A001

Bousquet, O., & Elisseeff, A. (2002). Stability and Generalization. *Journal of Machine Learning Research*, *2*(3), 499–526. doi:10.1162/153244302760200704

Bowles, C., Chen, L., & Guerrero, R. (n.d.). *Gan augmentation: Augmenting training data using generative adversarial networks*. Retrieved September 19, 2022, from https://arxiv.org/abs/1810.10863

Brnabic, A., & Hess, L. M. (2021). Systematic literature review of machine learning methods used in the analysis of real-world data for patient-provider decision making. *BMC Medical Informatics and Decision Making*, *21*(1), 1–19. doi:10.118612911-021-01403-2 PMID:33588830

Bunkhumpornpat, C., Sinapiromsaran, K., & Lursinsap, C. (2012). DBSMOTE: Density-based synthetic minority over-sampling technique. *Applied Intelligence*, *36*(3), 664–684. doi:10.100710489-011-0287-y

Calais, P. H., Pires, D. E. V., Guedes, D. O., Wagner, M., Hoepers, C., & Steding-Jessen, K. (2008). *A Campaign-based Characterization of Spamming Strategies*. Ceas.

Cambria, E., & White, B. (2014). Jumping NLP curves: A review of natural language processing research. *IEEE Computational Intelligence Magazine*, *9*(2), 48–57. doi:10.1109/MCI.2014.2307227

Carter, S., Tsagkias, M., & Weerkamp, W. (2011). *Twitter hashtags: Joint translation and clustering.* Academic Press.

Casari, A. (2017). *Mastering Feature Engineering Principles and Techniques for Data Scientists.* Oreilly Associates Inc.

Ceylan, Z., Bulkan, S., & Elevli, S. (2020). Prediction of medical waste generation using SVR, GM (1, 1) and Arima models: A case study for megacity Istanbul. *Journal of Environmental Health Science & Engineering, 18*(2), 687–697. doi:10.100740201-020-00495-8 PMID:33312594

Chaffar, S., & Inkpen, D. (2011). Using a heterogeneous dataset for emotion analysis in text. *Lecture Notes in Computer Science, 6657,* 62–67. doi:10.1007/978-3-642-21043-3_8

Chandra, N., Kumawat, S., & Srivastava, V. (2014). Various tagsets for indian languages and their performance in part of speech tagging. *Proceedings of 5th IRF International Conference.*

Chan, S., & Elsheikh, A. H. (2017). A machine learning approach for efficient uncertainty quantification using multiscale methods. *Journal of Computational Physics, 354,* 493–511. doi:10.1016/j.jcp.2017.10.034

Chatterjee, A., Narahari, K. N., Joshi, M., & Agrawal, P. (2019). Semeval-2019 task 3: EmoContext contextual emotion detection in text. *Proceedings of the 13th International Workshop on Semantic Evaluation.* 10.18653/v1/S19-2005

Chaurasia, V., & Pal, S. (2020). Application of Machine Learning Time Series analysis for prediction COVID-19 pandemic. *Research on Biomedical Engineering,* 1–13.

Chawla, N., & Bowyer, K. (n.d.). *SMOTE: Synthetic minority over-sampling technique.* Retrieved September 19, 2022, from https://www.jair.org/index.php/jair/article/view/10302

Chen, D., & Manning, C. D. (2014, October). A fast and accurate dependency parser using neural networks. In *Proceedings of the 2014 conference on empirical methods in natural language processing (EMNLP)* (pp. 740-750). 10.3115/v1/D14-1082

Cheng, J., Bernstein, M., Danescu-Niculescu-mizil, C., & Leskovec, J. (2017). Anyone can become a troll: Causes of trolling behavior in online discussions. *Proceedings of the ACM Conference on Computer Supported Cooperative Work, CSCW.* 10.1145/2998181.2998213

Cheng, L., Guo, R., Silva, Y., Hall, D., & Liu, H. (2019). Hierarchical attention networks for cyberbullying detection on the instagram social network. *SIAM International Conference on Data Mining, SDM 2019.* 10.1137/1.9781611975673.27

Cheng, M., Xu, Q., Lv, J., Liu, W., Li, Q., & Wang, J. (2016). MS-LSTM: A multi-scale LSTM model for BGP anomaly detection. In *Proceedings of the IEEE 24th International Conference on Network Protocols.* IEEE. 10.1109/ICNP.2016.7785326

Chen, Q., Zhu, X., Ling, Z., Wei, S., Jiang, H., & Inkpen, D. (2017). Enhanced LSTM for natural language inference. *Proceedings of the 55th Annual Meeting of the Association for Computational Linguistics (Volume 1: Long Papers).* 10.18653/v1/P17-1152

Chiche, A., & Yitagesu, B. (2022). Part of speech tagging: A systematic review of deep learning and machine learning approaches. *Journal of Big Data, 9*(1), 1–25. doi:10.118640537-022-00561-y

Chu, Z., Widjaja, I., & Wang, H. (2012). Detecting social spam campaigns on Twitter. Lecture Notes in Computer Science, 7341, 455–472. doi:10.1007/978-3-642-31284-7_27

Chui, M., Manyika, J., Bughin, J., Dobbs, R., Roxburgh, C., Sarrazin, H., Sands, G. & Westergren, M. (2012). *The Social Economy: Unlocking Value and Productivity through Social Technologies.* McKinsey Global Institute.

Chung, J., Gulcehre, C., Cho, K., & Bengio, Y. (2015). *Gated feedback recurrent neural networks.* arXiv:1502.02367v1.

Church, K. W. (2017). Word2Vec. *Natural Language Engineering, 23*(1), 155–162. doi:10.1017/S1351324916000334

Cirqueira, D., Pinheiro, M. F., Jacob, A., Lobato, F., & Santana, A. (2018, December). A literature review in preprocessing for sentiment analysis for Brazilian Portuguese social media. In *2018 IEEE/WIC/ACM International Conference on Web Intelligence (WI)* (pp. 746-749). IEEE. 10.1109/WI.2018.00008

Concepción-Sánchez, J., Molina-Gil, J., Caballero-Gil, P., & Santos-González, I. (2018). Fuzzy logic system for identity theft detection in social networks. *Proceedings - 2018 International Conference on Big Data Innovations and Applications, Innovate-Data 2018.* 10.1109/Innovate-Data.2018.00017

Cong, J., Ren, M., Xie, S., & Wang, P. (2019). Predicting Seasonal influenza based on SARIMA model in mainland China from 2005 to 2018. *International Journal of Environmental Research and Public Health, 16*(23), 4760. doi:10.3390/ijerph16234760 PMID:31783697

Conway, M., Hu, M., & Chapman, W. W. (2019). Recent advances in using natural language processing to address public health research questions using social media and consumergenerated data. *Yearbook of Medical Informatics, 28*(01), 208–217. doi:10.1055-0039-1677918 PMID:31419834

Cunliffe, D. (2019). Minority languages and social media. The Palgrave handbook of minority languages and communities, 451-480.

Cyril, C. P. D., Beulah, J. R., Subramani, N., Mohan, P., Harshavardhan, A., & Sivabalaselvamani, D. (2021). An automated learning model for sentiment analysis and data classification of Twitter data using balanced CA-SVM. *Concurrent Engineering, Research and Applications, 29*(4), 386–395. doi:10.1177/1063293X211031485

Das, D., & Bandyopadhyay, S. (2014). Emotion analysis on social media: natural language processing approaches and applications. In *Online Collective Action* (pp. 19–37). Springer. doi:10.1007/978-3-7091-1340-0_2

Data-efficient GANs with Adaptive Discriminator Augmentation. (n.d.). Retrieved March 30, 2023, from https://keras.io/examples/generative/gan_ada/

Demir, S. (2016, June). Context tailoring for text normalization. In *Proceedings of TextGraphs-10: the Workshop on Graph-based Methods for Natural Language Processing* (pp. 6-14). Academic Press.

Demszky, D., Movshovitz-Attias, D., Ko, J., Cowen, A., Nemade, G., & Ravi, S. (2020). GoEmotions: A dataset of fine-grained emotions. *Proceedings of the 58th Annual Meeting of the Association for Computational Linguistics*. 10.18653/v1/2020.acl-main.372

Deng, L. (2013). Three classes of deep learning architectures and their applications: A tutorial survey. In *APSIPA transactions on signal and information processing*. Cambridge University Press.

Derczynski, L., Ritter, A., Clark, S., & Bontcheva, K. (2013, September). Twitter part-of-speech tagging for all: Overcoming sparse and noisy data. In *Proceedings of the international conference recent advances in natural language processing ranlp 2013* (pp. 198-206). Academic Press.

Derczynski, L., & Bontcheva, K. (2014). Passive-aggressive sequence labeling with discriminative post-editing for recognising person entities in tweets. *Proceedings of the 14th Conference of the European Chapter of the Association for Computational Linguistics, 2*, 69–73. 10.3115/v1/E14-4014

Derczynski, L., Maynard, D., Rizzo, G., Van Erp, M., Gorrell, G., Troncy, R., Petrak, J., & Bontcheva, K. (2015). Analysis of named entity recognition and linking for tweets. *Information Processing & Management, 51*(2), 32–49. doi:10.1016/j.ipm.2014.10.006

Devi, G. D., & Kamalakkannan, S. (2020). Literature Review on Sentiment Analysis in Social Media: Open Challenges toward Applications. *Test Eng. Manag, 83*(7), 2466–2474.

Devika, R., Vairavasundaram, S., Mahenthar, C. S. J., Varadarajan, V., & Kotecha, K. (2021). A Deep Learning Model Based on BERT and Sentence Transformer for Semantic Keyphrase Extraction on Big Social Data. *IEEE Access : Practical Innovations, Open Solutions, 9*, 165252–165261. doi:10.1109/ACCESS.2021.3133651

Dey, R., & Salemt, F. M. (2017). Gate-variants of gated recurrent unit (GRU) neural networks. In *Proceedings of the IEEE International Midwest Symposium on Circuits and Systems*. IEEE. 10.1109/MWSCAS.2017.8053243

Dhaka, D., Kakar, S., & Mehrotra, M. (2022). Detection of spammers disseminating obscene content on Twitter. *International Journal of Business Intelligence and Data Mining, 21*(3), 265–289. doi:10.1504/IJBIDM.2022.125210

Dhaka, D., & Mehrotra, M. (2019, February).: Cross-Domain Spam Detection in Social Media: A Survey. In *International Conference on Emerging Technologies in Computer Engineering* (pp. 98-112). Springer. 10.1007/978-981-13-8300-7_9

Di Capua, M., Di Nardo, E., & Petrosino, A. (2016). Unsupervised cyber bullying detection in social networks. *Proceedings - International Conference on Pattern Recognition, 0*. 10.1109/ICPR.2016.7899672

Diestel. (n.d.). *Graph theory* (3rd ed.). https://sites.math.washington.edu/ billey/classes/562.winter .2018/2006

Dinakar, K., Reichart, R., & Lieberman, H. (2011). Modeling the detection of textual cyberbullying. *AAAI Workshop - Technical Report, WS-11-02.*

Ding, N., Xu, G., Chen, Y., Wang, X., Han, X., Xie, P., . . . Liu, Z. (2021). *Few-nerd: A few-shot named entity recognition dataset.* doi:10.18653/v1/2021.acl-long.248

Ding, Y., Ma, J., & Luo, X. (2022). Applications of natural language processing in construction. *Automation in Construction, 136,* 104169. doi:10.1016/j.autcon.2022.104169

Dixon, S. (2022). *Number of global social network users 2018-2022, with forecasts up until 2027.* https://www.statista.com/statistics/278414/number-of-worldwi de-social-network-users/#statisticContainer

Dredze, M., Paul, M. J., Bergsma, S., & Tran, H. (2013, July). Carmen: A twitter geolocation system with applications to public health. In AAAI workshop on expanding the boundaries of health informatics using AI (HIAI) (Vol. 23, p. 45). Citeseer.

Dughyala, N., Potluri, S., Sumesh, K. J., & Pavithran, V. (2021). Automating the Detection of Cyberstalking. *Proceedings of the 2nd International Conference on Electronics and Sustainable Communication Systems, ICESC 2021.* 10.1109/ICESC51422.2021.9532858

Du, H., Barut, E., & Jin, F. (2021). Uncertainty Quantification in CNN Through the Bootstrap of Convex Neural Networks. *35th AAAI Conference on Artificial Intelligence, AAAI 2021, 13B,* 12078–12085. 10.1609/aaai.v35i13.17434

Du, P., & Nie, J. (2018). Mutux at semeval-2018 task 1: Exploring impacts of context information on emotion detection. *Proceedings of The 12th International Workshop on Semantic Evaluation.* 10.18653/v1/S18-1052

Durgam, V. (2018). Social media and its role in marketing. *International Journal of Advanced Research in Management, 9*(2), 1-10.

Dzmitry, B., Kyunghyun, C., & Yoshua, B. (2014). Neural Machine Translation by Jointly Learning to Align and Translate. *Computation and Language.*

Ebba & Ovesdotter. (2008). *Affect Data.* http://people.rc.rit.edu/~coagla/affectdata/index.html

Edunov, S., Baevski, A., & Auli, M. (2019). *Pre-trained language model representations for language generation.* doi:10.18653/v1/N19-1409

Egele, M., Stringhini, G., Kruegel, C., & Vigna, G. (2013, February). Compa: Detecting compromised accounts on social networks. NDSS.

Egele, M., Stringhini, G., Kruegel, C., & Vigna, G. (2017). Towards Detecting Compromised Accounts on Social Networks. *IEEE Transactions on Dependable and Secure Computing, 14*(4), 447–460. doi:10.1109/TDSC.2015.2479616

Evang, K., Basile, V., Chrupała, G., & Bos, J. (2013, October). Elephant: Sequence labeling for word and sentence segmentation. EMNLP 2013.

Fan, A., Bhosale, S., Schwenk, H., Ma, Z., El-Kishky, A., Goyal, S., … Joulin, A. (2021). Beyond English-Centric Multilingual Machine Translation. *Journal of Machine Learning Research*, *22*(107), 1–48.

Farzindar, A. A., & Inkpen, D. (2015). Linguistic Pre-processing of Social Media Texts. In *Natural Language Processing for Social Media* (pp. 15–41). Springer International Publishing. doi:10.1007/978-3-031-02157-2_2

Farzindar, A. A., & Inkpen, D. (2020). Natural language processing for social media. *Synthesis Lectures on Human Language Technologies*, *13*(2), 1–219. doi:10.1007/978-3-031-02175-6

Fazil, M., & Abulaish, M. (2020). A socialbots analysis-driven graph-based approach for identifying coordinated campaigns in twitter. *Journal of Intelligent & Fuzzy Systems*, *38*(3), 3301–3305. doi:10.3233/JIFS-182895

Fernández-Gavilanes, M., Àlvarez-López, T., Juncal-Martínez, J., Costa-Montenegro, E., & González-Castaño, F. J. (2015). GTI: An unsupervised approach for sentiment analysis in Twitter. *Proceedings of the 9th International Workshop on Semantic Evaluation (SemEval 2015)*. 10.18653/v1/S15-2089

Fisher, H. L., Moffitt, T. E., Houts, R. M., Belsky, D. W., Arseneault, L., & Caspi, A. (2012). Bullying victimisation and risk of self harm in early adolescence: Longitudinal cohort study. *BMJ (Clinical Research Ed.)*, *344*(7855), e2683. Advance online publication. doi:10.1136/bmj. e2683 PMID:22539176

Fisher, T. (2009). ROI in social media: A look at the arguments. *J Database Mark Cust Strategy Manag*, *16*(3), 189–195. doi:10.1057/dbm.2009.16

Florian, R., Ittycheriah, A., Jing, H., & Zhang, T. (2003). Named entity recognition through classifier combination. In *Proceedings of the seventh conference on Natural language learning at HLT-NAACL 2003* (pp. 168-171). 10.3115/1119176.1119201

Fortunato, S. (2010). Community detection in graphs. *Physics Reports*, *486*(3-5), 75–174. doi:10.1016/j.physrep.2009.11.002

Foster, J., Cetinoglu, O., Wagner, J., Le Roux, J., Nivre, J., Hogan, D., & Van Genabith, J. (2011). *From news to comment: Resources and benchmarks for parsing the language of web 2.0*. Academic Press.

François-Régis, C. (2007). *UPAR7: A knowledge-based system for headline sentiment tagging*. doi:10.3115/1621474.1621568

Frantzi, K. T., Ananiadou, S., & Tsujii, J. (1998). The C-VALUE/NC-VALUE method of automatic recognition for multi-word terms. In *International conference on theory and practice of digital libraries* (pp. 585–604). Springer. 10.1007/3-540-49653-X_35

Frikh, B., Djaanfar, A. S., & Ouhbi, B. (2011). A new methodology for domain ontology construction from the Web. *International Journal of Artificial Intelligence Tools*, *20*(6), 1157–1170. doi:10.1142/S0218213011000565

Frommholz, I., al-Khateeb, H. M., Potthast, M., Ghasem, Z., Shukla, M., & Short, E. (2016). On Textual Analysis and Machine Learning for Cyberstalking Detection. *Datenbank-Spektrum: Zeitschrift fur Datenbanktechnologie: Organ der Fachgruppe Datenbanken der Gesellschaft fur Informatik e.V*, *16*(2), 127–135. Advance online publication. doi:10.100713222-016-0221-x PMID:29368749

Fung, Y. C., Lee, L. K., Chui, K. T., Cheung, G. H. K., Tang, C. H., & Wong, S. M. (2022). Sentiment Analysis and Summarization of Facebook Posts on News Media. In *Data Mining Approaches for Big Data and Sentiment Analysis in Social Media* (pp. 142–154). IGI Global. doi:10.4018/978-1-7998-8413-2.ch006

Gambäck, B., & Sikdar, U. K. (2017). *Using Convolutional Neural Networks to Classify Hate-Speech*. doi:10.18653/v1/W17-3013

Ganesan, M., & Mayilvahanan, P. (2017). Cyber Crime Analysis in Social Media Using Data Mining Technique. *International Journal of Pure and Applied Mathematics*, *116*(22).

Gao, H., Chen, Y., Lee, K., Palsetia, D., & Choudhary, A. (2012). *Towards Online Spam Filtering in Social Networks*. NDSS. doi:10.1016/j.carbon.2015.04.031

Gao, H., Hu, J., Wilson, C., Li, Z., Chen, Y., & Zhao, B. Y. (2010). Detecting and characterizing social spam campaigns. *Proceedings of the 10th Annual Conference on Internet Measurement - IMC '10*, 35. 10.1145/1879141.1879147

Gardiner, Raymond, & Rascal. (2002). *Calculation of graph similarity using maximum common edge subgraphs*. https://www.cs.princeton.edu/courses/archive/spring13/cos598 C/RASCAL.pdf

Garg, P., & Pahuja, S. (2020). Social media: Concept, role, categories, trends, social media and AI, impact on youth, careers, recommendations. In *Managing social media practices in the digital economy* (pp. 172–192). IGI Global. doi:10.4018/978-1-7998-2185-4.ch008

Gautama, A. K., & Bansal, A. (2022). A Predictive Model for Cyberstalking Detection on Twitter Using Support Vector Machine (Svm). *AIJR Abstracts*, 12.

Gautam, A. K., & Bansal, A. (2022). Performance analysis of supervised machine learning techniques for cyberstalking detection in social media. *Journal of Theoretical and Applied Information Technology*, *100*(2).

Gauthier, J. C. (n.d.). *Conditional generative adversarial nets for convolutional face generation*. foldl.me.

Gebreel, O. S. S., & Shuayb, A. (2022). Contribution of social media platforms in tourism promotion. *International Journal of Social Science, Education Communist Economies*, *1*(2), 189–198.

Gelli, F., Uricchio, T., Bertini, M., Del Bimbo, A., & Chang, S.-F. (2015). *Image Popularity Prediction in Social Media Using Sentiment and Context Features.* Advance online publication. doi:10.1145/2733373.2806361

Geng, Z., Shi, C., & Han, Y. (2022). Intelligent Small Sample Defect Detection of Water Walls in Power Plants Using Novel Deep Learning Integrating Deep Convolutional GAN. *IEEE Transactions on Industrial Informatics*, 1. Advance online publication. doi:10.1109/TII.2022.3159817

Gerguis, M. N., Salama, C., & El-Kharashi, M. W. (2016, December). ASU: An Experimental Study on Applying Deep Learning in Twitter Named Entity Recognition. In *Proceedings of the 2nd Workshop on Noisy User-generated Text (WNUT)* (pp. 188-196). Academic Press.

Gers, Schmidhuber, & Cummins. (1999). *Learning to forget: Continual prediction with LSTM.* Academic Press.

Gers, F. A., Schmidhuber, J., & Cummins, F. (2000). Learning to forget: Continual prediction with LSTM. *Neural Computation*, *12*(10), 2451–2471. doi:10.1162/089976600300015015 PMID:11032042

Ge, S., Qi, T., Wu, C., & Huang, Y. (2019). THU_NGN at semeval-2019 task 3: Dialog emotion classification using attentional LSTM-CNN. *Proceedings of the 13th International Workshop on Semantic Evaluation.* 10.18653/v1/S19-2059

Ghasem, Z., Frommholz, I., & Maple, C. (2015). Machine Learning Solutions for controlling Cyberbullying and Cyberstalking. *Journal of Information Security Research*, *6*(2).

Ghosh, R., Surachawala, T., & Lerman, K. (2011). *Entropy-based Classification of "Retweeting" Activity on Twitter.* https://arxiv.org/abs/1106.0346

Girvan, M., & Mark, E. J. (2002). Newman. Community structure in social and bio- logical networks. *Proceedings of the National Academy of Sciences of the United States of America*, *99*(12), 7821–7826. doi:10.1073/pnas.122653799 PMID:12060727

Golbeck, J. (2013). Network structure and measures. Analyzing the social web, 25–44.

Golladay, K. A. (2020). Identity theft: Nature, extent, and global response. In The Palgrave Handbook of International Cybercrime and Cyberdeviance. doi:10.1007/978-3-319-78440-3_40

Goodfellow, I. J., Pouget-Abadie, J., Mirza, M., Xu, B., Warde-Farley, D., Ozair, S., Courville, A., & Bengio, Y. (2014). Generative Adversarial Nets. *Advances in Neural Information Processing Systems, 27.* https://www.github.com/goodfeli/adversarial

Goyal, N., Du, J., Ott, M., Anantharaman, G., & Conneau, A. (2021). *Larger-scale transformers for multilingual masked language modeling.* doi:10.18653/v1/2021.repl4nlp-1.4

Gramlich, J. (2021, June). *10 Facts about Americans and Facebook.* Pew Research Center. https://www.pewresearch.org/fact-tank/2021/06/01/facts-about -americans-and-facebook

Grier, C., Thomas, K., Paxson, V., & Zhang, M. (2010, October). @ spam: the underground on 140 characters or less. In *Proceedings of the 17th ACM conference on Computer and communications security* (pp. 27-37). ACM.

Guo, Y., Dong, X., Al-Garadi, M. A., Sarker, A., Paris, C., & Aliod, D. M. (2020, December). Benchmarking of transformer-based pre-trained models on social media text classification datasets. In *Proceedings of the The 18th Annual Workshop of the Australasian Language Technology Association* (pp. 86-91). Academic Press.

Guo, L., Wen, Y. F., & Wang, X. H. (2018). Exploiting pre-trained network embeddings for recommendations in social networks. *Journal of Computer Science and Technology*, *33*(4), 682–696. doi:10.100711390-018-1849-9

Gupta, D., Tripathi, S., Ekbal, A., & Bhattacharyya, P. (2017). *SMPOST: parts of speech tagger for code-mixed indic social media text.* arXiv preprint arXiv:1702.00167.

Gupta, P., Perdisci, R., & Ahamad, M. (2018). Towards Measuring the Role of Phone Numbers in Twitter-Advertised Spam. *ASIA CCS '18 (ACM Asia Conference on Computer and Communications Security).* 10.1145/3196494.3196516

Gupta, S., Khattar, A., Gogia, A., Kumaraguru, P., & Chakraborty, T. (2018). *Collective Classification of Spam Campaigners on Twitter: A Hierarchical Meta-Path Based Approach.* doi:10.1145/3178876.3186119

Gupta, A., Lamba, H., & Kumaraguru, P. (2013). *1.00perrt#bostonmarathon#prayforboston Analyzing fake content on twitter. In 2013 APWG eCrime.* IEEE.

Gupta, N., Bhaskar, M., & Gupta, D. K. (2012). Macroenvironmental influence on Hepatozoon lacertilis infectivity to lizard Hemidactylus flaviviridis. *Journal of Environmental Biology*, *33*(1), 127–132. doi:10.1145/0000000.0000000 PMID:23033655

Gupta, S., Kuchhal, D., Gupta, P., Ahamad, M., Gupta, M., & Kumaraguru, P. (2018). Under the Shadow of Sunshine: Characterizing Spam Campaigns Abusing Phone Numbers Across Online. *Social Networks*, 67–76. Advance online publication. doi:10.1145/3201064.3201065

Hadni, M., Ouatik, S. A., Lachkar, A., & Meknassi, M. (2013). Hybrid part-of-speech tagger for non-vocalized Arabic text. *Int. J. Nat. Lang. Comput*, *2*(6), 1–15. doi:10.5121/ijnlc.2013.2601

Haidar, B., Chamoun, M., & Serhrouchni, A. (2017). A multilingual system for cyberbullying detection: Arabic content detection using machine learning. *Advances in Science. Technology and Engineering Systems*, *2*(6), 275–284. Advance online publication. doi:10.25046/aj020634

Haidar, B., Chamoun, M., & Serhrouchni, A. (2018). Arabic Cyberbullying Detection: Using Deep Learning. *Proceedings of the 2018 7th International Conference on Computer and Communication Engineering, ICCCE 2018.* 10.1109/ICCCE.2018.8539303

Hain, S., & Back, A. (2008). Personal Learning Journal – Course Design for Using Weblogs in Higher Education. *Electronic Journal of e-Learning*, *6*(3), 189–196.

Hakimov, S., Oto, S. A., & Dogdu, E. (2012, May). Named entity recognition and disambiguation using linked data and graph-based centrality scoring. In *Proceedings of the 4th international workshop on semantic web information management* (pp. 1-7). 10.1145/2237867.2237871

Halevy, A., Norvig, P., & Pereira, F. (2009). The unreasonable effectiveness of data. *IEEE Intelligent Systems*, *24*(2), 8–12. doi:10.1109/MIS.2009.36

Hallock, W., Roggeveen, A., & Crittenden, V. (2019). Firm-level perspectives on social media engagement: An exploratory study. *Qualitative Market Research*, *22*(2), 217–226. Advance online publication. doi:10.1108/QMR-01-2017-0025

Hammami, M., Friboulet, D., & Kechichian, R. (2020). Cycle GAN-based data augmentation for multi-organ detection in CT images via Yolo. *2020 IEEE International Conference on Image Processing (ICIP)*, 390–393. 10.1109/ICIP40778.2020.9191127

Han, B., & Baldwin, T. (2011, June). Lexical normalisation of short text messages: Makn sens a# twitter. In *Proceedings of the 49th annual meeting of the association for computational linguistics: Human language technologies* (pp. 368-378). Academic Press.

Han, D., & Liu, Q. (n.d.). *A new image classification method using CNN transfer learning and web data augmentation*. Elsevier. Retrieved September 20, 2022, from https://www.sciencedirect.com/science/article/pii/S0957417417307844

Han, B., Cook, P., & Baldwin, T. (2012, December). Geolocation prediction in social media data by finding location indicative words. *Proceedings of COLING*, *2012*, 1045–1062.

Haryadi, D., & Putra, G. (2019). Emotion Detection in Text using Nested Long Short-Term Memory. *International Journal of Advanced Computer Science and Applications*, *10*(6). Advance online publication. doi:10.14569/IJACSA.2019.0100645

Hasanzadeh, F., Jalali, M., & Jahan, M. V. (2014). Detecting communities in social networks by techniques of clustering and analysis of communications. In *2014 Iranian Conference on Intelligent Systems (ICIS)* (pp. 1–5). IEEE.

Hasbullah, S. S., Maynard, D., Chik, R. Z. W., Mohd, F., & Noor, M. (2016, January). Automated content analysis: A sentiment analysis on Malaysian government social media. In *Proceedings of the 10th International Conference on Ubiquitous Information Management and Communication* (pp. 1-6). 10.1145/2857546.2857577

Hecht, B., Hong, L., Suh, B., & Chi, E. H. (2011, May). Tweets from Justin Bieber's heart: the dynamics of the location field in user profiles. In *Proceedings of the SIGCHI conference on human factors in computing systems* (pp. 237-246). 10.1145/1978942.1978976

He, Z., & Tao, H. (2018). Epidemiology and Arima model of a positive rate of influenza viruses among children in Wuhan, China: A nine-year retrospective study. *International Journal of Infectious Diseases*, *74*, 61–70. doi:10.1016/j.ijid.2018.07.003 PMID:29990540

Hilte, L., Vandekerckhove, R., & Daelemans, W. (2019). Adolescents' perceptions of social media writing: Has non-standard become the new standard? *European Journal of Applied Linguistics*, *7*(2), 189-224.

Hochreiter, S., & Schmidhuber, J. (1997). Long short-term memory. *Neural Computation*, *9*(8), 1735–1780. doi:10.1162/neco.1997.9.8.1735 PMID:9377276

Holzman, L. E., & Pottenger, W. M. (2003). *Classification of emotions in internet chat: An application of machine learning using speech phonemes.* Academic Press.

Hoogeveen, D., Wang, L., Baldwin, T., & Verspoor, K. M. (2018). Web forum retrieval and text analytics: A survey. *Foundations and Trends® in Information Retrieval*, *12*(1), 1-163.

Hu, X., & Liu, H. (2012). Text analytics in social media. *Mining Text Data*, 385-414.

Huisman, M., van Rijn, J. N., & Plaat, A. (2021). A survey of deep meta-learning. *Artificial Intelligence Review*, *54*(6), 4483–4541. doi:10.100710462-021-10004-4

Hulea, M., Gavrilescu, M., de Marchi, S., Chatterjee, S., Hazra, D., Byun, Y.-C., & Kim, Y.-W. (2022). Enhancement of Image Classification Using Transfer Learning and GAN-Based Synthetic Data Augmentation. *Mathematics, 10*(9), 1541.

Hüllermeier, E., & Waegeman, W. (2021). Aleatoric and epistemic uncertainty in machine learning: An introduction to concepts and methods. *Machine Learning*, *110*(3), 457–506. doi:10.100710994-021-05946-3

Hussein, D. M. E. D. M. (2018). A survey on sentiment analysis challenges. *Journal of King Saud University. Engineering Sciences*, *30*(4), 330–338. doi:10.1016/j.jksues.2016.04.002

Hyndman, R. J., & Athanasopoulos, G. (2018). *Forecasting: Principles and practice.* OTexts.

Islam, M. M., Uddin, M. A., Islam, L., Akter, A., Sharmin, S., & Acharjee, U. K. (2020). Cyberbullying Detection on Social Networks Using Machine Learning Approaches. *2020 IEEE Asia-Pacific Conference on Computer Science and Data Engineering, CSDE 2020.* 10.1109/CSDE50874.2020.9411601

Jayasiriwardene, T. D., & Ganegoda, G. U. (2020, September). Keyword extraction from Tweets using NLP tools for collecting relevant news. In *2020 International Research Conference on Smart Computing and Systems Engineering (SCSE)* (pp. 129-135). IEEE. 10.1109/SCSE49731.2020.9313024

Jehl, L. E. (2010). *Machine translation for Twitter* [Master's thesis]. The University of Edinburgh.

Jere, R., Pandey, A., Singh, M., & Ganjapurkar, M. (2021, January). Leveraging Phone Numbers for Spam detection in Online Social Networks. In *2021 IEEE 19th World Symposium on Applied Machine Intelligence and Informatics (SAMI)* (pp. 119-124). IEEE.

Jiang, X., Hu, Y., & Li, H. (2009). A ranking approach to keyphrase extraction. In *Proceedings of the 32nd international ACM SIGIR conference on research and development in information retrieval*, SIGIR '09.

Jivani, A. G. (2011). A comparative study of stemming algorithms. *Int. J. Comp. Tech. Appl*, 2(6), 1930–1938.

Judd, J., & Kalita, J. (2013, June). Better twitter summaries? In *Proceedings of the 2013 Conference of the North American Chapter of the Association for Computational Linguistics: Human Language Technologies* (pp. 445-449). Academic Press.

Jurgens, D. A., Mohammad, S. M., Turney, P. D., & Holyoak, K. J. (2012). SemEval-2012 Task 2: Measuring degrees of relational similarity. **SEM 2012 - 1st Joint Conference on Lexical and Computational Semantics, 2*.

Jurgens, D., Finethy, T., McCorriston, J., Xu, Y., & Ruths, D. (2015). Geolocation prediction in twitter using social networks: A critical analysis and review of current practice. In *Proceedings of the International AAAI Conference on Web and Social Media* (Vol. 9, No. 1, pp. 188-197). AAAI.

Jusoh, S. (2018). A study on NLP applications and ambiguity problems. *Journal of Theoretical and Applied Information Technology*, 96(6).

Kakar, S., Dhaka, D., & Mehrotra, M. (2021a). Value-Based Behavioral Analysis of Users Using Twitter. In *Inventive Communication and Computational Technologies* (Vol. 145, pp. 283–294). Springer. doi:10.1007/978-981-15-7345-3_23

Kakar, S., Dhaka, D., & Mehrotra, M. (2021b). Value-based retweet prediction on twitter. *Informatica (Slovenia)*, 45(2), 267–276. doi:10.31449/inf.v45i2.3465

Kang, Y., Cai, Z., Tan, C. W., Huang, Q., & Liu, H. (2020). Natural language processing (NLP) in management research: A literature review. *Journal of Management Analytics*, 7(2), 139–172. doi:10.1080/23270012.2020.1756939

Karras, T., Aila, T., Laine, S., & Lehtinen, J. (2017). Progressive Growing of GANs for Improved Quality, Stability, and Variation. *6th International Conference on Learning Representations, ICLR 2018 - Conference Track Proceedings*. 10.48550/arxiv.1710.10196

Karras, T., Aittala, M., Hellsten, J., Laine, S., Lehtinen, J., & Aila, T. (2020). styleGAN_with Limited data. *Conference on Neural Information Processing Systems (NeurIPS 2020)*, 12104–12114.

Katoch, R., & Sidhu, A. (2021). An application of Arima model to forecast the dynamics of COVID-19 Epidemic in India. *Global Business Review*. Advance online publication. doi:10.1177/0972150920988653

Kaunain Sheriff, M. (2021). *Explained: What has changed in the second wave of Covid-19*. https://indianexpress.com/article/explained/explainedwhats-changed-in-second-wave-7289002/

Kaur, J., & Singh, J. (2019, October). Deep neural network based sentence boundary detection and end marker suggestion for social media text. In *2019 International Conference on Computing, Communication, and Intelligent Systems (ICCCIS)* (pp. 292-295). IEEE. 10.1109/ICCCIS48478.2019.8974495

Kawaguchi, K., Bengio, Y., & Kaelbling, L. (2022). Generalization in Deep Learning. *Mathematical Aspects of Deep Learning*, 112–148. doi:10.1017/9781009025096.003

Kenny, D. (2019). Machine translation. In *Routledge encyclopedia of translation studies* (pp. 305–310). Routledge. doi:10.4324/9781315678627-65

Ker, J., Wang, L., Rao, J., & Lim, T. (2017). Deep learning applications in medical image analysis. *IEEE Access : Practical Innovations, Open Solutions*, *6*, 9375–9389. doi:10.1109/ACCESS.2017.2788044

Khanbhai, M., Anyadi, P., Symons, J., Flott, K., Darzi, A., & Mayer, E. (2021). Applying natural language processing and machine learning techniques to patient experience feedback: A systematic review. *BMJ Health & Care Informatics*, *28*(1), e100262. doi:10.1136/bmjhci-2020-100262 PMID:33653690

Khanday, A. M. U. D., Khan, Q. R., & Rabani, S. T. (2021). Detecting textual propaganda using machine learning techniques. *Baghdad Sci. J*, *18*(1), 199–209. doi:10.21123/bsj.2021.18.1.0199

Khanday, A. M. U. D., Wani, M. A., Rabani, S. T., & Khan, Q. R. (2023). Hybrid Approach for Detecting Propagandistic Community and Core Node on Social Networks. *Sustainability (Basel)*, *15*(2), 1249. doi:10.3390u15021249

Khan, J., & Lee, S. (2021). Enhancement of Text Analysis Using Context-Aware Normalization of Social Media Informal Text. *Applied Sciences (Basel, Switzerland)*, *11*(17), 8172. doi:10.3390/app11178172

Kiela, D., Bartolo, M., Nie, Y., Kaushik, D., Geiger, A., Wu, Z., . . . Williams, A. (2021). *Dynabench: Rethinking benchmarking in NLP*. doi:10.18653/v1/2021.naacl-main.324

Kim, J., & Monroy-Hernandez, A. (2016, February). Storia: Summarizing social media content based on narrative theory using crowdsourcing. In *Proceedings of the 19th ACM Conference on Computer-Supported Cooperative Work & Social Computing* (pp. 1018-1027). 10.1145/2818048.2820072

Kinsella, S., Passant, A., Breslin, J. G., Decker, S., & Jaokar, A. (2009). The future of social web sites: Sharing data and trusted applications with semantics. *Advances in Computers*, *76*, 121–175. doi:10.1016/S0065-2458(09)01004-3

Kiperwasser, E., & Goldberg, Y. (2016). Simple and accurate dependency parsing using bidirectional LSTM feature representations. *Transactions of the Association for Computational Linguistics*, *4*, 313–327. doi:10.1162/tacl_a_00101

Kiran, S., Sai, C. R. S., & Pooja, M. R. (2019, March). A comparative study on parsing in natural language processing. In *2019 3rd International Conference on Computing Methodologies and Communication (ICCMC)* (pp. 785-788). IEEE. 10.1109/ICCMC.2019.8819687

Koehn, P., & Knowles, R. (2017). *Six challenges for neural machine translation*. doi:10.18653/v1/W17-3204

Koh, D. H. (2021). Evaluating Deep Learning Uncertainty Quantification Methods for Neutrino Physics Applications. *6th Workshop on Byesian Deep Learning, NeurIPS*.

Kornblum. (2008). *Cyberbullying grows bigger and meaner with photos, video*. https://abcnews.go.com/Technology/AheadoftheCurve/story?id=5 376341&page=1

Koshy, J. (2021). *Scientists see flaws in govt-backed model's approach to forecast the pandemic*. https://www.thehindu.com/news/national/governmentbacked-model-to-predict-pandemic-rise-and-ebb-lacks-foresightscientists /article34479503.ece

Kraemer, M. U. G., Tegally, H., Pigott, D. M., Dasgupta, A., Sheldon, J., Wilkinson, E., Schultheiss, M., Han, A., Oglia, M., Marks, S., Kanner, J., O'Brien, K., Dandamudi, S., Rader, B., Sewalk, K., Bento, A. I., Scarpino, S. V., de Oliveira, T., Bogoch, I. I., ... Brownstein, J. S. (2022). Tracking the 2022 monkeypox outbreak with epidemiological data in real-time. *The Lancet. Infectious Diseases*, *22*(7), 941–942. doi:10.1016/S1473-3099(22)00359-0 PMID:35690074

Kriesel, D. (2007). *A Brief Introduction to Neural Networks*. https://www.dkriesel.com/en/science/neural_networks

Krizhevsky, A., Sutskever, I., & Hinton, G. E. (2012). ImageNet Classification with Deep Convolutional Neural Networks. *Advances in Neural Information Processing Systems*, *25*, 1097–1105.

Kumar, A., & Gupta, T. (2012). Genetic Algorithm for Dynamic Capacitated Minimum Spanning Tree. International Journal of Computational Engineering and Management, 28-35.

Kumar, A., & Jaiswal, A. (2021). A Deep Swarm-Optimized Model for Leveraging Industrial Data Analytics in Cognitive Manufacturing. *IEEE Transactions on Industrial Informatics*, *17*(4), 2938–2946. Advance online publication. doi:10.1109/TII.2020.3005532

Kumar, A., Narapareddy, V. T., Aditya Srikanth, V., Malapati, A., & Neti, L. B. (2020). Sarcasm detection using multi-head attention based bidirectional LSTM. *IEEE Access : Practical Innovations, Open Solutions*, *8*, 6388–6397. doi:10.1109/ACCESS.2019.2963630

Kumar, A., & Sachdeva, N. (2021). Multimodal cyberbullying detection using capsule network with dynamic routing and deep convolutional neural network. *Multimedia Systems*. Advance online publication. doi:10.100700530-020-00747-5

Kwak, H., Lee, C., Park, H., & Moon, S. (2010). What is twitter, a social network or a news media? *Proceedings of the 19th international conference on World wide web*, 591–600. 10.1145/1772690.1772751

Lawaye, A. A., & Purkayastha, B. S. (2013). Towards Developing a Hierarchical Part of Speech Tagger for Kashmiri: Hybrid Approach. In *Proceedings of the 2nd National Conference on Advancement in the Era of Multidisciplinary Systems* (pp. 187-192). Academic Press.

Lawaye, A. A., & Purkayastha, B. S. (2014). Kashmir part of speech tagger using CRF. *Computer Science*, *3*(3), 3.

Lee, K., Caverlee, J., Cheng, Z., & Sui, D. Z. (2013). Campaign extraction from social media. *ACM Transactions on Intelligent Systems and Technology*, *5*(1), 1–28. doi:10.1145/2542182.2542191

Lemberger, P. (2017). *On Generalization and Regularization in Deep Learning*. https://arxiv.org/abs/1704.01312

Lenhart, A., Madden, M., Smith, A., Purcell, K., Zickuhr, K., Rainie, L., & Project, A. L. (2011). *Teens, Kindness and Cruelty on Social Network Sites*. PewResearchCenter.

Levi, G., & Hassncer, T. (2015). *Age and gender classification using convolutional neural networks.* . doi:10.1109/CVPRW.2015.7301352

Li, B., Fan, Y., Sataer, Y., Gao, Z., & Gui, Y. (2022). Improving Semantic Dependency Parsing with Higher-Order Information Encoded by Graph Neural Networks. *Applied Sciences (Basel, Switzerland)*, *12*(8), 4089. doi:10.3390/app12084089

Li, C., Wang, Z., Rao, M., Belkin, D., Song, W., Jiang, H., Yan, P., Li, Y., Lin, P., Hu, M., Ge, N., Strachan, J. P., Barnell, M., Wu, Q., Williams, R. S., Yang, J. J., & Xia, Q. (2019). Long short-term memory networks in memristor crossbar arrays. *Nature Machine Intelligence*, *1*(1), 49–57. doi:10.103842256-018-0001-4

Li, C., Weng, J., He, Q., Yao, Y., Datta, A., Sun, A., & Lee, B. S. (2012, August). Twiner: named entity recognition in targeted twitter stream. In *Proceedings of the 35th international ACM SIGIR conference on Research and development in information retrieval* (pp. 721-730). 10.1145/2348283.2348380

Li, H., Fei, G., Wang, S., Liu, B., Shao, W., Mukherjee, A., & Shao, J. (2017). Bimodal distribution and co-bursting in review spam detection. *26th International World Wide Web Conference, WWW 2017*. 10.1145/3038912.3052582

Lin, H., Jia, J., Guo, Q., Xue, Y., Li, Q., Huang, J., Cai, L., & Feng, L. (2014). User-level psychological stress detection from social media using deep neural network. *MM 2014 - Proceedings of the 2014 ACM Conference on Multimedia*, 507-516. 10.1145/2647868.2654945

Lipton, Berkowitz, & Elkan. (2015). *A critical review of recurrent neural networks for sequence learning*. arXiv preprint arXiv:1506.00019.

Li, T., Yu, K., & Wu, X. (2021). Hierarchical Cyber Troll Detection with Text and User Behavior. *Proceedings of 2021 7th IEEE International Conference on Network Intelligence and Digital Content, IC-NIDC 2021.* 10.1109/IC-NIDC54101.2021.9660415

Liu, D., & Hu, N. (2020). *GAN-Based Image Data Augmentation.* Stanford CS229 Final Project: Computer Vision.

Liu, B. (2012). Sentiment Analysis and Opinion Mining. *Sentiment Analysis and Opinion Mining*, 5(May), 1–108. doi:10.2200/S00416ED1V01Y201204HLT016

Liu, B., Ni, Z., Luo, J., Cao, J., Ni, X., Liu, B., & Fu, X. (2018). Analysis of and defense against crowd-retweeting based spam in social networks. *World Wide Web (Bussum)*, 1–23. doi:10.100711280-018-0613-y

Liu, J., Cheng, J., Wang, Z., Lou, C., Shen, C., & Sheng, V. S. (2022a). A Survey of Deep Learning for Named Entity Recognition in Chinese Social Media. In *International Conference on Adaptive and Intelligent Systems* (pp. 573-582). Springer. 10.1007/978-3-031-06794-5_46

Liu, J.-S., Ning, K.-C., & Chuang, W.-C. (2013). Discovering and charac- terizing political elite cliques with evolutionary community detection. *Social Network Analysis and Mining*, 3(3), 761–783. doi:10.100713278-013-0125-9

Liu, P., Guo, Y., Wang, F., & Li, G. (2022b). Chinese named entity recognition: The state of the art. *Neurocomputing*, *473*, 37–53. doi:10.1016/j.neucom.2021.10.101

Li, Y., Fang, C., Yang, J., Wang, Z., Lu, X., & Yang, M.-H. (2017). Diversified Texture Synthesis with Feed-Forward Networks. *2017 IEEE Conference on Computer Vision and Pattern Recognition (CVPR)*, 266-274. 10.1109/CVPR.2017.36

Loftus, T. J., Shickel, B., Ruppert, M. M., Balch, J. A., Ozrazgat-Baslanti, T., Tighe, P. J., Efron, P. A., Hogan, W. R., Rashidi, P. Jr, Upchurch, G. R., & Bihorac, A. (2022). Uncertainty-aware deep learning in healthcare: A scoping review. *PLOS Digital Health*, *1*(8), e0000085. doi:10.1371/journal.pdig.0000085 PMID:36590140

Lourentzou, I., Morales, A., & Zhai, C. (2017, December). Text-based geolocation prediction of social media users with neural networks. In *2017 IEEE International Conference on Big Data (Big Data)* (pp. 696-705). IEEE. 10.1109/BigData.2017.8257985

Madleňák, A. (2021). Geolocation Services and Marketing Communication from a Global Point of View. In *SHS Web of Conferences* (Vol. 92, p. 02040). EDP Sciences.

Maitama, J. Z., Haruna, U., Gambo, A. Y. U., Thomas, B. A., Idris, N. B., Gital, A. Y. U., & Abubakar, A. I. (2014, November). Text normalization algorithm for Facebook chats in Hausa language. In *The 5th International Conference on Information and Communication Technology for The Muslim World (ICT4M)* (pp. 1-4). IEEE. 10.1109/ICT4M.2014.7020605

Malouf, R. (2002). Markov models for language-independent named entity recognition. In *COLING-02: The 6th Conference on Natural Language Learning 2002 (CoNLL-2002)*. 10.3115/1118853.1118872

Manjunath, V. (2022, November). Mining Twitter Multi-word Product Opinions with Most Frequent Sequences of Aspect Terms. In *Information Integration and Web Intelligence: 24th International Conference, iiWAS 2022, Virtual Event, November 28–30, 2022 Proceedings, 13635*, 126.

Mansouri, S. A., & Piki, A. (2016). An exploration into the impact of blogs on students' learning: Case studies in postgraduate business education. *Innovations in Education and Teaching International, 53*(3), 260–273. doi:10.1080/14703297.2014.997777

Maple, C., Short, E., Brown, A., Bryden, C., & Salter, M. (2012). Cyberstalking in the UK: Analysis and recommendations. *International Journal of Distributed Systems and Technologies, 3*(4), 34–51. Advance online publication. doi:10.4018/jdst.2012100104

Marcus, G. (n.d.). *Deep Learning: A Critical Appraisal.* https://www.nytimes.com/2012/11/24/science/scientists-see-advances-in-deep-learning-a-part-of-artificial-

Marcus, M., Santorini, B., & Marcinkiewicz, M. A. (1994). Building a large annotated corpus of English: The Penn Treebank. *Computational Linguistics, 19*(2), 313–330.

Marsh, E., & Perzanowski, D. (1998). MUC-7 evaluation of IE technology: Overview of results. *Seventh Message Understanding Conference (MUC-7): Proceedings of a Conference.*

Maylawati, D. S. A., Zulfikar, W. B., Slamet, C., Ramdhani, M. A., & Gerhana, Y. A. (2018, August). An improved of stemming algorithm for mining indonesian text with slang on social media. In *2018 6th International Conference on Cyber and IT Service Management* (CITSM) (pp. 1-6). IEEE. 10.1109/CITSM.2018.8674054

McGee, J., Caverlee, J., & Cheng, Z. (2013, October). Location prediction in social media based on tie strength. In *Proceedings of the 22nd ACM international conference on Information & Knowledge Management* (pp. 459-468). 10.1145/2505515.2505544

Meftah, S., & Semmar, N. (2018, May). A neural network model for part-of-speech tagging of social media texts. In *Proceedings of the eleventh international Conference on Language Resources and Evaluation (LREC 2018).* Academic Press.

Mendoza, M., Poblete, B., & Castillo, C. (2010). Twitter under crisis: Can we trust what we rt? *Proceedings of the first workshop on social media analytics, 71*–79. 10.1145/1964858.1964869

Meng, R., Zhao, S., Han, S., He, D., Brusilovsky, P., & Chi, Y. (2017). *Deep keyphrase generation.* doi:10.18653/v1/P17-1054

Metzler, D., Cai, C., & Hovy, E. (2012, June). Structured event retrieval over microblog archives. In *Proceedings of the 2012 Conference of the North American Chapter of the Association for Computational Linguistics: Human Language Technologies* (pp. 646-655). Academic Press.

Mihalcea, R., & Tarau, P. (2004). TEXTRANK: Bringing order into text. *Proceedings of the 2004 conference on empirical methods in natural language processing.*

Mikheev, A., Moens, M., & Grover, C. (1999, June). Named entity recognition without gazetteers. In *Ninth Conference of the European Chapter of the Association for Computational Linguistics* (pp. 1-8). Academic Press.

Mireshghallah, F., Vogler, N., He, J., Florez, O., El-Kishky, A., & Berg-Kirkpatrick, T. (2022). *Non-parametric temporal adaptation for social media topic classification.* arXiv preprint arXiv:2209.05706.

Mishra, A. A., Edelen, A., Hanuka, A., & Mayes, C. (2021). Uncertainty quantification for deep learning in particle accelerator applications. *Physical Review. Accelerators and Beams, 24*(11), 114601. Advance online publication. doi:10.1103/PhysRevAccelBeams.24.114601

Mishra, P., Rajnish, R., & Kumar, P. (2016). Sentiment analysis of twitter data: Case study on digital india. In *2016 International Conference on Information Technology (InCITe)-The Next Generation IT Summit on the Theme-Internet of Things: Connect your Worlds* (pp. 148–153). IEEE. 10.1109/INCITE.2016.7857607

Miura, A., & Yamashita, K. (2007). Psychological and social influences on blog writing: An online survey of blog authors in Japan. *Journal of Computer-Mediated Communication, 12*(4), 1452–1471. doi:10.1111/j.1083-6101.2007.00381.x

MK, M. VAtalla, SAlmuraqab, NMoonesar, I.A. (2022). Detection of COVID-19 Using Deep Learning Techniques and Cost Effectiveness Evaluation: A Survey. *Frontiers in Artificial Intelligence, 5*, 912022. doi:10.3389/frai.2022.912022 PMID:35692941

Moers, T., Krebs, F., & Spanakis, G. (2018, January). SEMTec: social emotion mining techniques for analysis and prediction of facebook post reactions. In *International Conference on Agents and Artificial Intelligence* (pp. 361-382). Springer.

Mohammad, S. M. (2017). Challenges in sentiment analysis. In *A practical guide to sentiment analysis* (pp. 61–83). Springer. doi:10.1007/978-3-319-55394-8_4

Mostafa, M., Abdelwahab, A., & Sayed, H. M. (2020). Detecting spam campaign in twitter with semantic similarity. *Journal of Physics: Conference Series, 1447*(1), 012044. Advance online publication. doi:10.1088/1742-6596/1447/1/012044

Moussa, M. E., Mohamed, E. H., & Haggag, M. H. (2018). A survey on opinion summarization techniques for social media. *Future Computing and Informatics Journal, 3*(1), 82–109. doi:10.1016/j.fcij.2017.12.002

Musil, F., Willatt, M. J., Langovoy, M. A., & Ceriotti, M. (2019). Fast and Accurate Uncertainty Estimation in Chemical Machine Learning. *Journal of Chemical Theory and Computation, 15*(2), 906–915. doi:10.1021/acs.jctc.8b00959 PMID:30605342

Nagarajan, V. (2021). *Explaining generalization in deep learning: progress and fundamental limits.* https://arxiv.org/abs/2110.08922

Nakano, T., Suda, T., Okaie, Y., & Moore, M. J. (2016). Analysis of Cyber Aggression and Cyber-Bullying in Social Networking. *Proceedings - 2016 IEEE 10th International Conference on Semantic Computing, ICSC 2016*. 10.1109/ICSC.2016.111

Navamani, J. M. A., & Kannammal, A. (2015). Predicting performance of schools by applying data mining techniques on public examination results. *Research Journal of Applied Sciences, Engineering and Technology, 9*(4), 262–271. Advance online publication. doi:10.19026/rjaset.9.1403

Neunerdt, M., Trevisan, B., Reyer, M., & Mathar, R. (2013). Part-of-speech tagging for social media texts. In *Language Processing and Knowledge in the Web* (pp. 139–150). Springer. doi:10.1007/978-3-642-40722-2_15

Newall, M. (2018). *Cyberbullying: A Global Advisor Survey*. https://www.ipsos.com/sites/default/files/ct/news/documents/ 2018-06/cyberbullying_june2018.pdf

Newman, M. E. J., & Girvan, M. (2004). Finding and evaluating community struc- ture in networks. *Physical Review E: Statistical, Nonlinear, and Soft Matter Physics, 69*(2), 026113. doi:10.1103/PhysRevE.69.026113

Neyshabur, B. Sedghi, H., & Zhang, C. (2020). What is being transferred in transfer learning? Advances in Neural Information Processing Systems, 33, 512–523.

Nichols, J., Mahmud, J., & Drews, C. (2012, February). Summarizing sporting events using twitter. In *Proceedings of the 2012 ACM international conference on Intelligent User Interfaces* (pp. 189-198). ACM.

Nogueira dos Santos, Tan, Xiang, & Zhou. (2016). *Attentive pooling networks*. CoRR, abs/1602.03609.

Nordström, M. (2022). *AI under great uncertainty: Implications and decision strategies for public policy*. doi:10.1007/s00146-021-01263-4

Ohsawa, S., & Matsuo, Y. (2013). Like Prediction: Modeling Like Counts by Bridging Facebook Pages with Linked Data. *Proceedings of the 22Nd International Conference on World Wide Web Companion*, 541–548. 10.1145/2487788.2487992

Olah. (2015). *Understanding LSTM networks*. Academic Press.

Onaolapo, J., Mariconti, E., & Stringhini, G. (2016). What happens after you are Pwnd: Understanding the use of leaked webmail credentials in the wild. *Proceedings of the ACM SIGCOMM Internet Measurement Conference, IMC, 14-16-November-2016*. 10.1145/2987443.2987475

Oparin, I., Sundermeyer, M., Ney, H., & Gauvain, J. (2012). Performance analysis of Neural Networks in combination with n-gram language models. ICASSP.

Orlov, M., & Litvak, M. (2018). Using behavior and text analysis to detect propagandists and misinformers on twitter. In *Annual International Symposium on Information Management and Big Data* (pp. 67–74). Springer.

Palmer, D. D. (2000). Tokenisation and sentence segmentation. Handbook of natural language processing, 11-35.

Palmer, G., Du, S., Politowicz, A., Emory, J. P., Yang, X., Gautam, A., Gupta, G., Li, Z., Jacobs, R., & Morgan, D. (2022). Calibration after bootstrap for accurate uncertainty quantification in regression models. In NPJ Computational Materials (Vol. 8, Issue 1). doi:10.103841524-022-00794-8

Panayides, A. S., Amini, A., Filipovic, N. D., Sharma, A., Tsaftaris, S. A., Young, A., Foran, D., Do, N., Golemati, S., Kurc, T., Huang, K., Nikita, K. S., Veasey, B. P., Zervakis, M., Saltz, J. H., & Pattichis, C. S. (2020). AI in Medical Imaging Informatics: Current Challenges and Future Directions. IEEE Journal of Biomedical and Health Informatics, 24(7), 1837–1857. doi:10.1109/JBHI.2020.2991043

Papagiannopoulou, E., & Tsoumakas, G. (2020). A review of keyphrase extraction. *Wiley Interdisciplinary Reviews. Data Mining and Knowledge Discovery*, *10*(2), e1339. doi:10.1002/widm.1339

Patchin, J. W. (2022). *Summary of Our Cyberbullying Research (2007-2021)*. https://cyberbullying.org/summary-of-our-cyberbullying-research

Patel, C. (2022). *Visual Analysis of Spam Campaigns based on Network Modelling*. Academic Press.

Pekkala, K., & van Zoonen, W. (2022). Work-related social media use: The mediating role of social media communication self-efficacy. *European Management Journal*, *40*(1), 67–76. doi:10.1016/j.emj.2021.03.004

Pennington, J., Socher, R., & Manning, C. (2014). Glove: Global vectors for word representation. *Proceedings of the 2014 Conference on Empirical Methods in Natural Language Processing (EMNLP)*. 10.3115/v1/D14-1162

Peterson, A. A., Christensen, R., & Khorshidi, A. (2017). Addressing uncertainty in atomistic machine learning. *Physical Chemistry Chemical Physics*, *19*(18), 10978–10985. doi:10.1039/C7CP00375G PMID:28418054

Plaza-del-Arco, F. M., Molina-González, M. D., Ureña-López, L. A., & Martín-Valdivia, M. T. (2021). Comparing pre-trained language models for Spanish hate speech detection. *Expert Systems with Applications*, *166*, 114120. Advance online publication. doi:10.1016/j.eswa.2020.114120

Plested, J., & Gedeon, T. (2022). *Deep transfer learning for image classification: A survey*. https://arxiv.org/abs/2205.09904

Polignano, M., Basile, P., De Gemmis, M., & Semeraro, G. (2019). A comparison of word-embeddings in emotion detection from text using BiLSTM, CNN and self-attention. *Adjunct Publication of the 27th Conference on User Modeling, Adaptation and Personalization*. 10.1145/3314183.3324983

Polužanski, V., Kovacevic, U., Bacanin, N., Rashid, T. A., Stojanovic, S., & Nikolic, B. (2022). Application of Machine Learning to Express Measurement Uncertainty. *Applied Sciences, 12*(17), 8581. doi:10.3390/app12178581

Power, A., Burda, Y., Edwards, H., Babuschkin, I., & Misra, V. (2022). *Grokking: Generalization Beyond Overfitting on Small Algorithmic Datasets*. https://doi.org/ doi:10.48550/arxiv.2201.02177

Pradana, A. W., & Hayaty, M. (2019). The effect of stemming and removal of stopwords on the accuracy of sentiment analysis on indonesian-language texts. *Kinetik: Game Technology, Information System, Computer Network, Computing, Electronics, and Control*, 375-380.

Pradhan, A., Yatam, V. M., & Bera, P. (2020). Self-Attention for Cyberbullying Detection. *2020 International Conference on Cyber Situational Awareness, Data Analytics and Assessment*. 10.1109/CyberSA49311.2020.9139711

Pratt, T. C., Holtfreter, K., & Reisig, M. D. (2010). Routine online activity and internet fraud targeting: Extending the generality of routine activity theory. *Journal of Research in Crime and Delinquency, 47*(3), 267–296. Advance online publication. doi:10.1177/0022427810365903

Psaros A. F. Meng X. Zou Z. Guo L. Karniadakis G. E. (2022). *Uncertainty Quantification in Scientific Machine Learning: Methods, Metrics, and Comparisons*. https://arxiv.org/abs/2201.07766

Qian, F., Pathak, A., Hu, Y. C., Mao, Z. M., & Xie, Y. (2010). A case for unsupervised-learning-based spam filtering. *Performance Evaluation Review, 38*(1), 367–368. doi:10.1145/1811099.1811090

Radim & Sojka. (2010). Software Framework for Topic Modelling with Large Corpora. LREC 2010, 46-50.

Ragheb, W., Azé, J., Bringay, S., & Servajean, M. (2019). LIRMM-advanse at semeval-2019 task 3: Attentive conversation modeling for emotion detection and classification. *Proceedings of the 13th International Workshop on Semantic Evaluation*. 10.18653/v1/S19-2042

Raghu, M., Zhang, C., Kleinberg, J., & Bengio, S. (2019). Transfusion: Understanding Transfer Learning for Medical Imaging. *Advances in Neural Information Processing Systems, 32*. Advance online publication. doi:10.48550/arxiv.1902.07208

Ramanathan, U., Subramanian, N., & Parrott, G. (2017). Role of social media in retail network operations and marketing to enhance customer satisfaction. *International Journal of Operations & Production Management, 37*(1), 105–123. doi:10.1108/IJOPM-03-2015-0153

Rao, B., & Mitra, A. (2014). A new approach for detection of common com- munities in a social network using graph mining techniques. In *2014 Inter- national Conference on High Performance Computing and Applications (ICH-PCA)* (pp. 1–6). IEEE.

Rashid, U., Iqbal, M. W., Skiandar, M. A., Raiz, M. Q., Naqvi, M. R., & Shahzad, S. K. (2020). Emotion detection of contextual text using deep learning. *2020 4th International Symposium on Multidisciplinary Studies and Innovative Technologies (ISMSIT)*. 10.1109/ISMSIT50672.2020.9255279

Rather, I. H., Minz, S., & Kumar, S. (2023). *Hybrid Texture-Based Feature Extraction Model for Brain Tumour Classification Using Machine Learning*. doi:10.1007/978-981-19-4676-9_38

Rathod, S., & Govilkar, S. (2015). Survey of various POS tagging techniques for Indian regional languages. *International Journal of Computer Science and Information Technologies*, 6(3), 2525–2529.

Ray Chowdhury, J., Caragea, C., & Caragea, D. (2019, May). Keyphrase extraction from disaster-related tweets. In The world wide web conference (pp. 1555-1566). doi:10.1145/3308558.3313696

Řehůřek, R., & Sojka, P. (2010). *Software Framework for Topic Modelling with Large Corpora*. doi:10.13140/2.1.2393.1847

Rizki, A. S., Tjahyanto, A., & Trialih, R. (2019). Comparison of stemming algorithms on Indonesian text processing. *TELKOMNIKA*, 17(1), 95–102. doi:10.12928/telkomnika.v17i1.10183

Roberts, L. (2008). Jurisdictional and definitional concerns with computer-mediated interpersonal crimes : An Analysis on Cyber Stalking. *International Journal of Cyber Criminology*, 2(1).

Rodriguez, A., Argueta, C., & Chen, Y. L. (2019, February). Automatic detection of hate speech on facebook using sentiment and emotion analysis. In 2019 international conference on artificial intelligence in information and communication (ICAIIC) (pp. 169-174). IEEE. doi:10.1109/ICAIIC.2019.8669073

Romero, M., Interian, Y., Solberg, T., & Valdes, G. (2019). *Targeted transfer learning to improve performance in small medical physics datasets*. doi:10.1002/mp.14507

Roy, P. K. (2015). *Why online harassment goes unpunished in India*. https://www.bbc.com/news/world-asia-india-33532706

Roy, S., Bhunia, G. S., & Shit, P. K. (2021). Spatial Prediction of COVID-19 epidemic using Arima techniques in India. *Modeling Earth Systems and Environment*, 7(2), 1385–1391. doi:10.1007/s40808-020-00890-y

Roy, S. D., Lotan, G., & Zeng, W. (2015). The attention automaton: Sensing collective user interests in social network communities. *IEEE Transactions on Network Science and Engineering*, 2(1), 40–52. doi:10.1109/TNSE.2015.2416691

Rudrapal, D., Jamatia, A., Chakma, K., Das, A., & Gambäck, B. (2015, December). Sentence boundary detection for social media text. In *Proceedings of the 12th International Conference on Natural Language Processing* (pp. 254-260). Academic Press.

Rumahorbo, K. A., & Mutiaz, I. (2023). In-Press: Adolescent Responses to the Social Campaign Video on Kemdikbud. RI Account about Cyber-sexual Harassment. *Indonesian Journal of Visual Culture, Design, and Cinema*, 2(1), 107-116.

Sabharwal, R., & Miah, S. J. (2022). An intelligent literature review: Adopting inductive approach to define machine learning applications in the clinical domain. *Journal of Big Data*, 9(1), 1–18. doi:10.118640537-022-00605-3

Sadiq, S., Mehmood, A., Ullah, S., Ahmad, M., Choi, G. S., & On, B. W. (2021). Aggression detection through deep neural model on Twitter. *Future Generation Computer Systems, 114*, 120–129. Advance online publication. doi:10.1016/j.future.2020.07.050

Sadredini, E., Guo, D., Bo, C., Rahimi, R., Skadron, K., & Wang, H. (2018, July). A scalable solution for rule-based part-of-speech tagging on novel hardware accelerators. In *Proceedings of the 24th ACM SIGKDD international conference on knowledge discovery & data mining* (pp. 665-674). ACM.

Saeed, M. H., Ali, S., Blackburn, J., De Cristofaro, E., Zannettou, S., & Stringhini, G. (2022). TrollMagnifier: Detecting State-Sponsored Troll Accounts on Reddit. *2022 IEEE Symposium on Security and Privacy (SP)*, 2161–2175. 10.1109/SP46214.2022.9833706

Samarth, Homayoon, & Beigi. (2018). Multi-Modal Emotion recognition on IEMOCAP Dataset using Deep Learning. *Artificial Intelligence*.

Sampath, A., Durairaj, T., Chakravarthi, B. R., Priyadharshini, R., Cn, S., Shanmugavadivel, K., ... Pandiyan, S. (2022, May). Findings of the shared task on Emotion Analysis in Tamil. In *Proceedings of the Second Workshop on Speech and Language Technologies for Dravidian Languages* (pp. 279-285). 10.18653/v1/2022.dravidianlangtech-1.42

Sancheng Peng. (2022). *A survey on deep learning for textual emotion analysis in social networks.* doi:10.1016/j.dcan.2021.10.003

Sanchez, H., & Kumar, S. (2011). Twitter bullying detection. *Ser. NSDI, 12*, 15.

Sánchez, J., Monzón, N., & Salgado, A. (2018). An Analysis and Implementation of the Harris Corner Detector. *Image Processing On Line., 8*, 305–328. doi:10.5201/ipol.2018.229

Sang, E. F., & De Meulder, F. (2003). *Introduction to the CoNLL-2003 shared task: Language-independent named entity recognition.* arXiv preprint cs/0306050.

Sapountzi, A., & Psannis, K. E. (2018). Social networking data analysis tools & challenges. *Future Generation Computer Systems, 86*, 893–913. doi:10.1016/j.future.2016.10.019

Saravanaraj, A., Sheeba, J. I., & Devaneyan, S. P. (2016). *Automatic detection of cyberbullying from twitter. International Journal of Computer Science and Information Technology & Security.*

Saroj, A., & Pal, S. (2020). Use of social media in crisis management: A survey. *International Journal of Disaster Risk Reduction, 48*, 101584. doi:10.1016/j.ijdrr.2020.101584

Sarsam, S., Al-Samarraie, H., Alzahrani, A., & Wright, B. (2020). Sarcasm detection using machine learning algorithms in Twitter: A systematic review. *International Journal of Market Research, 62*(5), 578–598. Advance online publication. doi:10.1177/1470785320921779

Scherer, K. R., & Wallbott, H. G. (1997). *The ISEAR questionnaire and codebook.* Geneva Emotion Research Group.

Schuster, M., & Paliwal, K. (1997). Bidirectional recurrent neural networks. *IEEE Transactions on Signal Processing*, *45*(11), 2673–2681. doi:10.1109/78.650093

Segalin, C., Cheng, D. S., & Cristani, M. (2017). Social profiling through image understanding: Personality inference using convolutional neural networks. *Computer Vision and Image Understanding, 156*, 34-50. doi:10.1016/j.cviu.2016.10.013

Seidman & Foster. (1978). A graph-theoretic generalization of the clique concept. *The Journal of Mathematical Sociology, 6*(1),139–154. doi:10.1080/0022250X.1978.9989883

Seiler, S. J., & Navarro, J. N. (2014). Bullying on the pixel playground: Investigating risk factors of cyberbullying at the intersection of children's online–offline social lives. *Cyberpsychology (Brno), 8*(4). Advance online publication. doi:10.5817/CP2014-4-6

Shafie, L. A., & Nayan, S. (2013). Languages, code-switching practice and primary functions of Facebook among university students. *Study in English Language Teaching, 1*(1), 187–199. doi:10.22158elt.v1n1p187

Shahbaznezhad, H., Dolan, R., & Rashidirad, M. (2021). The role of social media content format and platform in users' engagement behavior. *Journal of Interactive Marketing, 53*(1), 47–65. doi:10.1016/j.intmar.2020.05.001

Shaheen, S., El-Hajj, W., Hajj, H., & Elbassuoni, S. (2014). Emotion recognition from text based on automatically generated rules. *2014 IEEE International Conference on Data Mining Workshop*. 10.1109/ICDMW.2014.80

Shalev-Shwartz, S., & Ben-David, S. (2013). Understanding machine learning: From theory to algorithms. Understanding Machine Learning: From Theory to Algorithms. doi:10.1017/CBO9781107298019

Sharma, A., Gupta, S., Motlani, R., Bansal, P., Srivastava, M., Mamidi, R., & Sharma, D. M. (2016). *Shallow parsing pipeline for hindi-english code-mixed social media text*. doi:10.18653/v1/N16-1159

Sharma, K., Zhang, Y., Ferrara, E., & Liu, Y. (2021, August). Identifying coordinated accounts on social media through hidden influence and group behaviours. In *Proceedings of the 27th ACM SIGKDD Conference on Knowledge Discovery & Data Mining* (pp. 1441-1451). ACM.

Sharma, P., & Moh, T.-S. (2016). *Prediction of Indian election using sentiment analysis on hindi twitter. In 2016 IEEE international conference on big data (big data)*. IEEE.

Sharp, T., Shreve-Neiger, A., Fremouw, W., Kane, J., & Hutton, S. (2004). Exploring the Psychological and Somatic Impact of Identity Theft. *Journal of Forensic Sciences, 49*(1). Advance online publication. doi:10.1520/JFS2003178 PMID:14979359

Sheel, A. (2021). *Global covid trends: The second wave and where we are headed*. https://www.livemint.com/opinion/online-views/global-covid-trendsthe-second-wave-and-where-we-are-headed-11623168003670.html

Sheikhalishahi, M., Mejri, M., & Tawbi, N. (2015). Clustering Spam Emails into Campaigns. *Proceedings of the 1st International Conference on Information Systems Security and Privacy,* 90–97. 10.5220/0005244500900097

Shelke, R., & Vanjale, S. (2022). Recursive LSTM for the Classification of Named Entity Recognition for Hindi Language. *Journal, 27*(4), 679–684. doi:10.18280/isi.270420

Shen, W., Wang, J., & Han, J. (2014). Entity linking with a knowledge base: Issues, techniques, and solutions. *IEEE Transactions on Knowledge and Data Engineering, 27*(2), 443–460. doi:10.1109/TKDE.2014.2327028

Shi, X. (2016). A Study on Factors Influencing the Click Through Rate, CTR, of Internet Ads by the Charging Mode of CPM (Cost per Mile) Based on Information Transfer. *International Journal of Simulation Systems, Science and Technology, 17*, 35.1-35.5. doi:10.5013/IJSSST.a.17.32.35

Shu, J., Xu, Z., & Meng, D. (2018). *Small Sample Learning in Big Data Era.* https://arxiv.org/abs/1808.04572

Siddique, T., Mahmud, M. S., Keesee, A. M., Ngwira, C. M., & Connor, H. (2022). A Survey of Uncertainty Quantification in Machine Learning for Space Weather Prediction. *Geosciences, 12*(1), 27. doi:10.3390/geosciences12010027

Singh, J., & Gupta, V. (2017). A systematic review of text stemming techniques. *Artificial Intelligence Review, 48*(2), 157–217. doi:10.100710462-016-9498-2

Singh, V. K., Ghosh, S., & Jose, C. (2017). Toward multimodal cyberbullying detection. *Conference on Human Factors in Computing Systems - Proceedings, Part F127655.* 10.1145/3027063.3053169

Singkul, S., Khampingyot, B., Maharattamalai, N., Taerungruang, S., & Chalothorn, T. (2019). Parsing thai social data: A new challenge for thai nlp. In *2019 14th International Joint Symposium on Artificial Intelligence and Natural Language Processing (iSAI-NLP)* (pp. 1-7). IEEE. 10.1109/iSAI-NLP48611.2019.9045639

Smatana, M., & Butka, P. (2016). Extraction of keyphrases from single document based on hierarchical concepts. In *IEEE 14th international symposium on applied machine intelligence and informatics (SAMI)* (pp. 93–98). IEEE. 10.1109/SAMI.2016.7422988

Smith, A., & Anderson, M. (2018). *Social Media Use 2018: Demographics and Statistics.* Pew Research Center. https://www.pewresearch.org/internet/2018/03/01/social-media-use-in-2018/

Smith, P. K., Mahdavi, J., Carvalho, M., Fisher, S., Russell, S., & Tippett, N. (2008). Cyberbullying: Its nature and impact in secondary school pupils. *Journal of Child Psychology and Psychiatry, and Allied Disciplines, 49*(4), 376–385. Advance online publication. doi:10.1111/j.1469-7610.2007.01846.x PMID:18363945

Solangi, Y. A., Solangi, Z. A., Aarain, S., Abro, A., Mallah, G. A., & Shah, A. (2018, November). Review on natural language processing (NLP) and its toolkits for opinion mining and sentiment analysis. In *2018 IEEE 5th International Conference on Engineering Technologies and Applied Sciences (ICETAS)* (pp. 1-4). IEEE.

Sood, S., & Vasserman, L. (2009). ESSE: Exploring mood on the web. *Proceedings of the 3rd international AAAI conference on weblogs and social media (ICWSM)*.

Sotudeh, S., Deilamsalehy, H., Dernoncourt, F., & Goharian, N. (2021). *TLDR9+: A large scale resource for extreme summarization of social media posts*. doi:10.18653/v1/2021.newsum-1.15

Speer, R., Chin, J., & Havasi, C. (2017). ConceptNet 5.5: An open multilingual graph of general knowledge. *Proceedings of the AAAI Conference on Artificial Intelligence*, *31*(1). Advance online publication. doi:10.1609/aaai.v31i1.11164

Speer, R., & Lowry-Duda, J. (2017). ConceptNet at semeval-2017 task 2: Extending word embeddings with multilingual relational knowledge. *Proceedings of the 11th International Workshop on Semantic Evaluation (SemEval-2017)*. 10.18653/v1/S17-2008

Sri Nandhini, B., & Sheeba, J. I. (2015). Cyberbullying detection and classification using information retrieval algorithm. *ACM International Conference Proceeding Series, 06-07-March-2015*. 10.1145/2743065.2743085

Ståhl, N., Falkman, G., Karlsson, A., & Mathiason, G. (2020). Evaluation of Uncertainty Quantification in Deep Learning. *Communications in Computer and Information Science, 1237*, 556–568. https://doi.org/ doi:10.1007/978-3-030-50146-4_41/FIGURES/4

Stahlberg, F. (2020). Neural machine translation: A review. *Journal of Artificial Intelligence Research*, *69*, 343–418. doi:10.1613/jair.1.12007

Straton, N., Mukkamala, R. R., & Vatrapu, R. (2015). *Big Social Data Analytics for Public Health: Predicting Facebook Post Performance using Artificial Neural Networks and Deep Learning*. Academic Press.

Stringhini, G. (2010). *Detecting spammers on social networks*. https://dl.acm.org/citation.cfm?id=1920261.1920263

Sundermeyer, M., Schlüter, R., & Ney, H. (2012). LSTM Neural Networks for Language Modeling. INTERSPEECH. doi:10.21437/Interspeech.2012-65

Sutaria, K., & Joshi, D. (2015). *An adaptive approximation algorithm for community detection in social network. In 2015 IEEE international conference on computational intelligence & communication technology*. IEEE.

Sutskever, Vinyals, & Le. (2014). Sequence to sequence learning with neural networks. *Advances in Neural Information Processing Systems*, 3104-3112.

Świechowski, M. (2022). *Deep Learning and Artificial General Intelligence: Still a Long Way to Go*. https://arxiv.org/abs/2203.14963

Szpyrka, M., Suszalski, P., Obara, S., & Nalepa, G. J. (2023). Email Campaign Evaluation Based on User and Mail Server Response. *Applied Sciences (Basel, Switzerland)*, *13*(3), 1630. doi:10.3390/app13031630

Tandon, H., Ranjan, P., Chakraborty, T., & Suhag, V. (2020). *Coronavirus (COVID-19): Arima based time-series analysis to forecast near future.* arXiv preprint arXiv:2004.07859.

Tang, H., Zhao, X., & Ren, Y. (2022). A multilayer recognition model for twitter user geolocation. *Wireless Networks*, *28*(3), 1–6. doi:10.100711276-018-01897-1

Tang, Y., Zhang, Y. Q., & Chawla, N. V. (2009). SVMs modeling for highly imbalanced classification. *IEEE Transactions on Systems, Man, and Cybernetics. Part B, Cybernetics*, *39*(1), 281–288. doi:10.1109/TSMCB.2008.2002909 PMID:19068445

Tao, S. Tianyi, Z., Guodong, L., Jing, J., & Chengqi, Z. (2018). Bi-Directional Block Self-Attention for Fast and Memory-Efficient Sequence Modeling. *Computation and Language.*

Tarihoran, N. A., & Sumirat, I. R. (2022). The impact of social media on the use of code mixing by generation Z. *International Journal of Interactive Mobile Technologies*, *16*(7), 54–69. doi:10.3991/ijim.v16i07.27659

Thara, S., & Poornachandran, P. (2018, September). Code-mixing: A brief survey. In *2018 International conference on advances in computing, communications and informatics (ICACCI)* (pp. 2382-2388). IEEE.

Thomas, K., Grier, C., Ma, J., Paxson, V., & Song, D. (2011). Design and evaluation of a real-time URL spam filtering service. *Proceedings - IEEE Symposium on Security and Privacy*, 447–462. 10.1109/SP.2011.25

Tiwari, A. S., & Naskar, S. K. (2017, December). Normalization of social media text using deep neural networks. In *Proceedings of the 14th International Conference on Natural Language Processing (ICON-2017)* (pp. 312-321). Academic Press.

Toleu, A., Tolegen, G., & Makazhanov, A. (2017). *Character-based deep learning models for token and sentence segmentation.* Academic Press.

Tomas, M. (2017). Advances in Pre-Training Distributed Word Representations. Academic Press.

Tran, C., Bhosale, S., Cross, J., Koehn, P., Edunov, S., & Fan, A. (2021). *Facebook ai wmt21 news translation task submission.* arXiv preprint arXiv:2108.03265.

Turney, P. D. (2000). Learning algorithms for keyphrase extraction. *Information Retrieval*, *2*(4), 303–336. doi:10.1023/A:1009976227802

Tyagi, R., Dwivedi, L. K., & Sanzgiri, A. (2020). *Estimation of effective reproduction numbers for COVID-19 using real-time bayesian method for India and its states.* Academic Press.

Utomo, M. N. Y., Adji, T. B., & Ardiyanto, I. (2018, March). Geolocation prediction in social media data using text analysis: A review. In *2018 International Conference on Information and Communications Technology (ICOIACT)* (pp. 84-89). IEEE. 10.1109/ICOIACT.2018.8350674

Van der Goot, R. (2019, October). An in-depth analysis of the effect of lexical normalization on the dependency parsing of social media. In *Proceedings of the 5th Workshop on Noisy User-generated Text* (pp. 115-120). Association for Computational Linguistics. 10.18653/v1/D19-5515

Van Hee, C., Jacobs, G., Emmery, C., DeSmet, B., Lefever, E., Verhoeven, B., De Pauw, G., Daelemans, W., & Hoste, V. (2018). Automatic detection of cyberbullying in social media text. *PLoS One*, *13*(10), e0203794. Advance online publication. doi:10.1371/journal.pone.0203794 PMID:30296299

Vasconcelos, C. N., & Vasconcelos, B. N. (2020). Experiments using deep learning for dermoscopy image analysis. *Pattern Recognition Letters*, *139*, 95–103. doi:10.1016/j.patrec.2017.11.005

Vathsala, M. K., & Holi, G. (2020). RNN based machine translation and transliteration for Twitter data. *International Journal of Speech Technology*, *23*(3), 499–504. doi:10.100710772-020-09724-9

Verma, P., Verma, A., & Pal, S. (2022). An approach for extractive text summarization using fuzzy evolutionary and clustering algorithms. *Applied Soft Computing*, *120*, 108670. doi:10.1016/j.asoc.2022.108670

Vijay, D., Bohra, A., Singh, V., Akhtar, S. S., & Shrivastava, M. (2018, June). Corpus creation and emotion prediction for Hindi-English code-mixed social media text. In *Proceedings of the 2018 conference of the North American chapter of the Association for Computational Linguistics: student research workshop* (pp. 128-135). 10.18653/v1/N18-4018

Villar-Rodríguez, E., Del Ser, J., Torre-Bastida, A. I., Bilbao, M. N., & Salcedo-Sanz, S. (2016). A novel machine learning approach to the detection of identity theft in social networks based on emulated attack instances and support vector machines. *Concurrency and Computation*, *28*(4), 1385–1395. Advance online publication. doi:10.1002/cpe.3633

Vinyals, O., Blundell, C., Lillicrap, T., Kavukcuoglu, K., & Wierstra, D. (2016). Matching Networks for One Shot Learning. Advances in Neural Information Processing Systems, 29.

Vo, B. K. H., & Collier, N. (2013). Twitter emotion analysis in earthquake situations. *Int. J. Comput. Linguistics Appl.*, *4*(1), 159–173.

Wang, J., & Perez, L. (2017). *The Effectiveness of Data Augmentation in Image Classification using Deep Learning*. https://arxiv.org/abs/1712.04621

Wang, L., & John, Q. (2017). Gan. Prediction of the 2017 French election based on twitter data analysis. In 2017 9th Computer Science and Electronic Engineering (CEEC) (pp. 89–93). IEEE.

Wang, Y., Li, J., Chan, H. P., King, I., Lyu, M. R., & Shi, S. (2019). *Topic-aware neural keyphrase generation for social media language*. doi:10.18653/v1/P19-1240

Wang, Y., Wang, S., Tang, J., Liu, H., & Li, B. (2015). Unsupervised sentiment analysis for social media images. In *IJCAI International Joint Conference on Artificial Intelligence* (pp. 2378-2379). International Joint Conferences on Artificial Intelligence.

Wang, B., Luo, H., Lu, J., Li, T., Zhang, G., Yan, Z., & Zheng, Y. (2019). Deep uncertainty quantification: A machine learning approach for weather forecasting. *Proceedings of the ACM SIGKDD International Conference on Knowledge Discovery and Data Mining*, 2087–2095. 10.1145/3292500.3330704

Wang, B., Wang, A., Chen, F., Wang, Y., & Kuo, C. C. J. (2019). Evaluating word embedding models: Methods and experimental results. *APSIPA Transactions on Signal and Information Processing*, *8*(1), e19. doi:10.1017/ATSIP.2019.12

Wang, C., Yang, B., Cui, J., & Wang, C. (2019). Fusing Behavioral Projection Models for Identity Theft Detection in Online Social Networks. *IEEE Transactions on Computational Social Systems*, *6*(4), 637–648. Advance online publication. doi:10.1109/TCSS.2019.2917003

Wang, C., Yang, B., & Luo, J. (2017). Identity Theft Detection in Mobile Social Networks Using Behavioral Semantics. *2017 IEEE International Conference on Smart Computing, SMARTCOMP 2017*. 10.1109/SMARTCOMP.2017.7947016

Wang, C., Zhu, H., & Yang, B. (2022). Composite Behavioral Modeling for Identity Theft Detection in Online Social Networks. *IEEE Transactions on Computational Social Systems*, *9*(2), 428–439. Advance online publication. doi:10.1109/TCSS.2021.3092007

Wang, D., Yu, J., Chen, L., Li, X., Jiang, H., Chen, K., Zheng, M., & Luo, X. (2021). A hybrid framework for improving uncertainty quantification in deep learning-based QSAR regression modeling. *Journal of Cheminformatics*, *13*(1), 1–17. doi:10.118613321-021-00551-x PMID:34544485

Wang, L., Zhang, K., Liu, X., Long, E., Jiang, J., An, Y., Zhang, J., Liu, Z., Lin, Z., Li, X., Chen, J., Cao, Q., Li, J., Wu, X., Wang, D., Li, W., & Lin, H. (2017). Comparative analysis of image classification methods for automatic diagnosis of ophthalmic images. *Scientific Reports*, *7*(1), 41545. doi:10.1038rep41545 PMID:28139688

Wang, S., Cao, J., & Yu, P. S. (2022). Deep learning for Spatio-Temporal data mining: A survey. *IEEE Transactions on Knowledge and Data Engineering*, *34*(8), 3681–3700. doi:10.1109/TKDE.2020.3025580

Wang, X., & Peng, Z. (2014). Method of moments for estimating uncertainty distributions. *Journal of Uncertainty Analysis and Applications*, *2*(1), 5. doi:10.1186/2195-5468-2-5

Wankhade, M., Rao, A. C. S., & Kulkarni, C. (2022). A survey on sentiment analysis methods, applications, and challenges. *Artificial Intelligence Review*, *55*(7), 5731–5780. doi:10.100710462-022-10144-1

Wan, L., Liao, J., & Zhu, X. (2008). Cdpm: Finding and evaluating com- munity structure in social networks. In *International Conference on Advanced Data Mining and Applications* (pp. 620–627). Springer. 10.1007/978-3-540-88192-6_64

Wei, C., Sprague, A., Warner, G., & Skjellum, A. (2008). Mining spam email to identify common origins for forensic application. *SAC '08: Proceedings of the 2008 ACM Symposium on Applied Computing*, 1433–1437. 10.1145/1363686.1364019

Wen, M., & Tadmor, E. B. (2020). Uncertainty quantification in molecular simulations with dropout neural network potentials. *npj Computational Materials*, 6(1), 124. Advance online publication. doi:10.103841524-020-00390-8

Wiebe, J., Wilson, T., & Cardie, C. (2005). Annotating expressions of opinions and emotions in language. *Language Resources and Evaluation*, 39(2), 165–210. doi:10.100710579-005-7880-9

Wong, S. C., Gatt, A., Stamatescu, V., & McDonnell, M. D. (2016). Understanding data augmentation for classification: when to warp? *2016 International Conference on Digital Image Computing: Techniques and Applications, DICTA 2016*. 10.1109/DICTA.2016.7797091

Woodward, D., Hobbs, M., Gilbertson, J. A., & Cohen, N. (2021). Uncertainty Quantification for Trusted Machine Learning in Space System Cyber Security. *Proceedings - 8th IEEE International Conference on Space Mission Challenges for Information Technology, SMC-IT 2021*, 38–43. 10.1109/SMC-IT51442.2021.00012

Wu, Y., Schuster, M., Chen, Z., Le, Q. V., Norouzi, M., Macherey, W., . . . Dean, J. (2016). *Google's neural machine translation system: Bridging the gap between human and machine translation.* arXiv preprint arXiv:1609.08144.

Wu, Y., Yang, Y., Nishiura, H., & Saitoh, M. (2018). Deep learning for epidemiological predictions. *The 41st International ACM SIGIR.* doi:10.1145/3209978.3210077

Xiao, J. (2019). Figure eight at semeval-2019 task 3: Ensemble of transfer learning methods for contextual emotion detection. *Proceedings of the 13th International Workshop on Semantic Evaluation.* 10.18653/v1/S19-2036

Xie, J., Kelley, S., & Szymanski, B. K. (2013). Overlapping community detection in networks: The state-of-the-art and comparative study. *ACM Comput. Surv.*, 45(4). doi:10.1145/2501654.2501657

Xie, Y., Yu, F., Achan, K., Panigrahy, R., Hulten, G., & Osipkov, I. (2008). Spamming botnets: Signatures and characteristics. *Computer Communication Review*, 38(4), 171–182. doi:10.1145/1402946.1402979

Xu, C. (2014). *Visual Sentiment Prediction with Deep Convolutional Neural Networks.* Available at: https://arxiv.org/abs/1411.5731

Xue, L., Barua, A., Constant, N., Al-Rfou, R., Narang, S., Kale, M., Roberts, A., & Raffel, C. (2022). Byt5: Towards a token-free future with pre-trained byte-to-byte models. *Transactions of the Association for Computational Linguistics*, 10, 291–306. doi:10.1162/tacl_a_00461

Yadav, V., & Bethard, S. (2019). *A survey on recent advances in named entity recognition from deep learning models.* arXiv preprint arXiv:1910.11470.

Yadav, J., Kumar, D., & Chauhan, D. (2020, July). Cyberbullying detection using pre-trained bert model. In *2020 International Conference on Electronics and Sustainable Communication Systems (ICESC)* (pp. 1096-1100). IEEE. 10.1109/ICESC48915.2020.9155700

Yamaguchi, Y., Amagasa, T., & Kitagawa, H. (2013, October). Landmark-based user location inference in social media. In *Proceedings of the first ACM conference on Online social networks* (pp. 223-234). 10.1145/2512938.2512941

Yan, D., Li, K., Gu, S., & Yang, L. (2020). Network-based bag-of-words model for text classification. *IEEE Access : Practical Innovations, Open Solutions*, *8*, 82641–82652. doi:10.1109/ACCESS.2020.2991074

Yang, C. I., & Li, Y. P. (2023). Explainable uncertainty quantifications for deep learning-based molecular property prediction. *Journal of Cheminformatics*, *15*(1), 1–14. doi:10.118613321-023-00682-3 PMID:36737786

Yang, C., Harkreader, R., Zhang, J., Shin, S., & Gu, G. (2012). Analyzing spammers' social networks for fun and profit: a case study of cyber criminal ecosystem on twitter. *WWW '12: Proceedings of the 21st International Conference on World Wide Web*, 71–80. 10.1145/2187836.2187847

Yang, H., Yuan, C., Xing, J., & Hu, W. (2017). SCNN: Sequential convolutional neural network for human action recognition in videos. *2017 IEEE International Conference on Image Processing (ICIP)*. 10.1109/ICIP.2017.8296302

Yang, M., Liang, Y., Zhao, W., Xu, W., Zhu, J., & Qu, Q. (2018). Task-oriented keyphrase extraction from social media. *Multimedia Tools and Applications*, *77*(3), 3171–3187. doi:10.100711042-017-5041-y

Yang, S., Lu, W., Yang, D., Li, X., Wu, C., & Wei, B. (2017). KEYPHRASEDS: Automatic generation of survey by exploiting keyphrase information. *Neurocomputing*, *224*, 58–70. doi:10.1016/j.neucom.2016.10.052

Yasmina, D., Hajar, M., & Hassan, A. M. (2016). Using YouTube comments for text-based emotion recognition. *Procedia Computer Science*, *83*, 292–299. doi:10.1016/j.procs.2016.04.128

Young, T., Hazarika, D., Poria, S., & Cambria, E. (2018). Recent trends in deep learning based natural language processing. IEEE Computational Intelligence Magazine, 13(3). doi:10.1109/MCI.2018.2840738

You, Q. (2015). *Robust Image Sentiment Analysis Using Progressively Trained and Domain Transferred Deep Networks.* AAAI. doi:10.1609/aaai.v29i1.9179

Zafarani, R., Abbasi, M. A., & Liu, H. (2014). *Social Media Mining: An Introduction.* Cambridge University Press. doi:10.1017/CBO9781139088510

Zakaryia, A., Mohammad, A. T., & Jaccomard, H. (n.d.). *Evaluation of Facebook Translation Service (FTS) in Translating Facebook Posts from English into Arabic in Terms of TAUS Adequacy and Fluency during Covid-19*. Academic Press.

Zarnoufi, R., Jaafar, H., & Abik, M. (2020). Machine normalization: Bringing social media text from non-standard to standard form. *ACM Transactions on Asian and Low-Resource Language Information Processing, 19*(4), 1–30. doi:10.1145/3378414

Zhang, X., Zhu, S., & Liang, W. (2012). Detecting spam and promoting campaigns in the Twitter social network. *Proceedings - IEEE International Conference on Data Mining,* 1194–1199. 10.1109/ICDM.2012.28

Zhang, J., & Tansu, N. (2013). Optical gain and laser characteristics of ingan quantum wells on ternary ingan substrates. *IEEE Photonics Journal, 5*(2), 2600111–2600111. doi:10.1109/JPHOT.2013.2247587

Zhang, L., Peng, T. Q., Zhang, Y. P., Wang, X. H., & Zhu, J. J. (2014). Content or context: Which matters more in information processing on microblogging sites. *Computers in Human Behavior, 31*, 242–249. doi:10.1016/j.chb.2013.10.031

Zhang, Q., Wang, Y., Gong, Y., & Huang, X. (2016). Keyphrase extraction using deep recurrent neural networks on Twitter. *Proceedings of the 2016 conference on empirical methods in natural language processing,* 836–845. 10.18653/v1/D16-1080

Zhan, N., & Kitchin, J. R. (2022). Uncertainty quantification in machine learning and nonlinear least squares regression models. *AIChE Journal. American Institute of Chemical Engineers, 68*(6), e17516. doi:10.1002/aic.17516

Zhao, Srivastava, Peng, & Chen. (2019). Long short-term memory network design for analog computing. ACM Journal on Emerging Technologies. *Computing Systems, 15*(1), 13.

Zhao, W. X., Jiang, J., He, J., Song, Y., Achanauparp, P., Lim, E. P., & Li, X. (2011, June). Topical keyphrase extraction from twitter. In *Proceedings of the 49th annual meeting of the association for computational linguistics: Human language technologies* (pp. 379-388). Academic Press.

Zhao, Z., Zhang, Z., & Hopfgartner, F. (2021, April). A comparative study of using pre-trained language models for toxic comment classification. In *Companion Proceedings of the Web Conference 2021* (pp. 500-507). 10.1145/3442442.3452313

Zhao, Z., Zhang, Z., Chen, T., Singh, S., & Zhang, H. (2020). *Image Augmentations for GAN Training*. https://doi.org/ doi:10.48550/arxiv.2006.02595

Zheng, C., Jiang, J. Y., Zhou, Y., Young, S. D., & Wang, W. (2020, July). Social media user geolocation via hybrid attention. In *Proceedings of the 43rd International ACM SIGIR Conference on Research and Development in Information Retrieval* (pp. 1641-1644). 10.1145/3397271.3401329

Compilation of References

Zhuang, L., Dunagan, J., Simon, D. R., Wang, H. J., Osipkov, I., Hulten, G., & Tygar, J. (2008). Characterizing botnets from email spam records. *Proceedings of the 1st Usenix Workshop on Large-Scale Exploits and Emergent Threats, 2*, 1–9. https://static.usenix.org/events/leet08/tech/full_papers/zhuang/zhuang.pdf%5Cnpapers2://publication/uuid/A045FDFA-4186-4 754-BD44-EB30103D1F2F

Zuo, Y., Ma, Y., Zhang, M., Wu, X., & Ren, Z. (2021). The impact of sharing physical activity experience on social network sites on residents' social connectedness: A cross-sectional survey during COVID-19 social quarantine. *Globalization and Health, 17*(1), 1–12. doi:10.118612992-021-00661-z PMID:33430894

About the Contributors

Ahmed A. Abd El-Latif received the B.Sc. degree with honor rank in Mathematics and Computer Science in 2005 and M.Sc. degree in Computer Science in 2010, all from Menoufia University, Egypt. He received his Ph. D. degree in Computer Science & Technology at Harbin Institute of Technology (H.I.T), Harbin, P. R. China in 2013. He is an associate professor of Computer Science at Menoufia University, Egypt. He is author and co-author of more than 130 papers in reputal journal and conferences. He received many awards, State Encouragement Award in Engineering Sciences 2016, Arab Republic of Egypt; the best Ph.D student award from Harbin Institute of Technology, China 2013; Young scientific award, Menoufia University, Egypt 2014. He is a fellow at Academy of Scientific Research and Technology, Egypt. His areas of interests are multimedia content encryption, secure wireless communication, IoT, applied cryptanalysis, perceptual cryptography, secret media sharing, information hiding, biometrics, forensic analysis in digital images, and quantum information processing. Dr. Abd El-Latif is an associate editor of Journal of Cyber Security and Mobility, and Mathematical Problems in Engineering.

Mohammed A. El-Affendi is currently a Professor of computer science with the Department of Computer Science, at Prince Sultan University, a Former Dean of CCIS, AIDE, the Rector, a Founder, and the Director of Data Science Laboratory (EIAS), a Founder and the Director of The Center of Excellence in CyberSecurity. His current research interests include data science, intelligent and cognitive systems, machine learning, and natural language processing.

* * *

Shakeel Ahamad is a research scholar at the School of Computer and Systems Sciences at Jawaharlal Nehru University, New Delhi. He completed his post-graduation in Computer Science and applications (2016) and graduated in statistics (2013) from Aligarh Muslim University, Aligarh UP, India. His research interests are performability, Reliability, and performance of safety-critical systems.

Marcellus Amadeus is a young scientist specialized in Natural Language Processing, Machine Learning, and Software Engineering. Amadeus already worked extensively with most of the available Machine Learning and Data Science frameworks and libraries and with both AWS and Oracle Cloud platforms. Amadeus is fluent in Python, SQL, and JavaScript, and is very comfortable with working under pressure and on complex projects. Amadeus has years of experience with the management of remote multi-cultural technical teams, and is self-taught in many things, from human languages to advanced mathematics.

Abhay Bhatia, Dr., is working as Assistant Professor in Department of Computer Science and Engineering at Roorkee Institute of Technology, Roorkee, Haridwar Uttarakhand. He is having more than 12 years of academic experience and worked with various reputed engineering institutions. He has completed his B.Tech in Computer Science and Engineering from AKTU (formely UPTU), M.Tech in Computer Science and Engineering from Rajasthan and Ph.D. in Wireless Sensor Networks. He is currently a member of IEEE as well as reviewer for several journals. He is having distinguish record of research papers with more than 15 International, Scopus and SCI papers. Moreover 3 patents are also in his bucket as a researcher with research area of Artificial Intelligence, Machine Learning, Image Processing and Wireless Sensor Network.

William Alberto Cruz Castañeda is currently AI Research Lead at Alana AI. Holds B.Sc. degree in computer sciences from Benemerita Universidad Autonoma de Puebla, México (2006). Master's and Ph.D. degrees in electrical engineering from the Federal University of Santa Catarina, Brazil (2011 and 2016 respectively). His lines of research interest include ubiquitous computing, machine learning, predictive models, decision-making, and natural language processing. Interests also include the design, development, and deployment of large-scale platforms to enable and enhance data-driven applications, in particular, to provide heterogeneous solutions.

Deepali Dhaka is working as a Senior Research Fellow in the Department of Computer Science, Jamia Millia Islamia, central university, Delhi, India. Her research area includes Machine Learning, NLP, Data Mining, Social Networks, and Deep Learning. She has worked as a Senior Software Engineer for 4 years in Aricent Altran Group. She has done her post-graduation in MSc. Informatics from Institute of Informatics and Communication, Delhi University and graduation BSc. Electronics(H) from S.G.T.B. Khalsa College, North Campus, Delhi University.

Ovais Bashir Gashroo is a Ph.D. student in the Department of Computer Science at Jamia Millia Islamia, New Delhi, India. His research interests include Natural Language Processing, Social media analysis, and Deep learning.

Ratneshwer Gupta did his Ph.D. in Component Based Software Engineering from Indian Institute of Technology, Banaras Hindu University, Varanasi (IIT-BHU), India. His research area is CBSE and SOA. He is serving as an Assistant Professor in School of Computer & Systems Sciences, JNU, New Delhi – 110067, India. He is actively involved in teaching and research for last 8 years. He has 16 research papers in International Journals and 16 research papers in international/national conference proceedings in his credit.

Vishwanath Kamath received the B.E degree in Electronics and Communications Engineering from Visvesvaraya Technological University, in 2005, M.S. degree in Software Systems from Birla Institute of Technology and Science, Pilani (BITS,Pilani) in 2013, M.Tech. degree in Data Science and Engineering from Birla Institute of Technology and Science, Pilani (BITS,Pilani) in 2021. He is currently working as a Research Engineer with Voice Intelligence Team, Samsung Research Institute Bangalore, India. His research interests include Machine Learning and NLP.

Arun Kashyap is Assistant Professor Department of CSE GL Bajaj institute of technology and management greater Noida.

Akib Mohi Ud Din Khanday received a master's degree in Information Technology from the Islamic University of Science and Technology, Awantipora, Jammu and Kashmir, India and a Ph.D. degree in Computer Sciences from the Baba Ghulam Shah Badshah University, Rajouri, Jammu and Kashmir, India, in 2022. He has worked as an Assistant Professor in the Department of Information Technology, S.P. College, Cluster University, Srinagar, J&K, India and the Department of Computer Science and Applications, Sharda University, India. He is currently working as a Post Doctoral Research fellow in the Department of Computer Science and Software Engineering-CIT, United Arab Emirates University, Al Ain. His research interests are Computational Social Sciences, NLP and Machine/Deep Learning. He has authored many research articles in the reputed journals and conferences. He has served as a reviewer in reputed journals over the years like Scientific Reports, Journal of Social Science and Humanities etc.

Anil Kumar is working as Assistant Professor in Department of Computer Science and Engineering at R.D. Engineering College Ghaziabad UP. He is having more than 17 years of academic experience and worked with various reputed engineering institutions. He has completed his B.Tech in Information Technology from AKTU (formely UPTU), M.Tech in Computer Science and Engineering from Rajasthan and Pursuing Ph.D. He is currently reviewer for several journals. He is having distinguished record of research papers with more than 12 International, Scopus and SCI papers. Moreover 2 patents are also in his bucket as a researcher with research area of Artificial Intelligence, Machine Learning, Deep Learning and Wireless Sensor Network.

Lokesh Kumar received a Ph.D. in Computer Science & Engineering from Glocal University.

Sushil Kumar received his Ph.D., M. Tech and MCA degrees in Computer Science from School of Computer and Systems Sciences, Jawaharlal Nehru University, New Delhi, India in 2014, 1999 and 1997 respectively, and B. Sc. degree in Mathematics from Kanpur University, India in 1993. He is currently working as Assistant Professor at School of Computer and Systems Sciences, Jawaharlal Nehru University, New Delhi, India. His research interest includes vehicular ad hoc networks, mobile ad hoc networks and wireless sensor networks. Dr. Kumar has published papers in International Journals and Conferences including IEEE, Springer, Elsevier, Inderscience, and Hindawi Publishing Corporation.

Neha Kumari is a research scholar and currently pursuing her Ph.D. in Computer Science at the School of Computer and Systems Sciences, Jawaharlal Nehru University, New Delhi, India. She did Mathematics (Hons.) from Miranda House, University of Delhi, India, and Masters in Computer Science and Applications from Guru Gobind Singh Indraprastha University, India. She worked as Assistant Professor in Nit Kurukshetra and St Stephens College Delhi University for nearly 1-2 years. She also worked as a software programmer in Busy Infotech Private Limited for 1 year.

Monica Mehrotra is presently working as a Professor in the Department of Computer Science, Jamia Millia Islamia (Central University). She completed her Ph.D. in Aug. 2007 from Jamia Millia Islamia. She has over twenty-five years of teaching experience. Her research interest areas include Data Mining, Information Retrieval, and social network analysis. She has authored two books published by Narosa Publishers titled 'Principles and practices of Software Engineering' and 'Software Project Measurement: Tools and Techniques'. She has published over 70 papers in international conferences & Journals of repute. She has won 'Excellent Researcher Award (female)' in 2nd International academic and research excellence awards (IARE – 2020) ceremony organized by GISR foundation on 3rd Oct, 2020. She is a member of IEEE.

Tawseef Ahmad Mir completed BCA from University of Kashmir in 2012. Completed MCA from Punjab Technical University in 2015 and presently pursuing Ph.D. in Computer Science from Baba Ghulam Shah Badshah University Rajouri, J&K-India. Areas of interest are Artificial Intelligence, Natural Language Processing.

Saima Saleem is a Ph.D. student in the Department of Computer Science at Jamia Millia Islamia, New Delhi, India. Her research interests include Natural Language Processing, Social media analysis, and Deep learning.

Jayantha Sarapanahalli received the B.E. degree in Computer Science Engineering from Visvesvaraya Technological University, in 2004. He is currently working as a Research Engineer with Voice Intelligence Team in Samsung Research Institute Bangalore, India. Some of his experiences include working in Mobile, Connected Car, AI with NLP, NLU for Voice Assistants. His research interests include Machine Learning and Natural Language Processing.

Vibhor Sharma is working as Assistant Professor in Swami Rama Himalayan University (SRHU), Jollygrant Dehradun. Sharma has more than 10 years of experience in academics, and has published widely in International Journals and Conferences his research findings related to Internet of things (IoT) and Data Mining. Sharma has a distinguished record of publication in academic journals with more than 25 papers in international level Journals and Conferences, International/National patents, Editorial board member and reviewer of journals.

Deepak Srivastava is working as Assistant Professor in Swami Rama Himalayan University (SRHU), Jollygrant Dehradun since August 2017. Sricastava has more than 11 years of experience in academics. Srivastava's Ph.D is in Computer Science & Engineering, M.Tech (CSE). Srivastava is also published widely in International Journals and Conferences his research findings related to Computer Network, Internet of things (IoT) and Machine Learning; and has distinguished record of publication in academic journals with more than 17 papers in International level Journals and Conferences, International/National patents, Editorial board member and reviewer of Journals.

Index

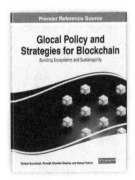

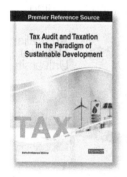

Printed in the United States
by Baker & Taylor Publisher Services